1919, The Year of Racial Violence
How African Americans Fought Back

This study recounts African Americans' brave stand against a cascade of mob attacks in the United States after World War I. The emerging New Negro identity, which prized unflinching resistance to second-class citizenship, inspired veterans and their fellow black citizens. In city after city – Washington, D.C.; Chicago; Charleston; and elsewhere – black men and women took up arms to repel mobs that used lynching, assaults, and other forms of violence to protect white supremacy; yet, authorities blamed blacks for the violence, leading to mass arrests and misleading news coverage. Refusing to yield, African Americans sought accuracy and fairness in the courts of public opinion and the law. This is the first account of this three-front fight – in the streets, in the press, and in the courts – against mob violence during one of the worst years of racial conflict in U.S. history.

David F. Krugler is Professor of History at the University of Wisconsin-Platteville. He is the author of *The Voice of America and the Domestic Propaganda Battles, 1945–1953* (2000) and *This Is Only a Test: How Washington, D.C., Prepared for Nuclear War* (2006).

1919, The Year of Racial Violence

How African Americans Fought Back

DAVID F. KRUGLER

University of Wisconsin-Platteville

CAMBRIDGE
UNIVERSITY PRESS

CAMBRIDGE
UNIVERSITY PRESS

32 Avenue of the Americas, New York NY 10013-2473, USA

Cambridge University Press is part of the University of Cambridge.

It furthers the University's mission by disseminating knowledge in the pursuit of
education, learning and research at the highest international levels of excellence.

www.cambridge.org
Information on this title: www.cambridge.org/9781107639614

First published 2015

A catalogue record for this publication is available from the British Library

Library of Congress Cataloguing in Publication data
Krugler, David F., 1969–
1919, the year of racial violence : how African Americans fought back / David F. Krugler,
University of Wisconsin, Platteville.
pages cm.
Includes bibliographical references and index.
ISBN 978-1-107-06179-8 (hardback) – ISBN 978-1-107-63961-4 (pbk.)
1. United States – Race relations – History – 20th century.   2. African Americans –
History – 1877–1964.   3. African Americans – Violence against – History –
20th century.   4. African Americans – Social conditions – 20th century.
5. Race riots – United States – History – 20th century.   6. Lynching – United States –
History – 20th century.   7. Racism – United States – History – 20th century   I. Title.
E185.5.K78   2014
305.80097309′04–dc23   2014024993

ISBN 978-1-107-06179-8 Hardback
ISBN 978-1-107-63961-4 Paperback

To Eric Pullin, friend and fellow historian

Contents

Acknowledgments

Books and their authors travel a long journey from idea to print. To my good fortune, a host of generous people have aided me during my trek, from my first thoughts on the book's subject to the final proofreading mark.

Professor Juliet E. K. Walker, now at the University of Texas, kindled my interest in African American history while I was a graduate student at the University of Illinois, and she taught me to think and read like a historian.

At the University of Wisconsin-Platteville, department chair Paula Nelson and college dean Mittie Nimocks Den Herder enthusiastically supported my 2007–2008 sabbatical. I also appreciate Mittie's endorsement of my application to the Institute for Research in the Humanities. Grants from UW-Platteville and the UW System Institute on Race and Ethnicity funded research trips. Paula Nelson and Carl Allsup wrote letters of recommendation. Kathy Lomax pointed me toward relevant fellowships. I am grateful to Elizabeth Throop, Dean of the College of Liberal Arts and Education, for providing a stipend for the costs of the book's images. Department chairs J. Elmo Rawling III and Nancy Turner approved grant applications and conference travel reimbursement. Becky Savoy helped me collect image permissions.

I benefited in more ways than I can count from the help of archivists, librarians, and scholars across the United States. At UW-Platteville's Karrmann Library, Lori Wedig cheerfully fulfilled my Universal Borrowing requests. Orville D. Menard shared his notes and thoughts on Tom Dennison and Omaha's 1919 riot. Stephanie Bayless handled my duplicating and photographic requests at the Butler Center for

Arkansas Studies. Staff at the Harold Washington, Sulzer, and Wood-son Libraries in Chicago helped me get through dozens of microfilm reels. Jane Aldrich and Molly French made copies for me in Charleston, South Carolina; Linda Piper sent materials from the Longview (Texas) Public Library. Marquette University Archivist Matt Blessing sent me a copy of Arthur Falls's memoir. For all their help, I want to acknowledge Doris Martinson, Knox County (Tenn.) Archives; Stephen G. McShane, Calumet Regional Archives, Indiana University Northwest; Gary R. Rosenberg, Douglas County (Neb.) Historical Society; Dennis Mihelich, history professor emeritus, Creighton University; Eric Yellin, associate professor of history, University of Richmond; Alan Lessoff, professor of history, Illinois State University; Daniel Greene, vice president for research and academic programs, Newberry Library; Joanne Ferguson Cavanaugh, Omaha Public Library; Faye Haskins, District of Columbia Public Library; Matthew Gilmore, H-DC editor; Joellen ElBashir, Cura-tor, Moorland-Spingarn Research Center at Howard University; and the staffs of the Newberry Library, Wisconsin Historical Society, Library of Congress, Chicago History Museum, and the National Archives in Wash-ington, D.C., and College Park, Md. Thanks are due to Arthur Waskow, Grif Stockley, and Theodore Kornweibel, Jr., for donating their invalu-able research materials to publicly accessible archives. Rachel Rooney and Brodie Austin, of the Newberry Library's Professional Development Programs for Teachers, invited me to lead several symposia on Chicago's 1919 race riot. I am grateful as well for the help of the Chicago-area teachers who took part in these symposia, especially Patricia Boughton, Greg Simmons, and Mike Torney. For their suggestions, I want to thank Laurie Matheson and Joe Spieler.

Historical conferences and lecture engagements offered opportunities to present my research to diverse audiences. At the 2007 Annual Confer-ence on Washington, D.C., Historical Studies, Bell Clement, Maurice Jackson, Jefferson Morley, and Dana Schaffer provided helpful feed-back. Thanks are due to Jonathan Coit for organizing a panel for the 2011 Annual Meeting of the Organization of American Historians and to Charles Lumpkins, Gregory Mixon, and Delia Mellis for their com-ments and advice. I appreciate the invitation from David Tucker and John Moser of Ashland University to give a Summer Institute lecture in 2011 for the Master of Arts in American History and Government program. Amy Parsons was a perceptive respondent when I delivered an address for the College of Liberal Arts and Education's Faculty Forum Series at UW-Platteville.

During Spring 2011, a fellowship at the Institute for Research in the Humanities at UW-Madison brought me into an extraordinary community of scholars, whose comments and ideas were immensely helpful. Susan Stanford Friedman, Craig Werner, and Jonathan Pollack were particularly generous with their time and suggestions.

At Cambridge University Press, Deborah Gershenowitz ardently backed my project and expertly shepherded the manuscript through peer and Press review. My thanks to Dana Bricken for her help during the publication process.

Many readers helped me improve my manuscript from the moment I drafted the first chapter. Roy Shaver read the manuscript in record time and offered much encouragement. The comments of Dawn Flood, an expert on Chicago history and a close friend, were incisive and beneficial. David Rowley provided background on pogroms; Joong-Jae Lee pointed me to relevant labor history sources. In 2010 and 2013, students in my course on African American history read drafts of two chapters as an assignment and offered helpful comments. The manuscript's peer reviewers provided many insightful recommendations. As editor of *Washington History*, Zachary Schrag of George Mason University helped me revise my chapter on Washington, D.C.'s riot for publication in the 2009 issue of the journal; Zach's guidance also sharpened my thinking about the role of white veterans in the racial violence of 1919. I am deeply indebted to my friend Eric Pullin, an associate professor of history at Carthage College, for his numerous close readings of my manuscript; his acumen and suggestions; and his good-natured prodding to work on my book "tomorrow, tomorrow. . . ."

Other friends and my family cheered me on as well. My ongoing card game with Mark Sethne, Reg Ihm, George Smith, and Mike Ira has long proven that Wednesday nights are better with euchre. A July 2012 trip to Barcelona that my wife Amy and I made with our friends Dorota and Zbigniew Kruczalak, Brian Sandberg, and Laura Kramer provided welcome respite from writing, as did our many dinner parties (especially Picasso Revisited, May 18, 2013). Brian, an associate professor of history at Northern Illinois University, encouraged me to apply to the Institute for Research in the Humanities when he was the Solmsen Fellow there, spent many hours talking to me about my book, and was always willing to meet me at Bookman's Corner on five minutes' notice. (And thanks to John Chandler for keeping me well supplied in used books.) The encouragement of the Pospisils – my sister Katie, brother-in-law Mike, and nieces Megan and Kayla – is much appreciated. My parents,

John and Dee Krugler, offered unwavering support, as they have for all my endeavors – I am, for so many reasons, a fortunate son. A fortunate spouse, too: Amy Lewis has traveled each step of this book's long journey with me. I want her to know how much her love, intellectual company, and companionship mean to me.

Source Abbreviations and Usage Note

The following abbreviations for primary sources are used in order to reduce footnote length. For the same reason, citations of secondary sources provide only an author's last name and a short title. The bibliography provides a complete list of the primary and secondary sources cited in the notes. In order to avoid obtrusive corrections, quotations in the text leave intact the original spelling and grammar of the sources.

Kornweibel Papers: Theodore Kornweibel Research Papers, 1910–1960, Newberry Library, Chicago, Ill.

NAACP Papers, Part 7, Series A: *Papers of the NAACP, Part 7: The Anti-Lynching Campaign, 1912–1955*, Series A: *Investigative Files, 1912–1955* (Frederick, Md.: University Publications of America, 1987).

NAACP Records: National Association for the Advancement of Colored People Records, Group I, Library of Congress, Washington, D.C.

RG 60, Glasser File: Records of the Department of Justice, Glasser File, U.S. National Archives and Records Administration, College Park, Md.

RG 65, OGF: Records of the Federal Bureau of Investigation, Old German File, U.S. National Archives and Records Administration, College Park, Md.

RG 80: Records of the Navy, General Correspondence of the Secretary of the Navy, 1916–1926, U.S. National Archives and Records Administration, Washington, D.C.

RG 125: Records of the Office of the Judge Advocate, Navy, Records of Proceedings of Courts of Inquiry, U.S. National Archives and Records Administration, Washington, D.C.

RG 159, Port Inspector: Record Group 159, Records of the Office of the Inspector General (Army), Port Inspector, Newport News and Norfolk, 1918–1920, U.S. National Archives and Records Administration, College Park, Md.

RG 165:   Record Group 165, Records of the War Department, General Staff, Military Intelligence Division, Microfilm Publication 1440, U.S. National Archives and Records Administration, College Park, Md.

RG 174, Division of Negro Economics: Record Group 174, Records of the Department of Labor, General Records, 1907–1942 (Chief Clerk's Files), Records of the Division of Negro Economics, U.S. National Archives and Records Administration, College Park, Md.

Waskow Notes: Arthur Waskow Notes on the NAACP 1919 Mob Violence File. (These notes are transcriptions that Waskow made in the late 1950s of the documents in the file, which was subsequently lost or destroyed prior to the deposit of the NAACP's records at the Library of Congress. Waskow's notes, which are held at the Wisconsin Historical Society, are the most complete copy of these invaluable historical records.)[1]

---

[1] Arthur Waskow to the author, February 11, 2008, in the author's possession.

Introduction

"In view of the sacrifices the negro soldiers made in this war to make the world safe for democracy it might not be a bad idea to make the United States safe for democracy."
– Colonel William Hayward, commanding officer of the 369th Infantry Regiment, Ninety-third Division (a.k.a. the Harlem Hellfighters), speaking in May 1919[1]

Aaron Gaskins was fed up. Never again would he submit to the pressure to buy Liberty Loans. Not one day more would he sit meekly at the back of the electric train during his morning commute from Alexandria, Virginia, to Washington, D.C. And no longer would he keep quiet about these indignities. On October 9, 1918, as his train crossed the Potomac River, Gaskins strode to the front and announced to the startled passengers: "I am as good as white people riding in this car." Gaskins, a tall black man with a scar on his cheek, loudly asked why he could not have the same rights as whites. Every morning he boarded the train with them in Alexandria and yet, because of the color of his skin, had to sit in the back until the car entered Washington. And this in the country that, Gaskins said, had just forced him to buy a bond for the war to make the world safe for democracy. "After this war is over," he proclaimed, referring to World War I, "we are going to get our rights – we will have a race war if we don't."[2]

---

[1] "Lynching Report Arouses Hayward," *New York Sun*, May 10, 1919, clipping in *NAACP Papers*, Part 7, Series A, reel 13, frame 1053.
[2] Francis Boyle to Harry A. Taylor, October 10, 1918, Case File 10218–284–1; S. J. DeVeau to Henry G. Pratt, November 17, 1918, Case File 10218–284–3; H.M. Raymond to

Gaskins's statement alarmed engineer William Smith. The federal government had warned Americans that the enemy, Germany, would try to damage homefront morale. To Smith, a black man demanding his rights in public seemed just the sort of trouble Germany might stir up, and he promptly reported the incident to the War Department's Military Intelligence Division. It dutifully investigated but found no evidence that German propaganda had swayed Gaskins. He led a modest life, worked at Washington's Union Station, and boarded in a house in Alexandria. The war ended a month later, and investigators dismissed the incident as the outburst of one angry black man.[3]

But plenty of other black Americans shared Gaskins's sentiment about equal rights and the war. In March 1919, attorney William L. Houston spoke at a reception for black soldiers who had just returned from France. Houston urged the men to now fight for democracy at home as they had done abroad.[4] Reverend Francis J. Grimké of Washington, D.C., offered the same message to black veterans during an April address, declaring that their military service in France would not help the race "unless you have come back with the love of liberty, equality, fraternity burning in your souls, and the determination to set other souls on fire with the same spirit."[5] Both men presaged the eloquent, forceful words of W. E. B. Du Bois. It is time, argued Du Bois in the May issue of the *Crisis*, to force America, the nation that disfranchises, robs, insults, and lynches us, to end its shame and fulfill its democratic promise: "We *return from fighting*. We *return fighting*. Make way for Democracy! We saved it in France, and by the Great Jehovah, we will save it in the United States of America, or know the reason why."[6]

Defenders of white supremacy did not make way for democracy. Jim Crow laws and customs held firm. So, too, did the decades-old disfranchisement of black men, the sharecropping that bound so many blacks

---

  Henry G. Pratt, November 20, 1918, Case File 10218–284–4 (both quotes), RG 165, copies in box 1, reel 5, Kornweibel Papers.

[3] Raymond to Pratt, November 20, 1918, Case File 10218–284–4. Such investigations were not uncommon. During World War I, the federal government maintained an extensive surveillance program of African Americans. See Kornweibel, *Investigate Everything*.

[4] Major W. H. Loving to General Churchill, March 17, 1919, Case File 10218 (no suffix number given), RG 165, copy in box 1, reel 1, Kornweibel Papers.

[5] "Address of Welcome Given at a Reception Tendered to the Men Who Have Returned from the Battle Front," April 24, 1919, *NAACP Papers*, Part 7, Series A, reel 2, frames 318–19.

[6] W.E.B. Du Bois, "Returning Soldiers," *Crisis* 18, no. 1 (May 1919), reprinted in Kerlin, *Voice of the Negro*, 35–7.

to twentieth-century serfdom and debt peonage, and the violence used to protect white supremacy. Between January and May 1919, more than twenty lynch mobs hanged, shot, burned, or dismembered two dozen African Americans.[7] "There are in this country 90,000,000 white people determined not to extend political and social equality to the 10,000,000 Negroes," Rep. James Byrnes (D-S.C.) declared on the floor of Congress, and the war, he said, had not in any way changed their position.[8] So Aaron Gaskins's prophecy came true: in 1919 America had a "race war," the most intense outbreak of racial conflict in the United States since Reconstruction.

Du Bois's and Byrnes's respective predictions pinpoint the major cause of the racial conflict. Wartime changes had unsettled the status quo of race relations based on the expectation of black subservience and white dominance. In particular, African Americans' military service molded the prewar New Negro movement into a potent force to confront the structure and practices of white supremacy. Well aware of this challenge, defenders of white supremacy acted swiftly, fiercely, and violently to suppress African Americans' efforts to secure political, economic, and social equality. Black resistance, which Gaskins, Du Bois, and Byrnes each anticipated, was the most prominent feature of the frequent violent clashes between blacks and whites that occurred right after World War I.

1919's Racial Conflict and African Americans' Three-Front War

Between late 1918 and late 1919, the United States recorded ten major race riots, dozens of minor, racially charged clashes, and almost 100 lynchings as white Americans tried to enforce the continued subjugation of black Americans in the postwar era. The major riots examined in this study took place in Charleston, South Carolina (May 1919); Longview, Texas (July 1919); Bisbee, Arizona (July 1919); Washington, D.C. (July 1919); Chicago, Illinois (July 1919); Knoxville, Tennessee (August 1919); Omaha, Nebraska (September 1919); Phillips County, Arkansas (October 1919); Gary, Indiana (October 1919); and Bogalusa, Louisiana (November 1919).[9] Nationally, the official death toll exceeded

---

[7] "The Lynching Industry, 1919," *Crisis* 19, no. 4 (February 1920), 183–6.

[8] The Editors, "A Reply to Congressman James F. Byrnes of South Carolina," *Messenger* vol. II, no. 10 (October 1919), 13.

[9] Tallies of 1919's racial clashes vary. Using the NAACP's file on 1919's mob activity, Arthur Waskow counts seven major riots and fifteen minor episodes. See Waskow, *From Race Riot*, 304–7. Citing W. E. B. Du Bois, Ann V. Collins counts twenty-six riots

150; the majority of the victims were black. Time and time again, white mobs provoked the violence and often had the sympathy and support of local law enforcement. Yet African Americans refused to surrender. Throughout 1919, they waged a three-front war against mob violence, not just to protect themselves but to also force the United States to recognize their constitutional rights.

On the first front, ordinary African Americans mobilized self-defense forces to repel armed white mobs that formed for many reasons: to drive blacks from industrial jobs or white neighborhoods; to punish blacks for their wartime prosperity; to "protect" white women against the alleged depredations of black men. Focusing on race riots as well as numerous lynchings, *1919, The Year of Racial Violence* tells the stories of the black men and women who rose, in city after city, to confront white mobs. In Longview, Texas, a black doctor organized a self-defense force to defend his friend from a lynching after city authorities refused to protect him. On Chicago's South Side, armed veterans of the all-black 370th Infantry Regiment, Ninety-third Division, donned their uniforms and patrolled to protect black residents from white ethnic gangs. In Knoxville, Tennessee, Joe Etter, a veteran of the Spanish-American War, lost his life while apparently trying to disarm state militia firing on black civilians; in Washington, D.C., teenager Carrie Johnson took up arms with her father to defend herself against a mob attacking their home. As the book describes the origins of postwar mob violence across America, it also relates the deeds and fates of these and many other ordinary black heroes.

The self-defenders came from many places within the black population. Black veterans and active-duty servicemen consistently repelled antiblack collective violence or resisted the assertion of white supremacy. Working class and professional black men also organized self-defense efforts: Arkansas sharecroppers, Indiana steel workers, the Texas doctor, a Chicago editor. Nor was armed resistance limited to men; black women took up arms to defend besieged homes in Washington and Chicago. Whether coordinated or unplanned, resistance to mob violence brought together diverse sections of the black population. African Americans' sustained, armed self-defense during the year of racial violence stands out as an early – and, as yet, understudied – landmark of the twentieth century

between April and October 1919. See Collins, *All Hell*, 71 n. 2. Cameron McWhirter puts the number of "major riots and mob actions" at twenty-five. See McWhirter, *Red Summer*, 13. My selection of major and minor riots and lynchings is not meant to be a definitive list; rather, it is based on the degree of resistance mounted by African Americans.

black freedom struggle. A major purpose of this book is to pinpoint the sources, features, and historical significance of this armed resistance.

The second front, the battle for the truth about the riots, opened even as the street clashes continued. Mainstream newspapers blamed African Americans for the riots, characterizing self-defense and armed resistance as unprovoked violence against whites. The black press, supported by the NAACP, fought back against these fallacious stories using eyewitness accounts, affidavits, and other evidence. At the same time, the black press celebrated resistance to mob violence and proclaimed the arrival of a "New Negro," one who had served his country in the fight to make the world safe for democracy. The New Negro now expected – now demanded – democracy in his native land. Across the country, black editors and writers lauded the manly virtues of armed resistance, issued calls for self-defense, and excoriated black leaders who urged restraint. These writers, who included William Monroe Trotter, Robert Abbott, James Weldon Johnson, A. Clement MacNeal, and many others, also demanded that white Americans and the federal government recognize and grant equality. The New Negroes warned that failure to make America safe for democracy invited further racial violence – not because uprisings were imminent, but because blacks refused to yield any longer to the violent enforcement of white supremacy.

On the third front, African Americans fought for justice. Hostile law enforcement officers and biased courts wrongfully arrested and prosecuted black self-defenders while letting white rioters go free. In city after city, white authorities pressed capital charges against blacks who had lawfully protected themselves against mob attacks, yet were portrayed as murderous criminals – lives thus hung in the balance as juries weighed the competing stories. Specially organized legal defense committees and the NAACP fought to right the scales of justice by providing attorneys for black defendants and by pressuring authorities to prosecute whites who had committed acts of violence. In one of the most successful legal battles, black attorneys in Washington won acquittals or dismissal of charges for numerous defendants, including Carrie Johnson, the teenager who defended her home against a white mob. In Chicago, a judge dismissed charges against A. Clement MacNeal and upbraided the state's attorney for prosecuting the editor for his self-defense actions. Success in court often required victory on the second front, the fight to publicize the facts about the riots, showing how intertwined the struggles were.

The racial violence of 1919 has received much attention, but four features make this book unique. First, while other studies focus primarily on the actions of mobbing whites, here African Americans are at the forefront of the story.[10] The book relates black veterans' massive resistance to white supremacy, explaining how returned black soldiers drew upon their military training and combat experience to halt mobs. In order to understand the scope and variety of black armed resistance, it is necessary to examine the ways in which black veterans led and inspired forceful stands against mob violence. Second, *1919, The Year of Racial Violence* describes how white paramilitary and patriotic associations fomented violence against blacks. During World War I, voluntary organizations such as the American Protective League (which enrolled 250,000 members) blurred the line between official and volunteer law enforcement, compelled support for the war, and quashed dissent. Vigilance became vigilantism, resulting in public violence that caused more than seventy deaths on the homefront.[11] The mustering out of soldiers and the founding of the American Legion swelled the ranks of voluntary vigilance associations after the war, as white veterans melded their military training with the practice of citizen policing. This book, as part of its analysis of black armed resistance, documents the extensive participation of white veterans, special deputies, home guards, and armed vigilantes in the postwar violence. Third, to deepen our understanding of the postwar backlash against African Americans, this study examines federal and state restrictions on arms sales to blacks. Fourth, and most important, *1919, The Year of Racial Violence* shows the year's racial violence from all significant sides: the fighting in the streets, the battle for the truth in the press, and the struggle for justice in the courts. Such an approach is needed because existing studies of 1919's racial violence generally focus on a single riot or court case.[12]

African Americans' three-front fight during 1919 fits into the historic spectrum of resistance to white supremacy in several ways.[13] Most obviously, the taking-up of arms to repel mobs was a direct – and dangerous – form of resistance. African Americans who purchased, carried, and used firearms did not act without forethought. At the same time black writers

---

[10] Waskow, *From Race Riot*; Collins, *All Hell*; Voogd, *Race Riots*.

[11] Capozzola, *Uncle Sam*, 3–20.

[12] Tuttle, *Race Riot* (Chicago); Stockley, *Blood in Their Eyes* (Arkansas); Cortner, *Mob Intent* (Arkansas); Whitaker, *On the Laps* (Arkansas). McWhirter, *Red Summer*, examines several race riots but does not treat the ensuing court battles.

[13] By "spectrum," I mean an array of resistance to white supremacy, from seemingly hidden or obscure forms (jokes, conversations, folklore) to overt acts (boycotts, mass protest, armed self-defense). My usage draws on Kelley, "We Are Not What We Seem."

and leaders denounced the state's failure to halt mob violence, they urged African Americans to arm, to do for themselves what authorities would not do. Veterans, drawing on their military training, did not rush head-long into armed battle with mobs but rather planned and organized their martial efforts. As another form of resistance, rebuttal of the dominant national narrative that blacks were responsible for the racial violence shows African American writers and leaders attacking the bias, misinformation, and stereotyping that excused white mob actions and justified state reprisals against blacks. The resistance was not merely rhetorical. As noted, establishing accurate, factual accounts of the mob violence was indispensible to the legal defense of African Americans charged with crimes against whites during riots. This interrelated resistance also cast a penumbra. Apprehension about armed blacks prompted some mobs to abandon or change their plans. In Omaha, for example, a white man warned a mob not to carry out an attack on the city's black neighborhood because of the expectation that its residents were armed.[14]

As a form of agency, the three-front fight was shaped by both national trends and local conditions. African Americans' wartime contribution and the concurrent New Negro movement (which are the subject of Chapter 1) provided national inspiration to resist racial violence, to "return fighting," but the individual responses of blacks much depended on local circumstances. In Chicago, for example, the Great Migration, the wartime movement of some 500,000 black southerners to northern cities, swelled the city's so-called Black Belt and greatly increased the number of black workers. Chicago's week-long riot in late July 1919 sprang from a variety of white efforts to enforce the boundaries of the Black Belt and to protect racial lines within the industrial workforce. For the black workers assaulted outside of Chicago's largest stockyard, self-defensive actions were an instinctive, life-saving response, whereas black veterans who took up arms to repel mobs attacking black-occupied homes were methodically acting to protect their community. The first action appears to be a natural human response to danger; the second, the premeditated deed of a set of individuals with a shared experience and history (military service). Both actions show agency and resistance, but failure to note their differences risks generalization.[15] Throughout the narrative, I have therefore tried to capture the unique features of black agency within each occurrence

---

[14] See Chapter 5.
[15] For more on the importance of contingency and particularity in understanding agency, see Johnson, "On Agency," and Emirbayer and Mische, "What Is Agency?"

of violence and resistance while also identifying the similarities of these episodes.

Mob Violence, White Supremacy, and the Roots of Black Resistance

It is helpful to situate 1919's racial violence in its historical context. Mob activity has a long history in the United States, from the colonial era to the twentieth century. During the eighteenth century, riots – which historian Paul Gilje defines as the extralegal actions of twelve or more people – commonly expressed dissatisfaction with a specific law enforcement act or regulation of property. Mob actions were a vital part of the American Revolution, as colonists regularly demonstrated their opposition to British policies through crowd actions. Starting in 1765, when the Stamp Act was introduced, hundreds of riots broke out in the colonies. Rioting remained common in the new republic, providing free men with an outlet to manage emerging social and economic tensions.[16]

Prior to the Civil War, mobs frequently targeted African Americans, especially in the urban North. (Mob violence was less common in the antebellum South, where slave owners and overseers used whippings, beatings, and other methods of physical harm to control the slave population.) Between 1824 and 1849, thirty-nine race riots broke out in northern cities. In each, whites reacted violently to actual or perceived challenges to white supremacy.[17] Columbia, Pennsylvania, experienced a wave of rioting in 1834 when white laborers attacked black artisans and craftsmen. In 1838, a mob destroyed a newly constructed abolition meeting hall in Philadelphia because it planned to allow nonsegregated gatherings – a step toward interracial equality, many whites feared. "Living together violently," as Richard Maxwell Brown puts it, was a fact of life for white and black Americans.[18]

After the Civil War, white opposition to abolition and to citizenship for African Americans ushered in a new era of racialized mob violence.

---

[16] Gilje, *Rioting in America*, 1–86. For more on colonial mob and vigilante violence, see Brown, *Strain of Violence*, 39–81.

[17] John M. Werner, "Race Riots in the United States during the Age of Jackson: 1824–1849" (Ph.D. diss., Indiana University, 1972), 4, 273ff., cited in Brown, *Strain of Violence*, 206 n. 41.

[18] Brown, *Strain of Violence*, 185–7 (quote on 185), 205–8. For more on antebellum northern race riots, see Gilje, *Rioting*, 87–91. For the national surge in antiabolitionist rioting during the 1830s, see Richards, *Gentlemen of Property*. For the prevalence of violence in the antebellum South, see Bruce, *Violence and Culture*, and Franklin, *Militant South*.

Reconstruction, directed by congressional Republicans and policed by federal troops, enabled black men's participation in the democratic process as voters and officeholders. Almost all of these newly enfranchised voters supported the Republican Party. In 1868, black Republicans held 85 of the 155 seats in the South Carolina legislature; all told, close to 800 black men served in the legislatures of the former Confederate states after the war. Although the Fifteenth Amendment did not enfranchise women, black women were politically active. They attended rallies, helped get out the vote, and supported men's runs for office.[19] Despite the presence of federal troops, white southerners deployed violence in a sustained campaign to topple the new Republican majorities, oust black officeholders, and disfranchise black voters. At times, the violence resembled warfare: between 1865 and 1875, whites in Louisiana killed 2,141 blacks and wounded another 2,115.[20] By 1877, the formal end of Reconstruction, the "redemption" of the South was complete: mob terrorism had suppressed black voting rights. That same year, the last federal troops were withdrawn from the South.[21]

The restoration of white-only rule enabled the creation of racial segregation, while the use of lynching to carry out vigilante justice continued the tradition of Reconstruction violence.[22] The number of black lynching victims in the United States rose steadily after 1865, particularly in the South. Between 1880 and 1930, 3,943 lynchings occurred in southern states (723 whites and 3,220 blacks). During the same period, by contrast, the Midwest experienced a total of 260 lynchings (181 whites and 79 blacks).[23] In his study of lynching in the South, Midwest, and West between the 1870s and 1940s, Michael J. Pfeifer argues that *rough justice* was the primary motive of mobs: rather than wait for the courts to act, mobs intervened to carry out swift death sentences. Vigilantism reflected widespread dissatisfaction with due process and the protection of accused criminals' rights. Rough justice thus helped protect social hierarchies and was viewed as a legitimate punishment of African Americans who defied white supremacy.[24] Much of 1919's rioting had rough justice

---

[19] Brown, "To Catch the Vision"; Hahn, *Nation Under*, 185, 217–19.
[20] Lemann, *Redemption*, 11.
[21] Shapiro, *White Violence*, 5–29.
[22] Key studies of American lynching include Brundage, *Lynching in the New South*; Wright, *Racial Violence in Kentucky*; Dray, *At the Hands*; Tolnay and Beck, *Festival of Violence*; Pfeifer, *Rough Justice* and *Roots of Rough Justice*.
[23] Brundage, *Lynching in the New South*, 7–8.
[24] Pfeifer, *Rough Justice*.

origins. In Knoxville, Tennessee, and Omaha, Nebraska, mobs stormed courthouses to attempt to lynch black men accused of crimes against white women. In Washington, D.C., mobs formed after a series of reported rapes. Rioting in Charleston, South Carolina, and Longview, Texas, aimed to punish blacks for defying Jim Crow or otherwise asserting equality with whites.

Rough justice was but one part of the ideology and practice of white supremacy. I use the term *white supremacy* to refer to the racial caste system entrenched throughout the United States during this era.[25] Built on a foundation of scientific racism, white supremacy depended on numerous fictions: that blacks were biologically inferior to whites, that Africans and African Americans were inherently uncivilized, that miscegenation endangered the so-called purity of the white race. As a system, white supremacy disfranchised and segregated African Americans; it exploited their labor; and it corrupted the courts, laws, and police, which used their authority and power to oppress blacks. As evidenced by the frequency of mob attacks and lynchings in the post-Civil War United States, violence was a mainstay of white supremacy.[26] This caste system was neither static nor uniform, however. Shaped by forces of class, gender, and local custom, the practice of white supremacy varied regionally. In Virginia, for example, the white upper class developed a "managed" system that used paternalism and token concessions to keep blacks subjugated. Virginia's elites were committed white supremacists, yet they disdained the Ku Klux Klan.[27] In Chicago, streetcars were not racially segregated as they were across most of the South, but Jim Crow still thrived up north: throughout 1918 and 1919, dozens of home bombings were used to try to keep African Americans contained to a specific neighborhood.[28] These bombings were just one example of the violence used to defend white supremacy after World War I.

The connection between mobs, white supremacy, and violence raises a question: what should organized attacks on African Americans be called? *Race riot* is the most commonly used term. Consider the titles of two important works on 1919's racial conflict: *From Race Riot to Sit-In, 1919 and the 1960s: A Study in the Connections between Conflict and Violence*, by Arthur Waskow; and *Race Riot: Chicago in the Red*

---

[25] For a comparative study of the origins and evolution of the racial caste system in the United States, see Frederickson, *White Supremacy*.

[26] Shapiro, *White Violence*.

[27] Smith, *Managing White Supremacy*, 3–75.

[28] Tuttle, *Race Riot*, 175.

Summer of 1919, by William M. Tuttle, Jr. For reasons of style, I use race riot throughout the book, but I ask readers to accept it as a synonym for *antiblack collective violence*, which more accurately (if less succinctly) describes 1919's racial conflict. Race riot implies that rioters of all races were equally responsible for the violence, but almost all of the year's conflict resulted from white-on-black violence. By meeting these attacks head-on, African Americans were not so much *rioting* as fighting back, counterattacking, repelling violence; above all, *resisting*. The word *riot* also suggests spontaneity, but antiblack collective violence during 1919 was deliberate, methodical, purposeful. Indeed, this was true of most American racial conflict occurring from the 1870s through the 1940s.

Some scholars, noting governmental sanction and support for mass violence against blacks, use *pogrom* to identify certain race riots. (Pogrom, derived from a Russian word for "smash, loot, destroy," was the name given to anti-Jewish collective violence in Russia during the nineteenth and early twentieth centuries. The Tsarist regime's support for these murderous rampages was a key component of pogroms.) Charles Lumpkins, for example, characterizes the riot that engulfed East St. Louis, Illinois, in July 1917 as an "American pogrom" because the city's white political and economic leaders deliberately used mass violence to halt blacks' quest for prosperity and equality. In her analysis of American race riots between 1898 and 1945, Ann V. Collins uses *pogrom* and *race riot* synonymously because the actions (or inaction) of authorities were common structural factors in the outbreak of white-on-black violence.[29] I have opted to use *pogrom* sparingly, using the word to describe just two of the riots treated in *1919, The Year of Racial Violence*: Longview, Texas, and Phillips County, Arkansas. Here the scope of civil authorities' support for white mob attacks was so great, and the intent to massacre blacks so obvious, that usage of *pogrom* appears appropriate.

Of course, for the targets of mobs taxonomy was a trifling matter – contending with the violence was the imperative. African American resistance to mob attacks between 1865 and the 1910s provided a foundation for the three-front fight against antiblack collective violence in 1919. After the Civil War, for example, black men and women recognized that protection of their rights required paramilitary mobilization, as evidenced by the actions of the Union League. Although it was supported by the Republican Party, the league was much more than a political organization. Black churches, fraternal lodges, and kin networks integrated the

---

[29] Lumpkins, *American Pogrom*; Collins, *All Hell*.

league's local councils into freed people's communities. The Ku Klux Klan and other white supremacist organizations set out to destroy the league, especially in South Carolina. These attacks met with armed resistance; anticipating conflict, many league councils had armed and drilled.[30] Although the restoration of white rule across the South by the end of the 1870s spelled an end to the league, after World War I black veterans followed the league's example of armed resistance to white supremacist mobs.

During the 1890s, journalist Ida B. Wells emerged as an eloquent proponent of resistance to mob violence and lynching. In her investigative works *Southern Horrors: Lynch Law in All Its Phases* (1892) and *A Red Record* (1895), Wells vividly exposed the myth that lynching was necessary (as so many white defenders of mob violence claimed) to protect white women from black men. Wells's path-breaking work documented the widespread practice of rough justice in America and exposed the gendered fiction underpinning Jim Crow, that the virtue of white women and the "purity" of the white race required vigilantism by white men. The black press, Wells contended, must establish the facts about mob violence and rebut claims that lynching was justifiable because of the alleged deeds of blacks.[31]

Wells also approved of armed resistance and of using legal means to end lynching. As she wrote, "a Winchester rifle should have a place of honor in every black home, and it should be used for that protection which the law refuses to give."[32] *That protection which the law refuses to give.* Because the cooperation of law enforcement enabled many lynchings, African Americans needed to compel white authorities to properly try accused criminals (whatever their race) and to bring lynchers to justice. Wells's call to action provides a framework for this study, for the journalist and reformer outlined the three-front battle against mob violence that emerged in 1919: armed self-defense, use of the black press, and pressure on law enforcement and the courts. Wells was more than a precursor; in 1919, she provided legal aid to jailed black self-defenders in Chicago and Arkansas.

---

[30] Hahn, *Nation Under,* 177–89, 265–6, 272–88, 302–10.

[31] Bederman, *Manliness and Civilization,* 45–76; Duster, *Crusade for Justice;* Royster, *Southern Horrors,* 1–41. African Americans also used testimonies of racial violence to advance political action against white supremacy from the end of the Civil War to World War I. See Williams, *They Left Great Marks.*

[32] Royster, *Southern Horrors,* 70.

The greatest demonstrations of black resistance occurred during several turn-of-the-century race riots.[33] The violence – which occurred in Wilmington, North Carolina, in 1898; Evansville, Indiana, in 1903; Atlanta, Georgia, in 1906; and Springfield, Illinois, in 1908 – had local causes but shared the basic purpose of protecting white supremacy by terrorizing and killing blacks and destroying their property. In each city, African Americans took up arms to protect themselves. In Wilmington, mobs and well-armed white supremacist groups attacked African Americans in order to restore white-only, Democratic Party control. During the riot twenty-five blacks faced down a larger force of white men, and snipers sporadically fired on the mobs.[34] In Evansville, approximately thirty black men assembled to drive away white vigilantes attempting to break into the county jail to lynch a black prisoner. Clashes between armed groups of whites and blacks ensued.[35] In Atlanta, false rumors of alleged assaults on white women by black men sparked a three-day riot in September 1906, but the antiblack collective violence had deeper sources: restoration of white hegemony and black subservience. White mobs that collectively numbered several thousand first attacked black businesses, visible signs of black prosperity and success, then targeted individual blacks. Georgia's Fifth Infantry Regiment mobilized to quell the rioting but also to curtail black self-defense measures. All told, thirty-two blacks and three whites died.[36] In Springfield, a mob thwarted from carrying out the lynching of two black prisoners instead attacked the city's black community. Black snipers fired on rioters from a saloon window, and twelve armed black men formed a patrol and fired on members of a mob leaving the site of one attack.[37]

The assertion of white supremacy that led to these mob attacks between 1898 and 1908 and the resistance mounted by African Americans presaged 1919's racial violence. Yet the intensity and frequency of both the postwar violence and black resistance suggest that they were not mere addenda to these turn-of-the-century episodes. Why so many race riots

---

[33] For an overview of Progressive-era racial violence and the responses of Wells and other black leaders, see Shapiro, *White Violence*, 91–144.

[34] Cecelski and Tyson, *Democracy Betrayed*, 3–15; Prather, "We Have Taken a City"; Gilmore, *Gender and Jim Crow*, 105–18.

[35] Butler, *Undergrowth of Folly*.

[36] Mixon, *Atlanta Riot*, 1, 64–110. See also Capeci and Knight, "Reckoning with Violence"; Bauerlein, *Negrophobia*; Godshalk, *Veiled Visions*.

[37] Senechal, *Sociogenesis of a Race Riot*, 21–54.

and pogroms in such a brief period? How and why did African Americans mount such sustained and varied resistance? Was it simply because the violence was so great? Answers to these questions can be found by first examining America's swift, sweeping mobilization for World War I.

1919, The Year of Racial Violence thus begins with a chapter on African Americans' transformative wartime experience and the emergent New Negro identity, which provided an ideology and purpose for black resistance during 1919. Rather than examine the year's violence in a riot-by-riot scheme, as many studies do, the book proceeds topically in order to foreground the three fronts of black resistance.[38] Chapters 2 through 6 focus on the first front, armed resistance and self-defense, in ten different locales: Charleston, South Carolina, Bisbee, Arizona, and Longview, Texas (Chapter 2); Washington, D.C. (Chapter 3); Chicago (Chapter 4); Knoxville, Tennessee, and Omaha, Nebraska (Chapter 5); and Phillips County, Arkansas, Gary, Indiana, and Bogalusa, Louisiana (Chapter 6). These five chapters are ordered chronologically, following the sequence of mob violence as it occurred. In several of these chapters, treatment of the second front, the concurrent struggle to correct inaccurate press coverage of the riots, is woven into the narrative. In order to enhance understanding of the scope of black armed resistance, Chapter 7 examines federal and state efforts to disarm African Americans. The next two chapters treat the third front: the struggle to secure justice after the riots ended. Chapter 8 looks at efforts to bring charges against white rioters and to secure due process for black defendants in Charleston, Longview, Washington, Chicago, and Omaha. Chapter 9 examines the sustained legal campaigns to overturn the death sentences delivered against black defendants in the wake of Knoxville's and Arkansas's riots. The final chapter analyzes African Americans' resistance to lynch mobs in both the South and the North, explaining how the struggle to end lynching fits into the three-front war. In the conclusion, I provide an overview of 1919's aftermath and offer my thoughts on the historical significance of African Americans' resistance to mob violence during 1919.

[38] Waskow, *From Race Riot*; McWhirter, *Red Summer*; Collins, *All Hell*.

World War I and the New Negro Movement

"The war to end all wars." For a brief time, Americans used this name to refer to the conflict that broke out in Europe in 1914, the war now known, of course, as World War I. The name is optimistic, confident, boundless in its ambition; and, given the global violence that engulfed the twentieth century, not a little naïve. In 1917, however, the war to end all wars articulated the special purpose President Woodrow Wilson stamped upon America's formal entry into the conflict. "The world must be made safe for democracy," he declaimed in his request to Congress for a declaration of war against Germany. For Wilson, this mission meant using an Allied victory to create an international organization of collective security, the League of Nations. Led by the United States and other democratic nations, the league would, Wilson hoped, deter aggression, promote the spread of democracy, and ultimately render war obsolete.[1]

To understand why and how African Americans fought a three-front war against mob violence during 1919, it is necessary to examine their responses to Wilson's mission. It was not an issue that preoccupied the president. Certainly Wilson hoped the nation's black citizens would support the war, but the problem of asking one group of Americans to fight abroad for the democracy denied to them at home did not unsettle Wilson, who was much more concerned with promoting patriotism to America's vast population of immigrants.[2] For African Americans, Wilson's call to war offered an opportunity to redress America's deficiencies. For doing

---

[1] For Wilson's war aims and internationalism, see Knock, *To End All Wars*.
[2] For the federal government's campaign to promote domestic support for the war, see Vaughn, *Holding Fast*.

their part to make the world safe for democracy, blacks expected restoration of voting rights in the South, an end to lynching and mob violence, and the dismantling of racial segregation.

The military service of almost 370,000 black men during the war created a potent force to carry out these goals. So, too, did the contributions of millions of black civilians who labored in defense factories, bought Liberty Loans, and followed volunteer rationing guidelines. Indeed, it is difficult to overstate just how profoundly the wartime service of African Americans steeled their determination to win their constitutional rights. Works by Adriane Lentz-Smith, Chad L. Williams, Nina Mjagkij, and Steven A. Reich detail and document the ways that blacks adapted Wilsonian rhetoric, redefined black manhood, redoubled the fight against Jim Crow through individual and collective resistance, and prepared to deploy their military training against white supremacists. Black veterans served as the vanguard in this war for democracy; they were, as Lentz-Smith puts it, "emblems and agents in this struggle." Black women were vital agents as well, lauding soldiers as their defenders and equals, resulting in a "cooperative notion of manhood that fused the aspirations of African American men and women."[3] As the wartime experiences of African Americans showed, these aspirations faced formidable obstacles.

Discrimination in the military was rampant. The marine corps refused to enlist blacks; the navy limited blacks to menial service occupations; and the army, which segregated its units, channeled most of its black conscripts and recruits into labor battalions. In May 1918, Colonel E. D. Anderson of the General Staff explained the War Department's reason for creating Services of Supply (SOS), as the labor battalions were officially called: the majority of black conscripts were, according to Anderson, of "the ignorant illiterate day laborer class." Unfit for combat, these men should "be organized in reserve labor battalions [and] put to work at useful constructive labor that furthers the prosecution of the war." Although Anderson did not oppose training "the cream of the colored draft" for combat, he and the General Staff believed the typical black soldier could best serve his country with a shovel, not a rifle, in his hands. Abuse and deprivation were common in the SOS units – one white officer joked that his men needed to be worked for three days, then whipped for another three. As if they were convicts, black soldiers were hired out

---

[3] Lentz-Smith, *Freedom Struggles* (quotes on 4 and 44); Williams, *Torchbearers of Democracy*; Mjagkij, *Loyalty in Time*; Reich, "Soldiers of Democracy" and "Great War."

to civilian contractors; in some instances, white officers kept the men's wages for themselves.[4] In Newport News, Virginia, soldiers of the 449th Reserve Labor Battalion wrote directly to Secretary of War Newton Baker to complain of being forced to work in the rain and on Sundays: "We did not think that we are in slavery again."[5] Adding insult to injury, white officers at Newport News habitually addressed and referred to black servicemen as "niggers" and "shines."[6] At the urging of Robert Moton, of the Tuskegee Institute, Baker hired Emmett Scott, Booker T. Washington's former secretary, to serve as his special assistant for black affairs. "It has been my policy to discourage discrimination against any persons by reason of their race," Baker told Scott, but that proved to be a difficult policy to enforce.[7]

The War Department refused to train black officers until an outcry from students and faculty at black universities led to the creation of a segregated officer training camp in Des Moines, Iowa.[8] Black troops and officers in the army's two segregated combat divisions, the Ninety-second and Ninety-third, contended with prevalent racism. Sixty years after the war, veteran Harry Haywood could still vividly recall the prejudice he witnessed while serving in France with the 370th Infantry Regiment, Ninety-third Division: the white officer who castigated an enlisted man for forgetting his mess hall ticket, the doctor who threatened to charge a convalescing sergeant with disobedience for refusing to remake his bed, the army bulletin informing French officers that the "vices of the Negro are a constant menace."[9] The commanding officer of the 372nd Infantry Regiment, Ninety-third Division, segregated the officers' mess and quarters during the Atlantic crossing; separate and unequal barracks also awaited the black officers in France.[10]

The combat readiness of the black divisions suffered as a result of this discrimination. The first regiment to arrive, the 369th, was put to work in December 1917 laying railroad track for a supply depot. Indeed, the War Department had ordered the regiment's deployment ahead of

[4] Barbeau and Henri, *Unknown Soldiers*, 100–1, 191–201 (quotes on 191 and 193).
[5] Unsigned letter from the "Boys of 449 Res. Labor Battalion" to the Secretary of War, December 3, 1918, box 1, no folder, RG 159, Port Inspector.
[6] Memorandum to the Port Inspector, October 13, 1919, box 6, folder "Investigations, October 1919," RG 159, Port Inspector.
[7] Beaver, *Newton D. Baker*, 224–31 (quote on 228).
[8] Scott, *Scott's Official History*, 82–91.
[9] Haywood, *Black Bolshevik*, 54–5, 73–5 (quote on 55). Harry Haywood's real name was Haywood Hall.
[10] Williams, *Torchbearers of Democracy*, 128–9.

schedule in order to halt escalating racial tensions at Camp Wadsworth in Spartanburg, South Carolina. The Ninety-second Division's commanding officer, General Charles C. Ballou, hurt morale by issuing a bulletin that appeared to order black servicemen to quietly accept racist treatment whenever they experienced trouble near their training camps. The field artillery regiments in the Ninety-second Division did not receive specialized training until just before leaving for France in June 1918.[11] In early 1918, the War Department assigned all four infantry regiments of the Ninety-third Division (369th, 370th, 371st, 372nd) to the French army, which had been promised American units. Although General John J. Pershing later characterized the transfer as temporary, the regiments served the duration of the war under French command. The troops wore American uniforms but were issued French gear, rations, and weapons. In practice and intention, the reassignment "cast African American troops as outside the U.S. Army, and, in a symbolic sense, outside of the nation itself," as Chad L. Williams observes.[12]

Despite these impediments, black troops consistently performed well in combat.[13] The achievements of the 369th were especially notable. Nicknamed the Harlem Hellfighters – the 369th was formed from a New York City-based National Guard unit – the regiment deployed to Chateau-Thierry during the Spring 1918 German offensive. In late May, Sergeant Henry Johnson earned international fame and the Croix de Guerre medal for repelling a German raiding party that attacked the observation post he was manning with Private Needham Roberts. In June, the regiment ousted German forces from Belleau Wood in fierce fighting. By mid-August, it had been on the lines for four straight months.[14] During the Fall 1918 Meuse-Argonne offensive to break the Germans' one-hundred-mile long defensive "Hindenburg Line," the 371st was dispatched to take a heavily guarded, strategic hill. A feigned surrender by German forces set a trap that decimated Company C, First Battalion, but the troops refused to yield and forced a German retreat.[15]

---

[11] Barbeau and Henri, *Unknown Soldiers*, 72–88, 111.

[12] Williams, *Torchbearers of Democracy*, 119–20 (quote on 120).

[13] A notable exception was the breakdown of the 368th Infantry Regiment, Ninety-second Division, during the September 1918 Meuse-Argonne offensive; however, a lack of support, training, and experience led to the failure. Deficient performance under fire afflicted some white units as well, but only in the case of the 368th was the race of the unit's officers singled out as the cause. See Williams, *Torchbearers of Democracy*, 138–40.

[14] Barbeau and Henri, *Unknown Soldiers*, 116–22.

[15] Williams, *Torchbearers of Democracy*, 135–8.

On the homefront, black men and women supported the war in ways that also advanced their goal to end racial discrimination. They raised funds for the Young Men's Christian Association (YMCA), which operated canteens for troops in the United States and France. Working with the American Library Association, the YMCA taught illiterate draftees to read and write. The Young Women's Christian Association (which, like the YMCA, maintained segregated programs) set up hostess houses at training camps. YWCA leaders wanted to aid not just soldiers, but also young black women, who could now contribute to the war effort in a structured, chaperoned environment.[16] Prominent black leaders served on local committees to aid the military's War Camp Community Service clubs for black servicemen. Washington, D.C., had one of the most active clubs; some of its events (picnics, recitals, taffy-pulls) attracted hundreds of participants. Yet the club's purposes extended beyond entertainment: "Every agency having for its object the development and advancement of the race is asked to cooperate with the club."[17] African Americans took part in the bandage-rolling campaign organized by the American Red Cross, while the National Association of Colored Graduate Nurses, aided by the black press, lobbied the Red Cross and the War Department to accept black nurses into national service.[18] E. Azalia Hackley, an accomplished concert singer, extolled black patriotism through pageants and festivals. Her elaborate wartime events, some of which featured hundreds of participants and drew thousands of spectators, prominently displayed African Americans' contribution to the Allied effort. A July 1918 pageant in Atlanta, for example, included 100 black soldiers from a nearby camp. At the same time, Hackley's inclusion of cherished spirituals in the musical repertoire subtly linked the antebellum freedom struggle to the current one.[19] A wartime slogan might have told African Americans, "*first* your Country, *then* your Rights," but, as these examples demonstrate, many believed they could serve both causes simultaneously.[20]

---

[16] Ibid., 97–103.

[17] "District of Columbia War-Camp Community Service of the War and Navy Departments Commissions on Training Camp Activities," March 1919, box C-374, folder "Military, General 1919, March," NAACP Records.

[18] Patterson, "Black Nurses."

[19] Karpf, "Get the Pageant Habit."

[20] The *Crisis* 16, no. 5 (September 1918), 217, cited in Mjagkij, *Loyalty in Time*, xxii. For more examples of African Americans' homefront contributions, see Mjagkij, *Loyalty in Time*, 121–40. Black support for the war was not, however, universal; opposition to conscription was common in the South. See Keith, *Rich Man's War*. For black apathy toward the war, see Kornweibel, *Investigate Everything*, 76–87.

The Great Migration was just as influential as the war. Between 1914 and 1920, more than 500,000 African Americans relocated from the rural south to northern cities. Floods and a cotton crop failure were two major sources of the migration. Southern blacks who sharecropped also yearned to escape debt peonage and the white supremacy upholding it. The outbreak of the war in August 1914 all but stopped European immigration to the United States, creating a labor shortage in northern factories. Labor recruiters fanned out across the South; migration clubs formed. Railroad depots bustled with black families boarding trains bound for Chicago, Detroit, Pittsburgh. Angered by the prospect of losing cheap labor, white southerners menaced would-be migrants and recruiters but failed to halt the exodus.[21] The arrival of so many new residents heightened racial tensions in the affected cities. Not surprisingly, two of these cities, Chicago and Gary, Indiana, experienced race riots in 1919; a third, East St. Louis, Illinois, was wracked by antiblack collective violence in July 1917.

The black population of East St. Louis had almost tripled between 1890 and 1917. Eager to obstruct interracial solidarity among their workers, employers encouraged animus against blacks. White resentment of rising black prosperity also precipitated violence: throughout May and June, a series of mob actions targeted blacks and black-owned property. The chief of police did nothing to stop the attacks, instead announcing his intention to crack down on black criminals. Black citizens prepared to defend themselves, drawing on the tradition of self-defense and the community institutions that southern migrants had brought with them. Black business owners obtained weapons in St. Louis; ceremonial marching by the Odd Fellows may have masked drilling. When mob attacks escalated on July 1, a black church bell served as a warning siren. Carefully placed black snipers subjected white drive-by shooters to crossfire. One attack by whites brought out an estimated counterforce of forty to seventy-five armed blacks. Still, the riot took a high toll. Three days of mob violence killed thirty-nine blacks and nine whites, while the targeting of black businesses and property caused three million dollars in damages.[22]

---

[21] Significant studies of the Great Migration include Arnesen, *Black Protest*; Grossman, *Land of Hope*; Trotter, *Great Migration*; and Marks, *Farewell*.

[22] Studies of the East St. Louis riot include Rudwick, *Race Riot*, which identifies economic competition as the riot's leading source; Lumpkins, *American Pogrom*, which emphasizes whites' alarm at black community-building; and McLaughlin, "Ghetto Formation and Armed Resistance," which analyzes black self-defense efforts. See also McLaughlin, *Power, Community, and Racial Killing*.

Another wartime race riot showed just how much African Americans' military service was antagonizing white supremacists. In Houston, Texas, white police officers perceived the nearby encampment of a black unit, the Twenty-fourth Infantry, Third Battalion, as a threat to their authority. On August 23, 1917, an officer pistol-whipped a black private who publicly questioned the humiliation of a black woman during her arrest. The assault followed several episodes of white police beating soldiers for breaking Jim Crow rules aboard streetcars. Fearing that his men might retaliate, the battalion's white commanding officer collected his men's arms. Rumors of a white mob, however, led to a mutiny – soldiers from two companies reclaimed their weapons and attacked whites in Houston's Sixth Ward. The army dealt harshly with the rebellion. The first of three courts martial tried sixty-three defendants and convicted fifty-eight, of whom thirteen were sentenced to death. Black commentators censured the mutineers but also pointed out that the aggressive actions of the police had abused the men of the Third Battalion until their discipline broke down. In this sense, the rebellion was a flashpoint in the growing struggle between black assertions of manhood and citizenship and the enforcement of white supremacy.[23]

The riots in East St. Louis and Houston were not the only episodes of wartime racial conflict. Fights between black and white troops broke out in training camps in Virginia and Maryland.[24] The backlash against southern migrants in northern industrial cities was not unique to East St. Louis. Chester, Pennsylvania, also experienced a race riot in July 1917.[25] In Chicago, a wave of bombings targeted the residences of blacks who moved into white neighborhoods and the offices of realtors selling homes to blacks.[26] The rapid expansion of the federal government created tens of thousands of jobs in Washington, D.C., and though the hiring policies of the Wilson administration limited black employment opportunities, whites resented the boost to black prosperity that the war brought. The same was true in Charleston, South Carolina, where the

---

[23] For treatment of the Houston mutiny as a conflict over black manhood and citizenship, see Lentz-Smith, *Freedom Struggles*, 43–79; for a full-length study of the mutiny, see Haynes, *Night of Violence*.

[24] Quander E. Hall to Captain Harry A. Taylor, October 11, 1918, Case File 10218–287–1, RG 165, copy in box 1, reel 5, Kornweibel Papers; Captain Harold F. Butler to G. B. Perkins, August 13, 1918, Case File 10218–199–1, RG 165, index card in box 7, card file box 9, Kornweibel Papers.

[25] See Chapter 10.

[26] Tuttle, *Race Riot*, 175–6.

Navy Yard and a new army port terminal created jobs for whites and blacks.

The clash between white supremacy and African Americans' expectations showed no signs of abating as the war continued. The nation's leading black writers, journalists, and editors recognized the need for an unflinching effort to remind all Americans why white supremacy must be destroyed as well as to rally African Americans to persevere in the domestic freedom struggle. This campaign added to and altered efforts already underway to promote racial uplift, unite communities within the African diaspora, and undermine the ideological and structural props of white supremacy. The wartime fashioning of this New Negro identity armed and readied, figuratively and literally, African Americans for 1919's antiblack collective violence.

The New Negro Movement

The New Negro is most often associated with the Harlem Renaissance of the 1920s, but the movement had its origins in earlier black self-help efforts. In the 1890s, the black elite, which comprised two percent of the black population, forged a racial uplift ideology based on middle class morality, self-improvement, and patriarchal authority. Proponents hoped such striving would abate white racism and win white allies to restore black men's political rights. Likewise, middle class black women advanced a bourgeois respectability for black women of all classes that prized sexual restraint and purity. Protecting black women (especially those who worked as domestic servants) from the sexual depredations of white men was, then, a necessary part of this campaign. For black men, whose manhood was constantly challenged and belittled by white supremacy, a similar respectability relied on their struggle to simultaneously resist emasculation and to establish an ideal identity for black men. Obtaining long-denied political rights, the rights of American *men*, was central to this initiative.[27]

The prewar New Negro identity emerged from the racial uplift ideology, but the New Negro was not merely a middle class striver seeking to cooperate with whites. Many black writers and activists believed the

---

[27] The definitive work on racial uplift ideology is Gaines, *Uplifting the Race*. For black women's promotion of bourgeois respectability, see Wolcott, *Remaking Respectability*. For black manhood during the late nineteenth and early twentieth centuries, see Ross, *Manning the Race*, and Summers, *Manliness and Its Discontents*.

New Negro must unite with blacks who lived outside of the United States. In 1913, black journalist and editor William H. Ferris published *The African Abroad, or His Evolution in Western Civilization, Tracing His Development under Caucasian Milieu.* Influenced by Social Darwinism, Ferris urged black men to adopt the traits that supposedly made "Anglo-Saxons" the world's master race: competitiveness, power, protection of racial purity. His cyclical reading of history led him to argue that people of African descent were at a low point, but following his prescriptions would restore Africans and the diaspora population to their rightful place at the forefront of the world's civilizations and races. Ferris was, as Kevin Gaines explains, a black nationalist seeking to bend the racial fictions that upheld white supremacy to blacks' advantage.[28]

Writer and activist Hubert Harrison, a contemporary of Ferris, was one of the most important internationally minded New Negroes. Born in the West Indies, Harrison emigrated to New York in 1900. A socialist for a time, Harrison's trenchant analysis of the international aspects of racial and class oppression led him to found the Liberty League and its newspaper the *Voice* in 1917. The first New Negro organization, the Liberty League called for a federal antilynching law, armed self-defense against mobs, cross-racial labor unity, and decolonization. In a 1917 essay explaining the league's principles, Harrison warned that if the state cannot halt mob violence, "then we should call upon our people to defend themselves against murder with the weapons of murder." Democracy for blacks in the United States, Harrison also wrote, depended on joining with 250 million Africans – "our brethren" – who want freedom and opportunity as well. Harrison celebrated blacks' armed resistance during the East St. Louis riot, even contending that if whites killed blacks who had done nothing wrong, then blacks must kill whites in order to protect their property and lives.[29] Harrison questioned the black elite's reliance on racial uplift ideology. True race consciousness, he argued, must come from the masses and take in radicals of all varieties in order to weaken the many forms of global white supremacy: colonialism, Jim Crow, antiblack collective violence.[30]

---

[28] Gaines, *Uplifting the Race*, 100–27.
[29] Harrison, *Hubert Harrison Reader*. For an overview of Harrison's life and ideas, see 1–30. Harrison's writings used here are: "Declaration of Principles [of the Liberty League]," *Clarion* (September 1, 1917) [89–92]; "The East St. Louis Horror," *Voice* (July 4, 1917) [94–5].
[30] Gaines, *Uplifting the Race*, 234–46.

The Liberty League and Harrison's ideas about race consciousness had a profound influence on Marcus Garvey and the Universal Negro Improvement Association (UNIA).[31] Born in Jamaica, Garvey settled in New York in 1916 and articulated a vision of racial solidarity that quickly attracted attention and followers. (The UNIA had almost 1,000 divisions in the United States, the Caribbean, and elsewhere by the mid-1920s.) Even a slight offense against a white man was taken as an offense to the entire white race, Garvey noted, but blacks do not as yet respond in kind to the minor humiliation of a fellow black. Fire must be fought with fire, Garvey said. He, too, celebrated blacks' armed resistance to white violence, but the ferocity of the attacks helped convince him that American-born blacks must emigrate to Africa to establish a homeland, a mission that would also help rid Africa of European colonialism. Like Harrison, Garvey saw the fight against mob violence within America as part of an international struggle. (Garvey and Harrison worked together briefly – Harrison edited the *Negro World*, the UNIA's newspaper – but doubts about Garvey's business ventures and ego led Harrison to break with Garvey in the early 1920s.)[32]

Socialism added texture to the New Negro identity. As noted, Harrison was a socialist, but disillusionment with racism within New York's Socialist Party prodded him toward his unique race-conscious, class activism.[33] Two other transplants to New York, Chandler Owen and A. Philip Randolph, remained committed to socialism. Owen, born in North Carolina in 1889, was a college graduate who attended Columbia University on a fellowship provided by the National Urban League. The son of a Florida tailor, Randolph was self-educated. The two men met in 1915 in New York, where they learned much about Marxism by listening to Harrison's renowned street corner lectures. In 1917, Owen and Randolph founded the *Messenger*, a monthly magazine devoted to the promotion of interracial class solidarity and an end to white supremacy in all its forms.[34]

Woodrow Wilson's wartime mission was as much an influence on New Negro identity as racial uplift, black nationalism, and socialism.

---

[31] Harrison, *Hubert Harrison Reader*, 1–30.

[32] For Garvey's response to white violence, see Shapiro, *White Violence*, 161–74. For an overview of Garvey's ideas and writings, see Hill and Bair, *Marcus Garvey, Life and Lessons*.

[33] Harrison, *Hubert Harrison Reader*, 1–30. For more on the radical features of New Negro identity, see Maxwell, *New Negro, Old Left*, 13–61, and Foley, *Spectres of 1919*, 1–69.

[34] Kornweibel, *No Crystal Stair*, 25–35.

Even before the president called on Americans to fight to make the world safe for democracy, black journalists, editors, and writers linked the war in Europe to the cause of freedom. Several editors compared German atrocities in Belgium to lynchings in the United States and the misdeeds of U.S. marines stationed in Haiti. In 1915, the *Chicago Defender* questioned the legitimacy of any possible U.S. involvement in Europe's war: how could a nation unwilling to snuff out rough justice within its own borders ethically intervene in the affairs of other nations?[35] Once the United States entered the war, writers appropriated the federal government's wartime propaganda. Attempts to inculcate patriotism within the so-called hyphenate Americans (recent European immigrants) invited the pointed reminder that Africans and their descendants had, for centuries, fought for the United States. As W. F. Cozart observed in the *Defender*, "the Negro has shown his loyalty and bravery from the time that Crispus Attucks fell a martyr on the Commons of Boston."[36] In their response to and adaptation of Wilsonianism and war mobilization, these writers used the New Negro identity to justify and encourage black resistance to mob violence. More than this: they hoped their efforts would force the state to bring rioters to justice and to ensure that all Americans, not just those of European descent, secured the rights and liberties guaranteed in the Constitution.

New Negro writers included William Monroe Trotter, fiery founder and editor of the *Boston Guardian*. Trotter was unrelenting in his criticism of segregated army officer training during the war and an early celebrant of black armed self-defense. "What men plant that shall they surely gather," he had warned in 1904. "As the south is sowing the storm, the whirlwind it must some day reap."[37] NAACP cofounder and *Crisis* editor W. E. B. Du Bois famously called on fellow black Americans to "close ranks," that is, to join together to fight in the war with the expectation of gaining their rights after an Allied victory.[38] In the *New York Age*, James Weldon Johnson continually linked the war to winning democracy at home. Harry Clay Smith, a three-term Ohio state

---

[35] Jordan, *Black Newspapers*, 36–45.

[36] W. F. Cozart, "To the White American," *Chicago Defender*, July 14, 1917, 2. For the black press's response to the U.S. entry into the war, see Jordan, *Black Newspapers*, 68–106.

[37] Fox, *Guardian of Boston*, 231–2.

[38] For differing views on Du Bois's "Close Ranks" editorial, see Jordan, "'Damnable Dilemma'" and Ellis, "W. E. B. Du Bois." For the NAACP's response to the war and the organization's postwar plans, see Schneider, *We Return Fighting*, 7–19.

legislator, founded the *Cleveland Gazette* and served as its editor for decades. Although he was a contemporary of Booker T. Washington, Smith had little patience for Washington's policy of accommodation. Smith and his fellow contributor Dr. William A. Byrd continually railed against Jim Crow and celebrated black resistance to racial violence and discrimination.[39] Robert Abbott's *Chicago Defender* was that city's leading black newspaper, known both for its salacious crime stories and for its unflagging encouragement of black migration to the North. National distribution extended the *Defender*'s influence, particularly in the South, but Abbott had a rival, the *Broad-Ax*, founded in 1895. Julius Taylor, the *Broad-Ax*'s publisher and editor, was, like Harry Clay Smith, a harsh critic of Booker T. Washington. J. Anthony Josey, a graduate of Atlanta University and the University of Wisconsin law school, founded the *Wisconsin Blade* in 1916. Wisconsin's black population was small, but the *Blade* was no less attuned to the denial of democracy to blacks than newspapers with greater circulation.[40]

Many of the New Negroes simultaneously supported the war and the domestic freedom struggle. James Weldon Johnson declared Wilson's war aims a "great trial" for the United States. Would the nation fulfill its ideals and constitutional guarantees once the Allies won their victory? Yet black editors had to choose their words carefully. The sweeping Espionage Act empowered the federal government to imprison anyone for even the mildest dissent, and agents of the Military Intelligence Division (MID) and the Department of Justice's Bureau of Investigation (BI) were avid readers of black publications. Nevertheless, black editors felt secure enough to present the government with several demands, including one for a federal antilynching law, after a national conference in Washington in June 1918. The president, breaking with his customary antipathy toward civil rights issues, denounced lynching in a statement the next month.[41]

Not all New Negroes supported the war, however. Socialists Chandler Owen and A. Philip Randolph pointedly asked why African Americans should fight to make the world safe for democracy when their own nation had stripped them of their constitutional rights and refused to protect them from mob violence. The men embarked on an antiwar lecture tour in the summer of 1918, traveling the country. Under constant

---

[39] Jordan, *Black Newspapers*, 21–3; Ross, "Democracy's Textbook."
[40] For details of the *Defender* and *Broad-Ax*, see Walker, "Promised Land"; for the *Wisconsin Blade*, see McBride, "Progress of 'Race Men.'"
[41] Jordan, *Black Newspapers*, 68–78, 98–133 (Johnson quote on 77).

surveillance by federal agents, Owen and Randolph were arrested in Cleveland, Ohio, and charged with violating the Espionage Act. Although a judge released them, Owen's failure to register for the draft later led to his imprisonment. (The married Randolph was exempt from conscription.) These disruptions prevented the *Messenger* from appearing regularly until March 1919, but neither man wavered in his opposition to the war.[42]

Whatever their position on the war, New Negro writers and editors entered the postwar period cautiously hopeful about making America safe for democracy. "What does the Negro expect out of the recent war?" asked J. Anthony Josey in the *Wisconsin Blade*. "He expects to be treated as a man in Mississippi as well as in Wisconsin ... he expects for himself and his dear ones absolutely the same treatment accorded every other citizen." The *Black Dispatch* (Oklahoma City) dedicated its January 10, 1919, issue to the Oklahoma state legislature, asking it to grant black men the right to vote. "If a man will submit in blood sacrifice his life upon the altar for your freedom – what is your responsibility?" The *Defender* echoed this question in a May 1919 editorial supporting a civil rights bill in Ohio: "When you send men to die upon foreign soil to uphold the rights of democracy you cannot deny its application at home."[43] The ferocity of white supremacy's reassertion during 1919 did not dampen the journalists' optimism or dilute their dedication. They had expected white opposition. The question was: how would the New Negro, tempered by war, respond to the backlash?

Armed resistance and the overall fighting spirit of blacks thus thrilled the New Negro journalists, who praised black self-defenders. In his survey of the black press in 1919, the white sociologist Robert Kerlin concluded, "self-defense is applauded and advocated by the entire colored press, with one exception."[44] No surrender, no cringing, declared the *Call* of Kansas City. "Since it is appointed unto all men once to die, how better can we die than in defending our lives, our homes, our rights from the attacks of white men?"[45] Across the South, blacks were organizing to protect themselves, reported the *New York Call*.[46] In the *Cleveland Gazette*,

[42] Kornweibel, *No Crystal Stair*, 29–35; Williams, *Torchbearers of Democracy*, 24–6.
[43] "What the Negro Expects Out of the War," *Wisconsin Weekly Blade*, May 10, 1919, 4; "What Black Men Are Thinking Today," *Black Dispatch*, January 10, 1919; "Putting Teeth in an Old Law," *Chicago Defender*, May 3, 1919, 20.
[44] Kerlin, *Voice of the Negro*, 23.
[45] Ibid., 77–8.
[46] Transcription of a clipping, *New York Call*, July 25, 1919, Waskow Notes, tab "U.S. Reaction."

Harry Clay Smith urged readers to arm themselves: "For more than fifteen years, *The Gazette* has been warning our people of this and all other large cities of the country to get ready for [race riots]." His colleague William Byrd vigorously defended counterattacks against mobs. We do not advocate violence, he wrote, but if violence is used to deny us our rights, it is foolish to be moderate. "Violence is the one remedy that will bring the white southern ruffians to their senses," he declaimed. "In taking this stand we do so because our backs are to the wall and it is either fight for life or lie down and die like a coward, which we will never do."[47] Chicagoan Fenton Johnson, editor and publisher of the magazine the *Favorite*, echoed that challenge. "Are we to be people, sons and daughters of Freedom, or are we to be doormats for the other races?"[48] If we fail to take our rights, the *Broad-Ax* of Chicago warned, "our descendants would curse our memory."[49] Mistreatment of African Americans was not new, the *Wisconsin Weekly Blade* observed, and so widespread it would "breed discontent among angels." But America is now taking notice because African Americans now "have the manhood to resent it – a healthy change."[50] In the September 1919 issue of the *Messenger*, Owen and Randolph published Claude McKay's poem "If We Must Die!" and proclaimed it a creed for the New Negro:

> If we must die, let it not be like hogs
>   Hunted and penned in an inglorious spot,
> While round us bark the mad and hungry dogs,
>   Making their mock at our accursed lot.
> If we must die, oh, let us nobly die.
>   So that our precious blood may not be shed
> In vain; then even the monsters we defy
>   Shall be constrained to honor us, though dead!
> Oh, kinsman! We must meet the common foe;
>   Though far outnumbered, let us still be brave,
> And for their thousand blows deal one death-blow!
>   What though before us lies the open grave?
> Like men we'll face the murderous, cowardly pack,
>   Pressed to the wall, dying, but – fighting back!

[47] Harry Clay Smith, "The Mob! A Warning," *Cleveland Gazette*, August 2, 1919, 2; "Dr. Wm. A. Byrd on Race Riots," *Cleveland Gazette*, August 30, 1919, 1.

[48] A. H. Loula, "In re: Race Rioting in Chicago," August 2, 1919, RG 65, OGF 369,914, reel 812.

[49] A. H. Loula, "In re: 'The Broad Ax' (Negro Newspaper)," August 6, 1919, RG 65, OGF 373,051, reel 820.

[50] *Wisconsin Weekly Blade*, September 18, 1919, in Kerlin, *Voice of the Negro*, 140.

The New Negro, with his "dauntless manhood, defiant eye, steady hand and a will of iron," commented the editors, would not shirk from confronting white mobs. Like McKay, Owen and Randolph intimated that the New Negro's willingness to die in this struggle would inflict heavy damage on those fighting to keep him subservient and weak.[51]

Long lauded as the New Negro's call to resistance, McKay's poem was not the first postwar celebration in verse of black self-defense. Song lyricist Andy Razaf (his works include "Ain't Misbehavin'" and "Stompin' at the Savoy") published "Don't Tread on Me" in the *Crusader* in April 1919. The title refers to the insignia of the 369th Regiment, the Harlem Hellfighters, which featured a coiled snake, poised to strike. Evoking the famous rallying cry from the American Revolution, Razak called on the race to make "Don't Tread on Me" a battle call: "Engrave it on your heart / It's time for us to 'do or die,' / To play a bolder part. / For by the blood you've spilled in France / You must – and will – be free / So, from now on, let us advance / With this, 'DON'T TREAD ON ME!'" Razak wrote many other poems featuring black veterans, who were presented as a vanguard who would keep white racists in check.[52]

The black self-defender was a distinctly masculine figure. When black male journalists wrote about the year's antiblack collective violence, they dwelled on men, especially veterans, but black women also praised armed resistance. Carita Owens Collins lauded black veterans for continuing the fight for democracy in her poem "Be a Man!": The "blood so freely spent on Flanders' field, / Shall yet redeem your race. / Be men, not cowards and demand your rights." Another poet, Georgia D. Johnson, bid black men to "spurn the handicap that binds you, taking what the world denies."[53] Mary Burrill's play *Aftermath*, published in the April 1919 issue of the *Liberator*, featured a black veteran who takes up arms to avenge the lynching of his father.[54] Yet black women were more than cheering spectators. In the UNIA, for example, the Black Cross Nurses ministered to sick members and operated soup kitchens. Modeled after

[51] "If We Must Die," *Messenger* vol. II, no. 9 (September 1919), 4. As printed, McKay's poem differed slightly from subsequent versions. In the *Messenger*, line five of the first stanza reads "If we must die, oh, let us nobly die"; in later versions, that line reads "If we must die, let it not be like hogs." See, for example, the version in Kerlin, *Voice of the Negro*, 186.

[52] Maxwell, *New Negro, Old Left*, 13–61 (see 42 for the text of "Don't Tread on Me").

[53] Georgia D. Johnson, "The Question," and Carita Owens Collins, "Be a Man!," in Kerlin, *Voice of the Negro*, 183–5.

[54] Tylee, "Womanist Propaganda," 157.

the Red Cross, the uniformed nurses exemplified ideal female traits such as nurture, service, and care. They provided a foil to the UNIA's all-male Universal African Legions, which embodied ideal male attributes of power, independence, and martial discipline. Both the nurses and the legions reinforced traditional gender norms; however, as Barbara Bair argues, they also forcefully rejected prevailing stereotypes about African Americans, that black men were a timid, oppressed underclass and that black women must serve whites, not their race.[55] In Texas, black women helped organize a number of NAACP branches during the war.[56] Two of these branches, San Antonio's and Austin's, provided legal help to black self-defenders jailed after the Longview, Texas, race riot in July 1919. As a vital part of the New Negro movement, black women supported or carried out activities that enabled resistance.

New Negroes were quick to recognize the link between manly armed resistance and the fight for political rights. Failure to grant equality, they warned, would only incur more armed resistance. In the *New York Age*, James Weldon Johnson wrote, "the Negro is in no temper to tamely submit to the kind of treatment which he has hitherto received, and he is not going to do it." In another editorial, Johnson went even further. Killing blacks to teach them a lesson will only backfire, he wrote. Thousands of black soldiers died in France, and their comrades are not afraid to face death in the same fight for freedom at home.[57] "Will Uncle Sam Stand for this Cross?" the *Defender* asked above a cartoon showing a white southerner pinning the "Croix de Lynch" on the chest of a uniformed black soldier.[58] No longer will blacks accept servitude and second-class citizenship, declared William Scarborough in the *Cleveland Gazette*. The only cure for the race riots was "justice – a willingness to accord to every man his rights – civil and political."[59] The editors of the *Houston Informer* resorted to capital letters to connect the war to black expectations: "THE BLACK MAN FOUGHT TO MAKE THE WORLD SAFE FOR DEMOCRACY, he now demands that AMERICA BE MADE AND MAINTAINED SAFE FOR BLACK

---

[55] Bair, "True Women, Real Men."
[56] Reich, "Soldiers of Democracy," 1490–3.
[57] James Weldon Johnson, "Views and Reviews," *New York Age*, August 2, 1919, 4, and September 13, 1919, 4.
[58] "Will Uncle Sam Stand for this Cross?," *Chicago Defender*, April 5, 1919, editorial page.
[59] "Pres. William S. Scarborough's Splendid Treatise on Race Riots and Their Remedy," *Cleveland Gazette*, September 20, 1919, 4.

FIGURE 1.1. Welcome Home Parade, Washington, D.C., February 27, 1919. The year of racial violence was underway when these black soldiers marched proudly down Pennsylvania Avenue in a parade honoring their service in the war to make the world safe for democracy. *Source:* U.S. Army Signal Corps. Courtesy of the National Archives, College Park, Md., Record Group 111, box 305, Photograph 111-SC-39897.

AMERICANS."[60] William Monroe Trotter credited President Wilson himself for this aspect of the New Negro movement. "The new spirit among the colored Americans of resisting attacks upon their lives is something for which President Wilson is chiefly responsible. His reiteration of noble sentiments and making our boys fight under their inspiration has given birth to a new spirit of manliness" (Figure 1.1).[61]

Many New Negroes, especially socialists, recognized that the domestic freedom struggle was part of an international movement. They celebrated Japan's efforts to add an antidiscrimination clause to the League of Nations charter during the Paris Peace proceedings. When Wilson rejected even a vague statement on the equality of nations, Chandler Owen and A. Philip Randolph criticized the president for protecting colonialism

[60] Kerlin, *Voice of the Negro*, 34.
[61] British Intelligence Service, "Negro Agitation," October 19, 1919, RG 65, OGF 3057, reel 304, 3.

and racial supremacy. In Harlem, public meetings and street corner lectures resounded with denunciations of the Allies for using their victory to protect, even expand, their colonial empires. (As Owen and Randolph piquantly observed, there was a big difference between "*peace* conferences and *piece* conferences.") The Caribbean-born Cyril Briggs, publisher of the *Crusader* and founder of the African Blood Brotherhood, called upon the Allies to grant full equality and rights to people of color, outlaw racial discrimination, and end the exploitation of Africa. W. E. B. Du Bois, recognizing the shared challenges and goals of the people of the African diaspora, helped organize the Pan-African Congress, held in Paris in February 1919. Its fifty-seven delegates put forward resolutions for graduated self-government in Africa and urged the Allies to use the League of Nations to protect the rights of Africans.[62] After his return from Paris, Du Bois publicly spoke about the similarities between the struggles of black Americans and Africans to escape the oppression of white supremacy.[63] Inspired by Wilson's vision of a postwar world based on the principle of self-determination, colonized peoples hoped the 1919 peace talks would result in sweeping decolonization. Hundreds of petitions arrived at the U.S. delegation's quarters in Paris as Koreans, Egyptians, and Indians, among many others, directly appealed to Wilson to dismantle colonial control of their respective homelands. If the Wilsonian Moment, as Erez Manela calls it, was short lived, its influence was long lasting. When the peace proceedings failed to advance self-determination for the non-Western world, protests broke out in the spring of 1919, propelling anticolonial nationalist movements in India and elsewhere.[64]

   Contempt for the so-called Old Crowd negroes was another feature of the New Negro movement. Although members of the Old Crowd were often not named, the pejorative typically referred to black clergy and community leaders who counseled restraint in the face of white mob violence and reliance on white authorities to keep the peace. Hubert Harrison criticized the Old Crowd for not doing enough to help blacks secure equality and opportunity.[65] William Byrd castigated ministers who called on blacks to stand down during riots. "Gentlemen, you are not

---

[62] Onishi, "New Negro of the Pacific," 191–213 (Owen and Randolph are quoted on 198). A firm stance against white supremacy and overtures to black leaders such as Marcus Garvey brought Japan considerable admiration and support among African Americans during the early twentieth century. See Horne, *Race War!*, 43–59.
[63] Contee, "Du Bois, the NAACP."
[64] Manela, *Wilsonian Moment*.
[65] Harrison, "As the Currents Flow," in *Hubert Harrison Reader*, 97–9.

rioting, but are doing your duty," Byrd addressed self-defenders, adding, "don't start anything but when something is started make it hot for them and finish it!"[66] The *Crusader* called on the "Old Negro" to pass in peace. Fifty years of quiescence and cowering brought only lynchings, Jim Crow, and disfranchisement, but now the New Negro led the race. "Can the Old Leaders deny that there is more wholesome respect for the Negro following the race riots... than there was before those riots and when there were only lynchings and burnings of scared Negroes and none of the fear in the white man's heart that comes from the New Negro fighting back?" Calvin Chase, of the *Washington Bee*, excoriated two black leaders who appeared before a Congressional committee to speak *against* a bill abolishing segregated railcars in the South. No longer could such men be trusted. "It is the young colored Americans who are defending the rights and the liberties of their people, and the old school politician is the dangerous element in society," wrote Chase.[67] James Weldon Johnson called them "rabbit-hearted," the supposed "leaders" who advised blacks to let southern whites take care of racial tensions.[68]

But not all clergy stood with the Old Crowd. In Boston in July 1919, the Reverend M. A. N. Shaw, of Boston, delivered a speech exhorting black men to stand and fight for their rights, sacrificing their lives if necessary. Ten thousand black men should die killing the same number of white men, Shaw declared, before a mob lynches another victim. In October, Shaw expounded upon the topics of white mob violence and black resistance in an address to the annual convention of William Monroe Trotter's organization, the National Equal Rights League. Race riots will cease, Shaw predicted, as blacks educate – and arm – themselves to act in their own defense. Shaw was careful to advise that blacks should never be the aggressors, but never should they back down.[69] In a letter to President Wilson, the Reverend J. G. Robinson of Chattanooga, Tennessee, warned that before blacks surrender to "many of the injustices which we have suffered the white men will have to kill more of them than the combined number of soldiers that were slain in the great world war."[70] These

---

[66] William Byrd, "Defend Lives to the Last!," *Cleveland Gazette*, September 20, 1919, 1.

[67] Kerlin, *Voice of the Negro*, 25, 28.

[68] James Weldon Johnson, "Views and Reviews," *New York Age*, October 11, 1919, 4.

[69] "Call on Negroes to Kill Lynchers by Wholesale," *Boston Herald*, July 14, 1919, clipping in Case File 10218–130, RG 165, copy in box 1, reel 1, Kornweibel Papers; "Negro Agitation," 2.

[70] "Race War May Come," *Advance* (Providence, R.I.), August 1919, clipping in *NAACP Papers*, Part 7, Series A, reel 6, frame 270.

clergy's celebration of armed resistance to white supremacy thus showed the profound influence of the New Negro movement on blacks' postwar expectations.

When he called on Americans to make the world safe for democracy, Woodrow Wilson surely did not anticipate that African Americans would embrace and mold this mission into a domestic freedom struggle. His unwavering, yet doomed, effort to secure Senate ratification of the Versailles Treaty in the summer of 1919 (and thus U.S. membership in the League of Nations) distracted the president from recognizing blacks' own determination to fulfill their aims. Wilson was in residence in the White House in July 1919 when black residents of Washington, D.C., put up armed resistance to a series of white mob attacks; but, weakened by illness and consumed by the treaty battle, he said little publicly about the riot or the fact that hundreds of troops were deployed to restore order. Instead, the president fretted that the violence sullied America's reputation as a model democracy.[71]

But the United States was not as yet a model democracy, as the New Negroes observed repeatedly. The "great trial" James Weldon Johnson had written about was still underway: would the nation itself become safe for democracy? African Americans were being tested, too. Would they capitalize on their military service and domestic support for the war to fight against the reassertion of white supremacy? That question, or to put it another way, that challenge, came first in Charleston, South Carolina, in December 1918, one month after declaration of the armistice that ended the Great War.

---

[71] "President Is Worried Over Foreign View of Riots Here," *Washington Times*, July 23, 1919, 1.

2

"We Return Fighting"

The First Wave of Armed Resistance

During World War I, African Americans resolved to make America safe for democracy. Four outbreaks of violence resulting from the enforcement of white supremacy between December 1918 and early July 1919 demonstrated just how difficult it would be for African Americans to secure equal rights and opportunities. In each instance, however, blacks fought back against their attackers: in Charleston, South Carolina (twice); in Bisbee, Arizona; and in Longview, Texas. The variety of the resistance reveals the determination of African Americans across the South to stand up to white supremacy. In Charleston's first riot, in December 1918, black soldiers briefly joined together with white servicemen to halt a white police officer's abuse of a black private. By late May 1919, when Charleston experienced a second riot, this biracial *esprit de corps* had evaporated, replaced by the unity of white civilians and servicemen, who joined together to attack the city's black residents. Not intimidated, black Charlestonians defended themselves. Six weeks later, a white mob comprised of civilians, soldiers, and law enforcement officers targeted the men of the Tenth Cavalry, a black army unit stationed at Fort Huachuca, Arizona. The troopers, asserting their rights as soldiers, resisted a forcible seizure of their sidearms by sheriff's deputies and police during a Fourth of July celebration in nearby Bisbee. Just a few days later, armed black men in Longview, Texas, successfully dispersed a lynch mob intent on punishing a prominent black resident for his perceived affront to whites.

African Americans had returned fighting, as W. E. B. Du Bois observed in the May 1919 *Crisis*: "We *return from fighting*. We *return fighting*. Make way for Democracy! We saved it in France, and by the Great

Jehovah, we will save it in the United States of America, or know the reason why."[1] Du Bois might well have added: "We *remain fighting*." For almost all of the African Americans who resisted white mob violence in Charleston, Bisbee, and Longview had remained in the United States during the war. Black veterans of the Western Front would play a significant role in armed resistance later in 1919, but during these early months, as these veterans were on their way home, civilians and servicemen stationed at domestic bases provided the first wave of armed resistance.

Charleston's Difficult Transition to Peace

For Private Clovie Sylvester, the war to make the world safe for democracy never went beyond Charleston. Sylvester served in the 349th Colored Labor Battalion, which remained stateside to clear roads, pull stumps, and load ships – the hard, physical labor of mobilization. And in Charleston, there was no shortage of chores for these uniformed work details – "the military equivalent of chain gangs."[2] Already home to a vast Navy Yard, Charleston became the headquarters for the U.S. Army's Southeastern Department in 1917. The army constructed a massive port terminal that began serving as a disembarkation point for returning troops even before it was completed (Figure 2.1).[3]

Given the hardship of labor battalion service, it is not surprising that Private Sylvester wanted to make the most of his leave on Sunday, December 8, 1918. That evening, he drank a half-pint of bootleg whiskey at a Charleston restaurant, then left, unsteadily, around 7 P.M. to return to North Charleston, where the 349th Colored Labor Battalion was stationed. If he was lucky, he could slip unnoticed into his quarters to sleep off the liquor. But Sylvester was not lucky. Policeman Thomas F. Fosberry was on traffic duty at Columbus and Meeting Streets when Sylvester sat down on a curb to wait for a streetcar. Fosberry, disgusted at the sight of an inebriated black soldier in uniform, arrested him and used a callbox to summon a police wagon.[4]

The incident quickly attracted a crowd of servicemen and curious civilians. A black sergeant asked Fosberry if he could take Sylvester back

---

[1] Kerlin, *Voice of the Negro*, 37.
[2] Barbeau and Henri, *Unknown Soldiers*, 90.
[3] Moore, "Charleston in World War I," 45–6.
[4] Statement of Private Clovie Sylvester, *Report of Investigation of Riot in Charleston, Sunday, December 8, 1918*, Case File 10218–272, RG 165, reel 4 (hereafter *Investigation of Riot*).

FIGURE 2.1. Navy Yard at Charleston, South Carolina. The U.S. Navy's massive yard and port facility, along with an army port terminal, made Charleston an important site of war mobilization, leading to racial tensions in December 1918 and again in May 1919. *Source:* U.S. Navy, Bureau of Yards and Docks. Courtesy of the National Archives, College Park, Md., Record Group 71, folder 71-CA-84H.

to camp; a white private wanted to know why Sylvester was under arrest. Angry that his authority was being questioned, Fosberry struck Sylvester in the face with his billy club.[5]

A sailor protested. "Remember, you are hitting a United States uniform."

"Fuck the uniform!" Fosberry shot back. "These sons of bitches" – meaning the black soldiers – "should not be in them."[6]

Fosberry's violent outburst transformed the crowd into a mob. Soldiers and sailors, white and black, rushed forward. They seized Sylvester

---

[5] My description of the incident is based on Major Thomas W. Davis, Judge Advocate, *Report of Investigation of Riots by Soldiers, Sailors and Citizens, Charleston, S.C., Sunday Night, December 8, 1918*, December 17, 1918, Case File 10218–272, RG 165, reel 4, 4–5 (hereafter *Davis Report*); Statements of Sergeant Sidney Cagnolatti and Private Fred Carrier, *Investigation of Riot*.

[6] Statement of Private Fred Carrier, *Investigation of Riot*, 10.

and grabbed Fosberry's club. Someone struck the police officer. As if Sylvester was a triumphant athlete, the mob carried him away, but police reinforcements soon swarmed round and regained custody of Sylvester. In the melee, the police also arrested black private Richard Proctor for allegedly grappling with Police Lieutenant Edward R. McDonald.[7]

Undeterred, a mob of approximately 200 white and black servicemen and civilians followed the police to their precinct house. The mob's leadership, which included black enlisted men, wanted Sylvester and Proctor released and Fosberry punished for insulting the uniform. Additional police, led by Chief Joseph Black, intercepted the crowd. Black identified himself and ordered everyone to disperse, but the mob remained until Black promised to reprimand Fosberry. However, Sylvester, Proctor, and four other black soldiers remained in jail, either charged with disorderly conduct or carrying concealed weapons. These arrests were "absolutely unwarranted," the army's judge advocate later concluded. These men were bystanders, and their so-called concealed weapons were mere pocket knives. Only one white serviceman was arrested; he was released that night.[8]

Scores of servicemen and civilians, black and white, drifted back to Columbus and Meeting Streets, the site of Sylvester's arrest, where they waited for streetcars. The Charleston Consolidated Railway Company practiced segregation. Black passengers, at the command of the conductor, were obligated to move to the rear seats. Private Fletcher Brewer and Sergeant Cyrus W. Perry of the 349th Colored Labor Battalion were filing through the front door of a car when Conductor H. M. Fail ordered them to enter through the rear.[9] As the two men turned to exit, a white bystander named Henry Heyward called on them to ignore Fail because they were soldiers.[10] Anticipating trouble, the motorman menaced Brewer with his iron switch stick. Perry seized the motorman's wrist, prompting Fail to pistol-whip Perry. "Pull him out," the bystander Heyward shouted, referring to Fail – "I want to beat his damned heart out." The ensuing melee left several men hurt. Fail fired his pistol, grazing Perry in the shoulder. Soldiers and sailors then beat up the motorman and Fail.[11]

[7] *Davis Report*, 6–7.
[8] *Davis Report*, 8, 11–14 (quote on 11); Statement of Chief of Police J. A. Black, *Investigation of Riot*.
[9] Statement of J. O. Brinson, *Investigation of Riot*.
[10] Excerpt of testimony, *State vs. Heyward and Pope*, in *Investigation of Riot*.
[11] Statements of Fletcher Brewer, Cyrus W. Perry, H. M. Fail, and J. O. Brinson; memorandum from police blotter, December 8, 1918, in *Investigation of Riot*.

Why had the conductor Fail and his motorman been so quick to threaten Private Brewer and Sergeant Perry? After all, the men had started to obey Fail and had not reacted to Heyward's goading – Brewer later said he never even noticed Heyward.[12] But Fail and his motorman were edgy, afraid they might confront mass defiance of segregation. The night before, two of their co-workers had struggled to enforce Jim Crow at that same stop. A dispatcher had required police help to clear black soldiers from a white-only car, while another group of black servicemen had refused a motorman's order to vacate his car. The riders had taunted the motorman by continually blowing the car's whistle.[13] Fail and his motorman, determined not to be similarly humiliated, inflamed the situation by physically threatening Brewer and Perry.

Henry Heyward, the white bystander, was arrested, along with his friend John Pope. Both men were charged with inciting a riot and disturbing the peace. Heyward's motive for urging Brewer and Perry to defy Conductor H. M. Fail's order remains obscure. At his trial, Heyward denied calling out to the black soldiers, but several witnesses contradicted him. Heyward, who worked in the streetcar yard, may have nursed a grudge against Fail, or perhaps Heyward and Pope simply wanted to keep the night's disturbances alive. (Heyward admitted he had joined the mob that had demanded the release of Private Clovie Sylvester.) Unconvinced by the witnesses' testimony, the jury acquitted both men.[14]

Major Thomas W. Davis, the judge advocate investigating the troubles of December 8, came to a firm conclusion: "the mistreatment of private Sylvester and the alleged cursing of the soldiers and the uniform by the policeman at Columbus and Meeting Streets was the real and efficient cause of all the trouble in Charleston that night." The Charleston police, by unjustifiably striking Sylvester, Proctor, and other black soldiers, incurred "the anger and indignation of the soldiers, and sailors."[15] Davis also blamed Fail, his motorman, Heyward, and Pope for exacerbating tensions at the streetcar stop. Yet the arrests and trials resulting from both incidents showed favoritism toward the locals. The police had arrested eight servicemen and only two civilians. Three black soldiers who could not pay their fines served either fifteen or thirty days on the chain gang.[16] Davis warned that this unfair treatment would not "create

[12] Statement of Fletcher Brewer, *Investigation of Riot*.
[13] Statements of W. H. Baker and R. E. Guyton, *Investigation of Riot*.
[14] Excerpt of testimony, *State vs. Heyward and Pope*, in *Investigation of Riot*.
[15] *Davis Report*, 15.
[16] Memorandum from police blotter, December 8, 1918; excerpt of testimony, *State vs. Heyward and Pope*, in *Investigation of Riot*.

a spirit of good feeling and cooperation between soldiers and civilians"
in Charleston.[17]

No one needed to tell that to Cyrus Perry, the black sergeant wounded
by Fail. Perry asked Emmett Scott to conduct an investigation. (Scott,
previously Booker T. Washington's secretary, now served as Secretary of
War Newton Baker's special assistant for black affairs.) "The People are
very bitter towards us here," Perry wrote, and "we are suffering a number
of thing heap upon us by the white People here."[18] Indeed, the actions of
the Charleston police and the streetcar employees revealed a distinct bias
toward servicemen in general and uniformed black men in particular.
Although Henry Heyward had urged Perry and Brewer to assert their
rights, his motive was hardly altruistic. Either to stir up trouble or to
harass H. M. Fail, he had involved the two black men. The result was a
"heap" of trouble for black servicemen.

The Redoubling of White Supremacy in Charleston and Beyond

The incident sparked by Private Clovie Sylvester's arrest demonstrates the
ambiguous status of black servicemen after the war's end. Fosberry, the
white police officer, roughed up his prisoner as an exercise of both white
supremacy and municipal authority. Servicemen, outraged at this affront,
set aside racial differences to protect one of their own and to demonstrate
the autonomy of the military. The armistice that ended World War I
was barely a month old, and considerable uncertainty existed over the
demobilization of servicemen and the transition to peace. Whites wanted
to reestablish prewar modes of white supremacy, while black servicemen
resolved to assert their rights. Although the military services practiced
segregation, in this instance a temporary but tenable biracial alliance
had cohered. For their part, Charleston's all-white police force and civil
authorities were anxious to secure peacetime control over the city. Harsh
punishments in local courts of the arrested soldiers rankled army officers,
who believed military justice provided the proper channels to punish the
offenders. Major General Henry G. Sharpe, the commanding officer of
the army's Southeastern Department, thus suggested to Charleston mayor
Tristam T. Hyde that all uniformed servicemen who were "accused of any
misdemeanor or improper conduct [should] be turned over to the Provost
Guard of this city for delivery to proper military authorities" who would

[17] *Davis Report*, 16.
[18] Sergeant Cyrus W. Perry to Emmett Scott, December 9, 1918, Case File 10218–272, RG
165, reel 4.

then give the men their day in a military court. "Experience in the past has shown this method . . . to be most effective in maintaining order and discipline among persons in the military service," Sharpe concluded.[19]

Sharpe's recommendations ignored the racial aspects of the Sylvester incident. A lack of discipline in the ranks had not perturbed Officer Fosberry – he was primed for an outburst because black men were serving in those ranks. Whites such as Fosberry, intent on protecting Jim Crow, hoped to see black enlisted men and officers mustered out as quickly and quietly as possible. Eight days *before* Charleston's trouble, a white army captain expressed his concern to the Military Intelligence Division (MID) about "the matter of converting the negro soldiers into civilians once more, and the strong probability that there will be numerous racial clashes in the South unless this matter is properly handled." According to the captain, himself a southerner, black soldiers were returning with "new ideas and social aspirations." Should these soldiers attempt to assert their equality with whites in the South, "an era of bloodshed will follow as compared with which the history of reconstruction will be mild reading, indeed."[20] As the incident in Charleston showed, the backlash was already under way.

And this was the case not just in Charleston. Across the South and the North, white supremacists revived Reconstruction-era methods of oppressing blacks. Alabama's governor reportedly convened a secret conference to discuss ways to handle returning black soldiers.[21] In January 1919, the Ku Klux Klan began organizing lodges in Georgia and Tennessee. According to the *St. Louis Argus*, a black newspaper, the Klan in Nashville was "preparing to inaugurate a system of crime and persecution in an attempt to take the heart out of the returned Negro soldier and reduce him to the same status that he occupied before the war." The Klan also organized in Pittsburgh, Pennsylvania, and posted menacing notices on the doors of residences and churches in the city's black neighborhood: "The war is over, negroes. Stay in your place. If you don't, we'll put you there."[22] Black veterans who continued to wear their uniforms – according to War Department regulations, servicemen could

---

[19] Major General Henry G. Sharpe to Tristam T. Hyde, December 20, 1918, Case File 10218–272, RG 165, reel 4.

[20] Captain F. Sullens to Major Brown, Office of the Chief of Staff, November 30, 1918, Case File 10218–289–1, RG 165, copy in box 1, reel 5, Kornweibel Papers.

[21] Ibid.

[22] "Secret Order to Oppose Negroes," *St. Louis Argus*, January 31, 1919; "Negroes Are Terrorized by Threats," *Pittsburgh American*, February 14, 1919, clippings in box C-313, folder "Subject File – KKK (Clippings) 1919 January–June," NAACP Records.

wear their uniforms up to three months after discharge – embodied whites' fears about African Americans using their wartime service to press for equality. As the army captain who had predicted racial violence put it, "the negro soldier strutting about in uniform three months after his discharge will always be a potential danger, especially if he happens to be of the type inclined to impudence or arrogance."[23] Veteran Wilbur Little, of Blakely, Georgia, found himself in exactly that danger when he defied the demand of white residents to take off his uniform. In April 1919, a mob beat him to death. Little was one of eleven black veterans lynched during 1919; overall, mobs lynched seventy-seven African Americans that year.[24]

The escalation of white supremacy evoked a forceful response from black editors and leaders. "Scheme after scheme has been inaugurated in the South to *Keep the Negro Down*," the *St. Louis Argus* wrote, but black soldiers who "stood in No Man's Land and defended the Stars and Stripes" will not back down, will not be stopped by the Ku Klux Klan. The *New York Tribune*, a white newspaper, echoed this sentiment. After noting African Americans' substantial contribution to the war, an editorial asked, "why any one should become excited over the return of negro soldiers from France is as perplexing to patriotic Americans as it is discouraging to the negroes themselves." One of the Pittsburgh ministers menaced by the Klan issued a public statement emphasizing the wartime service of blacks and declaring their determination to secure their rights.[25] As these statements suggest, many blacks believed a turning point was at hand. However, as historian Chad L. Williams observes, "African Americans lacked formal political influence, and, for this reason, the federal government, unswayed by the moral legitimacy of their claims, had little reason to consider the demands of black activists and reformers." Likewise, federal officials saw little reason to halt the spreading violence directed against blacks, including veterans, who continued to press for racial equality.[26]

[23] Sullens to Brown, November 30, 1918.

[24] "Army Uniform Cost Soldier His Life," *Chicago Defender*, April 5, 1919, clipping in *NAACP Papers*, Part 7, Series A, reel 10, frame 321; "The Lynching Industry, 1919," *Crisis* 19, no. 4 (February 1920), 183–6.

[25] "Undertaking the Impossible," *St. Louis Argus*, February 7, 1919; "Democracy at Home, Please," *New York Tribune*, February 20, 1919; "Negro Is Now on His Guard Says Minister," *Pittsburgh Leader*, February 21, 1919, clippings in box C-313, folder "Subject File – KKK (Clippings) 1919 January-June," NAACP Records.

[26] Williams, *Torchbearers of Democracy*, 213.

The friction between these forces produced the first major race riot of 1919. Not coincidentally, the violence broke out in Charleston, in the spring. Like the December 1918 incident, the May 1919 riot involved uniformed servicemen, but in this case, white sailors and soldiers joined with white civilians to attack black civilians.[27] The *esprit de corps* that had brought black and white servicemen together to defend the uniform in December had dissipated, replaced by the bond of race. The altered allegiances in Charleston reflected the national imperative to reassert white supremacy. At the same time, black Charlestonians' response to the attacks demonstrated that African Americans' determination to secure racial equality was not merely rhetorical.

Fighting Back in Charleston

Alexander Lanneau was upset. Born and raised in Charleston, the nineteen-year-old white salesman had always thought black Charlestonians knew "their place," but by May 1919, they had become troublesome and boisterous, he claimed. At times, whites "have to get off the sidewalk" because blacks no longer stepped aside for them.[28]

Blacks were indeed tired of stepping aside for whites. During the war, South Carolina's black citizens had purchased Liberty Bonds and had enlisted at high rates. Their patriotism nurtured forceful stands against discrimination. In May 1918, when the Navy Yard in Charleston revealed its intention to hire only white women for an on-base clothing factory, a protest organized by the local NAACP branch led to the hiring of 250 black women. In early 1919, black Charlestonians organized a successful campaign to change state law to allow the employment of black teachers at the city's segregated public schools.[29] Alexander Lanneau, like the streetcar employees involved in the December 1918 altercation, was determined to restore the prewar standard of quiescent blacks and dominant whites.

Lanneau found unexpected help from two white sailors, Robert Morton and Roscoe Coleman. The two teenagers – Morton was eighteen,

---

[27] Accounts of the May 1919 troubles in Charleston include Waskow, *From Race Riot*, 12–16; Tuttle, *Race Riot*, 23–5; Newby, *Black Carolinians*, 192–3; McWhirter, *Red Summer*, 41–9.

[28] *Record of Proceedings of a Court of Inquiry Convened at the Navy Yard, Charleston, S.C.*, May 27–June 19, 1919, File 9535, box 203, folder 4, RG 125, 238, 245–6 (hereafter *Court of Inquiry*).

[29] Hemmingway, "Prelude to Change."

Coleman only sixteen (he had lied about his age to enlist) – were fire-men third class at the Navy Yard. Morton already had a reputation as a troublemaker who started fights and disrupted movie showings. On Saturday, May 10, 1919, Morton and Coleman headed into the city to enjoy a night's leave. Around 7 P.M., a black man refused to step out of their way. Irked, they started following him; another sailor, George Washington Biggs, and two white civilians joined them. When the black man threw a brick, the white men chased him down an alley.[30]

Word of the incident spread fast. Lanneau rushed to join the mob, which clashed with several black men who had come to the defense of the man being chased. A barrage of rock-throwing ended when a black man fired a pistol into the air, scattering the white men.[31] Undeterred, Morton and his cohorts roamed the streets, looking for black pedestrians to attack. By 9 P.M., several white mobs ranging in size from six to sixty had formed. Two mobs armed themselves by looting Winchester rifles and twenty-two caliber ammunition from amusement galleries.[32]

False rumors, including a story that a black man had killed a white sailor, further emboldened the mobs. One stormed into a pool hall that catered to black men, who fought back with cue sticks, bottles, even billiard balls, hurling them at their attackers. A white sailor fell to the floor, unconscious. As the police rushed to the scene, the tumult spilled into the backyard. Fireman Third Class Jacob Cohen and another sailor, George Holliday, cornered an African American named Isaac Doctor, and, with looted rifles, shot him twice. Police Chief Joseph Black described what he saw after he pushed his way into the yard: a "negro lying on his back ... and these two sailors [Cohen and Holliday] were standing over him. They told me that they wanted him searched and that he had a pistol." When Black could not find the weapon, he arrested the two men, who were unfazed and jocular. Holliday and Cohen claimed that a naval officer had authorized them to shoot blacks who disobeyed orders to halt, but neither man could identify this officer. Their victim died at the hospital.[33]

---

[30] *Record of Proceedings of an Investigation Conducted at the Navy Yard, Charleston, S.C.,*
      May 13–19, 1919, File 9535, box 203, folder 4, RG 125, 1–12 (hereafter *Investigation Conducted*).
[31] *Court of Inquiry*, box 203, folder 3, 170–1; box 203, folder 4, 238–49; *Investigation Conducted*, 1–2.
[32] *Court of Inquiry*, box 203, folder 2, 91–5; box 203, folder 3, 180–5; *Investigation Conducted*, 17; Judge Advocate General, December 1, 1919, File 26251–21674, box 1289, RG 80.
[33] *Court of Inquiry*, box 202, folder 1, 47, 55, 84; box 203, folder 2, 108, 165–6; Joseph A. Black to T. T. Hyde, May 29, 1919, File 9535, box 203, folder 4, RG 125 (quote).

The arrival of the police did not deter the mobs, which continued to attack blacks and black-owned businesses for the next several hours. Six sailors and a civilian opened fire on James Frayer's cobbler shop, wounding Frayer's thirteen-year-old assistant Peter Irving, who was left paralyzed.[34] Another mob, in pursuit of a black porter, ransacked and vandalized W. G. Fridie's barbershop, even tearing down the ceiling fans. Black driver Edward Boston was making a delivery when several dozen sailors swarmed round his truck, jumped aboard, and beat him.[35]

Even African Americans who took precautions ran into trouble. Augustus Bonaparte waited more than two hours to leave a barber shop, whose owner had locked the door and lowered the shades after the looting of the amusement galleries. As Bonaparte walked down the street, several sailors jumped from a car and beat him with clubs and a hammer. Reeling from the assault, Bonaparte sought help. He passed a white policeman, who did nothing. Finally, a car stopped and gave Bonaparte a ride to the hospital, where he received twenty stitches.[36]

Although sailors had started and sustained the mob violence, white civilians were active participants. Alexander Lanneau spent two hours on the streets that night, joining with sailors and other civilians to pursue African Americans.[37] Two naval lieutenants later testified that they had seen large numbers of civilians in the mobs. According to a Charleston police officer, "it looked like the majority [of attackers] were civilians, at times."[38] George Washington Biggs, one of the first sailors to attack blacks, heard several civilians loudly advocating lynchings.[39] By one estimate, "at least one half of the mob were civilians."[40]

Alexander Lanneau and a naval officer, Lieutenant (j.g.) Nicklas, separately explained why civilians had joined with servicemen to attack blacks. Lanneau, who repeatedly denied he had done anything wrong, believed it was his duty to help the sailors in their fight with blacks. Nicklas, when asked if he thought the riot resulted from animosity between sailors and blacks, answered, "ill-feeling seemed to be general

34 Affidavit of James Frayer, Jr., May 22, 1919, Waskow Notes, tab "Charleston Riot"; "2 Dead; 27 Wounded in Street Rioting," *Charleston News and Courier*, May 12, 1919, clipping in Kirk Scrapbook, vol. 3, 34/622, South Carolina Historical Society.
35 *Court of Inquiry*, box 202, folder 1, 38, 103–4; box 203, folder 4, 251–2.
36 Affidavit of Augustus Bonaparte, May 22, 1919, Waskow Notes, tab "Charleston Riot."
37 *Court of Inquiry*, box 203, folder 4, 240, 243–4.
38 *Court of Inquiry*, box 202, folder 1, 36, 45, 64, 69 (quote).
39 *Investigation Conducted*, 3.
40 Commandant, Sixth Naval District to Solicitor, Department of the Navy, December 18, 1919, File 26283–2588, box 1775, RG 80.

as regards both civilians and enlisted personnel of the Navy. The only difference I could notice was that the sailors were perhaps a little more demonstrative."[41] Although Lanneau claimed to harbor no hatred toward blacks, his annoyance at the rising assertiveness of black Charlestonians, as previously noted, reveals his and other white civilians' primary motivation: to punish African Americans for forgetting "their place." It was a punishment many black residents refused to take without a fight.

At the first rumblings of trouble, black Charlestonians had dispersed a rock-throwing mob and tried to fend off the pool hall attack. As white violence increased, blacks continued to defend themselves and also began to retaliate. Protective measures included engaging the mobs, advance warning of approaching mobs, carrying weapons, and banding together. Many sailors who picked fights with blacks staggered away with cuts and broken bones; at least six enlisted white men sought treatment at the naval hospital. A group of blacks shouted warnings to black business owners so they could lock their doors. Other African Americans stood ready to face the mobs. One black veteran donned his uniform and roamed the streets, armed with a thirty-eight caliber pistol.[42] Armed black men risked arrest, however, as rioting sailors and civilians repeatedly claimed they were being shot at, prompting the police to stop, search, and arrest blacks with weapons. Police Lieutenant Edward McDonald, who had helped quell the December 1918 disturbance in Charleston, took in two armed black men in the course of dispersing sailors. Many black men were detained for carrying razors. A police sergeant, in pursuit of an armed black man, encountered a crowd of fifteen or so blacks gathered on a corner, ready to repel mobs.[43]

African Americans' self-defense and counterattacks duly impressed servicemen and the Charleston police. One naval officer witnessed bricks and bottles being hurled at mobs of sailors after 9 P.M. A policeman who searched a black-occupied tenement found piles of bricks on the porches. Around midnight, a touring car with several black riders opened fire on white servicemen standing outside the police station, wounding a provost guard (the equivalent of a military police officer) who had just arrived from the Navy Yard to restore order. A Charleston police officer claimed to see African Americans shooting at sailors on a different street. Recalling that night, a white sailor described seeing "one

[41] *Court of Inquiry*, box 202, folder 1, 36; box 203, folder 4, 243–4.
[42] *Court of Inquiry*, box 202, folder 1, 45; box 203, folder 3, 168, 199–200.
[43] *Court of Inquiry*, boxes 202–203, folders 1–2, 60, 80–2, 149, 156.

fellow get hit with a brick" and "another fellow getting carried out of a house."[44]

Although white enlisted men had initiated the night's violence, the defensive and retaliatory responses of African Americans, along with the false rumor that a black man had shot and killed a sailor, convinced whites that armed blacks had started the riot. "There is no doubt in my mind that the negroes were the aggressors," Lieutenant Nicklas later declared, even though at one point he had halted the assault of a lone black man by a mob of sailors and civilians.[45] This "blame the victim" attitude guided the Navy Yard's response to the tumult: commanding officers ordered troops to the city to stop and search African Americans, but not white civilians. In what proved to be a common feature of the racial violence of 1919, blacks now faced two hostile forces: the mobs themselves and the authorities attempting to restore order.

The first provost guards, about thirty sailors, arrived around 10 P.M. in response to a report that "negroes were firing on the whites in the City of Charleston." The guards had orders to clear the streets of civilians and enlisted men and to watch for black shooters. More troops, including soldiers and marines, soon arrived. Marine Captain Davis A. Holladay, whose troops were the target of the drive-by shooting, even authorized his men to fire on armed blacks who refused to halt when so commanded.[46]

William Brown, a young chauffeur, could not know about the patrolling marines' orders, though he was well aware that uniformed white sailors and marines were attacking African Americans. Just after midnight, he and a companion encountered three sailors and two marines, who ordered them to halt. When the two black men ran, the marines, Privates C. N. Woods and John Schumbacker, gave chase and opened fire, wounding Brown. His companion escaped unhurt.[47] "What are you shooting me for?" Brown cried out. "I was not doing anything." The marines upbraided him for ignoring their order, which Brown said he had not heard, and searched him without finding a weapon.[48] The commotion woke up Reverend T. B. Nelson, who watched from his porch as Brown was taken to a hospital. In a coincidence, Brown had just joined

---

[44] *Court of Inquiry*, box 202, folder 1, 29, 73, 87; box 203, folder 2, 150; box 203, folder 3, 210–11 (quotes).

[45] *Investigation Conducted*, 15.

[46] *Court of Inquiry*, box 202, folder 1, 45–6 (quote); box 203, folders 2–3, 150–1, 224.

[47] *Court of Inquiry*, box 203, folder 3, 175.

[48] Affidavit of T. B. Nelson, May 23, 1919, Waskow Notes, tab "Charleston Riot"; *Court of Inquiry*, box 203, folder 2, 160.

Nelson's congregation. When the pastor visited him, Brown told him he had only been trying to avoid the riot. Brown's wound became infected, and the young man died a week later.[49]

Like William Brown, Isaac Moses had to make a split-second decision about who was challenging him on the street. Around 1 A.M., he was hurrying home from his clothes-pressing shop when he heard an order to halt. He ignored the command, and two shots rang out. Both missed, Moses froze. Two marines ran up, berating him. When Moses said he did not know they were marines, they hit him in the head with a rifle butt and stabbed his leg with a bayonet. The marines searched him, took his money, and then arrested him for carrying a concealed weapon – his shaving razor. Moses was taken to the police station before receiving medical treatment.[50]

The dilemma for Brown and Moses was, of course, that the riot troops looked just like the rioters. The Charleston police even armed the first group of provost guards with billy clubs, the weapon of choice of many rioting sailors. The marines carried Springfield rifles, but in the dark who could distinguish these weapons from the looted Winchester rifles wielded by other rioting servicemen? A naval court of inquiry's questioning of Reverend T. B. Nelson about the shooting of William Brown reveals the difficulty black civilians faced:

Q. Do you know the difference between marines and sailors?
A. Yes, Sir, marines wear the khaki I believe, and the sailors wear blue, and white.

Q. Could these two men [the marines who ordered Brown to halt] not have been soldiers instead of marines?
A. Yes, Sir, they could have been, because the soldiers wear the same uniform.

Q. In other words, you would not be sure whether they were soldiers or marines?
A. *From what I heard later I understood that marines were doing guard duty on the streets that night*, and that is the reason I have been of the opinion that these men were marines [emphasis added].[51]

If a witness could not be sure who the servicemen were without subsequent information, then how could William Brown and Isaac Moses have

[49] *Court of Inquiry*, box 203, folder 2, 123–4, 131–3; "Dies as Result of the Rioting," *Charleston News-Courier*, May 17, 1919, 10.
[50] *Court of Inquiry*, box 203, folder 2, 157–8; Affidavit of Isaac Moses, May 22, 1919, Waskow Notes, tab "Charleston Riot."
[51] *Court of Inquiry*, box 203, folder 2, 125.

known who had ordered them to halt? Some of the riot troops themselves struggled to distinguish rioters from properly authorized guards. Private Schumbacker, giving his account of Brown's shooting, told the court of inquiry that he and Woods had encountered three sailors, two of whom were "evidently provost, having clubs in their hands, [who] said: 'There were two niggers at the next corner we went around and we had to stop them.'"[52] Schumbacker apparently did not care if the three sailors were actual provost guards; what mattered was that white servicemen had volunteered to help him and Woods carry out their orders to stop and search black civilians. In effect, rioting servicemen now had the opportunity to continue harassing and attacking African Americans by aiding the riot troops, who already believed blacks had incited the riot.

The Charleston police and the provost guards finally cleared the streets and ended the rioting around 3 A.M.[53] Rioting sailors were brought to the police station for transport to the Navy Yard. The police did not arrest or detain any white rioters, civilian or servicemen, with the exception of Jacob Cohen and George Holliday, who had shot Isaac Doctor at the pool hall, and Roscoe Coleman, for inciting a riot. Twelve black men, however, were arrested for carrying pistols, razors, or knives.[54] In keeping with the military's December 1918 proposal, the police gave the navy custody of Cohen, Holliday, and Coleman for possible court martial.

The riot took the lives of three black men: Isaac Doctor, William Brown, and James Talbot. (Talbot's shooters were never identified.) Another seven African Americans suffered gunshot wounds. One of these victims, Moses Gladden, was unable to work for months and could not support his wife and children. William Randall, a hack driver beaten and robbed by a mob of twelve sailors, died a month after the riot from a heart condition; his physician believed the attack hastened his death. W. G. Fridie's barber shop was almost totally ruined.[55]

The deaths, injuries, and damages suffered by Charleston's black community spurred a campaign to gather evidence of white servicemen's responsibility for the riot and to see that individual rioters were held accountable for their crimes. Numerous African Americans also filed

---

[52] *Court of Inquiry*, box 203, folder 3, 175.

[53] *Court of Inquiry*, box 203, folder 4, 265.

[54] "City Quiet After Riot," *Charleston American*, May 12, 1919, 1.

[55] *Court of Inquiry*, box 203, folder 4, 262, 266–7; Affidavit of William Randall, May 15, 1919, Waskow Notes, tab "Charleston Riot"; E. F. Smith to the Secretary of the Sixth Naval District, October 29, 1919, File 26283–2588, box 1775, RG 80.

civil suits to win compensation for their injuries or damages. In the weeks and months after the riot, the city's NAACP branch, aided by the Washington, D.C., branch, lobbied the secretary of the navy to investigate the riot, while black attorneys filed the civil suits. Although these efforts were only partially successful, they nevertheless opened up another front in the postwar fight against white mob violence: use of the courts to secure justice against rioters. Full treatment of this campaign, and those that followed other episodes of antiblack collective violence, can be found in Chapter 8. An outbreak of violence that occurred in Bisbee, Arizona, further demonstrates the extent of black armed resistance during the first half of 1919.

The Buffalo Soldiers' Fight

During World War I, the U.S. Army's Tenth Cavalry was stationed at Fort Huachuca in southern Arizona. Seasoned, professional soldiers, the men of the Tenth Cavalry were justly proud of their service and of their unit's illustrious history. Morale was high, reenlistment common – in the early 1910s, the Tenth had thirty or so troopers with more than twenty years of service. One of just two black regiments formed by Congress after the Civil War, the Tenth Cavalry had earned the nickname "Buffalo Soldiers" during the long campaigns to pacify the Indian tribes of the Western plains. In late 1913, the Tenth arrived in Arizona for border patrol, which embroiled the regiment in Mexico's civil war. For much of 1916, the Tenth forayed deep into Mexico as part of the so-called Punitive Expedition to capture Pancho Villa, who had raided Columbus, New Mexico.[56] During and after the war, the Tenth Cavalry remained at Fort Huachuca (Figure 2.2).

Their meritorious service did not shield the black troopers from racist treatment by officers and civilians. A white lieutenant designated the first rows of Fort Huachuca's theater for white soldiers only. (The order was rescinded after black NCOs protested the segregation.) The posting of Lieutenant Colonel Charles Young, the army's highest-ranking black officer, to Fort Huachuca in 1916 incensed several junior white officers, who resented having a black superior officer. Although Young ably led the Second Squadron during the Mexican mission, he was eased into retirement after a routine medical examination revealed heart trouble. In 1918, a Bisbee candy store clerk refused to serve Sergeant Walter Stewart

---

[56] Work, "Their Life's Blood"; Glass, *History of the Tenth Cavalry.*

FIGURE 2.2. Troop A of the U.S. Tenth Cavalry. The black troopers of the Tenth Cavalry had a long, distinguished service record when this photograph was taken in 1915. In Bisbee, Arizona, in July 1919, the Tenth Cavalry became the target of white law enforcement officers and vigilantes who refused to accept the troopers' uniform as an emblem of equality. *Source:* U.S. Army Signal Corps. Courtesy of the National Archives, College Park, Md., Record Group 111, Cabinet 25, Drawer 1, folder "Cavalry: Tenth U.S. Cavalry Regiment (Old West) #1 of 2," Photograph 111-SC-83535.

and his date. "This uniform means the same thing a white man's does," Stewart angrily told the clerk. Despite this hostility, the troopers frequently visited Bisbee and neighboring towns for social activities. Bisbee, Douglas, and Globe each had small black communities that sponsored dances and other gatherings for the Tenth. Several troopers married local women, who organized social groups.[57]

Bisbee still simmered with the tensions that had earned the mining town of 8,000 national notoriety in June 1917, when the International

[57] Work, "Their Life's Blood," 356–7, 362–7 (quote on 367); Shellum, *Black Officer*, 229–54.

Workers of the World (IWW or Wobblies) had called a strike. The Phelps-Dodge Company, which operated the Copper Queen Mine and owned many of Bisbee's other businesses, joined with other mine operators and Sheriff Harry Wheeler to deport picketing workers. Wheeler deputized a force of 2,000 men, drawn from the ranks of the Citizen's Protective League and the Bisbee Workman's Loyalty League, two recently formed vigilante forces. On July 12, this posse fanned out across Bisbee and accosted male residents, demanding to know if the men were working. If their answer was no, the posse arrested them. City officials censored the telephone and telegraph lines while more than 1,100 men, 90 percent of whom were foreign-born, were packed into railroad cattle cars and dumped in Hermanas, New Mexico. The deportation led to a federal investigation and numerous indictments, but city officials and the vigilantes remained defiant, even patrolling the town borders to keep out the deportees, hundreds of whom were veterans, Bisbee property holders, and Liberty Bond purchasers. No wonder Bisbee was known as "a pretty tough town," as Fred Watson, one of the deported men, recalled decades later.[58]

Bisbee also had earned a reputation as a "white man's camp." In the 1880s, the town had prohibited the settlement and employment of Chinese immigrants. Mexicans and Americans of Hispanic descent lived and worked in Bisbee, but the mines refused to hire them for high-paying jobs. A dual wage structure existed as well: whites were paid higher wages than Latinos for the same work. White male miners cultivated a sense of manhood that prized rugged individualism, patriotism, and their ability to support a family solely on their earnings. Being white and native-born was an essential component of this manhood.[59]

The 1919 Fourth of July parade thus presented the working class white men of Bisbee with an opportunity to showcase their Americanism while excluding those who did not belong. For the town's elites, especially the mine operators, holiday ceremonies that celebrated whiteness and nativism helped keep the Wobblies at bay. But what about the Tenth Cavalry? To not invite the 800 troopers to take part in the parade would

---

[58] Taft, "Bisbee Deportation"; Laurie and Cole, *Role of Federal,* 240–5; Watson, "Still on Strike," 171–84 (quote on 171); Benton-Cohen, *Borderline Americans,* 198–238.

[59] Benton-Cohen, "Docile Children." For more treatment of whiteness and other racial categories in Arizona during this period, see Benton-Cohen, *Borderline Americans.* Notable studies of whiteness include Roediger, *Wages of Whiteness;* Jacobson, *Whiteness of a Different Color;* Hale, *Making Whiteness.*

look unpatriotic, yet the men's race threatened to crack the façade of this racialized Americanism. Bisbee's leaders and law enforcement officers also feared that the Wobblies might exploit the parade to publicly advocate their creed of industrial solidarity based on racial and ethnic equality.[60]

Racial tensions surfaced in Bisbee a few days before the Fourth of July, when the Tenth Cavalry's baseball team played against the local, all-white team. Arguments broke out in the stands during the game. The army's MID and the Department of Justice's Bureau of Investigation (BI) suspected that Wobblies had caused the trouble by conspicuously cheering for the black troopers. According to one report, the Wobblies were also warning the black troopers that they would be mistreated in Bisbee on the Fourth of July. Bisbee's leaders, as well as the BI and MID, believed the Wobblies wanted the black troopers to "start trouble at the least provocation" during the holiday.[61]

As these reports show, federal agents and military officers were closely watching IWW activity in Arizona. The 1917 deportation had crippled the union, but an army sergeant warned after the war that the IWW was "working very quietly" in the Bisbee district to regain strength.[62] In April 1919, an infantry officer assured his commander that his company could handle any problems that might arise in the mines near the town of Jerome, where "agitators" were active.[63] Although an intelligence officer had concluded in June that the "high state of morale and discipline" in the Tenth Cavalry "naturally precludes the existence of Bolshevism," the baseball game renewed concerns about the IWW.[64] BI agent O. L. Tinklepaugh traveled to Bisbee on July 1 in order to monitor the Wobblies and to prevent demonstrations, especially in Brewery Gulch, the red-light district.[65]

[60] Special Agent Tinklepaugh, "In Re: Riot between Soldiers, 10th Cavalry & Civil Officers, Bisbee, Arizona, on July 3, 1919," Case File 10218–348–4, 2; Captain Forrest D. Wright to Commanding General, July 6, 1919, Case File 10218–348–5, 2, RG 165, reel 5.

[61] "Re – Disorders July 3rd," July 12, 1919, Case File 10218–348–1, RG 165, reel 5.

[62] Sgt. G. L. Stancliff to Capt. H. S. Dickey, November 9, 1918, box 3, folder "Arizona (Military Intelligence Inserts)," RG 60, Glasser File. For an overview of the IWW's postwar travails, see Dubofsky, *We Shall Be All*.

[63] Lt. Eugene H. Mitchell to Commanding Officer, Second Battalion, Nineteenth Infantry, April 1, 1919, box 3, folder "Arizona (Military Intelligence Inserts)," RG 60, Glasser File.

[64] Lt. Robert Scott Israel to Director of Military Intelligence, June 23, 1919, box 3, folder "Arizona (Copper and IWW 1917–18–19)," RG 60, Glasser File.

[65] Tinklepaugh, "In Re: Riot," 2.

The Tenth Cavalry arrived in Bisbee on July 3. While the troopers set up their bivouac two miles outside of town, the officers checked into the Copper Queen Hotel. The segregation extended to the night's activities, too. The officers attended a ball in their honor at a country club; the troopers, a dance at the Silver Leaf, a black club in Brewery Gulch.[66] They were not the only soldiers in Bisbee. Provost guards from the all-white Nineteenth Infantry were on duty to maintain order. As far as Chief of Police J. A. Kempton and Sheriff James McDonald were concerned, keeping the peace in Bisbee was a local responsibility, not a federal or military duty.

That evening, two suspected Wobblies addressed black servicemen as they arrived at the Silver Leaf, telling them that the Copper Queen company would make them "eat out of the garbage cans like yellow curs." The speech attracted the attention of provost guards and police officers, who hurried to the scene, but the speakers fled before they got there.[67] Just the fact that some of the troopers had been listening made them troublemakers in the eyes of local law enforcement. The sight of so many black men in uniform also angered the white provost guards, who saw an emblem of equality they refused to accept. Furthermore, the sidearms the troopers were permitted to carry greatly troubled both the police and provost guards.

As Chief of Police Kempton later admitted, he and his men had disarmed the black troopers: "In the afternoon it was noticed that practically all of the colored soldiers coming up town bore Army automatics concealed on their persons, most of them carrying them inside their blouses or in other places where they were not visible. I immediately started taking the guns from these men."[68] The provost guards also had orders to disarm the troopers.[69] According to Kempton, his officers disarmed thirty to forty black men without incident; the provost guards also had no trouble obtaining custody of the sidearms.

As the police and provost guards became more aggressive, however, tensions mounted. Outside the Silver Leaf, a provost guard insulted a passing trooper, who allegedly punched the guard.[70] Then, as Kempton and his men were forcibly escorting several black soldiers out of the club,

---

[66] Tinklepaugh, "In Re: Riot," 2–3; Work, "Their Life's Blood," 369–70.
[67] "Re – Disorders July 3rd."
[68] Tinklepaugh, "In Re: Riot," 8.
[69] Wright to Commanding General, July 6, 1919.
[70] "Pistol Shot Exchanged Following Insult," *Chicago Whip*, July 9, 1919, 1; "Civilians Battle Tenth Cavalry," *Chicago Defender*, July 12, 1919, 1.

"one of them who had been acting mean throughout the affair continued to drop behind and curse," the chief recalled. "I told him to shut up and move along, whereupon he turned to me and said, 'Fuck you, I am a United States soldier and don't have to!'" Kempton could hardly believe the soldier's insolence. He struck the man on the head with his club and arrested him.[71] For the men of the Tenth, it was time to make a stand.

Agent Tinklepaugh was patrolling the center of Bisbee when he encountered Kempton and Deputy Sheriff Joe Hardwick, who told him a riot was underway. A carload of deputies and policemen pulled up, and the group sped into Brewery Gulch. White civilians surged around the officers, shouting that the black soldiers were firing their weapons. Kempton spotted two black soldiers forty yards ahead and ordered them to halt. The men refused and fired at him, Kempton later claimed. Then, as reported by Tinklepaugh, Kempton said "colored soldiers came out of the club a short distance beyond and there followed a regular pitched battle between us, the other police officers joining us before it was over with." One witness estimated that the police and enthusiastic white vigilantes fired between 100 and 200 shots. Their ammunition depleted, the police rushed back to the stationhouse to rearm themselves. Several troopers were wounded, as well as a deputy sheriff and a Mexican woman caught in the crossfire. Meanwhile the provost guards continued to accost black troopers and demand that they surrender their weapons. Those who ran were fired upon, as were several carloads of soldiers trying to leave town.[72]

Although Tinklepaugh squarely blamed the troopers for having "given trouble," the actions of local law officers, especially Hardwick, alarmed him. "On this occasion [Hardwick] almost completely lost his head as was demonstrated by the readiness with which he fired upon any negroes who did not give themselves up immediately." Hoping that the Tenth's officers could defuse the situation, Tinklepaugh tracked down Lieutenant Ryder at the Copper Queen Hotel and dispatched him to Brewery Gulch. The BI agent hoped to find more officers at the Tenth Cavalry's bivouac, but they were all attending the dance at the country club. Black troopers swarmed round his car, imploring the federal agent to take them into Bisbee so they could defend their comrades. After coaxing the troopers off his car's running board, Tinklepaugh drove to the country club, where he told Colonel George P. White, the Tenth's commanding officer, that

[71] Tinklepaugh, "In Re: Riot," 8.
[72] Tinklepaugh, "In Re: Riot," 3–4 (quote on 3); Work, "Their Life's Blood," 369–70.

a gunfight had wounded and possibly killed several of his men. To Tinklepaugh's disgust, White "appeared very indignant at having his social
duties infringed upon."[73]

Meanwhile, Lieutenant Ryder, accompanied by Chief Kempton, went
into the Silver Leaf Club and asked the black troopers present to place
their weapons on the bar. None did. Ryder then ordered them to disarm –
again, not a man obeyed. A sergeant spoke up: the troopers did not want
to surrender their weapons for fear of being beaten up by whites. As a
compromise, Kempton promised to protect the troopers if they left town
immediately. With Ryder in front, the troopers lined up outside the club,
still bearing their sidearms, and marched out of Brewery Gulch.

Not all of the troopers were compliant, however, leading to a final
altercation. *Bisbee Daily Review* editor B. P. Guild noticed one soldier
take up position behind a telephone post, his weapon in hand. Guild
called out a warning, catching the attention of Deputy Hardwick. The
trooper rejoined his comrades, but when he started to lag, Hardwick shot
him without warning. Several troopers rushed to his aid; fearing another
outbreak of violence, Kempton and his men disarmed and arrested these
soldiers. Still, the shooting did not disrupt the formation, and the black
troopers continued on their way out of town. All told, the police and
vigilantes had wounded five troopers and assaulted eight; approximately
seventy-five troopers had been stripped of their weapons. The rest of the
evening passed without incident, and the Fourth of July celebration took
place as planned the next day. The police and sheriff released the jailed
troopers to their officers and all charges were dropped. To Tinklepaugh's
relief, the suspected Wobblies did not disrupt the parade. The men of the
Tenth returned to Bisbee and marched proudly "as though nothing had
happened." Afterward, they returned to their camp, where they spent the
day.[74]

The troopers of the Tenth Cavalry may have marched as if all was
well, but neither they nor their officers forgot the attacks and abuse they
had suffered. Lieutenant Colonel F. S. Snyder, acting for Colonel White,
interviewed troopers and witnesses to the shootout. His report excoriated
Bisbee's policemen and deputy sheriffs, accusing them of nothing less than
a conspiracy to "hunt down the troopers." Snyder observed that vigilantes
had eagerly fired weapons during the shootout, and he absolved his men

[73] Tinklepaugh, "In Re: Riot," 4–5, 10.
[74] Tinklepaugh, "In Re: Riot," 5–6, 10 (quote on 10); Work, "Their Life's Blood," 369–70.

of the death of the Mexican woman, citing a witness who saw a civilian officer, not a trooper, fire the shots that killed her.[75]

Three other witnesses corroborated Snyder's findings. Agent Tinklepaugh, no friend of the troopers, concluded that civil authorities "went to extremes when they attempted, after the first trouble broke out, to disarm and jail all of the soldiers found on the streets." As a result, numerous troopers "who were absolutely innocent of any connection with the affair were roughly handled."[76] White cab driver W. E. Beath was taking a black sergeant into Bisbee from the Tenth Cavalry's camp when several "Bulls" (police or deputies) stopped his car and arrested the trooper to keep him away from Brewery Gulch. Beath later witnessed two other police officers beat and arrest a black civilian sitting outside the railroad depot. M. E. Cassidy, a mining company employee, told an army officer that the "ill feeling for the negros on the part of civilians" was a primary cause of the riot.[77] Determined to keep their town free of individuals who threatened the racial and class hierarchy, Bisbee's "Bulls" had wielded the same tools used in the 1917 deportation: vigilantism, violence, and unlawful arrests.

The military's recognition that Bisbee's civil officers had provoked the black troopers helps explain why they were not punished for their part in the riot. So, too, does the lack of injuries to white civilians and law enforcement officials. (Only one sheriff's deputy was wounded.) If the men of the Tenth had killed law officers and white residents, they might well have suffered the fate of the men of the Twenty-fourth Infantry stationed in Houston in 1917. Although Colonel White broke three sergeants down to the rank of private later that month, it is not clear if the demotions resulted from the men's actions during the riot.[78]

Bisbee's leaders hoped to put the trouble behind them. In his story in the *Bisbee Review*, B. P. Guild pointedly avoided mentioning that most of the Tenth Cavalry's officers had been absent during the shootout.[79] Meanwhile city authorities took steps to get rid of Deputy Sheriff Joe

75 Wright to Commanding General, July 6, 1919; "Denies Troops Are Responsible for Bisbee Riot," *Chicago Whip*, August 8, 1919, 9 (quote).
76 Tinklepaugh, "In Re: Riot," 9–10.
77 Wright to Commanding General, July 6, 1919.
78 Special Orders [number illegible on original], July 17, and Special Orders No. 137, July 19, 1919, box 23A, book "Special Orders 1919–1920," Record Group 391, Records of Regular Army Mobile Units, World War I Organization Records Cavalry, 1916–1921, U.S. National Archives and Records Administration, College Park, Md.
79 Tinklepaugh, "In Re: Riot," 9.

Hardwick, who was likely responsible for shooting each of the five wounded troopers. Even in a town known for tolerating "quick draw" officers, Hardwick went too far on July 8 when he unholstered his gun during a heated argument with Kempton and the provost marshal of the Nineteenth Infantry. Hardwick was soon removed from his position.[80]

For the black troopers, the troubles of July 3, 1919, served as another reminder that their uniform did not as yet mean "the same thing a white man's does," as Sergeant Walter Stewart had asserted in 1918. Refusing to be treated as anything less than soldiers of the U.S. Army, the troopers had resisted disarmament and unlawful arrests. Like the enlisted men in the 349th Colored Labor Battalion in Charleston, the Tenth Cavalry had been targeted by white law enforcement officials determined to protect civil authority and white supremacy. In Arizona, however, white enlisted men had *not* come to the black troopers' aid. Instead, provost guards from the Nineteenth Infantry had allied with Bisbee's police and sheriff's deputies. Both the Charleston incident of December 1918 and the Bisbee altercation revealed that the active military service of black men remained a flashpoint in the immediate postwar period. These events also showed that black servicemen would resist mistreatment, in and away from their forts or camps. As an enlisted man wrote in a letter addressed to the secretary of war, "now the colored men has awoken up to their sence of their duty and [are] asking to be treated like men."[81] An outbreak of racial violence in Longview, Texas, soon demonstrated that this awakening was not limited to black soldiers.

Fighting Back in Longview

In 1919, S. L. Jones and Dr. C. P. Davis were both respected members of the black community in Longview, an east Texas town in Gregg County. Davis was a physician, Jones a teacher and news agent. Both men had recently encouraged Gregg County's black cotton growers to sell their bales in Galveston rather than to local white brokers. This advocacy, along with the creation of black-owned cooperative stores in Longview, did not sit well with white residents, who held a slight majority in the county of 16,700 people.[82] However, Longview's antiblack violence had

---

[80] District Intelligence Officer to the Department Intelligence Officer, July 10, 1919, Case File 10218–348–6, RG 165, reel 5.

[81] Unsigned letter posted from Columbus, N. Mex., July 12, 1919, Case File 10218–347–1, RG 165, reel 5.

[82] Tuttle, "Violence in a 'Heathen' Land," 325–6.

its sources in an ill-fated love affair. In June, Lemuel Walters, a black man, was allegedly discovered in the bedroom of a white woman in a nearby town. He was arrested and jailed. According to the *Longview Daily Leader*, law enforcement officers put him on a train to Louisiana on the evening of June 17, but the next morning, Walter's bullet-riddled body was found beside the tracks outside of Longview. His death, the newspaper reported, was a mystery.[83]

S. L. Jones heard a different account when he delivered copies of the *Chicago Defender* to the jail's black inmates a few days later. Four prisoners – three black, one white – told him that ten white men had come to the jail on June 17 and taken Walters away. (Notably, the men had the keys to the cells.) Jones shared this story with Dr. Davis and other prominent black citizens. A delegation visited county judge Erskine H. Bramlette and asked for his help in launching an investigation. The judge promised to cooperate, but Jones and Davis soon realized he was not acting in good faith. Bramlette asked the delegation to keep quiet – to avoid tipping off the men who had taken Walters, he said – but no one was arrested in the days to come. At the judge's request, Jones had identified the inmates he had spoken with; these men were soon moved to other jails.[84] Jones and Davis were not sure what to do next. Each day they waited gave authorities more time to cover up the killing of Lemuel Walters, but if they publicized the murder, they risked the enmity of one of the county's most powerful white men. As they considered their options, the *Chicago Defender* broke the story about the murder and Walters's alleged affair with a white woman.

By 1919, the *Defender* was the most widely read black newspaper in the South. Its actual circulation exceeded the stated figure of 130,000, for subscribers widely shared their copies. The paper's publisher, Chicago businessman Robert Abbott, cultivated the support of railroad porters and traveling black entertainers to bring the *Defender* to the attention of black southerners. Abbott's editorial stance further cemented the weekly newspaper's popularity. An unflinching critic of racial discrimination, Abbott published detailed, lurid accounts of lynchings and other acts of violence against blacks. The *Defender*'s coverage of mob actions incensed southern whites, who also reviled its policy of encouraging black migration to the North. Suppression of the newspaper was common during the

---

[83] Clipping, *Longview Daily Leader*, July 12, 1919, Longview Riot File, Longview Public Library.

[84] Tuttle, "Violence in a 'Heathen' Land," 325–6.

war. A BI agent in Jacksonville, Florida, predicted that circulation of the *Defender* "will create a spirit of unrest and possible disloyalty."[85] Police throughout the South confiscated copies and harassed news agents; local and state authorities asked federal agencies such as the BI for help in censoring the newspaper.[86]

When the July 5 edition of the *Defender* arrived in Longview, someone gave a copy to two brothers of the white woman alleged to have been Walters's lover. A front page article reported the coverup of the kidnapping and murder of Walters, adding that the "sheriff of the jail gladly welcomed the mob, and acknowledged recognitions from the men as they passed in the gate to seize the prisoner." To the brothers' horror, the article also claimed that Walters's lover had "declared she loved him, and if she were in the North would obtain a divorce and marry him."[87] Who was the *Defender*'s source for this story? The brothers blamed S. L. Jones, the *Defender*'s agent in Longview. On Thursday, July 10, they drove into Longview to find him, determined to avenge the honor of their disgraced sister. They accosted Jones in front of the courthouse. He denied being the source of the article, but the men beat him with a wrench anyway. Although Jones managed to escape and have his injuries treated, his life was still in danger, not just from his attackers, but also from a growing number of Longview's white residents.[88]

The *Defender*'s article challenged white supremacy at several points. It implicated the sheriff in a lynching, accused city officials of a conspiracy, and boldly claimed that a white woman was in love with a black man. Adding insult to injury, the *Defender* had suggested this love could have blossomed in the North. Whether or not Jones was the *Defender*'s source – and he continued to deny it – hardly mattered to much of Gregg County's white population. As the distributor of the *Defender*, Jones had to pay the price for the "false and scurrilous article which was printed in a Chicago paper, reflecting upon a white woman in this county, the citizenship in general and the [city and county's] officials."[89] The beating, though

[85] Edward S. Chastell, "In re: Chicago Defender (newspaper)," April 24, 1917, RG 65, OGF 5911, in *Federal Surveillance of Afro-Americans*, reel 9, frame 39.

[86] Grossman, *Land of Hope*, 44, 74–88; Tuttle, "Violence in a 'Heathen' Land," 326; Tuttle, *Race Riot*, 89–92.

[87] "Police Work to Keep Lynching a Secret," *Chicago Defender*, July 5, 1919, 2.

[88] Tuttle, "Violence in a 'Heathen' Land," 326–7; "The Riot at Longview, Texas," *Crisis* 18, no. 6 (October 1919), 297–8.

[89] "Race Riot in Longview, Two White Men Killed, Four Negroes Killed," *Gilmer Daily Mirror*, n.d.; clipping, *Longview Daily Leader*, July 12, 1919 (quote), Longview Riot File.

vicious, did not suffice. To atone for the transgression against white supremacy, Jones had to accept exile from Longview – or worse.

Thursday evening, Jones received word that he would be lynched if he did not leave town by midnight. His friend Dr. C. P. Davis went to city hall to see what would be done to stop the lynch mob. Davis found the mayor conferring with several other officials. When the white men demanded Davis remove his hat before speaking, the doctor could no longer contain his anger. "Yes! That's all 'you all' say to a colored man who comes to talk serious business to you," he retorted. "'Take off your hat.' I am not going to do it. I want to know what protection we colored citizens are going to have tonight." The chief of police sternly warned Davis to "be careful"; still defiant, Davis stormed out. A white man followed him, but Davis let him see that he was armed, and he backed off. Davis drove to Jones's house, where two dozen black men had gathered to defend the teacher. As if he was a veteran sergeant from the Tenth Cavalry, Davis "posted men where they could safeguard every side from which an attack could be made," including outhouses and a corn patch, and ordered the men not to open fire unless he shot first. He also sternly warned them "under no circumstances to shoot into white people's houses." The guards in place, Davis reconnoitered the center of Longview, where he saw an armed mob preparing to move out from the fire station. He returned to Jones's home and offered the volunteer defenders a final chance to leave if anyone "did not feel like risking his life in defense of Prof. Jones." Not a man budged.[90]

At midnight the mob surrounded the house. Four white men stepped onto the back porch and summoned Jones. When he didn't answer, the men rammed the door – Davis opened fire, followed by his men. The defensive barrage surprised and confused the attackers, who fired back blindly. Three whites were wounded; a fourth took several blows to the head from a rifle butt and crawled beneath a nearby house. By one estimate, between 100 and 150 shots were fired during the next half-hour. None of the defenders were wounded, and the mob retreated to the town square. When they realized they had left their wounded behind, leaders quickly dispatched cars to retrieve them. The identities of the injured white men suggest that the mob came from a cross-section of Longview.

---

[90] "Interview with Prof. S. L. Jones and Dr. C. P. Davis, late of Longview, Texas, at Olivet Church, Chicago, Illinois," August 18, 1919, excerpted in Tuttle, "Violence in a 'Heathen' Land," 327–30 (all quotes; hereafter cited as Jones and Davis Interview); clipping, *Longview Daily Leader*, July 12, 1919.

One was a businessman, another a fireman. The man who crawled under a porch was a recently returned veteran.[91]

This initial victory did not lull Davis into a false sense of security. The intrepid physician again went into town for more reconnaissance. He overheard white men "talk of going back but no leader could be found to start the trip." Unnoticed, he hurried back to Jones's house and briefed the defenders, who remained on guard for a few more hours and then dispersed. Davis continued to observe the home from a safe distance. As he kept up his vigil, Davis heard the bell ringing at the fire station – a call for reinforcements for the white mob.[92]

By four in the morning, approximately 1,000 white men had amassed in Longview. Still lacking clear leadership, they waited for daybreak. A hardware store was looted for rifles and ammunition, then the revived mob set out for Jones's house. After circling without being fired upon, the mob set the unoccupied home ablaze. Encouraged by this first strike, the mob fanned out. Jones's neighbors, a married couple, were shot and their home torched. The meeting place of the Negro Business Men's League was burned. Davis's medical office and home were the next targets. Still fearful of being ambushed, members of the mob first surrounded the office. When they were convinced it was undefended, they set it on fire. Davis's wife and children were inside his house, though, and some in the mob were apparently reluctant to burn them alive: "After some talk, they allowed a colored man to go in and take the women and children away" before lighting the house on fire.[93]

Davis and Jones remained marked men. Davis sought refuge with his wife's family, hiding in their attic with a gun. A mob barged into the home, but Marion Bush, Davis's father-in-law, convinced its leaders that Davis was not there. At dawn, Davis dressed in a soldier's uniform and hopped a freight train. Outside of Longview he waited for a passenger train at a depot, continuing to pose as a soldier. In his telling, "knowing that anyone looking for him would be looking for a doctor, he bought some popcorn, some red pop and some other refreshment and walked

[91] Jones and Davis Interview; "More Troops Ordered Sent to Longview," *Dallas Morning News*, July 13, 1919, 1; "Longview Is Quiet After Race Rioting," *Dallas Morning News*, July 12, 1919, 1; clipping, Longview Daily Leader, July 12, 1919; "Longview Is Quiet Under Troop Guard," *Waco Times-Herald*, July 12, 1919, Longview Riot File.

[92] Jones and Davis Interview.

[93] Jones and Davis Interview (quote); "Story apparently prepared for *Crisis* or other NAACP publication, no date on MS., no author, in NAACP Mss.," Waskow Notes, tab "NAACP Probes."

around the railroad track and toward the station, throwing the bottle in the air, drinking from it ostentatiously and eating and singing, like a simple 'darky.'" He eventually made his way to Chicago. Jones also managed to leave Longview undetected. Fortunate to escape with their lives, both men had left behind their families, not knowing who would care for them.[94]

The mob still continued to hunt for Jones and Davis, leading to another tragedy for Davis's family. The sheriff and a deputy called on Marion Bush, who allegedly fired several shots at them and fled. Did, in fact, the sheriff or his deputy fire first? Might Bush have merely fled without firing a shot? Without his testimony, these questions cannot be answered. Early Sunday morning, armed vigilantes encountered Bush near a rural schoolhouse three miles from Longview. According to them, Bush was carrying a rifle and opened fire after being ordered to halt. They returned fire, killing Bush, the riot's first and only fatality.[95]

Even before the killing of Marion Bush, Longview mayor G. A. Bodenheim was reconsidering the rough justice he had unleashed. He had not expected Longview's black men, led by Dr. Davis, to stand their ground against the mob intent on lynching S. L. Jones. Now four members of the mob were hurt, and the smoking ruins of several homes and buildings dotted his city. Bodenheim was also upset that the police had arrested only four suspects in the citywide hunt for the two dozen men who had defended Jones. On Friday, July 11, the mayor asked Texas governor W. P. Hobby to send Texas National Guard troops and Texas Rangers. The rangers and the soldiers, drawn from cavalry brigades, began arriving that night. The guardsmen set up their encampment on the courthouse grounds and started patrolling the black neighborhood. To prevent additional looting, commanding officer General R. H. McDill stationed armed sentries outside of Longview's hardware stores. The rangers and soldiers also helped enforce a 10:30 P.M. curfew declared by Bodenheim.[96]

Friday night passed without additional violence, but Longview and the outlying areas remained tense. The killing of Marion Bush and the arrest of two black residents for being armed prompted Bodenheim to

94 Jones and Davis Interview.
95 "More Troops Ordered Sent to Longview," *Dallas Morning News*, July 13, 1919; "Gregg County Now Under Martial Law," *Dallas Morning News*, July 14, 1919, 1, Longview Riot File.
96 "Longview Is Quiet After Race Rioting," *Dallas Morning News*, July 12, 1919; "Longview Is Quiet Under Troop Guard," *Waco Times-Herald*, July 12, 1919, Longview Riot File; *Biennial Report of the Adjutant General of Texas*, 27–8.

ask the governor to impose martial law and to send more troops. On Sunday, July 13, McDill ordered all citizens, black and white, to turn in their weapons. He also proscribed public gatherings. Longview's black residents promised to cooperate with the guardsmen and rangers, but, as one black man told military officers, they would "defend themselves if attacked." By Monday, 281 enlisted men, twenty-two officers, and ten rangers were in Longview. Most left on July 16; three officers and forty enlisted men remained until martial law was lifted two days later.[97]

Black resistance did not cease with the restoration of civil order. The arrest of the men who had defended S. L. Jones led Longview's black residents, aided by the NAACP, to mount a vigorous legal defense campaign for these men. At the same time, blacks hoped to see charges brought against the white men who had attacked Jones's home and committed arson. For their part, Jones and Dr. Davis struggled to obtain compensation for the total loss of their assets and savings. Like the black residents of Charleston who had suffered damage in that city's riot, Jones and Davis used civil suits to proceed. (For the outcomes of this fight for justice, see Chapter 8.)

The antiblack collective violence that swept across Charleston, Bisbee, and Longview shared many characteristics. In all three locales, white military and civil authorities organized or condoned mob violence against African Americans. Whites initiated the violence, and blacks responded with armed self-defense. For the most part, African Americans acted with restraint at the onset of trouble. In May 1919 in Charleston, for example, the first targets of white violence sought to avoid confrontation by trying to elude the sailors and civilians harassing them. In Bisbee, military regulations permitted the soldiers of the Tenth Cavalry to carry sidearms while on leave and in uniform; the men drew their weapons only after being fired upon. In Longview, black residents first sought the protection of the law and the city government. Only after they learned that the mayor and the police chief were plotting mob violence did they assemble a paramilitary self-defense force.

African Americans' actions in Charleston, Bisbee, and Longview demonstrated that postwar armed resistance to white mob violence was

[97] "More Troops Ordered Sent to Longview," *Dallas Morning News*, July 13, 1919; "Gregg County Now Under Martial Law," *Dallas Morning News*, July 14, 1919; "Longview Is Quiet Under Troop Guard," *Waco Times-Herald*, July 12, 1919 (quote), Longview Riot File; *Biennial Report of the Adjutant General of Texas*, 27–8.

no aberration. Blacks were striking back against white mobs, even when outnumbered, even with the knowledge that white control of the economy, police power, and justice system threatened crushing retribution. At points this resistance was reflexive – the frayed tempers of the men of the Tenth Cavalry, for example. Black self-defenders in Charleston, Bisbee, and Longview were much more than individuals who had "had enough," however; their actions also show deliberation over what actions to take. In Charleston, some residents *chose* to avoid mobbing whites, while others opted to defend their residences or fight back when attacked. The troopers in Bisbee chose to ignore their white commanding officer's order to relinquish their sidearms inside the Silver Leaf Club. This decision, technically insubordination, prompted Bisbee's chief of police to seek a rapprochement that allowed the troopers to keep their weapons. In Longview, Dr. C. P. Davis chose to organize a unit of self-defenders because authorities refused his request for protection for his friend S. L. Jones. Resistance was not borne of desperation in these instances; it resulted from consideration of the available options.

These forms of resistance, and the choices underlying them, did not go unnoticed. Just as whites used violence to deter and punish black strivings for equality and opportunity, so, too, could blacks use armed self-defense to deter racially motivated rioting. As George Towns, a district organizer for the NAACP, remarked about the black men who had repelled the mob from S. L. Jones's doorstep, "Longview is going to have a very wholesome restraint upon other smaller places."[98] And not just small towns: ten days after Longview's troubles, black armed resistance in Washington, D.C., also yielded a "very wholesome restraint."

[98] George Towns to James Weldon Johnson, September 22, 1919, box C-4, folder "General Correspondence Sept. 18–25, 1919," NAACP Records.

3

Fighting a Mob in Uniform

Armed Resistance in Washington, D.C.

During the Great War, the 372nd Infantry Regiment, Ninety-third Division, faced two enemies: its white officers and the Germans. The regiment was formed from four existing black National Guard units, including the First Separate Battalion of the District of Columbia. Arriving in France in mid-April 1918, the 372nd soon found itself in the trenches of the Western Front, first in the Argonne West sector. The regiment took part in the Meuse-Argonne offensive, going "over the top" on September 28, with artillery shells "falling like hail." The 372nd helped force a German retreat, capturing sixty enemy soldiers and many artillery cannons. It stayed on the front for more than a week, until its relief by a French regiment.[1]

Whether in or out of the trenches, the black enlisted men and officers of the 372nd chafed under their white command. In a breach of military protocol, Colonel Glendie Young ordered the officers to eat with enlisted men. "I wouldn't make a god-damned one of these black sons-of-a-bitch an officer if I didn't have to," Young complained to other white officers. No wonder Rayford Logan, a newly commissioned black officer, called the colonel a "Negro-hater." Young was soon transferred, but his replacement promptly asked General John J. Pershing to remove the regiment's black officers, claiming that "racial distinctions which are recognized in civilian life naturally continue to be recognized in military life." Although Pershing rejected the request, the regiment's

[1] Scott, *Scott's Official History*, 239–43 (quotes on 241); Barbeau and Henri, *Unknown Soldiers*, 129.

66

deteriorating morale alarmed French general Mariano Goybet, who questioned the unit's combat readiness due to these racial tensions.[2]

Rayford Logan was just one of the almost 600 black Washingtonians serving in the 372nd. Their record in France put the lie to their white officers' low expectations. Two hundred men suffered wounds; more than thirty were killed. Many, such as Sergeant Ira Payne, came home with the Croix de Guerre. Payne charged a German machine gun nest, shot two of the gunners, and captured the others. Two privates, Charles E. Cross and Benjamin Butler, received the same medal for braving enemy shells to deliver messages from headquarters to the trenches.[3] All three men had begun their military service in the First Separate Battalion of the District of Columbia, which, prior to its incorporation into the 372nd, had guarded the White House. Even this duty had aroused animosity. In September 1917, a white officer requested the unit's removal from the White House grounds because of "the unsettled condition of the country at large, and of Washington in particular, especially in connection with the negro question."[4]

Black soldiers guarding the White House, then risking their lives in France under the command of hostile white officers: the juxtaposition was more than symbolic. For Rayford Logan, the glaring contradiction between America's mission and its treatment of black servicemen led him to remain in France after the war – he dreaded coming home to ongoing racism.[5] But Logan was the exception. Almost all of Washington's native sons returned, marching down Pennsylvania Avenue in a victory parade in February 1919.

As Logan feared, domestic racism was as strong as ever, especially in the military. In March, the chief of staff of the Ninety-second Division at Fort Meade, Maryland, rebuffed the request of three black officers for peacetime commissions, telling them he did not want blacks in the army.[6] With the approval of Secretary of War Newton Baker, the decision was overturned, but for two black lieutenants, Osceola McKaine and Charles

[2] Williams, *Torchbearers of Democracy*, 128–32 (Young and Logan quotes on 128); Barbeau and Henri, *Unknown Soldiers*, 128–9 (replacement quote on 128).

[3] Scott, *Scott's Official History*, 251–2.

[4] Capt. C. J. Harvey to the Chief of Staff, September 5, 1917, box 6, folder "Washington, D.C. (1917, 1919)," RG 60, Glasser File.

[5] Williams, *Torchbearers of Democracy*, 269.

[6] W. H. Loving to Churchill, March 3, 1919, Case File 10218-331-2, RG 165, copy in box 1, reel 5, Kornweibel Papers.

Lane, the problem went beyond one racist officer. "Until we have colored officers commanding white men we do not want white officers commanding colored men," they told an audience at the Howard Theater. "If satisfaction cannot be had from the Secretary of War we will go to Congress. We owe no special allegiance to a government that discriminates, segregates, and permits lynching and burning at the stake."[7] Shortly after being mustered out, veterans of the 372nd gathered in Washington to listen to speakers who urged them to fight for democracy at home. As an observer from the army's Military Intelligence Division (MID) reported, the "thought of fighting for democracy abroad and expecting democracy at home seems to be the key note and when the soldiers themselves are not using the expression, they can always find some one to express their sentiments on these public occasions."[8] For the MID, the thought of several hundred black veterans in Washington fighting for democracy was unsettling. What if the men resorted to violence? Fears of an uprising led the MID to maintain its surveillance of black veterans. Events soon showed, however, that a different set of ex-servicemen posed a threat to law and order in Washington.

Postwar Uncertainties and Tensions

In the summer of 1919, Washington continued to cope with wartime growing pains. Its population had fallen from an April 1918 peak of 526,000 to 455,000, but the city still had almost 100,000 more residents than it did before the United States entered the war. A persistent housing shortage kept rents high and rooms crowded. The War and Navy Departments winnowed their ranks of civilian employees, but the return of Washingtonians from military service mitigated the departures.[9] So, too, did the arrival of hundreds of white veterans mustering out from nearby camps or forts in Virginia and Maryland. These men, who were not residents of Washington, drifted into the city, hoping to find work.

---

[7] Newton Baker to George Foster Peabody, June 18, 1919, copy in box 1, reel "Newton-Baker – George Peabody," Kornweibel Papers; W. H. Loving to General Marlborough Churchill, June 11, 1919, box 113–1, folder 12, Walter H. Loving Papers, Moorland-Spingarn Research Center (quote).

[8] Loving to Churchill, March 17, 1919, Case File 10218 [no suffix], RG 165, copy in box 1, reel 1, Kornweibel Papers.

[9] Abernethy, "Washington Race War," 310; Buchholz, "Josephine: The Washington Diary," 6.

Few found jobs. The unemployed white veterans – many still in their uniforms – milled in the streets, went to the movies, killed time in Washington's near-beer saloons and pool halls.[10] They socialized with active-duty white soldiers, sailors, and marines stationed in Washington. (The army had mustered out most of its black soldiers, the marine corps refused to enlist blacks, and the navy only allowed blacks to serve as stewards.) These servicemen came from East Potomac Park, barrack grounds of the Sixty-third Infantry; the Marine Barracks near Capitol Hill; Bolling Field, an army base; the naval air station along the Anacostia River; and the Navy Yard. On any given weekend night, hundreds of white veterans and servicemen roamed the District. Washington had gone dry on November 1, 1917, but a loophole allowed possession of liquor for personal consumption. Enterprising residents drove to Baltimore, loaded their cars with crates of whiskey, and sold it in the District. On July 1, 1919, Congress outlawed the transport of liquor between states, but vigorous enforcement failed to staunch the flow of alcohol into the District.[11] Veterans and active-duty servicemen thirsting for something stronger than weak beer went to Bloodfield, a rough neighborhood in Southwest Washington, where black entrepreneurs controlled the illicit liquor trade. Here, too, were many of the city's brothels. Boisterous white men sometimes started fights, and armed black men occasionally robbed whites looking for whiskey, adding to racial tensions.[12]

Lingering confusion over authority in the wake of war was another problem, and not just in Washington. To mobilize the public to support the war, the federal government had relied extensively on voluntary associations to promote patriotism, "Americanize" immigrants, suppress dissent, and safeguard the homefront. The American Protective League, which enrolled more than a quarter million men, was a prominent example. Across the country, its volunteers reported public utterances of dissent or criticism of the government to local police so that the speakers could be arrested for disorderly conduct or riot incitement.[13] Similar associations proliferated, often with state sanction. (Two examples: the Bisbee Workman's Loyalty League and the Citizen's Protective League that had

---

[10] Abernethy, "Washington Race War," 311–12.

[11] *Annual Report of the Commissioners*, 200–1; "Crooks Reap Harvest," *Washington Post*, June 2, 1919, 2.

[12] Arthur Waskow Interview with West A. Hamilton, undated notes, Waskow Notes, tab "D.C. Riot"; "Lured into Autos," *Washington Post*, July 7, 1919; F. M. Kemon, "In Re: Race Riots in Washington," July 31, 1919, RG 65, OGF 369,936, reel 812.

[13] Jensen, *Price of Vigilance*, 135–6.

helped Bisbee authorities deport striking mining workers in June 1917.) Vigilantes avidly and often violently targeted socialists, radicals, draft resisters, and African Americans. As historian Christopher Capozzola observes, "coercive voluntarism made America's first world war both its most democratically mobilized homefront as well as its most violent," with mob and public violence causing more than seventy deaths in the United States during the war.[14] Even with the war's end, no one could instantly snuff the hyperpatriotic eagerness for a fight. Encouraged by the federal government, many voluntary vigilance groups expected to keep up their civic policing after the war. The Justice Department even asked for the American Protective League's help in case of a domestic communist revolt.[15]

The continued existence of voluntary vigilante associations and the presence of so many idle veterans did not alarm Major Walter H. Loving, the MID's only black officer, and the team of white officers that had closely surveilled black Washingtonians throughout the war. Instead, they turned their attention to socialists, labor leaders, or anyone advocating racial equality. When Chandler Owen and A. Philip Randolph, the black publishers of the socialist monthly the *Messenger*, spoke in Washington on the subject of "Bolshevism, a Menace or a Promise," Loving took down every word. When lieutenants McKaine and Lane demanded equality in the army, Loving was listening, too. And when a white tailor reported that a black employee claimed to preach at secret meetings of local blacks, a MID officer excitedly believed he had uncovered evidence of a clandestine, subversive society.[16]

While the MID stealthily observed black Washington, the Metropolitan Police (Washington's city police) searched for an apparent serial rapist. Black teacher Louise Simmons was the first victim. On her way to work on June 25, 1919, a man dragged her into a woods and attempted to rape her. Simmons described her assailant in detail: black, five feet, six inches tall, 150 pounds, wearing a blue coat and pants. Within five days, two more assaults occurred in Northwest Washington. The victims, both

[14] Capozzola, *Uncle Sam Wants You*, 3–20, 123–31 (quote on 10–11).
[15] Jensen, *Price of Vigilance*, 238.
[16] H. B. Arnold to Major Henry G. Pratt, June 18, 1919; W. H. Loving to Churchill, June 1, 1919 (quote); Remarks of A. Philip Randolph, May 30, 1919, Case File 10218–296–19, RG 165, reel 5; K. A. Wagner to Henry G. Pratt, November 22, 1918, Case File 10218–283–1, RG 165, copy in box 1, reel 5, Kornweibel Papers. For more on federal surveillance of African Americans during World War I, see Kornweibel, *Investigate Everything*.

white, said their assailant was a dark-skinned young black man wearing a blue coat. On July 5, a white government clerk was raped in a woods in Somerset, Maryland, just over the District line. She offered the same description of her attacker as the other victims. All of the assaults occurred within one and a half miles of each other.[17]

Chief Raymond Pullman immediately assigned forty officers to hunt for the suspect, urging them to "bend every effort to get the brute." Soon, sixty more officers, Montgomery County (Md.) deputy sheriffs, and hundreds of volunteers had joined the manhunt. In an action that further blurred the line between law enforcement and vigilantism, Pullman authorized the Home Defense League to patrol as a police auxiliary. A wartime volunteer force, the Home Defense League closely resembled the American Protective League, and its members eagerly embraced their new duty. Sweeping roundups of black men ensued. Inspector Clifford Grant, chief of detectives of the Metropolitan Police, promised to continue arresting "suspects" until the rapist was found – in a previous case, he remarked, the police had detained no fewer than 136 individuals until they found their man.[18] By July 10, the police had questioned more than 100 black men, taking many from their homes without warrants. Crowds of white men accosted black men on the street to interrogate them; one mob carried a long rope.[19] Washington's newspapers gave the manhunt front page coverage, often using provocative phrases: "Negro Fiend Pursued by 1,000 Posse" announced a headline in the July 7 issue of the *Washington Herald*. "Trouble seems to be brewing in Washington," the same paper reported, but "the police laugh at the possibility of racial affrays."[20]

The police force's draconian tactics and the roaming vigilantes were no laughing matter to black Washingtonians. "The recent outrages," observed the *Washington Bee*, the city's black weekly, referring to the sexual assaults, unfairly "cast suspicion on other innocent colored

[17] "Assaults and Rape Cases," notes given by Chief of Police Raymond Pullman to Herbert Seligmann, July 23, 1919, box G-34, folder "DC Branch 1919 March-July," NAACP Records; "Mrs. Sewall Assaulted," *Washington Bee*, June 28, 1919, 1 (the *Bee* incorrectly gave Louise Simmons's last name as Sewall); "Believe Same Negro Attacked Two Women," *Washington Evening Star*, July 1, 1919, 2; "Girl War Worker Is Negro's Victim," *Washington Evening Star*, July 6, 1919, 1.
[18] "Girl War Worker"; "Hunt of Women's Assailant Grows," *Washington Evening Star*, July 7, 1919, 1 (quotes).
[19] "Woods Scoured in Hunt for Negro," *Washington Evening Star*, July 8, 1919, 1.
[20] "Negro Fiend Pursued by 1,000 Posse," *Washington Herald*, July 7, 1919, 1; "Police Tactics in Fiend Search," *Washington Herald*, July 10, 1919, 1 (quote).

civilians," who trust and obey the law.[21] The local branch of the NAACP directed its opprobrium at the press. In a letter sent to all four dailies on July 9, the branch warned that their coverage was "sowing the seeds of a race riot."[22]

By mid-July, the police had identified Forrest Eaglan, a former golf caddy, as a suspect, despite a lack of evidence. After seeing Eaglan, two of the victims declared he did not attack them. Even so, the police decided to hold him "until proof of his innocence can be established."[23] They also arrested another man for two of the assaults. The *Washington Evening Star*'s editorial writers praised the police for using "sensible methods" and predicted that the arrests "will greatly relieve the community and ease the strain under which it has been suffering for nearly a fortnight."[24]

They were wrong.

The First Mob

Elsie Stephnick's shift ended late on Friday, July 18. Recently married, the nineteen-year-old white woman worked at the Bureau of Engraving and Printing, at 14th and B Streets (now Independence Avenue), SW. Shortly after 10 P.M., she encountered two black men as she walked home. According to the *Evening Star*, the men accosted her but ran when she screamed.[25] Were they trying to rob Stephnick? Assault her? What was said? Newspaper accounts varied, but all of the city's dailies lingered on the race of Stephnick's alleged attackers ("Negro Thugs," to the *Washington Times*), emphasized their purported menacing intent, and elaborated on Stephnick's escape.[26]

Like so many young Washingtonians, Stephnick had a military connection; her husband, John, was a civilian employee of the navy's aviation department. On learning that the police had questioned Bloodfield resident Charles Ralls about the incident, John apparently became convinced that Ralls was one of the men who had menaced his wife. As word of

[21] "Recent Outrages," *Washington Bee*, July 12, 1919.
[22] "Additional Notes," *Branch Bulletin* vol. III, no. 8 (August 1919), no page number given.
[23] "Former Caddy Latest Arrest in Fiend's Case," *Washington Herald*, July 14, 1919, 1.
[24] "Women Identify Assault Suspect," *Washington Evening Star*, July 15, 1919, 22; "Police Success," *Washington Evening Star*, July 16, 1919, 6 (quotes).
[25] "Woman Attacked on Way from Work," *Washington Evening Star*, July 19, 1919, 10.
[26] "Assaults and Rape Cases"; "Negroes Attack Girl," *Washington Post*, July 19, 1919, 2; "Screams Save Girl from 2 Negro Thugs," *Washington Times*, July 19, 1919, section 2.

Ralls's identity spread throughout the military establishment, a group of servicemen called for their comrades and veterans to assemble near the Knights of Columbus hut for enlisted men at 7th Street and Pennsylvania Avenue, NW, at 10 P.M. on Saturday to find Ralls (Figure 3.1 shows a map of the area).

Sailors, soldiers, and marines strolled 9th Street and Pennsylvania Avenue, giving the word. They had no trouble recruiting a mob. Earlier that day, three black men had robbed a sailor at gunpoint near the Navy Yard. A fistfight in Southwest over bootlegged whiskey left several battered sailors eager for revenge against the black men who had bested them. And, as one white sailor freely informed his black barber during a shave, servicemen from the South were angry that the police had not as yet halted the assaults of white women. Back home, he said matter-of-factly, if whites didn't get results one way, they used another.[27]

The result was a mob in uniform. By 10:30 P.M., more than one hundred white servicemen in uniform had gathered at 7th and Pennsylvania. Ralls's house was half a mile away. Brandishing pipes, clubs, sticks, and pistols, the men thronged south on 6th and 7th Streets or crossed the Mall. Eager civilians fell in, swelling the crowd. George Montgomery, a fifty-five-year-old African American, was out buying produce when he encountered the mob on C Street. Blows from clubs and sticks knocked him to the sidewalk. Other black passers-by suffered similar beatings. The mob spotted Ralls walking with his wife and began beating them. The couple broke free and bolted home, shots ringing out behind them. The mob tried to break in, but Ralls's neighbors and friends rallied to his defense – a return fusillade scattered the mob and wounded a sailor. Servicemen fired back as black residents locked their doors and prepared to defend their homes.

The police responded with their own uniformed reinforcements, consisting of marines from the nearby barracks and soldiers from the Sixty-third Infantry stationed at East Potomac Park. (The infantry unit had served as the District's wartime provost guard until June 15, when regular patrols had ceased.) Anxious police officers sought out the mob's self-appointed spokesmen and apparently struck a deal: there would be no arrests if everyone went home. The mob reluctantly dispersed. Private E. H. Moore, stationed at Bolling Field, boasted that he had "got three"

---

[27] "Men in Uniform Attack Negroes," *Washington Evening Star,* July 20, 1919, 1; "Attacks on Women Lead to Race Riots," *Washington Post,* July 20, 1919, 1; Kemon, "In Re: Race Riots in Washington."

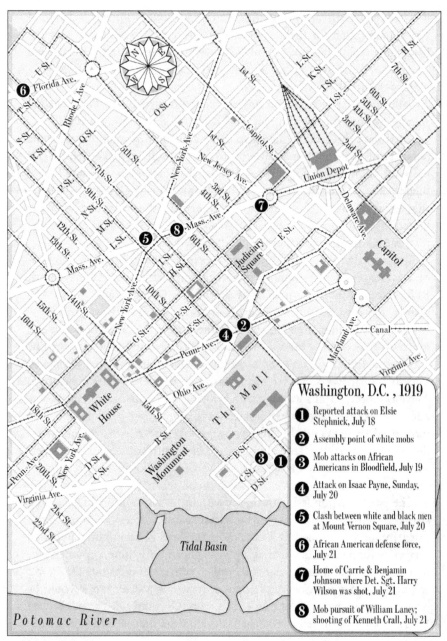

FIGURE 3.1. Map of Washington, D.C., 1910. *Source:* C. S. Hammond & Company Atlas, 1910.

blacks before the police took away his lead pipe. To African Americans watching warily from their houses, the police appeared interested only in breaking up the crowd rather than also identifying the servicemen, veterans, and civilians guilty of assault and attempted home invasion.

Outside of Southwest, the police arrested scattered troublemakers, many of them in uniform. A white sailor who assaulted blacks on the Mall spent the night in jail, as did four black men charged with disorderly conduct. To prevent the mob from reforming, the police arrested Private Moore when he returned to 7th and Pennsylvania. One of the alleged mob leaders, a petty naval officer from the Anacostia air station, was apprehended on the same corner. Throughout the night, beat cops patrolled the streets and alleys of Southwest. Tensions ran high between the white officers and black residents. When two white patrolmen approached a black man in an alley at 4 ½ and D Streets, the man fired a pistol, the officers reported, wounding one of them.[28]

The local branch of the NAACP saw the violence as the military's responsibility, and it asked Secretary of Navy Josephus Daniels to restrain the sailors and marines who had joined the mob. Referring to the May Charleston riot, the branch suggested that immediate "drastic action" could prevent a similar outbreak of violence in Washington. Daniels ignored the request.[29] While President Wilson, recently returned from Europe, spent the humid Sunday aboard the USS *Mayflower* on the Potomac River, hundreds of white sailors, soldiers, and marines in khaki and blue uniforms milled around the central business district, discussing the previous night's fracas. As night fell, they gathered on corners, joined by recently mustered-out servicemen and men in civilian clothes. Some spoke openly of carrying out a lynching. Some carried clubs and sticks; others wrapped rocks in handkerchiefs.[30] An angry force was mobilizing, and Pennsylvania Avenue, as wide as a plaza, made a good battlefield. Streetcars ran down the center of the thoroughfare, offering vulnerable targets, and black passengers headed uptown had to transfer at the

---

[28] "Men in Uniform"; "Attacks on Women" (Moore quote); "Policeman Is Shot During Riot," *Washington Times,* July 20, 1919, section 2; "Two Shot; 4 Hurt in D.C. Race Riots," *Washington Herald,* July 20, 1919, 1.

[29] "Additional Notes."

[30] Wilson's cruise is noted in John L. Sullivan to Joseph E. Murphy, July 20, 1919, box 13, no folder, Record Group 87, Records of the Secret Service, Daily Reports of Agents on White House Detail, 1902–1936, U.S. National Archives and Records Administration, College Park, Md. For the gathering of white servicemen, see "Score of Negroes Hurt as Race Riot Spreads," *Washington Herald,* July 21, 1919, 1–2.

expansive intersection between 7th and 9th Streets, the very spot where the mob had congregated the previous night.

Shortly after 9 P.M., several white servicemen and civilians set upon Isaac Payne, a young black man, at 9th Street and Pennsylvania Avenue. They beat him and dislocated his collarbone before police arrived. The arrest of Payne's assailants only emboldened jeering onlookers to form another mob. They followed the police to the First Precinct stationhouse, just three blocks away, and called for the men's release. Denied, the mob headed to the streetcar transfer on 7th Street and began attacking black men as they disembarked. "Keep them where they belong," some whites shouted as they gave chase. More than thirty police officers could not, or would not, halt the mob – a critical failure, for it proved to white rioters that they could assault blacks at will. Like a fast-growing cell, the mob split and spread. In forces ranging from two to twenty or more, white men fanned out across the central business district. Some even hired taxis to search for victims.[31] Meanwhile, scores of black Washingtonians were returning home from crosstown visits, trips to the theaters, or jobs. Others were enjoying an evening walk. By the time most realized what was happening, their chance to escape had vanished.

Francis L. Thomas, age seventeen, was riding the 7th Street streetcar around 11:15 P.M. when white sailors and soldiers jumped aboard and started "beating [him] unmercifully from head to foot." Then they threw him through the streetcar window. Just before he lost consciousness, he heard the cries of the other three black passengers, two of them women, "pleading whith the Lord to keep them from being killed." When he revived, Thomas was so battered that he had to crawl home.[32] Similar boardings and beatings occurred on the 14th Street line, while other white rioters seized blacks from passing automobiles. White civilians served as scouts, pointing out targets – "There he goes!" – for the mobs advancing up Pennsylvania Avenue.[33] In front of the Raleigh Hotel, on 12th Street, a black man fell to the ground after a vicious beating; another man was

[31] "Score of Negroes Hurt" (quote). The *Washington Post* reported that a mob seized Payne after police arrested him for a "minor charge," but other accounts do not include this detail. See "Scores Are Injured in More Race Riots," *Washington Post*, July 21, 1919, 1.

[32] Francis L. Thomas statement, undated, box G-34, folder "DC Branch 1919 March-July," NAACP Records; Garnet Wilkinson to Archibald Grimké, undated letter, box 39-28, folder "July 1919," Archibald Grimké Papers, Moorland-Spingarn Research Center.

[33] "Service Men Beat Negroes in Race Riot at Capital," *New York Times*, July 21, 1919, 1.

assaulted outside the Washington Post building one block west. Just after midnight, a white soldier chased a black man to the northeast corner of the Treasury Building's lawn and struck him with a stone slung in a handkerchief. Two black men accosted in front of the White House, next to the Treasury Building, managed to escape. The black historian Carter G. Woodson was walking on Pennsylvania Avenue when he saw a mob at the corner of 8th Street. He hurried away as shots rang out and the mob chased another black man. Policemen observed many of the chasings and beatings without intervening. When a white civilian asked three officers why no one was trying to stop the rioting, one exclaimed, "that is what we would like to know!"[34]

Not all black Washingtonians were caught off-guard. Directly north of the central business district, Uptown (now known as Shaw) was home to Washington's prominent black businesses, theaters, and restaurants.[35] Even before the attack on Isaac Payne, residents gathered at 7th Street and Florida Avenue, NW, to defend their neighborhood. While they moved south on 7th Street, white rioters came north from Pennsylvania Avenue. The two crowds clashed at Mount Vernon Square, site of the stately Carnegie Library. Around 1 A.M., a street battle between hundreds of blacks and whites broke out on L Street between 9th and 10th Streets, just north of the library. Few white rioters reached Uptown itself; those who did, an hour later, retreated after a brief brawl with the more than one hundred young black men still lining the intersection of 7th and Florida.[36]

Sunday night's rioting brought no deaths, but more than a dozen African Americans were hospitalized with serious injuries – internal bleeding, broken bones, severe lacerations – while as many as 100, by one estimate, suffered minor injuries or did not seek hospitalization.[37] After two days of antiblack collective violence, Washingtonians awoke Monday morning wondering whether the disturbances were finished. Black

[34] "Scores Are Injured" (quote); "Race Riot at Capital," *New York Age*, July 26, 1919, 1; Woodson, *Negro in Our History*, 531–3.
[35] Fitzpatrick, "Great Agitation for Business," 61–9.
[36] Lt. Robert Dawson to Major G. Q. Peters, July 22, 1919, Case File 10218–350-4, RG 165, copy in box 1, reel 6, Kornweibel Papers; Abernethy, "Washington Race War," 316–17; "Race Riot at Capital"; "Service Men Beat Negroes"; "Scores Are Injured"; W. E. Hawkins, "When Negroes Shot a Lynching Bee into Perdition," *Messenger* vol. II, no. 9 (September 1919), 28–9.
[37] "Score of Negroes Hurt"; "Scores Are Injured."

residents and veterans asked themselves a second question: what would *they* do to stop the white mobs if the riot continued?

An Army or a Mob?

Secretary of War Newton Baker proved more interested in imposing order than Secretary of the Navy Daniels. Recognizing that the trouble in Washington might reprise the violence of the 1917 Houston and East St. Louis riots, he ordered the commanding officer at Fort Myer to send cavalry. He then told Louis Brownlow, president of the D.C. Board of Commissioners, that he would order as many troops into the city as needed and would cancel nonessential leaves for servicemen stationed in and near the District.[38]

But Baker was not the only person issuing military orders. That day, the *Washington Post* issued its own call to arms in a now-notorious front page story:

It was learned that a mobilization of every available service man stationed in or near Washington or on leave here has been ordered for tomorrow evening near the Knights of Columbus hut, on Pennsylvania avenue between Seventh and Eighth streets.

The hour of assembly is 9 o'clock and the purpose is a "clean-up" that will cause the events of the last two evenings to pale into insignificance.[39]

Monday's *Washington Times* also wrote about the planned nine o'clock meeting, sans the lurid prediction.[40] As the prior rioting showed, white servicemen needed no advertising to muster up mobs, but the *Post* and *Times* articles greatly alarmed black residents, who now expected the mob to attempt another attack on Uptown.

In response, African Americans sought their own armed protection – preferably one with the legitimacy of military service. Told by Brownlow of the impending arrival of troops, a delegation from the local NAACP branch asked why black soldiers (such as those who had served in the 372nd) were not being included in this force. After all, active-duty white servicemen had started the riot. The answer, that the army had discharged its black soldiers, failed to placate the four men, who were in no mood for

---

[38] Major General Henry Jervey to the Adjutant General, July 21, 1919, box 6, folder "Washington, D.C. (1917, 1919)," RG 60, Glasser File; "'No More Rioting Here,' Military Men Decree," *Washington Times*, July 21, 1919, 1.

[39] "Scores Are Injured."

[40] "Desperadoes Shoot as Car Speeds Past U.S. Hospital," *Washington Times*, July 21, 1919, 1.

excuses. Black Washingtonians "would not receive a square deal from the white soldiers," they told Brownlow and Chief of Police Pullman, both of whom balked at the delegates' proposal to "commission some of the discharged colored soldiers and officers" for riot duty. Instead, the chief and commissioner sought assurances that blacks would not fight back. It is your duty to preserve order and peace, the delegation replied indignantly, declaring that the black men of Washington "had determined not to stand up and be shot down like dogs, but they were prepared to protect their families and themselves and would do so at all hazard."[41]

Denied a chance to defend themselves as soldiers, blacks armed themselves privately. An estimated 500 firearms were sold on Monday, prompting the police to ask weapons dealers to suspend sales.[42] When the gun dealers complied, black bootleggers turned their smuggling operation into an "underground railway" by driving to Baltimore to buy weapons and ammunition they then handed out to black Washingtonians.[43] "It was splendid," remarked an observer, to see the "poolroom hangers-on and men from the alleys and side streets, people from the most ordinary walks of life," preparing to defend their community from mobs.[44] In the early evening, Neval Thomas, one of the four men who had visited Brownlow, walked through Uptown, marveling at the 2,000 blacks thronging Florida Avenue and U Street from 6th to 14th Streets. Many declared "their purpose to die for their race, and defy the white mob," expected because of the *Post*'s mobilization announcement. Thomas found the spectacle inspirational, especially when the crowd started patrolling the surrounding blocks. Just as white veterans were deploying their military training to carry out mob violence, black veterans and emulative civilians were drawing on their wartime experience in the cause of self-defense.[45]

---

[41] Neval Thomas to Archibald Grimké, July 28, 1919, box 39–28, folder "July 1919," Archibald Grimké Papers; unsigned summary of riot, July 28, 1919, box G-34, folder "DC Branch 1919 March–July," NAACP Records (quotes). For detailed analysis of the NAACP delegation's meeting with Brownlow and Pullman, see Mellis, "The monsters we defy," 272–81.

[42] "500 Guns Bought in D.C., Police Say," *Washington Post*, July 22, 1919, 1; "Race Riot at Capital."

[43] "Riots in Washington," *Chicago Whip*, July 25, 1919, 1 (quote); W. H. Loving to M. Churchill, August 10, 1919, Case File 10218–350-7, RG 165, copy in box 1, reel 6, Kornweibel Papers.

[44] "Negroes of Washington Were Forced to Defend Themselves," *New York Age*, August 2, 1919, 1.

[45] Thomas to Grimké, July 28, 1919 (quote); W. Wright, "In Re: Race Riots in Washington," July 22, 1919, RG 65, OGF 369,936, reel 812.

In addition to the 372nd Regiment, Washington's black veterans included men from the 368th Regiment, Ninety-second Division. They, too, had fought in the Meuse-Argonne offensive and had struggled against deep-set racism. As the MID noted, "these officers and soldiers returning to their homes in Washington have told their grievances and, in some instances, as reported to [the MID], have boasted of their ability to handle guns and of their determination to use the arms in their possession rather than submit to unjust treatment." According to the MID, these men then joined the black self-defense force.[46] At Howard University, ROTC officers purportedly got ready to distribute weapons and ammunition from their magazine. Fair-skinned black veterans "passed" into white mobs to monitor their intentions.[47] Whatever the source of their military training, black Washingtonians were ready to use it against the mobs.

Meanwhile, the cavalry Newton Baker had called in took up positions downtown. Two hundred marines arrived from Quantico, Virginia. Half were immediately dispatched, in details of between fifteen and twenty-five men, to six police precincts, while the other half joined soldiers from the Sixty-third Infantry for street patrols along Pennsylvania Avenue.[48] Additional infantrymen, carrying sidearms and rifles with fixed bayonets, shared guard duty with police officers outside station houses. Some of these troops were just as confused about their duty as the white and black veterans now preparing to fight as civilians. "Ain't it hell how things change," remarked one soldier posted on Pennsylvania Avenue. "Here I was last night down here with the boys. Tonight I am supposed to shoot them down if it becomes necessary."[49]

As twilight approached, the city braced for calamity. W. W. Wright, Acting Agent-in-Charge for the Bureau of Investigation (BI), went to 7th Street and Florida Avenue, NW, to observe the crowd. (Earlier that day, Chief Pullman had requested the BI's help, so seven agents were put on the streets with police.) The same sight that drew Neval Thomas's praise unsettled the white federal agent. Although Wright experienced no hostility, "the aspect was sinister and it looked as if trouble might

---

[46] Major J. E. Cutler to Churchill, July 23, 1919, Record Group 165, Records of the War Department, General Staff, Military Intelligence Division, File 2198 (hereafter RG 165, File 2198).

[47] Williams, *Torchbearers of Democracy*, 249.

[48] Memorandum for Major General William G. Haan, July 22, 1919; Major C. H. Wells to Major General William G. Haan, July 26, 1919, RG 165, File 2198.

[49] "Notes of Last Night's Rioting," *Washington Post*, July 22, 1919, 4.

break out at any moment."[50] Another white man, reporter Paul O'Neill, shared that sentiment. "There was tension in the air," he said of the corner, "much like the lull preceding a storm." At the Eighth Precinct station house, at the corner of 9th and T Streets, Captain Robert Doyle delivered a pep talk to his white officers while black residents continued to patrol outside. "The devil is abroad tonight," said Doyle. "Don't turn your back on anyone. Shoot to kill if necessary."[51] Detective Sergeant Harry Wilson, reporting for duty, tried to remain upbeat. That day, he had received a postcard from his wife, who was in Toronto with their baby daughter – they were returning home in a few days.[52] Theodore Micah Walker, a young African American, tried to be prudent. A night watchman at the Treasury Department, the Howard University medical student had to pass through the same streets where so many beatings had occurred the previous night. Walker slipped a thirty-eight caliber revolver into his jacket before mounting his motorcycle to go to work.[53] William Laney also worried about being attacked while he was out that night. The black navy veteran had moved to Washington just two months earlier and worked as a residential janitor.[54] He, too, carried a pistol, a thirty-two Colt automatic. Benjamin Johnson and his seventeen-year-old daughter Carrie, also known as Clara, hoped they would not need to leave their small brick house just east of Judiciary Square, but, like the black residents of Southwest on Saturday night, they were ready to defend their home if attacked.

The first trouble came in Uptown. Neval Thomas saw members of the U Street crowd board streetcars and beat several white passengers, including uniformed marines. A small mob halted a streetcar and hurled bricks through its windows. A few blocks south, a white mob chased a black delivery driver, who sped through a gauntlet of rocks and gunfire. Patrolling marines hurried to the intersection and scattered the attackers.[55]

---

50 Wright, "In Re: Race Riots."
51 Paul O'Neill, "Eye-Witness Account of Battles Near 8th Precinct," *Washington Times*, July 22, 1919, 2.
52 "Take Care of Self, Dear, Last Message of Wife to Detective Who Was Slain," *Washington Times*, July 22, 1919, 3.
53 "One Riot Victim Dies; Troops Quiet Capital; Crowds Quit Streets," *Washington Post*, July 24, 1919, 1; "Washington Letter," *New York Age*, August 2, 1919, 4.
54 "Negro Held for Death of Youth Shot During Riot," *Washington Times*, July 27, 1919, 1; "Reopen Inquest of Victim," *Washington Times*, July 28, 1919, 2.
55 Thomas to Grimké, July 28, 1919; O'Neill, "Eye-Witness Account"; Wright, "In Re: Race Riots."

Captain Doyle, fearing all-out rioting, ordered infantrymen and police officers to disperse the hundreds of blacks gathered at 6th and T. (That night, police captains exercised considerable discretion in the use of the riot troops.) Jabs from the soldiers' bayonets forced some blacks to jump back but also drew taunts. Inspector Clifford Grant arrived in a car and ordered the crowd to leave. When no one moved, the police drew their weapons and advanced. Shots rang out, and Patrolman J. C. Bunn fell to the street, wounded. The infantrymen opened fire, as did the police; armed members of the crowd fired as they fled.[56]

Who shot first? The answer is lost to history, if ever it was known – the dusk-dimmed tumult that ensued surely scattered any eyewitnesses, leaving to the mists of their memories knowledge of what happened. What occurred next, though, is no mystery: the Metropolitan Police set out to wrest back control of the city. And that meant clearing the streets and sidewalks of blacks. For most officers, the shooting of Bunn scrubbed away the distinction (if it had existed) between African Americans carrying weapons for protection or assembling for self-defense and those targeting whites or clashing with the police and riot troops. Paul O'Neill, who spent the night roaming the streets of Uptown, saw clearly drawn battle lines: "Practically the only fights staged were those between policemen, men in military service and the negroes."[57] Black residents, angry at the mass arrests during the citywide hunt for the serial rapist and the lack of protection against white mobs, regarded the police and troops as their enemies. BI agent Wright remarked, "these press reports [of the so-called mobilization] having been generally read, the colored people believed that such an attack would be made and had armed themselves in anticipation."[58] This mutual antagonism engulfed Uptown and neighboring blocks in a veritable two-front war, as black residents contended with both white mobs and hostile authorities.

At 8th Street and Florida Avenue, a brick struck an officer in the leg. A bullet whirred past another officer a few blocks away. BI agent M. A. Joyce, riding along with police and marines on several riot calls, reported being fired on repeatedly.[59] Captain Doyle remained unfazed, even when two marines carried in a wounded patrolman, Herbert

[56] O'Neill, "Eye-Witness"; "Flash News Briefs Detail," *Washington Times*, July 22, 1919, 3.
[57] O'Neill, "Eye-Witness."
[58] Wright, "In Re: Race Riots."
[59] "Flash News Briefs Detail"; M. A. Joyce, "In Re: Race Riots in Washington," July 23, 1919, RG 65, OGF 369,936, reel 812.

Glassman. An army truck rushed him to the hospital while the marines excitedly described how they had opened fire on several armed blacks, who had shot back. "Now, what you should have done is this," Doyle instructed the marines: "One of you should have stayed by to protect Glassman and the other should have jumped in the automobile and run down the shooters' car."[60]

Brutal treatment of black prisoners by the police stoked further conflict. Paul O'Neill counted between 75 and 100 prisoners at the Eighth Precinct, all of them black. The police treated the "submissive" prisoners fairly, O'Neill claimed, but the "belligerent were promptly dealt with." He described men with split scalps, swollen eyes, and blood-stained collars.[61] One officer struck an "unruly" man with his nightstick right in front of two black men who had just told the desk sergeant they had come to ensure fair treatment of prisoners.[62] Later that night, a local black businessman met with Captain Doyle to discuss the treatment of arrested black men. While they talked in Doyle's private office, almost thirty officers burst into the adjoining room and began beating and kicking an unresisting black prisoner. "I rushed through the crowd and standing over the man demanded that these officers treat him as a man and a human being," the businessman recalled, and he stood by until the man struggled to his feet and was taken to a cell (Figure 3.2).[63]

Escalating hostility between white police and black residents brought Detective Sergeant Harry Wilson and Benjamin and Carrie Johnson together, with tragic consequences. The Johnsons lived in a house at 220 G Street, NW, next to Ball Court, a crowded block with numerous alley dwellings. In the surrounding neighborhood, which lay beyond the cavalry cordon, white residents far outnumbered blacks. Mobs laid siege to the homes of blacks, who fired rifles and pistols from windows. Wilson, accompanied by Inspector Grant and five other detectives, arrived on the scene sometime after 10 P.M. Police and soldiers already there struggled to halt a white crowd estimated at 1,000 from surging toward the Johnson home. The detectives decided to arrest black residents, including one man who had fled from a mob at his doorstep. Wilson may have been pursuing this man or trying to halt gunfire from a second story window when he

[60] O'Neill, "Eye-Witness."
[61] Ibid.
[62] Wright, "In Re: Race Riots."
[63] Swan M. Kendrick, Horace G. Anderson, and George E. C. Hayes, "In re a Conversation with Commissioner Brownlow," July 22, 1919, box G-34, folder "DC Branch 1919 March–July," NAACP Records.

Negro rioter being taken into police station, and group of troops that form part of the military detail that has been on duty in Washington for several nights helping the police keep down disorder.

FIGURE 3.2. Arrest of African Americans. Front page coverage of Washington's race riot perpetuated the myth that black men were the cause of the trouble, but the menacing glares of onlookers point to a root cause of the violence: racial hatred. *Source: Washington Times*, July 24, 1919. Courtesy of the Library of Congress.

broke through the Johnson's front door, followed by Detective Patrick O'Brien. The two men cautiously climbed the staircase in the darkened house, Wilson taking the lead. "I'm younger than you," he reportedly told his partner. "Let me go first."[64]

Moments later, more than a dozen shots had been fired, Wilson lay dying, and the Johnsons each had multiple gunshot wounds, none fatal. (Figure 3.3.) According to Grant, who entered the home after O'Brien, he and Wilson had to force their way into an unlit bedroom upstairs, where Carrie, hiding under the bed with her father, shot Wilson twice. Grant, O'Brien, and another detective responded with a volley of shots aimed beneath the bed. It is not clear, however, if Wilson or any of the detectives identified themselves after breaking into the Johnson home. And if the Johnsons were shot while huddled under a bed, why then did police investigators later extract nineteen bullets from the room's *walls*, not the floor?[65] Wherever they had hidden, father and daughter were trapped. A hostile crowd packed the street outside, armed men had breached their door. Carrie, just seventeen, may have fired because she was scared, resented the intrusion into her home – or both.[66] As she awaited transport to a hospital, a bystander unwittingly revealed how black Washingtonians' self-defense and armed resistance were now deterring white rioters: only the fear of more trouble, he spitefully told the wounded girl, was keeping a rope off her neck.[67]

Like the Johnsons, Theodore Micah Walker and William Laney had to make split-second decisions in harrowing conditions. Walker was riding his motorcycle on 15th Street, headed to his job at the Treasury Department, when two white men knocked him to the pavement and began beating him. They ran after Walker pulled out a revolver, but an armed white mob remained on a nearby streetcar platform. Alone and exposed,

---

[64] "Mobs in Race Clash Surge Through Streets," *Washington Evening Star*, July 22, 1919, 2 (quote); "House Where Detective Was Killed by Negress," *Washington Times*, July 22, 1919, section 2; Herbert Seligmann to Herbert Croly, August 4, 1919, Waskow Notes, tab "D.C. Riot."

[65] "Johnson Girl Is Held," *Washington Post*, July 23, 1919, 3; "Negro Caddie Formally Charged with Assault on Miss Mary Saunders," *Washington Times*, July 26, 1919, section 2.

[66] The *Washington Post* characterized Carrie Johnson as "scared" ("Johnson Girl Is Held"), but the *New York Age* described her as resentful of the police break-in to her home; see "Race Riot at Capital," *New York Age*, July 26, 1919, 1. For analysis of media coverage of the shooting, see Mellis, "'Literally Devoured': Washington, D.C., 1919."

[67] "Mobs in Race Clash Surge Through Streets."

House Where Detective Was Killed By Negress

Sniping shots fired from the second story window of the house with open door and window by a seventeen-year-old colored girl attracted the attention of Headquarters Detectives O'Brien and Wilson last night. Both made a rush for the door, Wilson reaching the entrance first and pushing through the door. He gained the second story, and entering the room where the sniper hid, fell as a bullet pierced his heart. He died on his way to the Emergency Hospital. The girl, Carrie Minor Johnson, was arrested.

FIGURE 3.3. Home of Benjamin and Carrie Johnson, 220 G Street, NW. Father and daughter Benjamin and Carrie Johnson were defending their home against white rioters when seven detectives from the Metropolitan Police broke through the front door, resulting in the fatal shooting of Detective Sergeant Harry Wilson. *Source: Washington Times*, July 22, 1919. Courtesy of the Library of Congress.

Walker exchanged shots with the mob, then fled, unharmed. A patrolman chased and arrested him. Walker protested that he had not aimed at the crowd, that he had only fired warning shots, but Louis Havlicek, a marine private, lay wounded on the platform.[68]

Laney, the navy veteran, sheltered with a married couple at 617 Massachusetts Avenue, NW. He ventured out to 7th Street to search for his friend's children when a white mob spotted him. "Catch the nigger!" the rioters shouted. Laney ran to the building's backyard and drew a revolver, but the mob turned its fury upon a nearby home, battering the door and breaking windows. Laney had two choices: stay hidden, and hope the mob forgot about him, or make a break for his home, about a mile away. Gun in hand, Laney sprinted to Massachusetts Avenue. The mob gave chase, shooting; Laney returned fire. In the exchange, Kenneth Crall, a nineteen-year-old white man, fell to the street, fatally wounded; two other white rioters suffered minor wounds. Laney escaped unhurt.[69]

White mobs continued to stalk and attack African Americans, in the streets and in their homes. James E. Scott, a veteran, boarded a streetcar just after midnight. "Where are you going nigger?" a white soldier demanded when Scott tried to sit. A chorus of threats rose from the other white passengers: "Lynch him," "Kill him," "Throw him out of the car window." Several men seized Scott, but he pushed his way to the rear and leapt from the car, reeling from a sharp blow to the head. The conductor pointed a revolver at Scott and fired three shots, all errant. Only then did Scott notice a black woman aboard the car. "What became of her I do not know," he said later.[70]

White rioters tried repeatedly to break through the cavalry cordons on N Street, to advance on Uptown, and along the Mall, to attack Bloodfield, but the troops from Fort Myer held firm. Like dammed water, the thwarted crowds coursed through side streets, their shouts punctuated by gunfire and clanging ambulance bells. They brawled with roving bands of black men, who raced forward to the fight. The rioters threw

---

[68] "One Riot Victim Dies"; "Held for Death of Riot Victim," *Washington Herald*, July 25, 1919, 2.

[69] "Shots Fatal to Crall Came from Housetop," *Washington Evening Star*, July 22, 1919, 3; "Negro Held for Death"; "Reopen Inquest of Victim"; "Laney Is Held as Crall's Murderer," *Washington Evening Star*, July 29, 1919, 19; O'Donnell, "Courting Science, Binding Truth," 297–303 (quote on 297).

[70] James E. Scott statement, August 4, 1919, box G-34, folder "DC Branch 1919 March-July," NAACP Records; Michael Schaffer, "Lost Riot," *Washington City Paper*, April 3, 1998.

punches, swung clubs, slashed one another with knives and razors, and fired revolvers, ferocious and fast battles that ceased as soon as police or soldiers rushed in, "the wreck of one or more of the victims lying in the street." Blacks living outside of Uptown and Bloodfield remained barricaded in their homes, repulsing both mob and police raids with gunfire, and, as dawn broke, "the race struggle became a house-to-house battle."[71] A few small mobs reached Bloodfield, but Uptown remained impregnable. All night, a crowd of several hundred roamed U Street, a self-appointed protective cordon. BI agent M. A. Joyce, a white man, walked alone through the crowd around 1:30 A.M. He drew hateful stares and muttered threats – one woman told him he "better damned sight move on or he will be headed for the morgue" – but no one attacked him.[72]

The tally of dead, wounded, and injured grimly exposed the wide swath of Monday's violence. Randall Neale, black, fatally shot in the chest by marines at 7th and T Streets, NW. Robert Broadus, black, wounded by a Sixty-third infantryman at 3rd and K Streets, SW. Phelon Eatman, white, stabbed by four black men at 22nd and N Streets, NW. William H. Thomas, white, wounded at 7th Street and Pennsylvania Avenue, NW, by George Dent (alias Gentry), black, himself shot five times by a police detective. (Amazingly, Dent lived.) Sadie Harris, black, shot in the leg at 18th and U Streets, NW, by white teenagers. Throughout the night, injured rioters and victims staggered, limped, or were carried into the city's hospitals from ambulances, army trucks, and private vehicles. Overwhelmed physicians and nurses struggled to treat a bloody array of lacerations, concussions, fractured skulls and kneecaps, broken jaws, gunshot wounds. In addition to Detective Sergeant Harry Wilson, Kenneth Crall, and Randall Neale, a black man named Thomas Armstead was killed on Monday night, bringing the death toll to four. At least sixty-nine men and women of both races received hospital treatment, but the number of injured was likely much greater; neither James Scott nor Francis Thomas, for example, went to an emergency room after their streetcar beatings.[73]

[71] "Nation's Capital Held at Mercy of the Mob," *Washington Post*, July 22, 1919, 1, 5 (quotes on 5).
[72] Joyce, "In Re: Race Riots in Washington."
[73] "Flash News Briefs Detail"; "Toll of Dead and Wounded in Last Night's Rioting," *Washington Times*, July 22, 1919, 4; "Where Serious Rioting Took Place," *Washington Post*, July 22, 1919, 1.

The identities of the perpetrators of violence showed the consequences of the tepid response to the first outbreak of antiblack violence. African Americans had armed themselves because authorities had not halted white mob attacks. Even as they acted to stop subsequent attacks on blacks, the first troops deployed in Washington treated black self-defenders as their enemy. Numerous injuries and shootings of African Americans thus resulted from altercations with these soldiers and marines. Although the Metropolitan Police had failed to stop the first wave of antiblack violence, many officers blamed African Americans for the riot, as revealed by the brutal treatment of black prisoners. Meanwhile, whites continued to attack blacks, leading to black retaliation against whites. Late Monday night, Secretary of War Newton Baker realized that the spreading violence required drastic action.

Haan Takes Command

On Baker's authority, the adjutant general of the army called in hundreds of troops from nearby bases: from Camp Humphries, Virginia, 150 Engineer Corps troops; from Camp Meade, twenty-five Tank Corps troops and a full battalion (400 men) of the Seventeenth Infantry.[74] Baker had no intention, however, of suspending civil authority. "No, no, no, there will be no martial law," he declared on Tuesday. Baker met briefly that afternoon with President Wilson, who deferred to his judgment. Acute diarrhea and anxiety over the Senate debate on the Versailles Treaty left Wilson with neither the energy nor desire to deal with the rioting.[75] In turn, Baker entrusted General William Haan to restore order.

Baker had delegated wisely. Haan had quashed looting in San Francisco after the 1906 earthquake and had just returned home from France to a hero's welcome. The fifty-six-year-old general enjoyed a much-deserved reputation for action and certitude. "There couldn't be a better man to handle the Washington situation," enthused one reporter.[76] Haan did not want the assignment but accepted it with the equanimity of a

[74] Adjutant General of the Army to the Commanding General, Camp Humphries, July 24, 1919; Adjutant General of the Army to the Commanding General, Camp Meade, July 24, 1919, box 6, folder "Washington, D.C. (1917, 1919)," RG 60, Glasser File.

[75] "Martial Law Not Needed, Says Sec. Baker," *Washington Times*, July 23, 1919, 2; "President Wilson Ill," *Washington Post*, July 22, 1919, 1.

[76] "Capital Kept Calm by Federal Troops," *New York Times*, July 24, 1919 (quote); Laurie and Cole, *Role of Federal Military Forces*, 284.

career army man. "Someone has to do it," he confided to a fellow officer, "and it might as well be me."[77]

Haan took charge at five o'clock Tuesday afternoon, tellingly setting up his command in Chief of Police Pullman's office. Right away, he fired off General Order Number One to his officers and troops. You are here to help the police, he told them, and should arrest "all persons whomsoever [are] creating disorder." The order also banned public assemblies and stipulated that anyone found on the streets "will be kept moving." With nightfall approaching, Haan and his staff scrambled to strategically position troops throughout the city. The cavalry cordoned off K Street from 14th to North Capitol Streets, the Sixty-third Infantry spread out through Bloodfield. Forty sailors from the USS *Mayflower*, which had taken President Wilson on his Potomac cruise days earlier, reported for patrol duty along Pennsylvania Avenue. Additional marines and soldiers beefed up the existing detachments at police precincts, while hundreds of servicemen waited in reserve at East Potomac Park, the Marine Barracks, and Camp Meigs, in Northeast Washington.[78] In all, 60 officers and 1,153 enlisted men were on riot duty. Haan, a cigar poking from beneath his full gray mustache as he reclined in Pullman's chair, exuded confidence. Although small mobs of black and white men had skirmished throughout the day, "conditions will be normal again," he predicted. "Yes, I believe it's all over. Of course, there may be one or two sporadic, individual cases of lawlessness, but the riot danger is over."[79]

James Weldon Johnson thought otherwise. The field secretary for the NAACP, he arrived in Washington from New York at 8:30 P.M. As his train approached Union Station, he noticed a growing tension in his car: "It showed itself in the air of the passengers as they read the newspapers, with their glaring headlines telling of the awful night before and intimating that the worst was yet to come." When he arrived in Uptown for a briefing about the riot, he expected to see widespread fear, even panic. Instead, he found residents "calm and determined, unterrified and unafraid," and he marveled at the steely resolve of black Washingtonians to again defend themselves and their homes, if necessary, against white

[77] Haan to Major General Thomas H. Barry, July 30, 1919, box 5, folder "Correspondence July–August 1919," William G. Haan Papers, Wisconsin Historical Society.

[78] General William Haan to the Chief of Staff, August 1919 (no day given); map of troops' placement, RG 165, file 2198.

[79] "Troops Ready to Act If Rioting Is Resumed in Capital, Says Haan," *Washington Times*, July 23, 1919, 1 (quote); "Gen. Haan in Command After Wilson Confers with Baker on Riots," *Washington Post*, July 23, 1919, 1.

mobs. Community efforts to restore peace also impressed Johnson.[80] Two of the city's most distinguished black residents, Emmett Scott, who served as a special assistant to Newton Baker, and Judge Robert Terrell, the city's only black justice, had posted a public appeal for law and order. Scott and Terrell squarely blamed white servicemen for the riot but, after acknowledging the desire to retaliate, called upon all law-abiding blacks to work with whites to end mob violence so "that men who shared the sacrifices and hardships of the late war, as well as all other members of our Race, may mutually share in the finer rewards which should come out of a fair settlement of the reconstruction and readjustment problems which face us on every side."[81] The Parents' League of D.C., normally devoted to education issues, issued a similar appeal to its 20,000 members but also urged self-defense, advising "our people, in the interest of law and order and to avoid the loss of life and injury, to go home before dark and to remain quietly and to protect themselves."[82]

Haan's optimism proved premature, but Tuesday night's rioting was not as severe as Johnson had feared. Intermittent cloudbursts deterred many would-be rioters from taking to the streets. The worst incidents occurred near the Carnegie Library. Ensign L. S. Moore and the *Mayflower* crew spent the early evening breaking up small mobs of white men searching for blacks and black-occupied homes to attack. Armed black men, either retaliating or defending themselves and their homes, clashed with the mobs and the sailors. The sporadic gunfire unnerved area residents, and most stayed indoors.[83]

But Haan could not control everyone who believed himself an enforcer of order, including two white members of the Home Defense League who stationed themselves at 9th and M Streets, NW. Isaac Halbfinger, a paperhanger, told his worried wife that he would call her throughout the night. His young partner, Benjamin Belmont, a Russian immigrant, had just left the military and worked at the post office. The two men believed they had official approval to patrol the streets, due to Chief Pullman's prior request for the Home Defense League's help and the instructions they received that night at the Second Precinct station house.

---

[80] "The Riots: An N.A.A.C.P. Investigation," *Crisis* 18, no. 5 (September 1919): 241–4 (quotes on 241 and 242).

[81] Kerlin, *Voice of the Negro*, 76–7.

[82] "Riots 1919 – Washington, D.C.," Vertical File, Moorland-Spingarn Research Center; "Conditions Normal at Capital," *New York Age*, August 9, 1919, 1.

[83] "Gen. Haan in Command"; "Home Guard Is Shot Dead," *New York Times*, July 23, 1919; Report of Ensign (T) L.S. Moore, July 25, 1919, RG 165, file 2198.

However, neither man was one of the 300 league volunteers recently commissioned by the Metropolitan Police as special officers, authorizing them to carry weapons and wear badges. Both men wore civilian clothes and were unarmed. Once again, the distinction between civilians and sworn law officers or active-duty servicemen had blurred; to a casual observer, Halbfinger and Belmont would have looked like two ordinary civilians.[84]

To a black man disembarking from a streetcar at 10:30 P.M., Halbfinger and Belmont went from mundane to menacing when they accosted him. Halbfinger, seeing a bulge in the man's back pocket, demanded he stop so they could search him for a weapon. The black man refused, leading to a struggle. He shot Halbfinger in the chest, Belmont in the abdomen, then fled to a nearby alley. Belmont survived; Halbfinger died almost immediately. Police and the crew of the *Mayflower* rushed to the corner and began a house-to-house search on the adjoining block, where many African Americans lived. These intrusions led to more gunfire, but the shooter was never caught.[85]

Tuesday's incidents did not rattle Haan, and another night of vigorous patrolling by his troops finally quelled the violence. The cavalry continued to guard K Street on Wednesday, while the crew of the *Mayflower* returned to the vicinity of Pennsylvania Avenue. They spent the evening searching black pedestrians for weapons. The other troops also remained on duty, in full strength, including forty-six troops from the Seventeenth Infantry posted to the State, War, and Navy Building in case rioting broke out again near the White House.[86] At midnight, a burst of shots shattered the windows of a streetcar on 14th Street, but no one was hurt.[87] BI agent F. M. Kemon braced for another tumultuous night, but "witnessed nothing of a disorderly nature" as he roamed the streets and visited police station houses with his partner. Dozens of anxious spouses and family members of policemen rang the news desk of the *Washington Times* to

---

[84] "Negro's Bullet Ends Guard's Life Struggle with Victory in Sight," *Washington Times*, July 23, 1919, section 2; "Halbfinger Home Stricken by Grief" and "Defense League Warns Members Not to Police," *Washington Evening Star*, July 23, 1919, 2–3; "Negro Kills Defense League Patrolman and Shoots His Companion," *Washington Times*, July 23, 1919, 2; "Caution with Guards," *Washington Post*, July 24, 1919, 2.

[85] "Negro Kills Defense League Patrolman"; Report of Ensign L.S. Moore; NAACP, unsigned summary of riot, 4.

[86] Report of Ensign L.S. Moore; Commanding Officer, Detachment 17th Infantry, to Major General Haan, July 27, 1919, RG 165, file 2198.

[87] "One Riot Victim Dies."

ask if the "trouble" had resumed, hanging up with relief at the answer.[88] "The city is now under control," Haan declared. "Our problem now is only to keep [conditions] normal and to insure the city against any return of rioting."[89] On Thursday, July 24, the general relieved half of the cavalry troops and shrunk the number of marines and infantrymen at each police station house to twenty. A modest detachment of Sixty-third Infantrymen should "appear from time to time on the streets merely as an indication that some troops are still in the City after Saturday night [July 26]," Haan advised the army chief of staff. This reconstituted provost guard of thirty-five men began patrolling the central business district from 7 P.M. to midnight on July 27; Haan relieved the remaining riot troops by July 31.[90]

The rapid end to rioting greatly impressed Newton Baker. "General Haan's judgment that he has the situation well in hand is justified," he told the president. Baker also credited black Washingtonians for helping to restore peace: "The attitude of the colored people, particular of their leaders, is reported to have been helpful generally" by keeping residents in their homes.[91] But Wilson showed scant interest in the contribution of local black leaders. Instead, the president, who had spent most of the year to date in Paris, hammering out the Versailles Treaty, worried that news abroad about the riots would, in the words of the *Washington Times*, "make a detrimental impression in countries where heretofore America had been regarded as the foremost exponent of social equality and justice."[92]

Assigning Blame

As the infantry patrolled Pennsylvania Avenue, Washingtonians and out-siders alike scrambled to explain why the riot had occurred. Commissioner Louis Brownlow, resentful that "wets" blamed the mob violence on enforcement of dry laws, countered that opponents of Prohibition

[88] Kemon, "In Re: Race Riots in Washington"; "Wives of Guards Worry at Home," *Washington Times*, July 24, 1919, section 2.

[89] "Riot Shot Claiming a Second Policeman," *Washington Post*, July 25, 1919, 1.

[90] Major General William G. Haan to the Chief of Staff, July 24, 25, and 26, 1919 (quote on July 26); Colonel R.M. Beck, Jr., Orders No. 1 [*sic*], July 27, 1919, RG 165, file 2198.

[91] Newton Baker to Woodrow Wilson, July 23, 1919, box 11, folder "General Correspondence, Woodrow Wilson 1919," Newton Baker Papers, Library of Congress.

[92] "President Is Worried Over Foreign View of Riots Here," *Washington Times*, July 23, 1919, 1.

had stirred up trouble to demonstrate that crime had increased due to the alcohol ban. However, Brownlow privately told Emmett Scott and James Weldon Johnson that white resentment of black Washingtonians' prosperity had prompted some of the attacks.[93] The *New York Times* pinned the riot on the "criminal element among the negroes," incompetent police, and "exasperated" white men. The *Washington Post* largely agreed, rebuking the police for allowing "hoodlums of both colors" to roam the streets before the riot.[94]

White mob attacks had deeper sources. As Brownlow had observed, the prosperity of the city's black middle class angered whites of lesser means. So did the federal government's employment of blacks. Although the Wilson administration had demoted or denied promotion to African American civil servants, forcing many to quit or accept menial positions as janitors, laborers, and messengers, many white federal workers, especially those from the South, "deeply resent[ed] the idea that colored people should have Government positions" at all, as Joseph Manning, a white southerner, explained. Dining in a Washington restaurant a few days after the riot ended, Manning overheard two white men, one of them a Georgian, discuss the continuing need to "do something to terrorize" black Washingtonians – apparently the mob attacks had not sufficed. Others agreed. "I am astonished at the resistance put up by these Washington niggers," a white Democrat from Alabama told Manning. "These folk in Washington will have to find some other way to teach [them] their place."[95] In a letter home to Montgomery, Alabama, a white female employee of the War Department bitterly complained that black residents thought they ran the city. Describing the riot, she praised white men for taking the law into their hands.[96] The attempted invasions of Uptown, particularly U Street, further demonstrated the deployment of mob violence to reassert white supremacy and defile, if not destroy, visible signs of African American accomplishment.[97]

93 "Brownlow Talks on Riots in Secret," *Washington Post*, July 24, 1919, 2; "The National Situation," *Branch Bulletin* vol. III, no. 8 (August 1919), no page number given.
94 "Race War in Washington," *New York Times*, July 23, 1919; "Public Order and Safety," *Washington Post*, July 23, 1919, 6.
95 Joseph C. Manning, "Inside Facts of the Washington Riots," *Cleveland Gazette*, August 23, 1919, 1. For racial discrimination against African American federal workers during Wilson's presidency, see Yellin, *In the Nation's Service*, 113–31; Yellin, "It Was Still No South to Us."
96 "A Sidelight on the Washington Riot," *New York Age*, August 16, 1919, 4.
97 Fitzpatrick, "Great Agitation for Business," 73.

Other observers blamed tensions raised by wartime mobilization. A military intelligence officer accused black veterans of the 368th Infantry, many of whom were District residents, of starting the riot. He also declared the trouble "a logical outcome" of propaganda urging African Americans to demand and obtain equality.[98] George Foster Peabody, a confidante of Newton Baker and a philanthropic supporter of black educational institutions, traced the riot to wartime discrimination against blacks, which led "conscienceless and more ignorant Negroes" to retaliate against white women.[99]

But what about the white servicemen who had attacked blacks? No one could truthfully deny that white men in uniform had started the riot, but were they active-duty, recently discharged, or both? Newton Baker and General Haan shifted the blame toward veterans. Haan told Baker that "nothing has come to my notice that is at all conclusive that any soldiers still in the Army had any part in this mixup." Baker agreed, though he was more circumspect when speaking to reporters: "There is a considerable number of discharged men [in the District], many of them still in uniform, but, of course, the War Department has no jurisdiction or control over them."[100] However, active-duty servicemen had joined uniformed veterans in the nightly frays, even after Haan canceled nighttime leaves. On Tuesday, July 22, the riot's third night, an army captain had learned of yet another planned "mobilization": at nightfall, one group of soldiers would carry out diversionary disturbances near Pennsylvania Avenue while other groups would shoot blacks in Uptown and Bloodfield. (The plan was not carried out.)[101] William H. E. Church, an enlisted man in the Twenty-eighth Balloon Company stationed at Aberdeen, Maryland, was arrested on July 21 with four other white men in a vehicle pursuing blacks in another car. In some cases, arrested servicemen came from the ranks of troops entrusted with restoring civil order: two privates arrested on Sunday night listed their address as East Potomac Park, the barrack grounds of the Sixty-third Infantry.[102] As previously noted, two

98 Major J. E. Cutler to General Churchill, July 23, 1919, RG 165, file 2198.
99 Peabody to Baker, July 24, 1919, box 10, folder "General Correspondence, Aug.–Dec. 1919," Newton Baker Papers.
100 Haan to the Secretary of War, July 24, 1919, RG 165, file 2198; for Baker's statement, see "Race Riot at Capital."
101 Capt. Horace T. Jones to Lt. Col. Brown, July 22, 1919, Case File 10218 [no suffix number provided], RG 165, copy in box 1, reel 1, Kornweibel Papers.
102 "Notes of Last Night's Rioting"; "High Spots in Night of Rioting," *Washington Herald*, July 21, 1919, 1.

FIGURE 3.4. This nation's gratitude. Published on the front page of Washington's black newspaper, this cartoon poignantly depicted how white mob violence betrayed the democratic ideals for which black and white Americans had fought in the First World War. *Source: Washington Bee,* July 26, 1919. Courtesy of the Washingtoniana Division, D.C. Public Library.

of the ringleaders of the first mob attack, on Saturday night, were active-duty servicemen. In an environment where voluntary vigilance thrived and the distinction between soldier and civilian remained blurred, white veterans and active-duty servicemen had banded together to become a mob in uniform (Figure 3.4).

In the riot's aftermath, black Washingtonians openly celebrated the resistance they had mounted against this mob in uniform. *Washington Bee* publisher Calvin Chase lauded "the determination of the black man to protect his home, his wife and his children" when the police failed to do so. "The Negroes' conduct was indeed heroic and noble," said Neval Thomas. "It was one of reprisal but it was effective, and pursued with beautiful purpose and self-sacrifice." Mary Church Terrell, wife of Judge Robert Terrell and a distinguished advocate of equality for women and African Americans, remarked that the "general slaughter of Negroes (tho. I don't favor using that word) for some one offense won't be suffered any longer. It shows that Washington has awakened and I'm glad of it."[103] Dr. J. Milton Waldron, preaching the Sunday after the riot, told an enthusiastic congregation of 350 at the Shiloh Baptist Church that "we are dealing with a new negro and not with the old slave."[104] James Weldon Johnson went home to New York "disquieted, but not depressed over the Washington riot; it might have been worse. It might have been a riot in which the Negroes, unprotected by the law, would not have had the spirit to protect themselves."[105] Black journalist William Monroe Trotter, recently returned from France, traveled to Washington to deliver his praise in person. "I [must] express my great satisfaction at the noble way in which the people of my race defended themselves during the recent race riot in this city," he told his audience. Trotter also spoke for many when he expounded on the root cause of antiblack collective violence, not just in Washington, but across the nation: "There will be no peace until white Americans . . . make up their minds to give the colored Americans equal justice and let them share the democracy at home for which our brave soldiers fought and died abroad."[106]

The soldiers themselves agreed. Even before the riot had ended, a leaflet entitled "Be Ye Also Ready for We Know Not When They Will Return" had circulated throughout black Washington. The League for Democracy, formed by black officers of the Ninety-second Division, was responsible:

Lest we forget the Democracy for which our men fought and died; lest we forget to strike our enemies the death blow when the lives of our mothers, fathers, wives, sweethearts, sisters and brothers are sought by the white intruder; lest we forget the vile, insidious propaganda directed against us in this the Nation's Capital by infamous Pseudo-Americans and the press; lest we forget vows and oaths made and taken to right our wrongs without fear and without compromise after the war; we do solemnly declare to lash ourselves to our gallant tars, and expire together in one common cause, fighting for a safe and decent place to live in.

---

[103] "The Rights of the Black Man," *Washington Bee*, August 2, 1919; Thomas to Grimké, July 28, 1919; Mary Church Terrell letter, August 18, 1919, box 5, folder "Correspondence July–September 1919," Mary Church Terrell Papers, Library of Congress.

[104] As reported by H. D. Knickerbocker et al. to Major Henry G. Pratt, July 28, 1919, Case File 10218–352–1, RG 165, copy in box 1, reel 6, Kornweibel Papers, 6.

[105] "The Riots: An N.A.A.C.P. Investigation," 243.

[106] As reported by W. H. Loving to M. Churchill, August 12, 1919, Case File 10218–345–1, RG 165, copy in box 1, reel 6, Kornweibel Papers.

Rather than admiring the patriotism the leaflet expressed, the BI and MID, determined to root out the source of this "agitation," scoured Washington to find the author.[107]

They never did.

---

[107] For "Lest We Forget" as the motto of the League for Democracy, see Williams, "Vanguards of the New Negro," 357. For the text of "Lest We Forget!," see Loving to Churchill, August 10, 1919, Case File 10218–350–7, RG 165, copy in box 1, reel 6, Kornweibel Papers. For the investigation, see Col. A. B. Coxe to Frank Burke, August 12, 1919; Assistant Director, Bureau of Investigation to Raymond Pullman, August 15, 1919, RG 65, OGF 372,102, reel 818.

4

Blood in the Streets

Armed Resistance in Chicago

"There has been considerable negro hunting today, and considerable excitement in some sections of the city. Some sniping."
– Major General Leonard Wood's diary entry about Chicago,
July 29, 1919.[1]

Michigan and Wabash Avenues were a sea of spectators on February 17, 1919. Several hundred thousand Chicagoans amassed to cheer the men and officers of the 370th Regiment, Ninety-third Division, the black unit better known locally as the Eighth Illinois National Guard. The regiment had just returned from France, where its men had earned the nickname the "Black Devils" from the Germans for their tenacity in combat. Disembarking at the La Salle Street station, the troops "greeted the city with a whoop – the kind that caused the blood to curdle in the Germans' veins." In formation the men marched several blocks to a coliseum, where a crowd of 60,000 kept up the adulations. A host of high-ranking army officers feted the men, praising their bravery and sacrifices. A call to remember the dead evoked tears. Mayor William "Big Bill" Thompson's surprise appearance drew cheers – he was popular with Chicago's black voters. When he shouted "that justice and equality of citizenship . . . shall open the doors of opportunity to you," the crowd roared its approval.[2]

---

[1] Leonard Wood Diary, July 29, 1919 entry, box 12, folder "Diary Jan. 1st – Dec. 31, 1919," Leonard Wood Papers, Library of Congress.

[2] "Throngs Greet 8th: 'Black Devils' Are Welcomed by Multitudes Amid Thundering Applause," *Chicago Defender*, February 22, 1919, 3.

No one could deny that the "Old Eighth" – the only American unit fully commanded by black officers during the Great War – had done its part to make the world safe for democracy. In September 1918, Company F had seized the Hindenburg Cave, a German headquarters at Mont des Signes. Sergeant Matthew Jenkins and his men charged 150 yards to besiege the heavily defended prize. Lacking food and water, Company F withstood several counterattacks during the next two days. In one of the war's last battles, Company C routed an enemy artillery and machine gun position, earning its soldiers the French Croix de Guerre.[3]

How could the men of Company C and their comrades know that just five months after their hometown victory parade, they would once again don their uniforms, take up arms, and even pin their medals to their chests to return to the front lines? This time, the battlefields were not called Hindenburg or Mont des Signes; the names were far more familiar to the men of the Old Eighth: Michigan and Wabash Avenues, La Salle Street, and Canaryville.

"They Shall Not Pass"

Canaryville was a small neighborhood with an outsized reputation. Its name reputedly came from the "wild canaries," sons of the Irish immigrants who lived there. Located on Chicago's South Side, Canaryville was just a mile long (40th to 47th Streets) and less than a mile wide (Wentworth Avenue to Halsted Street). Other preponderantly Irish neighborhoods straddled Canaryville on its northern and southern edges. West of Halsted, the commercial street, was the sprawling 425-acre Union Stock Yard, "Hog Butcher for the World" and the biggest employer of neighborhood men. But the border that mattered most was Wentworth Avenue, on Canaryville's eastern side. Today, the Dan Ryan Expressway (Interstate 90/94) runs parallel to Wentworth, forming a barrier as formidable as Chicago's reverse-flowing river. In 1919, the blocks later razed to make way for the expressway were part of Chicago's Black Belt, where approximately 90 percent of the city's African American residents lived. And the "wild canaries," with the support of their elders, were determined to see that blacks remained there.[4]

---

[3] Scott, *Scott's Official History*, 214–30; Williams, *Torchbearers of Democracy*, 105–6.
[4] James R. Barrett, "Canaryville," and Dominic A. Pacyga, "Union Stock Yard," in Grossman, *Encyclopedia of Chicago*. Holt and Pacyga, *Chicago*, 133, identify 39th and 49th Streets as the northern and southern boundaries of Canaryville.

During the 1910s, Chicago's black population increased by almost 150 percent, rising from 44,103 to more than 109,000 by 1920. Historically, the Black Belt encompassed the area between 12th and 31st Streets (north to south) and Wentworth to Wabash Avenues (west to east). During the years of the Great Migration, the Black Belt's boundaries expanded south to 39th Street and east to Lake Michigan, but the need for adequate housing stock remained acute. A survey of 274 black families catalogued the deficiencies of their living space: sodden plaster falling from ceilings due to toilet and pipe leaks, walls shot through with rat holes, privies in yards. Few residents had electricity or furnaces, yet leases for these dilapidated dwellings exceeded, by 15 to 25 percent, the price whites paid for superior homes and apartments. Not surprisingly, black Chicagoans were frequent movers, seeking, as one man put it, a "better house and a better neighborhood."[5] However, the Black Belt, especially the entertainment and business district known as "the Stroll" (State Street between 26th and 39th Streets), was also an incubator of New Negro identity.[6]

White Chicagoans living directly south and east of the Black Belt had, by 1919, resolved to hold the line against black settlement on their blocks. In the communities of Kenwood and Hyde Park,[7] white residents rallied one another with rhetoric worthy of the nation's now-idle wartime propagandists: "Shall we . . . run like rats from a burning ship, or shall we put up a united front and keep Hyde Park desirable for ourselves? It's not too late." Realtors eager to buy low from panicked whites claimed property values were on a downward spiral. At a May 1919 meeting of the Kenwood and Hyde Park Property Owners Association, one speaker claimed that the aggregate value of homes had dropped $250 million because blacks were moving into the area. "If someone told you that there was to be an invasion that would injure your homes to that extent, wouldn't you rise up as one man and one woman, and say as [French] General Foch said: 'They shall not pass'?"[8] The threat of violence was not merely rhetorical.

---

[5] Chicago Commission, *Negro in Chicago*, 152–65 (quote on 154); Tuttle, *Race Riot*, 163–4. For an overview of the pre-riot Black Belt, see Drake and Cayton, *Black Metropolis*, 61–4.

[6] Baldwin, *Chicago's New Negroes*, 21–52.

[7] Kenwood and Hyde Park, though designated as "communities," were (and remain) part of the city of Chicago. Other residential areas – Canaryville and Back of the Yards, for example – were classified as "neighborhoods."

[8] Chicago Commission, *Negro in Chicago*, 117–19 (quotes on 118–19).

Between March 1918 and July 1919, twenty-five bombings targeted the homes of African Americans and the homes or offices of black and white realtors; fourteen of these attacks came in the first seven months of 1919.[9] Most of the bombings occurred in the area between 39th and 47th Streets and State Street and Cottage Grove Avenue. In March, a bomb exploded outside of the real estate office of African American entrepreneur Jesse Binga. A bomb packed with lead and gravel exploded at the door of Mrs. Gertrude Harrison's home two months later. Early on the morning of June 4, the S. P. Motley family was jolted awake by dynamite exploding beneath the porch of the neighboring house. The Motleys, whose own home had been bombed in July 1917, were now accused of facilitating the sale of the other home to a black family. Yet another bombing in the first half of 1919 blew out windows and collapsed ceilings in an apartment building at 3365 Indiana Avenue, killing a six-year-old girl.[10]

The NAACP dispatched Assistant Secretary Walter White to Chicago to investigate. With his fair skin and blue eyes, White easily passed at a June meeting of the property association. White listened as speaker after speaker vilified blacks and discussed ways to thwart rentals and sales to African Americans. Although the topic of bombs was not broached, White reported that "inflammatory and incendiary remarks, tending to create a spirit of great racial animosity and ill will, were made by various speakers."[11] Another association gathering grew menacing as members urged less talk and more action. When someone warned that blacks were arming themselves and would fight back if attacked, causing bloodshed, a Kenwood resident retorted, "bloodshed, nothing!" He then boasted about knocking down a black man near his home. Another man declared, "if we can't get them out any other way we are going to put them in with the bolsheveki and bomb them out."[12]

Many bombings occurred soon after property association meetings. The "bomb squad" was not as large as the unlawful posse that had roamed the streets of Washington, but its spirit of vigilantism was just as fervent. The bombers' identities remained shadowy, but their methods suggested they had the covert approval, even direct aid, of the property associations, realtors, and mortgage lenders. Targets usually received

[9] Tuttle, *Race Riot*, 175.

[10] Chicago Commission, *Negro in Chicago*, 123–9, 133; Tuttle, *Race Riot*, 176; "Bomb Throwers Are Still Active," *Chicago Defender*, May 24, 1919, 19.

[11] Affidavit by Walter F. White, January 14, 1920, Waskow Notes, tab "NAACP Probes."

[12] Interview, John Shillady with Mrs. Meta Harvey, August 3, 1919, Waskow Notes, tab "NAACP Probes."

advance warnings. In several cases, the bombs exploded in the period between the home purchase and public announcement of the sale or occupancy. One bombing in April occurred at 2 A.M.; within minutes, white neighbors in daytime clothing had congregated outside the damaged home. "It would appear strange," commented the *Chicago Defender*, "that people would be fully dressed at this early hour." Despite eyewitness descriptions of the vehicles delivering the bombs, the police made no arrests during the first half of 1919.[13]

No bombings occurred in Canaryville and the adjoining neighborhoods of Bridgeport and Back of the Yards. Here, residents had an even more powerful force to deploy than bombs: "athletic clubs." The Dirty Dozen. The Sparklers. Our Flag. Ragen's Colts. For years, boys and young men had flocked to these gangs, dividing the blocks west of Wentworth Avenue as their turf. The membership and activities of the Colts, the most powerful gang, revealed the intertwined Irish-American, political, and class dimensions of these gangs. In command of the twenty blocks lying between 43rd and 63rd Streets, the Colts took their name from their sponsor, Cook County Commissioner Frank Ragen, who paid for their clubhouse and funded sporting events and social activities. In return, the Colts served as muscle for Ragen and the Democratic Party, menacing suspected Republican voters at polling places. The Hamburg Athletic Club, in Bridgeport, enjoyed the patronage of Alderman Joseph McDonough and could later boast it groomed the city's most powerful mayor: Richard J. Daley, a member since his teens, was elected club president in 1924, when he was twenty-two. The young men in these clubs came from working class homes; many of their fathers worked at Union Stock Yard or served on the police force.[14] The Colts were a "very disturbing element," recalled Augustus L. Williams, a black Chicago lawyer. If African Americans crossed Wentworth, the "Irish really cracked their skulls."[15]

Or worse, as the family of Joseph Robinson discovered. The Robinsons had recently moved to Chicago from New Orleans and settled at 514 West 54th Place, which placed them west of Wentworth Avenue. In 1910, between 5 and 10 percent of the residents on the blocks around the Robinsons' home were African American; by 1919, that percentage had

[13] Chicago Commission, *Negro in Chicago*, 123, 127–32; Tuttle, *Race Riot*, 178; "Bomb Throwers Still Operate Unmolested," *Chicago Defender*, April 12, 1919, 1.

[14] Tuttle, *Race Riot*, 32–3, 199–200; Cohen and Taylor, *American Pharaoh*, 21, 27–30.

[15] Arthur Waskow, notes on interview with Augustus L. Williams, July 1959, Waskow Notes, tab "Chicago NAACP & Defense."

almost doubled, but all-white blocks bordered this enclave on its eastern and western edges.[16] On the night of June 21, 1919, Joseph Robinson was out walking when Ragen's Colts attacked and killed him. Part of the same gang also assaulted Charles Mitchell, a black veteran. Mitchell lived in the Black Belt, but he was visiting a black family who lived just two blocks from the Robinsons. The mob beat Mitchell before he managed to escape.[17]

The attacks were not random. Three weeks earlier, 150 Colts had descended on 54th Place, knocked out streetlights, then broke windows and doors in several homes. Residents called the police, who, tellingly, did not arrive until after the troublemakers had dispersed. According to a white resident, this was not unusual because many of the marauders were the sons or relatives of policemen assigned to the Stock Yards Station, the closest precinct house.[18] The Colts and other gangs also freely attacked African Americans in parks west of Wentworth "under cover of darkness."[19]

By late July 1919, battle lines between whites and blacks were firmly set in Chicago. In Kenwood and Hyde Park, whites colluded to obstruct the sale of homes to black buyers and used bombs to attempt to drive out black residents. In Canaryville and other west-of-Wentworth neighborhoods, well-organized athletic clubs constantly menaced African Americans. In both locales, law enforcement ignored, even sanctioned, these acts of terrorism; in both, the violence took the lives of African Americans.

Friction in the Union Stock Yard added to the volatility of race relations. For many years, major Chicago employers had replaced striking white workers with black laborers. In one case, black workers walked off the job when they learned they were crossing a picket line, but the belief that blacks were strikebreakers remained strong among white laborers. During the war, biracial organization of the stockyards, where more than 10,000 blacks worked, became a priority for the newly formed Stockyards Labor Council. The obstacles were considerable. In addition to the pernicious stereotype of blacks as scabs, many white craft workers

---

[16] See maps 3 and 4 in Tuttle, *Race Riot*, 72–3.

[17] "Ragan's [*sic*] Colts Start Riot," *Chicago Defender*, June 28, 1919, 1.

[18] Ibid.

[19] "Ruffianism in the Parks," *Chicago Defender*, July 12, 1919, editorial page. To highlight the spreading violence directed at blacks nationwide, the *Defender* began juxtaposing stories about southern lynchings with articles on attacks on blacks in Chicago. See Doreski, "From News to History," 639–40.

believed association with blacks impugned their trade and talents. Black workers resented this racism. They also worried about losing their jobs if they joined a union. By May 1919, an estimated 10,000 black laborers were unemployed, and the packers admitted they were letting blacks go at a faster pace than whites. A yard-wide unionization drive begun in June included direct appeals to black workers, but by July 26, when the unions voted to strike in two days if the packers refused their demands, only 25 percent of African Americans were organized, compared to 90 percent of whites.[20]

Unchecked white vigilantism, coupled with workplace tensions, had brought Chicago's South Side to a breaking point. (Figure 4.1.) At the previous sites of racial violence – Charleston, Bisbee, Longview, and Washington, D.C. – a seemingly minor incident had sparked mob attacks on blacks. In each city, African Americans' resistance had intensified to match the level of antiblack collective violence. In Charleston, for example, black residents had hurled bricks at marauding white servicemen; in Bisbee, the troopers of the Tenth Cavalry had drawn their sidearms; in Longview, armed black citizens had set a trap for a lynch mob. The scope of Washington's violence had surpassed all three of these episodes. As a result, black self-defense measures in the nation's capital had been formidable, even featuring paramilitary patrols by hundreds of armed black men. Chicago's racial violence, however, was the worst yet. In keeping with the year's pattern of resistance, black Chicagoans' armed self-defensive measures thus exceeded those used in the other cities.

The Spark

Sunday, July 27, was especially hot, the temperature hitting 100 degrees Fahrenheit by the afternoon.[21] Many Southsiders sought relief at the 25th and 29th Street beaches. Five young black men, including seventeen-year-old Eugene Williams, set out into the lake aboard their homemade raft, planning to paddle to a post located about 1,000 feet from the 29th

[20] Tuttle, *Race Riot*, 112–56; Halpern, *Down on the Killing Floor*, 44–65; George E. Haynes, "Negro labor situation in Chicago, Ill., and other localities following recent race disturbances at Chicago," August 27, 1919; Haynes to the Secretary of Labor, June 19, 1919, File 8/102-C, box 18, RG 174, Division of Negro Economics. For more on economic and housing competition as sources of racial friction in Chicago in 1919, see Abu-Lughod, *Race, Space, and Riots*, 43–66.

[21] Graham Taylor Diary, entry for July 27, 1919, box 4, Diaries, 1911–1937, Graham Taylor Papers, Newberry Library.

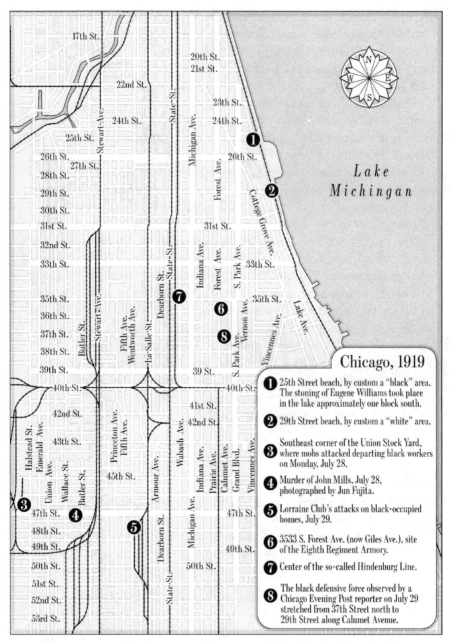

❶ 25th Street beach, by custom a "black" area. The stoning of Eugene Williams took place in the lake approximately one block south.

❷ 29th Street beach, by custom a "white" area.

❸ Southeast corner of the Union Stock Yard, where mobs attacked departing black workers on Monday, July 28.

❹ Murder of John Mills, July 28, photographed by Jun Fujita.

❺ Lorraine Club's attacks on black-occupied homes, July 29.

❻ 3533 S. Forest Ave. (now Giles Ave.), site of the Eighth Regiment Armory.

❼ Center of the so-called Hindenburg Line.

❽ The black defensive force observed by a Chicago Evening Post reporter on July 29 stretched from 37th Street north to 29th Street along Calumet Avenue.

FIGURE 4.1. Map of Chicago, 1910. *Source:* Rand McNally Standard Map, 1910.

Street beach.[22] As they drifted by the breakwater near 26th Street around 2 P.M., a twenty-three-year-old white man named George Stauber began throwing rocks at them. The boys were seventy-five feet away and, for several minutes, effortlessly dodged the rocks. "As long as we could see him," one of the rafters, John Harris, told historian William Tuttle fifty years later, "he could never hit us, because after all a guy throwing that far is not a likely shot." Harris and his friends even treated the barrage as a game, calling out to one another as the stones hurtled through the air.

Then came a one-in-a-million shot. In a moment's distraction, Eugene Williams looked away and a large rock struck him in the forehead. Dazed, he slipped underwater. Harris tried to save him but had to break free when his panicked friend seized his ankle and pulled him down. As Stauber fled the breakwater and ran south, Harris dove from the raft, swam ashore, and raced north.[23] Stauber went to the 29th Street beach, by custom and self-enforcement a white-only area, perhaps hoping to escape identification as the rock thrower. Harris, well aware of these Jim Crow rules, was headed toward the black-only beach at 25th Street to summon a lifeguard.

He was too late – Eugene Williams had drowned. Divers recovered his body half an hour later. In the meantime, Harris and his friends had come to the 29th Street beach, accompanied by a black detective sergeant named William Middleton, to look for Stauber. When they spotted him, Patrolman Daniel Callahan, who was white, refused to make an arrest and prevented Middleton from taking Stauber into custody. Refusing to give up, Harris and his friends rushed back to 25th Street to tell black beachgoers what had happened.[24]

A lakefront racial clash seemed imminent. To be precise, *another* lakefront clash seemed imminent. Earlier that afternoon, a group of blacks had entered the 29th Street beach and announced their intention to swim. Angry white men ordered them to leave. They did but returned with reinforcements – blacks from 25th Street. A hail of rocks and stones drove out the whites, who stormed back with their own reserves. As if crudely reenacting a battle from the Great War, a fight "ensued between the colored men from the north side angle of the beach and the white men at a

---

[22] Tuttle, *Race Riot*, 3–5.

[23] Tuttle, *Race Riot*, 6–7 (quote); "Man Accused of Starting Riot," *Chicago Whip*, August 9, 1919, 1.

[24] Tuttle, *Race Riot*, 7; "Riot Sweeps Chicago," *Chicago Defender*, August 2, 1919, 1; "First Rioter's Confession Obtained," *Chicago Evening American*, August 2, 1919, 1.

vantage point to the south, many stones being thrown by men on both sides across the angle of the beach." Women and children caught in the crossfire ran for shelter.[25]

The rock fight abated during the search for Eugene Williams. Blacks and whites remained on the beach, watching intently; quickly, "awe gave way to excited whispers."[26] Only George Stauber, John Harris, and the other three rafters knew the exact circumstances of the drowning, but the crowd spread their own, unverified accounts: a barrage from white men during the rock fight had prevented Williams from coming ashore; a direct hit from this hail had caused him to drown; a white boy had swum out to drown Williams. The rumors dwelled on the victim's vulnerability, depicting a desperate boy's strength ebbing as a legion of merciless whites caused his death.[27]

With John Harris's identification of George Stauber, fact and rumor converged. Stauber had caused Eugene Williams's death, but had he acted alone? Was he part of a gang? Patrolman Callahan's refusal to arrest Stauber looked like yet another dereliction of duty to blacks: just as the police condoned Ragen's Colts' assaults and the Kenwood–Hyde Park bombings, they now allowed a white who had killed a black teenager to go free. Crimes against blacks were not really crimes, it seemed, as long as they protected racial segregation in Chicago. When Callahan arrested a black man on the complaint of a white man, the black crowd refused to tolerate any more injustice. Around 6 P.M., rocks rained down on an arriving patrol wagon. A black man named James Crawford drew a handgun and shot at white police officers, who fired back and killed Crawford. Armed members of the crowd also opened fire.[28] The nation's fifth race riot in three months was underway. By the time it ended a week later, thirty-eight men (twenty-three black, fifteen white) had lost their lives, 537 men and women (342 black, 178 white, and 17 of unknown race) suffered injuries, and approximately 1,000 people were forced out of their homes.[29]

---

[25] Chicago Commission, *Negro in Chicago*, 4; Tuttle, *Race Riot*, 5; Peter Hoffman, Coroner, *Report of the Coroner's Jury on the Race Riots*, November 3, 1919, box 38, folder 1980, Graham Taylor Papers, 9 (quote).

[26] Chicago Commission, *Negro in Chicago*, 4.

[27] Some of these rumors later appeared in print. See Hoffman, *Report*, 9–10; Chicago Commission, *Negro in Chicago*, 4.

[28] Tuttle, *Race Riot*, 8; Hoffman, *Report*, 28; Chicago Commission, *Negro in Chicago*, 5.

[29] Chicago Commission, *Negro in Chicago*, 1. The October 1919 riot in Phillips County, Arkansas, most likely claimed more lives than Chicago's riot, but a precise death toll in Arkansas remains difficult to determine. See Chapter 6.

Chicago's upheaval followed a familiar pattern. A small-scale incident had become a flashpoint for fast-spreading violence. In Charleston, a black man had allegedly failed to step aside for two white sailors; in Longview, whites had accused a black man of impugning the honor of a white woman. The precipitating causes of racial conflict in Bisbee and Washington also appeared to be minor, but the intensity of white-on-black attacks in all four cities revealed a greater mission: protection of the structure and practice of white supremacy. The same was true in Chicago, where the violence that engulfed the city after the drowning of Eugene Williams advanced the purpose of driving black residents from majority white neighborhoods. Like Washington's police, many of Chicago's officers treated black self-defenders as criminals. And like the troopers in Bisbee and the black residents of Charleston, Longview, and Washington, black Chicagoans undertook an array of self-defensive actions. The initial response to the beach incident, however, was retaliatory.

The Blaze

After the exchange of gunfire at the 29th Street Beach, roving black men began attacking whites. According to the *Chicago Defender*, white riders were pulled from street cars near 35th and State, approximately two miles from the beach, and beaten. The mob also pulled drivers and passengers from automobiles. Nine white men were beaten or stabbed; gunfire wounded a tenth. Thelma Shepherd, a young black woman, was aboard a streetcar. As she recalled, "police cars were coming from all directions, what seemed to be hundreds of people were yelling and pushing, and it seemed for a minute like something absolutely crazy was going on." By 8 P.M., the *Defender* reported, "the whole South Side was in an uproar."[30] As news of the beach fracas and attacks on whites spread to Canaryville, Bridgeport, and other white neighborhoods, the athletic clubs swung into action. Armed with bats, knives, and pistols, they crossed Wentworth and began attacking African Americans. During the next six hours, gangs beat twenty-seven blacks, stabbed seven, and shot four (none fatally).[31]

The riot had reached a crucial stage, as Lieutenant Donald C. Van Buren recognized. Van Buren was assigned to the Chicago office of the

---

[30] "Riot Sweeps Chicago"; Chicago Commission, *Negro in Chicago*, 5; "A Report on the Chicago Riot by an Eye-Witness," *Messenger* vol. II, no. 9 (September 1919), 13; for Shepherd's account, see Hartfield, *Another Way Home*, 52–3.

[31] Tuttle, *Race Riot*, 32–3; Chicago Commission, *Negro in Chicago*, 5.

U.S. Army's Military Intelligence Division (MID). At 8:30 P.M., one of the MID's volunteer agents, a Red Cross ambulance driver, informed Van Buren that a race riot had broken out. Police and reserves were being mobilized, but the two men spent the next several hours serving as self-appointed auxiliaries. They rushed a wounded white teenager to a hospital and patrolled the streets of the Black Belt, where they saw police officers gathered on corners and black men and women thronging the sidewalks. Although Van Buren believed the riot was ending, he was ready to intervene if the circumstances changed.[32]

Cooperation between the military, police, and volunteers during race rioting was not unusual. Federal agents and military officers had worked closely with the police in Charleston, Bisbee, and Washington, D.C. In Bisbee and Washington, vigilante organizations such as the Home Defense League had also been authorized to intervene in the riots. The actions of Van Buren and his driver revealed yet again the blurred line between official and volunteer authority; and, as it had in the other cities, such cooperation spelled trouble for African Americans in Chicago.

Van Buren was mistaken; the riot was only just beginning. At 8 A.M. Monday, Mayor Thompson returned from an out-of-state trip. A veteran police officer recommended he call in the state militia, but Thompson shrugged off the advice. The chief of police, John J. Garrity, had told him that a cordon around the Black Belt would halt additional clashes. However, Garrity's plan offered no protection to blacks trying to get to their jobs.[33] Indeed, it all but encouraged Ragen's Colts and the other athletic clubs to assault black stockyard workers, to besiege streetcars carrying black passengers through white neighborhoods, and to attack black-occupied homes beyond the cordon. Although Garrity assured a delegation of black leaders that he would request state militia if needed, Thompson was loath to ask for help from Governor Frank Lowden, whom he despised.[34]

Black laborers arrived at Union Stock Yard on Monday morning without trouble. By mid-afternoon, however, gangs had congregated near the gates, wielding clubs and bats as they waited for the 3 P.M. shift to end.[35] Departing black workers were trapped. If they ran east, they

---

[32] Lt. Donald C. Van Buren, "Race Riots in Chicago," July 28, 1919, Case File 10218–353-2, RG 165, copy in box 1, reel 6, Kornweibel Papers.

[33] Tuttle, *Race Riot*, 34–5.

[34] "300 Armed Negroes Gather; New Rioting Starts; Militia Next," *Chicago Daily News*, July 28, 1919, 1; Tuttle, *Race Riot*, 203–7.

[35] Chicago Commission, *Negro in Chicago*, 9, 15.

went straight into Canaryville. To the south and west lay another hostile white neighborhood, Back of the Yards, while railroad tracks and a creek blocked escape to the north. That afternoon and evening, white mobs assaulted thirty black men in and near the yard.[36] Black workers who boarded streetcars at platforms inside the yard still faced danger. Henry Goodman was aboard an eastbound car when a delivery truck pulled across the tracks. Three white men forced Goodman and the other black passengers to disembark and began beating them. Another mob halted a streetcar as it crossed into Canaryville. A hail of stones and bricks shattered windows, then the mob began attacking black riders. One, John Mills, fled east – the Black Belt was just four blocks away. He only made it one block. The mob surrounded him and delivered a fatal beating.[37]

A good Samaritan saved Leo Falls, a black teenager, from a similar fate. When gang members boarded his streetcar, a white man hid Falls under his own seat. According to Falls's brother, "it was only the action of this man that prevented [Leo] being dragged off and killed." Similar interventions saved the lives of other African Americans, but in the case of John Mills, a crowd estimated at 2,000 gathered as fifty or so young men killed him.[38] A police station was located a few blocks away, but officers arrived too late to save Mills. Evidence also suggests that some police were reluctant to interfere with the athletic clubs. One policeman recognized members of the Our Flag Club but insisted they were not Mills's assailants because they did not run away when the patrol arrived. A Ragen's Colt later boasted that the "coppers" had been "fixed and told to lay off on club members"; another claimed that an officer always rode along with a carload of Colts during the riot so he could wave off patrolmen.[39]

Jun Fujita captured on film one of the most vicious gang attacks. Born in Hiroshima, Japan, Fujita immigrated to the United States in 1915 and went to work for the *Chicago Evening Post* as a photographer. Unafraid to put himself in the riot, Fujita photographed a dozen teenagers and boys – one looks no older than ten – racing through a backyard

---

[36] Pacyga, *Polish Immigrants*, 215–16.

[37] Hoffman, *Report*, 10–11, 30; Chicago Commission, *Negro in Chicago*, 10–11.

[38] "Arthur G. Falls, Reminiscence, 1962," Marquette University Department of Special Collections and University Archives, 74 (hereafter "Falls Reminiscence"; all citations refer to the upper-right pagination on the ms.); Chicago Commission, *Negro in Chicago*, 22.

[39] Chicago Commission, *Negro in Chicago*, 11–12 (quotes), 15.

FIGURE 4.2. Mob running with bricks. White mobs, many drawn from the ranks of South Side gangs and "athletic clubs," relentlessly pursued and attacked African Americans during Chicago's riot, causing numerous deaths and hundreds of injuries. *Source:* Photographer Jun Fujita, ICHi-65495. Courtesy of the Chicago History Museum.

(Figure 4.2). A viewer, unaware of the context, might think the boys are at play, lighting a firecracker, say, or running to a ballgame. The older boys crowd around the rear of a house. Two peer beneath the porch, one waits with a large rock gripped in his right hand. And now a close-up: the foot of an exterior staircase. At the first step lies a black man – bleeding, battered, dying. A young white male in a dark shirt and engineer's cap has just hurled a heavy rock at the man's head. A second young white man stands close, a brick in his hand, winding up; his face is a blur. The victim's head and the striking stone are also blurry, but the thrower's sleeve and hand are focused, frozen forever at the end of his follow-through. It is nothing less than the snapshot of a murder.[40]

---

[40] One of Fujita's photographs was published on the front page of the *Chicago Evening Post* on July 30, 1919. The caption reads, "here is a remarkable picture of the race riot

Who are these boys? Presumably, Fujita's photographs could have been used to identify the victim's murderers, but only if people who knew the boys spoke up. As a detective asking questions in Canaryville remarked, "it is a pretty tough neighborhood to try to get any information out there; you can't do it."[41] Witnesses remained silent, participants kept mum, police arrived late. In another of Fujita's photographs, three uniformed police officers linger at the murder scene, the killers long gone.

And who is the slain man? His identity depends on where Fujita was standing. Of the twenty-three deaths of African Americans documented in the Cook County Coroner's Jury's report, only two fit the scenes photographed by Fujita: that of John Mills, already described; and that of Edward W. Jackson, who was killed by a white mob in Canaryville at 9 A.M. Tuesday. In Fujita's fourth picture, a figure looking at the camera casts a shadow. If the backyard depicted faced east, then he is looking into the morning sun, placing him at the attack on Edward Jackson. If the backyard faced west, then an afternoon sun cast the shadow; and Mills was killed at 5:35 P.M. on Monday. The identity of the victim depends on another factor: was he already dead when the police found him? If so, then he cannot be Jackson, who survived for a week before succumbing to his injuries. The policeman in another photograph seems to show no sense of urgency (Figure 4.3). It thus appears that the dead man in the photograph is John Mills.[42]

Assured of the opportunity to attack African Americans at will, white rioters spent Tuesday and Wednesday (July 29–30) terrorizing blacks living near or beyond the Black Belt's border of Wentworth Avenue. Just as white veterans and servicemen had mobilized in Washington, the Lorraine Club, an athletic club, recruited participants for a mob attack against black-occupied homes on Wentworth between 47th and 48th Streets. The marauders shattered windows, fired guns, and looted as the residents fled. Ten blocks south, the aptly named Sparklers tried three times to burn down a house. At dusk on Wednesday, some 200 Ragen's Colts laid siege to African Americans living in nine houses located three

in the black belt, showing rioters attacking the home of a negro who has been pursued for blocks." The photographs described in the text were published in Chicago Commission, *Negro in Chicago*; the original prints are held at the Chicago History Museum.

[41] Chicago Commission, *Negro in Chicago*, 12.

[42] It is possible that Fujita photographed a murder not recorded in the coroner's report. This seems highly unlikely, however, given the fact that policemen are present in the sequence of photographs.

FIGURE 4.3. Victim of a mob. Evidence suggests that the dead man in the photograph is John Mills, chased by a mob from a street car and, in the words of the Coroner's Jury, "overtaken by the mob and struck and beaten to death by unknown white men" at approximately 5:35 P.M. on July 28, 1919. *Source:* Photographer Jun Fujita, ICHi-65494. Courtesy of the Chicago History Museum.

blocks west of Wentworth. Moving down the block, they knocked down doors, hurled furniture into yards, and set fires. Like well-briefed soldiers, the attackers knew exactly which homes to hit.[43] These vigilante evictions were an escalation of the previous attacks carried out by Ragen's Colts and the other clubs. For months, gangs had targeted African Americans living in or passing through the west-of-Wentworth neighborhoods. The spillover of Sunday's beach melee offered the gangs an enticing opportunity to finish the job, to permanently expel blacks from their fledgling enclaves.

[43] Chicago Commission, *Negro in Chicago*, 14–15; Tuttle, *Race Riot*, 54–5; "U.S. and State Act to Curb Race Riots; New Clashes Bitter," *Chicago Daily News*, July 30, 1919 (home edition), 1. The Chicago Commission on Race Relations incorrectly reported the date of the Ragen's Colts' attack as Tuesday, July 29; it actually occurred the next day. See Tuttle, *Race Riot*, 55 n. 36.

Fighting Fire with Fire

Black men such as Harry Haywood were determined to see that the gangs did not roam unchecked. Haywood was a veteran of the Eighth Illinois (370th Regiment, Ninety-third Division). After mustering out in April, the twenty-one-year-old went to work as a waiter on the New York–Chicago route of the Michigan Central. When he and other black crew members disembarked in Chicago at 2 P.M. on Monday, July 28, a white trainman warned them to be careful. "There's a big race riot going on out there," he said, also sharing a rumor that two black soldiers had been killed that morning. Recalling the racism that he and his comrades had endured in France, Haywood had no trouble believing the news. Even though Haywood as yet knew little about the riot, he intuitively grasped that its causes sprang from ongoing efforts, in the armed services and across the country, to preserve the prewar status of black subjugation. "I had been fighting the wrong war," he realized. "The Germans weren't the enemy – the enemy was right here at home. These ideas had been developing ever since I landed home in April, and a lot of other Black veterans were having the same thoughts."[44]

Haywood also knew exactly what he was going to do: reunite with his brothers-in-arms at the regiment's South Side armory. He was not the only one with that idea. According to the *Chicago Evening Post*, armed veterans were guarding the armory and had put up signs reading "Recruits Wanted."[45] After learning that the west-of-Wentworth gangs planned to come down 51st Street that night, Haywood and his comrades set up a defensive position in an apartment building overlooking the street. In addition to army-issue Springfield rifles, the men had a Browning submachine gun. "We didn't ask where it had come from," said Haywood, but he surmised that the weapon had been taken from the armory. The men spent the night watching, the submachine gun mounted by the window. "Fortunately for [the gangs], they never arrived and we all returned home in the morning," Haywood remembered.[46]

---

[44] Haywood, *Black Bolshevik*, 1–2.

[45] "Blacks Fight Guards at County Jail," *Chicago Evening Post*, July 29, 1919, 1.

[46] Haywood, *Black Bolshevik*, 81–3 (quotes on 82). Although the Chicago Commission on Race Relations later asserted that no rifles were taken from the Eighth Illinois Armory (see *Negro in Chicago*, 21), Lieutenant Donald Van Buren reported, "it is believed that the negro element, in particular, are using army rifles." See Van Buren, "Race Riots in Chicago," July 29, 1919, Case Files 10218-353-6 (quote) and 10218-353-11, RG 165, copies in box 1, reel 6, Kornweibel Papers.

The defensive preparations of the Eighth Illinois's veterans were not unique. A group of black men went to a public school to take rifles used in cadet training. Although it is not clear if they succeeded – accounts varied – black Chicagoans found many other ways to arm themselves.[47] Haywood's fellow crew members had purchased revolvers and ammunition while their train was in Michigan. One black-occupied house on State Street served as a magazine, holding several hundred rounds of thirty-eight and forty-eight caliber cartridges. Two women and sixteen men, including a uniformed veteran, shared seven firearms and ammunition in several flats on 22nd Street. A black man arrested for carrying concealed weapons purportedly told a police captain, "I've been getting ready for a war of my own," adding that he was supplying his friends with ammunition obtained from Georgia.[48]

As had happened in Washington, the spike in weapons and ammunition purchases alarmed authorities and gun dealers. A city ordinance required residents to obtain a permit to buy revolvers but did not restrict the possession of handguns and other firearms. Nevertheless, one dealer contacted police after taking a telephone order for weapons and ammunition totaling $3,000 from a man he believed was black.[49] An alderman asked the city's corporate counsel if police had the right to enter homes to search for weapons.[50] In Gary, Indiana, thirty miles southeast of Chicago, police arrested two black Chicagoans for purchasing revolvers. The presiding judge, who was white but also happened to be the president of Gary's NAACP branch, fined the men $210 each.[51] These restrictions did not, however, prevent black Chicagoans from arming themselves.

Monday evening, thousands of African Americans lined the streets of the Black Belt, especially along State Street and 35th Street (Figure 4.4).

[47] According to a black lawyer in Chicago, approximately 100 rifles were taken. See "A Report on the Chicago Riot." According to the MID, Chicago's police had previously secured all the weapons. See Francis D. Hanna, Memorandum #2, n.d., Case File 10218–353–7, RG 165, copy in box 1, reel 6, Kornweibel Papers. According to the *Chicago Daily News*, forty-one Enfield rifles were removed, though most were recovered. See "Regulars Round Up 13,000 Army Rifles," *Chicago Daily News*, July 30, 1919 (box score edition), 3.

[48] Haywood, *Black Bolshevik*, 1; "Police Make Many Arrests for Murder," *Chicago Daily News* July 29, 1919 (home edition), 3; "Human Munitions Truck Arrested," *Chicago Evening American*, August 1, 1919, 2 (quote); "U.S. and State Act."

[49] "Race Riots in City Spread," *Chicago Daily News*, July 29, 1919 (home edition), 3; "Regulars Round Up."

[50] "New Riots Spread in Negro Belt," *Chicago Evening Post*, July 28, 1919, 1.

[51] Mary White Ovington to Judge William Dunn, August 8 and 16, 1919; Dunn to Ovington, August 11, 1919, Waskow Notes, tab "NAACP Probes."

FIGURE 4.4. Crowd in front of a storefront. During Chicago's riot, African Americans gathered on street corners in the riot zone to share news and to form self-defense forces. The men shown in this photograph stand outside the office of black Chicago businessman Jesse Binga, who was the target of a bombing in March 1919 intended to stop him from brokering the sale of homes in white-occupied neighborhoods to African Americans. *Source:* Photographer Jun Fujita, ICHi-65481. Courtesy of the Chicago History Museum.

Estimates of the crowds ranged from 1,500 to 25,000. One black witness described the crowd as a "Hindenburg line." Led by veterans, armed black men formed squads and kept in touch by telephone. "Discharged soldiers were among those active in stimulating the resistance of the Negroes," reported George Haynes, who came to investigate the riot for the U.S. Labor Department. The MID's officers and observers claimed to see black veterans in uniforms without the required discharge chevrons.[52]

[52] "Chicago Rebellion: Free Black Men Fight Free White Men," *Messenger*, vol. II, no. 9 (September 1919), 31–2 (first quote); "A Report on the Chicago Riot"; Haynes, "Negro labor situation," 6 (second quote); Van Buren, "Race Riot – Chicago," August 4, 1919, Case File 10218–353–29, RG 165, copy in box 1, reel 6, Kornweibel Papers; Chicago Commission, *Negro in Chicago*, 32.

Arthur Falls, whose brother had narrowly escaped a streetcar beating, took comfort in knowing that if a mob targeted the family home, "most of the colored families were well-armed and numbers of them had had army experience."[53] Chief Garrity's decision to concentrate his forces meant police were patrolling almost every major corner in the Black Belt, but that night, they shared the duty of keeping the peace with thousands of black civilians and veterans. Mutual distrust and animosity soon brought bloodshed.

By 8 P.M., African Americans had surrounded the Angelus, an apartment building housing black and white families. Rumors circulated: a black woman had been killed, a white mob was coming, a white sniper had fired from a window. Two black officers – one was Detective Sergeant William Middleton, who had tried to arrest George Stauber for causing Eugene Williams's drowning – tried to find the alleged sniper but conflicting statements frustrated their efforts. Meanwhile, some sixty white officers faced a hostile crowd, a tense stand-off resembling the one in Washington two weeks earlier. When blacks began hurling bricks, the police opened fire; some in the crowd shot back. The exchange killed four men, three black and one white.[54]

The melee outside the Angelus Building was, as the Coroner's Jury put it, an instance of "violent and uncontrollable rioting." Newspapers offered similar characterizations. To the Chicago Commission on Race Relations, it was an example of the "anger-provoking power of rumor."[55] But the black mob was also an offshoot of the State Street defensive line. As the MID reported, a crowd of "2,500 armed whites . . . [had] formed near South 35th and State Streets" that afternoon. In addition, white veterans wearing army uniforms with red discharge chevrons "were racing through the [Black Belt], in an automobile, armed with revolvers carried in holsters on their belts." The police had not stopped the car, the MID further reported, because they "thought they were working under Government orders."[56] To African Americans, the police's failure to stop the white veterans seemed part of a pattern rather than a mistake. Who would stop the mob of 2,500 armed whites if not blacks themselves? As Arthur Falls said, "most of the police in this area were of Irish descent and

---

53 "Falls Reminiscence," 78.
54 "U.S. and State Act"; Chicago Commission, *Negro in Chicago*, 31–2; Hoffman, *Report*, 22–3, 37–9.
55 Hoffman, *Report*, 23; Chicago Commission, *Negro in Chicago*, 32.
56 Crockett to MID, July 28, 1919, box 4, folder "Chicago, Ill. #1," RG 60, Glasser File (first quote); R. H. Uhlemann et al., "Race Riots in Chicago," July 29, 1919, Case File 10218-353-18, RG 160, copy in box 1, reel 6, Kornweibel Papers (second quote).

were labeled, rightly or wrongly, as Irish Catholics; and for most colored people in Chicago the term Irish Catholic was synonymous with the word enemy."[57] As black Washingtonians had, black Chicagoans increasingly viewed the police as but another mob in uniform.

That same night, "sniping done from windows, alleyways, and roofs" wounded two white police officers in the Black Belt. In another example of the blurred lines that distinguished police, military, and civilian authority, Lieutenant Van Buren and a volunteer agent helped police search the scene and question witnesses.[58] Another shooting took the life of black police officer John Simpson. At 7:30 P.M., Simpson was trying to disperse a black mob pursuing a white man near an elevated station when one or more black men fired revolvers at Simpson.[59] Although hundreds of African Americans mobilized only for self-defense, some blacks targeted the police, who, like Washington's police, acknowledged no difference between self-defense and retaliation.

Elsewhere on the South Side on Monday, African Americans defended themselves against roving groups of white men. Three black stockyard workers had just left work when a mob brandishing clubs boarded their streetcar. The cornered men fought back. One, Joseph Scott, fatally stabbed his assailant. The police arrested Scott but not the attacking whites. Scott spent a week in jail without medical attention to his injuries, treatment described by the Coroner's Jury as "a travesty on justice and fair play."[60] Close to midnight, six or so white men and boys surrounded three black couples walking home from the theater. "Let's get the niggers! Let's get the niggers!" the mob shouted. Outnumbered, the three black men, two of whom were army officers, defended their party. Lieutenant Louis C. Washington, who had served with the Eighth Illinois, suffered a stab wound; Lieutenant Michael V. Browning, a gunshot to the leg. One of the whites, a teenager, was stabbed in the chest – his comrades ran from the scene, leaving him to bleed to death. The Coroner's Jury was unequivocal in its judgment, finding that "the group of colored people, en route to their home, were acting in an orderly and inoffensive manner, and were justified in their acts and conduct during said affray." The police arrested Washington but none of his attackers.[61]

---

[57] "Falls Reminiscence," 77.
[58] Van Buren, "Race Riots in Chicago," Case File 10218–353–6.
[59] Hoffman, *Report*, 32–3.
[60] Hoffman, *Report*, 17–18.
[61] Tuttle, *Race Riot*, 41–2; Chicago Commission, *Negro in Chicago*, 24–5 (first quote); "Indict 14 More for Riot; Plan to Try 50 Soon," *Chicago Tribune*, August 6, 1919, 2; Hoffman, *Report*, 21–2 (second quote).

Black defensive and deterrent measures, led by the men of the Eighth Illinois, continued throughout Tuesday. In the afternoon police arrested a dozen or so uniformed, armed veterans who had been guarding stores and patrolling in the Black Belt since Sunday night. Although the men claimed they had been deputized by a white police sergeant, the police jailed them.[62] That same afternoon, thirty-five men from the Eighth Illinois converged at the Cottage Grove police station to demand the release of an arrested comrade. Lieutenant Van Buren could hardly believe their audacity. "These soldiers were armed, and were doing police duty without anyone in authority directing their effort," he complained, oblivious that such a judgment also applied to whites who had deputized themselves.[63]

As Van Buren well knew, the riot had overwhelmed the police – he was, after all, helping investigate shootings. Another witness reported seeing police officers sitting on a curb while riot calls flooded South Side precincts. "The consensus of opinion," Van Buren reported, is "that the rioting would continue for a number of days or weeks to come, and that it would require all available troops in this territory to suppress it." Some of the men he talked to – other MID officers, volunteer agents, and police officers themselves – even proposed a quarantine of the Black Belt, with state troops stopping all traffic in and out except for the delivery of food and other essentials.[64] Yet army officers and white volunteers refused to recognize as legitimate African Americans' own efforts to keep the peace.

With 80 percent of the police spread throughout the Black Belt, white mob attacks shifted from the stockyard to the Loop, the commercial district. On Tuesday morning, Arthur Falls and his father William were walking to their jobs at the main post office when a mob surrounded them. As Arthur recalled, "I had been struck twice and was fighting back when I suddenly saw an opening in the circle." Like black Washingtonians William Laney and Theodore Micah Walker, Arthur, just seventeen years old, had to make a split-second decision: keep fighting or try to escape? Arthur sprinted toward the opening, hoping to draw part of the mob away from his father. The ploy worked. Arthur outran his attackers, lowered his shoulder to knock down a man trying to block his way,

---

[62] "Eleven Colored Soldiers Held," *Chicago Daily News*, July 29, 1919 (box score edition), 1; R. H. Uhlemann et al., "Race Riots in Chicago," Case File 10218–353–18.

[63] Memorandum, Lt. Donald Van Buren, July 29, 1919, Case File 10218–353–12, RG 165, copy in box 1, reel 6, Kornweibel Papers.

[64] Van Buren memorandum, Case File 10218–353–6.

and reached the post office. His father arrived an hour later – six white men had intervened to save him.[65] In another incident, white men in military uniform dragged a black porter out of a barbershop.[66] Other white servicemen – it is not clear if they were veterans, active-duty, or both – joined with civilians to attack blacks. One mob robbed and shot Paul Hardwick, rolling his body into the gutter near Adams and Wabash, one of Chicago's busiest intersections. Confident that the police would not intervene, the men lingered to divide Hardwick's belongings. Similar assaults continued unchecked for several hours.[67]

Meanwhile, Mayor Thompson continued to equivocate. On Monday afternoon, he had requested mobilization but not deployment of state militia. At the governor's order, the state's adjutant general, Brigadier General Frank S. Dickson, instructed the Eleventh Regiment of the Illinois National Guard and the First, Second, and Third Infantries of the Illinois Reserve Militia to report to their Chicago armories.[68] By nightfall, 3,500 militia were garrisoned in Chicago, but Thompson still clung to his hope that Garrity's men could do the job. The militia spent Tuesday in their barracks even as violence raged mere miles away. African Americans would need to continue defending themselves, and they did so in various ways.

At 6 A.M. on Tuesday, William Henderson and another black man walked through Canaryville to their jobs at Union Stock Yard. Brave men, these two – only a few dozen of the thousands of blacks employed at the yard came to work that day. Henderson and his companion defended themselves against a mob, stabbing one of their attackers before fleeing. The mob caught Henderson and beat him severely. When the police arrived, they arrested only Henderson. A few hours later, 150 white men amassed outside a black-occupied home on State Street and started throwing rocks. One of the inhabitants, Emma Jackson, allegedly shot and killed one of the rock throwers.[69] A *Chicago Evening Post* reporter who accompanied a police captain on a drive across the South Side on Tuesday observed an "awesome spectacle" on Calumet Avenue between

---

[65] "Falls Reminiscence," 79–84 (quote on 81).

[66] "The Personal History of Robert Lucas Donigan," Chicago History Museum, 47.

[67] Chicago Commission, *Negro in Chicago*, 19–20; Hoffman, *Report*, 21.

[68] John Oglesby to the Adjutant General of Illinois, July 28, 1919, and Special Orders No. 121a, July 28, 1919, Chicago Commission on Race Relations Records, Minutes 1919–1920, microfilm roll 30–11, Library of Congress.

[69] Tuttle, *Race Riot*, 44–6; Hoffman, *Report*, 18–20; Chicago Commission, *Negro in Chicago*, 28.

29th and 37th Streets: armed blacks standing guard outside every home.[70] At twilight, Samuel Johnson, the first black to move onto 60th Street west of Wentworth Avenue, opened fire on an attacking mob, killing one member. Arthur Falls listened with dread to the gunfire from his home on 61st Street – the Falls did not own firearms. "I would fight until the point that I was killed," Arthur resolved, but the "spirited defense by the people in the neighborhood" deterred more attacks.[71] At 9 P.M., armed blacks on State Street fired on four white drive-by shooters who had wounded a black passer-by. A police wagon then blocked the white men's vehicle, causing it to crash.[72] In this instance, black self-defense, combined with effective policing, squelched an attack that could have caused more bloodshed.

Monday and Tuesday's self-defense mobilization sometimes over-lapped with retaliation against whites. African Americans near 35th and State killed an elderly peddler, Casmero Lazeroni, on Monday about 4:30 P.M. That same afternoon, three black men fatally stabbed a white shop owner. Corporal Paul Bullack, just discharged from the army, reported being attacked at 39th and State by a uniformed black soldier who asked what he was doing in that neighborhood. "Before I could answer," Bul-lack said, "he hit me on the jaw." On Tuesday morning, a small mob of black men fatally stabbed a white shopowner at 51st and Dearborn.[73]

In some cases, the line between retaliation and self-defense is not easy to discern.[74] William Otterson was in a car with another white man on Monday evening when a black mob attacked them at 35th and Wabash. A brick fractured Otterson's skull, killing him. Were Otterson and his companion merely driving by, or were they sniping? In another incident, two black men signaled a white driver to stop; when he ignored the order, the men opened fire. The driver, who escaped unhurt, called the police, who brushed off the incident and told him to go home.[75] Had these

---

[70] "Post Reporter Shot at on Tour of Riot Zone," *Chicago Evening Post*, July 29, 1919 (home edition), 1.

[71] Hoffman, *Report*, 15–16; "Falls Reminiscence," 85–90 (quote on 88).

[72] "The Chicago Riots," *Branch Bulletin* vol. III, no. 10 (October 1919), 94; Affidavit of Count J. Teffner, August 22, 1919, Waskow Notes, tab "Chicago NAACP & Defense."

[73] Hoffman, *Report*, 23–6; Lt. Donald C. Van Buren, "Race Riots in Chicago," July 29, 1919, Case File 10218-353-10, RG 165, copy in box 1, reel 6, Kornweibel Papers (quote).

[74] At several points during Chicago's riot, self-defense transformed into clashes with police or attacks on whites. See Coit, "Changed Attitude," 242–5.

[75] Van Buren, "Race Riots in Chicago," July 31, 1919, Case File 10218-353-16, RG 165, copy in box 1, reel 6, Kornweibel Papers; Chicago Commission, *Negro in Chicago*, 39.

black men carried out a retaliatory attack, or had they set up a roadblock because the police were absent?

The Fictional Riot

In their coverage of the riot, Chicago's daily newspapers did not distinguish between self-defense and retaliation. "A group of twelve discharged negro soldiers, all armed, terrorized small groups of whites in various parts of the south side this afternoon. The men are believed to be former members of the 8th regiment." So reported the *Chicago Daily News* on Tuesday, July 29, spinning a lurid tale of armed black men advancing in formation as they "blazed away" at whites. According to the *Daily News*, women fainted, frantic whites scurried to their homes, and a bullet ricocheted off a policeman's badge. By the time additional police arrived, the black soldiers had fled. A similar account appeared in the *Chicago Tribune*.[76] The stories read like a script for a northern version of *Birth of a Nation*, with uniformed black veterans again featured as villains. The men featured in the article were most likely the dozen veterans who had claimed that a white police sergeant had deputized them on Sunday night. The Coroner's Jury later lauded these men for "their valuable service in patrolling, quieting the excited colored population, and relieving the grave fears of the women and children that white mobs were about to break through from west of Wentworth Avenue and burn their homes."[77] There is no evidence that the men charged white crowds, but stories depicting blacks as marauders abounded in Chicago's newspapers.

On Wednesday, the *Daily News* printed the unsubstantiated accounts of Alderman Joseph McDonough, sponsor of Bridgeport's Hamburg Athletic Club, and State Representative Thomas Doyle. McDonough described a carload of black men racing through Bridgeport, firing at whites. Doyle falsely claimed that the men gunned down a woman and a young boy and asserted that black residents had stockpiled enough ammunition to sustain years of guerilla warfare. The *Daily News* referred to blacks as "snipers" but said little about the activities of the athletic clubs.[78] An article about African Americans arrested for carrying

---

[76] "Troops Moving on Chicago as Negroes Shoot into Crowds," *Chicago Daily News*, July 29, 1919 (home edition), 1; "One Death in 14 Hours Puts Total at 26," *Chicago Tribune*, July 31, 1919 (final edition), 1–2.

[77] Hoffman, *Report*, 5.

[78] "Storm Mayor with Demand for Troops to Quell Race Riots," *Chicago Daily News*, July 30, 1919 (box score edition), 1; Chicago Commission, *Negro in Chicago*, 28.

weapons used a mocking tone. "'Bos, I was jus' carryin' this yere razor long wif me for to clean my fingernails wif,' was the ingenious explanation of one negro," read the newspaper's description of Ellsworth Richardson, a student at the Moody Bible Institute.[79] In a similar fashion, the *Tribune* described the scene at a police station as "Uncle Tom's Cabin in a modern setting," as blacks waiting for police escorts "huddled" together "like fugitive slaves of the ante-bellum south."[80] According to the *Chicago Evening American*, "tough Negroes from the West and North sides had made their way into the riot zone to take their stand at the side of their racial brothers."[81] In the *Herald-Examiner*'s version of the Eighth Illinois's visit to its armory, several thousand men stoned the building, broke down doors, and wounded or hurt more than fifty people as they seized hundreds of weapons. In another article, the same newspaper cited a man "whose name is withheld" that African Americans had stockpiled more than 2,000 Springfield rifles and a stock of soft-nosed bullets. Several newspapers incorrectly reported that black men were assaulting white women.[82]

The black press was not immune from exaggeration, either. The *Defender*, for example, reported a gruesome, false story about a white mob smashing a baby against a telegraph pole and slashing the mother "into ribbons."[83] The *Defender* was a weekly, though, and its first issue with riot coverage did not appear until Saturday, August 2. (White-owned presses refused to publish a special edition of the *Defender* during the riot.) The *Chicago Whip*, the *Defender*'s up-and-coming rival, produced an edition on July 31, but white authorities confiscated and destroyed as many copies as they could find.[84] Chicago's dailies thus had six days to print falsehoods and fabrications, to traffic in stereotypes and fears: latter-day Nat Turners bent on murdering whites (black veterans who "blazed away"; the "snipers" who allegedly gunned down a woman and child); dim-witted minstrel characters (Ellsworth Richardson); and so-called fiends and brutes intent on raping white women. Black Chicagoans,

---

[79] "Negro Rioters Draw Heavy Fines in Court," *Chicago Daily News*, July 31, 1919 (home edition), 3.

[80] "Riot Refugees Flee to Police Fearful of Mob," *Chicago Tribune*, July 31, 1919 (final edition), 2.

[81] "State Troops Bring Quiet to Riot Zone," *Chicago Evening American*, August 1, 1919, 2.

[82] Chicago Commission, *Negro in Chicago*, 17, 28–9 (quote on 29).

[83] "Riot Sweeps Chicago."

[84] "Shuts All Saloons in Race Riot Area," *Chicago Daily News*, August 1, 1919 (home edition), 1; "Chicago Rebellion: Free Black Men."

menaced by gangs and mistreated by the police, now also confronted, as had blacks in Washington, a white-written narrative about the riot that cast them as the wrongdoers.[85] Countering fiction with fact was vital not just for the sake of history but also to ensure that justice was served fairly and fully.[86]

Extinguishing the Blaze

By Wednesday morning, the death toll had risen to thirty-one. More than 250 blacks and approximately 140 whites were injured. *Chicago Evening Post* photographer Jun Fujita, who had captured the killing of John Mills on film, flew over the Black Belt on Wednesday and took an aerial photograph of armed men on a rooftop and large crowds of black men gathered on corners.[87] Governor Lowden had come to Chicago, but he still needed the mayor's request to deploy troops. Thompson continued to insist the police could quell the disorder, but few shared his optimism. "Demands that state troops take charge... fell in an avalanche today on Mayor Thompson," the *Daily News* reported. Most of the twenty-five aldermen present at a special council meeting voiced approval of using troops. Jesse Binga, the black realtor and banker whose office had been bombed in March, warned the state's attorney that black residents, unable to leave their homes to work or to shop, now faced hunger and deprivation (Figure 4.5). A black woman and five children were found hiding in their home; they had been without food for two days. Those who ventured out found empty shelves – deliveries to the Black Belt had practically ceased. Not surprisingly, Binga and other black leaders urged immediate deployment of troops. As pressure mounted, the mayor clumsily tried to shift the blame back on Lowden, contending that the governor could activate the troops without a mayoral request. "Nothing except rotten politics is preventing the calling out of troops," an alderman grumbled.[88]

---

[85] For more on the newspapers' errors and bias, see Chicago Commission, *Negro in Chicago*, 26–32.

[86] Blacks editors and writers also used differing narratives about the riot and black self-defense to refine New Negro identity. The *Defender*'s Robert Abbott, for example, argued that assertions of black manhood, spurred by military service, had incurred a white backlash, leading to the riot. See Coit, "Changed Attitude," 248–56.

[87] "Riot Snipers Photographed from Airplane," *Chicago Evening Post*, July 31, 1919 (home edition).

[88] Chicago Commission, *Negro in Chicago*, 40; "Storm Mayor with Demand" (first quote); "Police Aid Starving Negroes," *Chicago Daily News*, July 30, 1919 (home edition), 1; Tuttle, *Race Riot*, 50–4 (second quote).

FIGURE 4.5. Neighborhood children raiding an African American family's home. A primary purpose of Chicago's antiblack collective violence was to drive blacks out of majority-white neighborhoods bordering the city's Black Belt. As the size – and age – of this crowd reveals, that mission had widespread support. *Source:* ICHi-40052. Courtesy of the Chicago History Museum.

Late Wednesday night, Thompson finally capitulated. The troops, now 6,200 strong, dispersed from their armories, taking up positions between 18th and 55th Streets and Wentworth and Indiana Avenues, a zone encompassing the Black Belt and part of Kenwood and Hyde Park. Lowden did not, however, declare martial law. Although the militia remained under the command of Brigadier General Dickson, the police retained civil authority, using the troops either as reserves or as patrols. The Third Infantry covered the district between 31st and 38th and State and Halsted Streets, for example, while the Eleventh Infantry patrolled the area just to the south. Beleaguered police officers expressed relief, even joy. "Thank God!" one exclaimed. "We can't stand up under this much longer!" Although the First Infantry experienced no trouble, other militia tangled with the athletic clubs. As rain began to fall, many white rioters quit for the night.[89]

By Thursday morning, July 31, the troops were firmly in control of the Black Belt, and deliveries of food, ice, and other necessities resumed. Grateful black residents thronged round trucks to buy provisions as militia stood guard.[90] The soldiers "unquestionably prevented mob formations, raids, and 'sniping,'" enthused the Chicago Commission on Race Relations, praising the troops' discipline and efficacy. One regimental commander said his men were "welcomed into the [riot] zone, of course, by everybody, and I'd say especially by the colored people." All of the troops were white, but they did not favor rioting whites as the police had. The militia officers, drawn from Chicago's middle and upper classes, were prosperous and socially connected bankers, businessmen, and public officials. For men such as Brigadier General LeRoy T. Steward (day job: Superintendent of the Chicago Post Office), the phrase "athletic club" meant membership in the downtown Illinois Athletic Club, not a Canaryville gang. For their part, the "wild canaries" reviled the militia, taunting them constantly but only making a few attempts to break through the cordon along Wentworth.[91]

The riot's last gasp came on Saturday, August 2, when arsonists started a blaze in the Back of the Yards neighborhood that gutted some fifty homes. Almost all of the displaced residents were Polish and Lithuanian immigrants who worked at the stockyard. Blame quickly fell on African Americans. Witnesses offered conflicting accounts: one claimed to see a

---

[89] Chicago Commission, *Negro in Chicago*, 41–2 (quote); Tuttle, *Race Riot*, 55.

[90] Tuttle, *Race Riot*, 56–7.

[91] "Many I.A.C. Men Among Troops in Riot Zone," *Chicago Evening American*, August 2, 1919, 2; *Who's Who in Chicago*, 935; Chicago Commission, *Negro in Chicago*, 42 (quotes).

truck loaded with black men; another reported seeing blacks run from a barn just before it ignited. But it was unlikely that African Americans would set foot in such a hostile neighborhood. As a stockyard superintendent commented, "there isn't a colored man, regardless of how little brains he'd have, who would attempt to go over into the Polish district and set fire to anybody's house over there. He wouldn't get that far." Some police accused white gang members in blackface of lighting the fires, in an apparent attempt to revive the riot, but they had no evidence to support the charge. The arsonists were never identified.[92]

Thirty-eight men (twenty-three black, fifteen white) died in Chicago's week-long riot; more than five hundred men and women were hurt. The scope of the violence, which exceeded that of Washington's, prompted an exhaustive investigation of its causes. At the urging of more than eighty prominent Chicagoans, Governor Lowden formed the Chicago Commission on Race Relations (CCRR) less than a month after the riot's outbreak. The CCRR's twelve members – six white, six black – held thirty conferences and took almost 2,000 pages of testimony from 175 experts. A dozen field investigators amassed sheaves of housing, crime, and employment data. The CCRR interviewed riot witnesses and victims as well as police officers. Its final report, published in 1922, was more than 600 pages long. The CCRR attributed Chicago's riot to widespread racial inequities and discrimination in housing, recreation, employment, policing, and the courts. The CCRR also faulted Chicago – its government, employers, and white and black citizens – for inadequately responding to the recent influx of black southerners.[93] Although the CCRR noted that a "growing race solidarity" had animated black armed resistance, and its narrative documented numerous instances of black self-defense, the commission did not dwell on this aspect of the riot.[94] The CCRR also did not analyze Chicago's upheaval within the context of the year's spreading racial violence.

---

[92] Chicago Commission, *Negro in Chicago*, 20–1 (quote); D. T. Hammond, August 2, 1919, and Lt. Van Buren, August 2, 1919, Case File 10218–353–21, RG 165, copies in box 1, reel 6, Kornweibel Papers.

[93] For an overview of the Chicago Commission's work, see the commission's progress report for December 21, 1920, box 115, folder 753, Victor Lawson Papers, Newberry Library. For the commission's recommendations, see *Negro in Chicago*, 595–651. For a critical evaluation of the commission and a review of the scholarship on it, see Hudson, "The Negro in Chicago."

[94] Chicago Commission, *Negro in Chicago*, 46.

Yet black armed resistance was one of the most notable features of Chicago's riot, especially when compared to the self-defensive measures taken in Charleston, Bisbee, Longview, and Washington. In those four cities, African Americans had responded to attacks by whites with increasing degrees of coordination. In Charleston and Bisbee, self-defense had been instinctive and reactive. (Recall the blacks in the Charleston pool hall who fought off attacking sailors with billiard balls, the troopers in Bisbee who reached for their sidearms when police and deputies harassed them.) In Longview, the resistance was preemptive; Dr. C. P. Davis had hastily deployed a volunteer force to protect his friend S. L. Jones from a lynch mob. In Washington, black self-defenders had rushed in weapons from Baltimore and organized a paramilitary force to halt mob incursions into black neighborhoods. The League for Democracy, a black veterans' group, had even posted fliers celebrating and justifying armed resistance. In Chicago, self-defense measures reached their highest levels yet during 1919; not coincidentally, black veterans figured prominently in these efforts. Donning their uniforms, veterans of the Eighth Illinois had taken up arms and roved the streets to halt white mobs and drive-by shooters. But these veterans had plenty of civilian comrades, as evidenced by the number of black residents who had defended their homes or thronged State Street as part of the so-called Hindenburg Line.

Black Chicagoans themselves sensed that something extraordinary had happened – indeed, was *still* happening. After the riot, a Bureau of Investigation agent interviewed Ida B. Wells, who now lived in Chicago. She emphatically rejected his suggestion that radical elements like the IWW were behind the city's racial clash. "Her statement was the old, old story about the maltreatment of the colored people in the South," the agent scornfully reported. "She further stated that the black race had become exasperated with the treatment it has received at the hands of the United States Government; and the Negroes of America are now ready to demand their rights as Citizens, even if they have to take up arms and die fighting for these rights."[95] At a post-riot gathering, a black Chicagoan declared:

The recent race riots have done at least one thing for the colored race. In the past we Negroes have failed to appreciate what solidarity means. We have, on the contrary, been much divided. Since the riot we are getting together and devising ways and means of protecting our interests. The recent race riots have convinced us that we must take steps to protect ourselves. Never again will we be found

[95] "In re: Race Rioting in Chicago From July 27th to July 31," August 6, 1919, RG 65, OGF 369,914, reel 812.

unprepared. It is the duty of every man here to provide himself with guns and ammunition. I, myself, have at least one gun and at least enough ammunition to make it useful.[96]

For all the bloodshed and destruction, African Americans had found cause to celebrate: the New Negro – resolute, unafraid, proud, armed, determined to make America safe for democracy – had arrived. Chicago's antiblack collective violence exceeded even the intensity and scope of Washington's riot, which had broken out less than two weeks earlier. From the clamor of the street clashes in both cities, African American self-defenders had raised a clarion signal: more mob action would incur, not deter, more armed resistance.

---

[96] Chicago Commission, *Negro in Chicago*, 46–7. Black clergy in Chicago did not, however, celebrate this spirit of resistance. Many urged their congregations to accept segregation as the price of racial peace. See Carter, "Making Peace with Jim Crow."

5

Armed Resistance to the Courthouse Mobs

Knoxville, Tennessee, and Omaha, Nebraska, did not appear to be likely sites of racial violence in 1919. Knoxville's mayor, John McMillan, had recently spurned a Ku Klux Klan organizer's request for support and had publicly denounced the Klan in an address to black leaders.[1] Omaha, an industrial city on the banks of the Missouri River, did not have a large black population. In his response to a NAACP questionnaire about the racial conflict spreading across the nation, Omaha's chief of police succinctly observed that "we have had no race riots here."[2] In August and September, however, Knoxville and Omaha experienced race riots after massive mobs formed to lynch black men accused of crimes against white women. The mobs stormed the courthouses in both cities and attacked black residents, who responded with individual and collective acts of self-defense. In a resemblance to Chicago and Washington, Knoxville's armed resistance featured roving groups of black men who repelled or slowed down bands of white attackers. Although black self-defense in Omaha was more dispersed and sporadic than in Knoxville, it prevented a mob from mounting an attack on Omaha's black neighborhood. As was the case in Charleston, Bisbee, Longview, Washington, and Chicago, black self-defenders in Knoxville and Omaha confronted not only mobbing whites but also hostile police, troops, and volunteer vigilantes. If the courthouse riots demonstrated that no city or locale in the United States was immune from antiblack collective violence in 1919, then African

[1] Lamon, "Tennessee Race Relations," 69.
[2] Marshall Eberstein to Mary White Ovington, August 9, 1919, box C-4, folder "General Correspondence Aug. 7–12, 1919," NAACP Records.

Americans' actions in Knoxville and Omaha demonstrated that armed resistance was no aberration.

The Charge against Maurice Mays

For Maurice Mays, Friday, August 29, 1919, was a busy day. In his early thirties, the Knoxville native was handsome, with almond eyes, smooth cheeks, and a sublimely confident expression. Posing for a portrait as a young man, he offered a pensive look, gazing directly at the camera, lips caught between a smile and a frown, chin propped on folded fingers. His taste for fine clothes and beautiful women made it easy to dismiss him as a dandy, but Mays had many interests and diversions. For a time he owned a café and briefly served as a deputy sheriff. He also knew the law from the other side: his arrest record included charges, but no convictions, for gambling and carrying a concealed weapon.[3]

That Friday, the start of the Labor Day weekend, Mays was canvassing for the city's white mayor, John McMillan; the election was just a week away. Mays and his adoptive father William rented a horse and buggy and gave out campaign cards to black voters, a crucial bloc of McMillan's supporters. In an exception to southern disfranchisement, black men could vote in Knoxville if they paid a poll tax – or someone paid it for them. Along with the cards, the Mays had poll tax receipts to hand out. The grateful McMillan, a banker, provided the young man with loans for his business ventures, but the men shared more than financial and political ties. Maurice's birth mother, a black maid named Ella Walker, had worked for the McMillan family when John was a teenager. She left Knoxville after William Mays and his wife, a black couple, adopted Maurice, and the line on the birth certificate for the baby's father was never filled in. Although neither McMillan nor Mays said so openly, both privately admitted that they were father and son.[4]

After dropping off William and returning the buggy around 8 P.M., Mays meandered downtown Knoxville, chatting with friends and handing out more poll tax receipts. Until he returned to his rented room at 12:30 A.M., Mays was never alone for more than a few minutes, and a friend gave him a ride home in his taxi.[5] At 3:30 A.M., Deputy

---

[3] Lakin, "Dark Night," 6–8.

[4] Lakin, "Dark Night," 6–8; *State vs. Mays* 145 Tenn. 118 (1921), 254–5, Transcript of Record, Knox County Archives.

[5] *State vs. Mays*, 260–72.

Sheriff Thomas Kirby and Knoxville police officers John Hatcher and Andy White pounded on Mays's door. William Mays was with them. As a confused Maurice watched, the officers searched his room. Do you have a flashlight, a pocketbook, a revolver? they demanded. Only a revolver, Mays said, pointing to his dresser. The officers took turns examining the weapon and sniffing the barrel. "What is the trouble, what has happened?" Maurice asked, but the officers refused to tell him. White picked up Maurice's shoes and scratched the soles. "What do you scrape them shoes for," William asked, "there is no mud on them," but White continued. Get dressed, the policemen told Maurice, finally explaining that they wanted a woman to see him. The officers drove to a street two miles away. White left the vehicle and returned with a distraught young white woman: mussed hair, eyes red from crying, unable to walk unaided. She looked at Mays and declared: "He is the man." Mays protested that he had never been on that block, but the officers promptly charged him with murder and jailed him.[6]

The woman who had identified Mays was Ora Smyth, a young mill worker.[7] She was staying with her twenty-seven-year-old cousin Bertie Lindsey whose husband was looking for work in Ohio. The Lindseys lived in a three-room house on Eighth Avenue in North Knoxville. The women slept in the same bed, and before retiring at 11 P.M., they had opened the back door to get fresh air. At 2:20 A.M., a terrified Bertie shook Ora awake – someone was in the bedroom. Smyth later claimed he was "a negro standing by the bed with a pistol in one hand and a flash light in the other." When Bertie disobeyed an order to stay in the bed, the intruder fatally shot her and fled with her pocketbook. Smyth ran to the neighbors, Emmett and Gertrude Dyer, and woke them up. After Gertrude opened the door, both women saw a man on the street, flashlight in hand, running down a muddy alley. Smyth was certain she had just seen her cousin's killer. Gertrude later described the man as "tolerably heavy" and wearing a "dingey gray suit" but could not describe his skin color.[8]

Patrolman Andy White had already been in the neighborhood earlier that night, investigating calls about two attempted home break-ins. He and his driver, a black officer named Jim Smith, also responded to the

---

[6] *State vs. Mays*, 276–9.

[7] Smyth was her married name; in August 1919, her surname was Parsons.

[8] Lakin, "Dark Night," 5–6; *State vs. Mays*, 15–19, 26–32, 66 (quotes on 26 and 66); "Killed in Effort to Escape Negro," *Knoxville Journal and Tribune*, August 31, 1919, 1.

Lindsey shooting. Even before they arrived, White had a suspect in mind: Mays. As Smith recalled, White believed "that God Damned Maurice Mays killed that woman." This was not the first time Smith heard White disparage Mays. White frequently mocked Mays's good looks and had declared that the "son-of-bitch" should be in the state prison. The officer had arrested his nemesis on trumped-up charges several times, but his apparent aim to pin the Lindsey shooting on Mays drastically escalated the grudge.[9]

The case against Mays was weak. Ora Smyth likely was in shock when she identified him, and he was the only man shown to her. Mays's shoes were clean, but Smyth and Gertrude Dyer had seen the suspect run into a muddy alley. Mays owned a thirty-eight revolver, the same type of weapon used to shoot Bertie Lindsey, but Mays's gun had not recently been fired. Jim Smith disdainfully recalled the eagerness of Andy White and other officers to detect a scent of powder in the barrel. "I seen them smelling it and looking like they were all dissatisfied about it, kept smelling it over and over." Gapers crowded into the Lindsey house, making it impossible to gather evidence. Neither the flashlight nor Lindsey's stolen pocketbook were found in Mays's room. A prowler with a flashlight had been spotted outside two houses just blocks from the Lindsey home, but the police did not investigate to determine if the incidents were connected. One had occurred around midnight, when Mays was still downtown.[10] The flimsiness of the evidence did not, however, concern the hundreds of Knoxville residents who hoped to see rough justice delivered swiftly.

Knoxville's Riot

News of the Lindsey murder and Mays's arrest flashed across Knoxville on Saturday, and a crowd soon gathered around the city jail. When Police Chief E. M. Haynes transferred Mays to the county jail in the courthouse a few blocks away, the crowd followed. Newspaper coverage inspired rumors – Mays had killed Bertie because she was pregnant with his baby, for example – and stirred talk of a lynching.[11] The Knox County

---

[9] Lakin, "Dark Night," 8; *State vs. Mays*, 355–65 (quotes on 356 and 359). The grudge against Mays stemmed in part from Mays's alleged relationships with white women. See Lamon, "Tennessee Race Relations," 76.

[10] "Killed in Effort"; *State vs. Mays*, 282, 381–3; Lakin, "Dark Night," 8–10 (Smith quote on 8).

[11] Lakin, "Dark Night," 10–11.

Courthouse, a veritable castle of stone walls and turrets, seemed impregnable, but Sheriff William Cate decided to covertly move Mays out of town anyway. Cate ordered the prisoner to don a wig and dress, whisked him to a waiting car, and put him on a train to Chattanooga. Cate himself went along as a guard.[12]

A mob could not lynch an absent man. But what if its leaders suspected that the prisoner was hidden somewhere in the courthouse? As rumors spread that Mays remained inside, Cate's deputies permitted a self-appointed "committee" to see for themselves that the prisoner was gone.[13] Rather than appease the crowd, the tours – three of them – fueled more rumors. "I don't believe [Mays is] any more in Chattanooga than I am," a man grumbled. One woman claimed she had seen deputies on the roof lower Mays into the chimney with a rope.[14] At 7 P.M., a white man named Jeff Claiborne pushed his way to the front. Although he had already toured the cell block, he proposed that a search party composed of men who knew Mays by sight conduct yet another search. The mob cheered and began chanting, "tear down the jail." Rocks rained down, a deputy fired a warning shot, armed members of the mob fired back; the siege was underway. Two dozen men heaved an improvised battering ram into the iron door, which held, but then a stick of dynamite blew out a barred window. Men swarmed through the breach. Some tried to unlock the main door, others began battering the formidable interior doors sealing the cell blocks.[15]

The melee inside the jail masked the mob's disparate goals. Several cadres searched for Mays, scrutinizing every room and nook. Rioters poked through the coal bin and peered into the furnace boiler. Flashlights swept the roof, a man clambered up the chimney to look down the shaft. Prisoners in cells were questioned repeatedly: where is Mays? They gave the same answer that the deputies had. Meanwhile, looters and excitement-seekers mixed with the would-be lynchers. The mob ransacked Sheriff Cate's apartment inside the courthouse and looted the locker containing the prisoners' possessions. The discovery of twenty-five

[12] "Sheriff Cate Searches for Escaped Prisoners," *Knoxville Journal and Tribune,* September 1, 1919, 2; Lakin, "Dark Night," 11.

[13] "County Jail Wrecked by Mob in Frantic Search for Negro," *Knoxville Journal and Tribune,* August 31, 1919, 1.

[14] "Crowd Partly Wrecks Jail," *Knoxville Sentinel,* September 1, 1919, 12.

[15] "Crowd Partly Wrecks Jail" (quote); "County Jail Wrecked by Mob"; Testimony of Tom Day, *State vs. Martin Mays,* No. 509 (Supreme Court of Tennessee, Eastern Division, June 7, 1920), Transcript of Record, Knox County Archives, 18–21.

gallons of whiskey brought men running to the basement. Vandalism was rampant; rioters even smashed toilet bowls and ripped out water pipes.[16] For still other members of the mob, the riot offered an opportunity to carry out a different type of rough justice – the freeing of prisoners. Amid the looting, a dozen or so men toiled to break into the upper cell blocks, which housed white prisoners.[17] Jailer Earl Hall was certain these men had intended to mount a jail break all along, pointedly observing that no one tried to break into the cell block that housed black prisoners. Mays could not be hidden in a cell for whites without being easily spotted, so the men could not claim they were trying to find him.[18] When the locks were finally broken, grateful white prisoners abandoned their cells and blended into the throngs of rioters.

National Guard troops rushed into the city to break up the riot. Unlike Washington's and Chicago's officials, Knoxville authorities wasted no time deploying troops. Coincidentally, the all-white Tennessee Fourth Infantry was at nearby Camp Sevier. When news of the riot reached the encampment, the Fourth Infantry's commander, General E. B. Sweeney, mobilized 150 troops and arrived at the courthouse at 10 P.M. The crowd outside the jail booed as the soldiers forced their way into the jail. Rioters inside resisted the soldiers, who retreated. After warning that his men would open fire upon his order, Sweeney conceded the crowd's desire for rough justice. "I have as much respect for a white woman as any man in the south," he announced. "The negro who committed the murder this morning should be hanged. Hell is too good for him." But, he concluded, the judicial process had to be followed.[19]

Sweeney's appeal, backed by a second advance of his troops, ended the courthouse riot. By this time, approximately 11 P.M., the mob had achieved its aims. Would-be lynchers now knew that Maurice Mays was, in fact, gone; looters had stolen everything of value; vandals had wrecked all they could; and white prisoners had escaped. The mob's desire to inflict

---

[16] "Crowd Partly Wrecks Jail"; "12 Prisoners Are Liberated at Jail," *Knoxville Journal and Tribune*, September 1, 1919, 1; Testimony of William Cate, *State vs. Martin Mays*, 7–9.

[17] "Two of Fifteen Prisoners Who Escaped from County Jail Saturday Night Voluntarily Return," *Knoxville Sentinel*, September 1, 1919, 10; "Grand Jury To Take Action," *Knoxville Sentinel*, September 2, 1919, 1.

[18] "Damage to Jail May Be $15,000," *Knoxville Sentinel*, September 1, 1919, 11.

[19] "Crowd Partly Wrecks Jail" (quote); "Gov. Roberts Reviews Troops," *Knoxville Journal and Tribune*, August 30, 1919, 7; "Bloody Riots Follow Attack on Jail," *Knoxville Journal and Tribune*, August 31, 1919, 1.

violence remained unabated, however, as the black residents of Knoxville soon discovered.

Holding the Line at Vine and Central

Liston Dantzler, a young black man, had heard a rumor that a race riot was going to break out in Knoxville even before the storming of the courthouse. He did not let the gossip change his plans, though. That night he took his girlfriend to a dance, then went to the Bowery, the city's red-light district, to play craps. Around midnight, the sound of machine gun fire startled him and his fellow gamblers. Gunfire in this neighborhood was not altogether rare, but a machine gun? Dantzler could no longer ignore the day's excited chatter and tumult – a race riot had indeed broken out, right around him.[20]

Joe Etter was not surprised. Etter was a lean man with a carefully groomed mustache who owned a secondhand clothing store (Figure 5.1). A veteran of the Spanish-American War, Etter expected the mob to continue its rampage by attacking the city's black neighborhood, which was just blocks from the courthouse. He armed himself and waited, reputedly telling his young wife that if there was a race riot, he intended to be in the thick of it.[21]

He was not the only black resident of Knoxville to make – and keep – such a promise. Black men armed themselves and took up positions in alleys, stores, and residences. Dr. Joseph Carty, a white man who owned a drugstore in the Bowery, sensed a change in the typical Saturday scene. "As the evening advanced," Carty recalled, "I noticed that the feeling was growing in bitterness." Around 11 P.M., the first armed white men from the jailhouse mob arrived in the neighborhood. Shots rang out. Although Carty could not tell who fired first, he witnessed the swift response of black Knoxville's defenders: black men "poured down to the corner of Vine and Central from every direction... in a few minutes, there were more than a hundred of them, according to my calculations."[22] Other

---

[20] Liston Dantzler interview with Joe Crump, 1980, Knoxville, Tenn., Beck Cultural Exchange Center.

[21] Mary Etter interview with Ann Wilson, May 19–23, 1979, Beck Cultural Exchange Center; Lakin, "Dark Night," 17.

[22] "Eye-Witness Tells Story of Beginning of Race Riots," *Knoxville Journal and Tribune*, September 1, 1919, 2.

FIGURE 5.1. Portrait of Joe Etter. Joe Etter, a veteran of the Spanish-American War and the owner of a small business, lost his life during Knoxville's race riot. Reputedly, Etter died trying to prevent troops from the Tennessee Fourth Infantry, which had been ordered into the city to restore order, from firing on blacks. *Source:* Beck Cultural Exchange Center, Inc. Courtesy of the Beck Cultural Exchange Center, Inc.

black defenders stationed themselves at the Fifth Avenue bridge to prevent rioters from attacking from another side.[23]

Who were these men? Joe Etter was one, and he likely had fellow veterans as comrades-in-arms: approximately 400 black men from Knoxville and Knox County had served in the army during World War I, and many had seen action on the Western Front.[24] The use of barricades hints at

[23] "Boy Seriously Hurt by Bullets," *Knoxville Sentinel*, September 1, 1919, 11.
[24] "Negro Soldiers Parade Tuesday," *Knoxville Sentinel*, September 15, 1919, 13.

military training, while the defenders' familiarity with the buildings and
alleys of the neighborhood suggests that the men also came from the
ranks of clerks, cooks, and porters who worked in the Bowery. Many of
Knoxville's leading black men belonged to a gun club; is it possible they
mobilized, using their sport rifles and shotguns?[25] Whatever the identity
of Knoxville's black defenders, they held their ground.

White rioters came on foot and in cars, advancing down several streets.
As word spread that the black defenders were armed, whites broke into
shops and stole hundreds of rifles and handguns from five businesses.
(Late-arriving looters at the C. M. McClung Company had to settle for
knives and razors from the cutlery department.)[26] Still, whites failed to
penetrate the defensive cordon at Vine and Central. A white man fired
a revolver as he drove his vehicle straight at the barricade, but a return
fusillade forced him to veer away.[27]

The Fourth Infantry troops hurried from the county jail to Vine
Avenue, where they were met by rioters who claimed – untruthfully –
that armed black men were robbing white men. In a remarkable reversal,
whites fell in behind the guardsmen they had reviled earlier.[28] The rioters
now regarded the soldiers as allies who could help them attack blacks. The
Fourth's officers, intent on ousting black defenders from their positions,
did not disperse the vigilantes. As had happened in Charleston, Bisbee,
Washington, and Chicago, the line between rioters and peacekeepers had
disappeared, yet again forcing African Americans to confront multiple
enemies.

Blacks opened fire. By one account, "civilians and guardsmen kept up
their steady advance down Vine avenue." Return fire from the troops
and rioters forced the defenders to withdraw from Vine and Central to
windows and doorways. Guardsmen hurriedly assembled two machine

[25] Jeannine Hunter, "Gun Club Members May Have Joined in 1919 Race Riot," *Knoxville News-Sentinel*, February 12, 2003, clipping in the "Knoxville, TN, History, 1919–1939" Subject File, McClung Historical Collection.

[26] "Machine Guns Are Used by Soldiers to Quell Mob," *Knoxville Journal and Tribune*, August 31, 1919, 1; "Firearms in Stores Taken," *Knoxville Sentinel*, September 1, 1919, 13; Carson Brewer, "'Guest of Honor' Missed Knoxville's 1919 Racial Necktie Party," *Knoxville News-Sentinel*, March 11, 1979, C-4. There was only one reported instance of blacks looting a store for arms. See "Many Stores Looted by Mob," *Knoxville Journal and Tribune*, September 1, 1919, 1.

[27] "Two Killed in Street Battle," *Knoxville Sentinel*, September 1, 1919, 7; "Machine Guns Are Used."

[28] "Two Killed in Street Battle"; "Hold-Up Reports Start New Riot," *Knoxville Journal and Tribune*, August 31, 1919, 2.

gun nests on Vine as white rioters urged them to fire on a group of black men. Mistaking this encouragement as an order, two gunners opened fire, killing one of their own officers, Lieutenant James Payne.[29] As the soldiers and civilians advanced down Vine, Joe Etter strode toward them, firing his revolver. All his shots missed, but a rifle barrage killed him instantly. An infantry captain later said Etter was calm and deliberate, even unhurried, when he made his move.[30] According to Etter's widow Mary, however, the undertaker said her husband had been shot with a machine gun. Mary thus believed Etter had died storming the machine gun nest. After the accidental death of Lieutenant Payne, did the guardsmen spray the buildings on Vine with machine gun fire, prompting Etter's charge? Or did Etter die as the captain claimed, approaching the line of soldiers and civilians? Like the names of the boys in Jun Fujita's photographs of Chicago's riot or the identity of the man who sparked the shoot-out between police and black defenders in Washington, the answer remains elusive. Whatever his motive, Etter certainly knew the risks he was taking. That night, he had not just told Mary he was going to be in a race riot; he had also predicted he would die in it.[31]

Black self-defensive measures did not cease with Etter's death. For several hours, intermittent shooting between the troops, white civilians, and black men rang out. While the Fourth Infantry remained in the machine gun nests, white civilians scattered to alleys and doorways. Streetlights had been shot out, engulfing the area in darkness. Blacks regrouped on Vine and fired on a small crowd, prompting calls to storm their barricade. Officers scrambled to halt the civilians, pointing out the hazards of charging a fixed position in the dark. But more armed rioters were rushing to Vine, eager for action. As a reporter observed, "several civilians were handling their firearms carelessly and endangering the lives of the soldiers by shooting at every moving object." Some were drunk on the contraband whiskey seized during the jail riot. Realizing at last the danger posed by their civilian "reserves," army officers ordered troops to clear the streets. Additional guardsmen arrived from Camp Sevier, and by 3 A.M. the shooting had mostly ceased.[32]

[29] "Two Killed in Street Battle" (quote); "Officer's Death Was Accident," *Knoxville Journal and Tribune*, September 1, 1919, 2; "First Hit by Sniper's Shot," *Knoxville Journal and Tribune*, September 2, 1919, 2.

[30] "Two Killed in Street Battle"; "Negro Defied Death," *Knoxville Sentinel*, September 1, 1919, 7.

[31] Mary Etter interview.

[32] "Machine Guns in Main Battle of Riot" (quote) and "Police Arrest 16," *Knoxville Journal and Tribune*, September 1, 1919, 1–2.

Casualties were surprisingly few, given the number of shooters. Approximately 150 guardsmen and officers, accompanied by hundreds of white rioters, had confronted an estimated 100 blacks.[33] Yet only three men, including Lieutenant James Payne and Joe Etter, were killed. Twenty-two white civilians, all male, suffered gunshot wounds. One police officer and a deputy sheriff were also wounded. Only four black men were shot, though the figure may have been higher; newspapers based their figures on hospital records, so those who did not seek medical care for minor wounds were not included.[34] The dark streets and the use of cover by shooters likely helped reduce fatalities and injuries.

Daybreak found the black neighborhood around Vine and Central under virtual martial law, as hundreds of troops from the Tennessee Fourth Infantry set up checkpoints, patrolled, and disarmed black residents. Liston Dantzler had to work that morning; guardsmen stopped him twice to pat him down. He was lucky, in a way – another black man was searched seven times during a three-block walk. The soldiers stopped all African Americans, including women and children, even ministers hurrying to their churches. "The indignities which colored women suffered at the hands of these soldiers would make the devil blush for shame," fumed James Cary, the president of Knoxville's recently chartered NAACP branch. One guardsman unwrapped a loaf of bread to inspect it; another ordered a woman to open her umbrella. Streetcars were halted so passengers could be examined. Worried that blacks living outside of Knoxville might bring in arms, soldiers checked black passengers as they disembarked from trains. Guardsmen wounded three blacks who allegedly resisted searches. By Sunday evening, military authorities claimed to have confiscated more than 100 firearms from blacks. Cary vigorously disputed that assertion, contending that the soldiers found only pocket knives.[35]

In a now-familiar pattern, peacekeeping forces had wrongly blamed the latest outbreak of violence on blacks. The spillover of the courthouse

---

[33] "Machine Guns Are Used"; "Eye-Witness Tells Story."

[34] "Known Casualties," *Knoxville Journal and Tribune*, September 1, 1919, 1; Lakin, "Dark Night," 20.

[35] "118 Deputies as Patrolmen," "3rd Battalion Leaves Tonight," "Even a 'Rain Stick' Sometimes Suspicious," and "Law and Order Restored," *Knoxville Sentinel*, September 1, 1919, 1, 11–12, 14; "Situation Seems Under Control," "Negroes Searched As They Leave Trains," and "Four Negroes Are Wounded Resisting Search by Soldiers," *Knoxville Journal and Tribune*, September 1, 1919, 1–3; "Riot Arrests Begin," *Journal and Tribune*, September 2, 1919, 1; Liston Dantzler interview; James Cary to John Shillady, September 18, 1919, box G-198, folder "Knoxville, Tenn., 1915–1935," NAACP Records (quote).

riot to Vine and Central had presented black defenders with a potentially deadly dilemma: surrender to soldiers who were advancing alongside a mob or repel a combined force that seemed intent on killing them. Sunday's quarantine of Knoxville's black neighborhood was, in effect, an extension of the alliance between soldiers and white civilians. Although General Sweeney claimed that white men were also being searched, James Cary saw "low class white men" jeering blacks as they were being searched or even accosting them afterward without intervention from the guardsmen (Figure 5.2).[36]

The white press also blamed blacks for the second riot. The *Knoxville Journal and Tribune* pinned the shoot-out on "a riotous mob of negroes who were reported to have been spreading terror among whites in that section of the city." Newspapers outside of Tennessee took a similar line. The *New York Times* incorrectly blamed the looting of stores for arms on blacks; the *Omaha Bee* headlined its coverage, "Soldiers Turn Rapid Fire Gun on Blacks." Although Knoxville's white residents knew the weekend's troubles had begun with an attempted lynching at the county jail, fears of a black uprising gripped the city for days to come.[37]

In response to these fears, the city commission and Mayor John McMillan authorized the Knox County sheriff and city police to swear in 250 white men as special deputies and officers. Once again, white volunteers were being used as agents of law enforcement. The volunteers were issued firearms and authorized to patrol the streets outside of the zone controlled by the infantry troops. Most of the police volunteers remained in plain clothes – "secret service men," the *Knoxville Sentinel* dubbed them – so they could carry out their surveillance undetected. The police asked them to call in regularly, even if they spotted no trouble. Police dispatchers calmly told anxious citizens calling in reports of trouble that "we have a squad of men patrolling your district and they have just called and reported there is nothing to the rumor."[38] These patrols helped spread the view that black residents were responsible for the city's riot.

For New Negro writers, however, the Knoxville riot offered more proof of African Americans' readiness to take up arms in self-defense. As James Weldon Johnson put it, Knoxville demonstrated "a fact which has

---

[36] "Law and Order Restored"; Cary to Shillady, September 18, 1919.
[37] "Officer's Death Was Accident" (quote); "Troops Fight Race Rioters in Knoxville," *New York Times*, September 1, 1919, 1; "Soldiers Turn Rapid Fire Gun on Blacks," *Omaha Bee*, August 31, 1919, 1; Lakin, "Dark Night," 23.
[38] "250 Specials Patroling City," *Knoxville Journal and Tribune*, September 1, 1919, 3; "118 Deputies as Patrolmen" (quotes).

FIGURE 5.2. Tennessee Fourth Infantryman frisking a black man. African Americans' self-defense efforts during Knoxville's racial violence prompted white authorities to quarantine the black neighborhood and search all residents for weapons, as seen here. Invasive personal searches of women and children prompted a protest from the city's NAACP branch. *Source:* William J. MacArthur, *Knoxville: Crossroads of the New South* (Tulsa, Okla.: Continental Heritage Press, 1982). Courtesy of the East Tennessee Historical Society.

already been proclaimed to the country by the Washington and Chicago riots: The Negro will no longer allow himself to be mobbed free of cost. Those who indulge in mobbing him now and hereafter have got to pay the cost, and pay it in lives."[39] In the *Cleveland Gazette*, William Byrd praised Knoxville's black residents for making "a brave stand."[40] A black sailor expressed similar sentiment at a gathering in Montclair, New Jersey, much to the alarm of a listening Bureau of Investigation agent. Referring to Knoxville, the bluejacket declared that force had to be met with force. "This sentiment was approved by all present and is general among the Negro service men," the agent reported.[41]

The defensive stand mounted by Knoxville's black residents certainly offered evidence that white mobs, even those reinforced by armed troops, could not riot unchecked. By halting the mob at Vine and Central, black self-defenders undoubtedly protected the neighborhood and its residents from considerable property damage and physical harm. In the months to come, resistance to mob violence in Knoxville took on a new form: the struggle to ensure that Maurice Mays received a fair trial. Mays had escaped the lynch mob's noose, but he was brought back to Knoxville to be tried for the murder of Bertie Lindsey. Given the prejudicial atmosphere in the city against Mays, was it possible for him to receive a fair trial? In the aftermath of Knoxville's riot, Mays's adoptive parents and Knoxville's NAACP branch led a long, difficult campaign to see that Mays was not convicted of a crime he did not commit. That effort was only just underway when a courthouse riot that eerily resembled Knoxville's broke out in Omaha. Also at the center of this riot: a black man falsely accused of attacking a white woman.

The Origins of Omaha's Courthouse Riot

We do not know much about the life of Will Brown. He was born in the late 1870s or the early 1880s, place unknown. He likely received little schooling and went to work at a young age. An undated photograph catches him in a pensive pose, as if daydreaming, his lips pursed together, eyes aimed away from the camera's lens (Figure 5.3). We might be tempted to see a forlorn face, but his expression is inscrutable, ambiguous; above

---

[39] "More of the Fruits of Lawlessness," *New York Age*, September 6, 1919, 1.
[40] "The Tennessee Riot," *Cleveland Gazette*, September 20, 1919, 1.
[41] "In re: Negro Radical Activities in New York, N.Y.," September 1, 1919, RG 65, OGF 258,421, reel 672.

WILL BROWN, VICTIM OF MOB'S WRATH

FIGURE 5.3. Portrait of Will Brown, circa 1919. In the fall of 1919, laborer Will Brown was falsely accused of raping a young white woman, prompting an outbreak of antiblack collective violence in Omaha, Nebraska. *Source:* RG2467–8. Courtesy of the Nebraska State Historical Society.

all, private. In 1914, Brown was living in Cairo, Illinois, a hardscrabble town wedged between the Ohio and Mississippi Rivers. A few years later, the African American laborer made his way to Omaha, where he found work in the city's sprawling stockyards, possibly as a strikebreaker. By September 1919, he was living in South Omaha, close to the yards, in a ramshackle house he shared with Henry Johnson, also black, and Virginia Jones, a white woman.[42]

---

[42] For the photograph of Will Brown, see *Omaha's Riot in Story and Picture*. Brown's biographical sketch is drawn from "Officers Keep Mob Off Negro," *Omaha Bee*, September

About Tom Dennison we know much more, although the facts of his life are obscured by hazy legends of the Wild West. Dennison settled in Omaha in 1892, at the age of thirty-four, already a man of renown and wealth. As a teenager, he left the Nebraska farm of his Irish parents to rove the Great Plains and Western states. He husked corn in Iowa, blacksmithed in Kansas, prospected for gold in Colorado. It was said he shot a man in a mining camp. It was also said he orchestrated the train robbery of diamonds worth $15,000, but he beat those charges at trial. A big man, six feet tall and beefy, he operated several casinos in Colorado before coming to Omaha. His low voice commanded attention, as did his fashionable suits (adorned with diamond pins), and he had the cool, level gaze of the gambler who always wins. He quickly set up a lucrative numbers game in Omaha's Third Ward, teeming with saloons, brothels, and bought cops. A political operation followed, and, by the early 1900s, the "Gray Wolf" was reliably mobilizing ward-heelers, floaters, and ballot box stuffers to deliver electoral victories for the city's established Republican political machine. By 1918, however, even a boss as formidable as Dennison could not find shelter from the winds of Progressivism. A reform slate won office, and the new mayor, Edward Smith, directed his police commissioner to curtail vice and weed out corrupt cops.[43] From a saloon's backroom, Dennison plotted his comeback. His plan was simple, but it required patience. And a patsy. Preferably a man of few means and fewer friends, an itinerant laborer, say, or a strikebreaker who had just arrived in town; most importantly, a man with dark skin.

In the summer of 1919, Omaha, gateway to the West, was "a city in ferment." Years of growth had established it as an industrial center and pushed its population to 190,000. Omaha's packers slaughtered meat by the tons; the city's plants smelted iron, milled flour, brewed beer. Beginning in June, a series of strikes roiled the city. The Teamsters struck first, then streetcar workers and livestock handlers walked off their jobs. By September, railway workers and steam plant engineers had struck. Rising food prices and rents added further to the city's discontent, as did enforcement of Prohibition.[44]

The postwar turmoil presented both hazard and opportunity for black residents. Though an outlier on the path of the Great Migration, Omaha

27, 1919, 1; "Say Negro Lynched Had Trouble in Cairo," *Morning Omaha World-Herald* (hereafter *MOWH*), September 30, 1919, 1; Larsen and Cottrell, *Gate City*, 168.

[43] Davis, "Gray Wolf."

[44] Lawson, "Omaha, a City"; Larsen and Cottrell, *Gate City*, 127–44.

saw its African American population rise from 5,143 to 10,315 during the 1910s. By some measures, the black community was thriving: 100 black-owned businesses, twenty fraternal organizations, more than forty churches. The newly chartered NAACP branch had an active membership. The wartime boom had brought more jobs and higher wages, but the *Omaha Monitor*, the city's weekly black newspaper, worried that returning white veterans would oust blacks from their jobs.[45] For their part, unemployed white veterans resented the employment of blacks, while the hiring of black replacement workers agitated striking white workers. The actual number of black strikebreakers is difficult to determine – it may have been nominal – but white veterans and laborers believed that hundreds of black men were moving to Omaha to cross picket lines. "We are reliably informed that a carload of Negroes is again being imported from East St. Louis, in order to break [our] strike," declared a pamphlet distributed by the Teamsters in July. The next month, the *Omaha Bee* claimed that 500 blacks had just arrived to take the jobs of striking packinghouse workers.[46]

Meanwhile, vice and crime seemed to grow worse. Despite crackdowns, prostitution thrived. In August, two men murdered their families and took their own lives.[47] News of sexual assaults caused the most alarm. On March 15, 1919, the *Bee* reported the sexual assault of a white woman by a black man. It was, the newspaper asserted, the fifth such attack in a month.[48] By the summer, the *Bee* was publishing a lurid series of assault reports. Bessie Kroupa, nineteen, lashed to a tree in a vacant lot and raped by a black man. Margaret Larsen, eleven, bound and gagged by a black burglar. Anna Glassman, twelve, tied up in her home and sexually assaulted by a tall black man missing a hand – "One-Armed Negro Forces Way Into Home" read the *Bee*'s subhead.[49] By late September, the *Bee* had run stories about the assaults of twenty-one women, all white save one. Sixteen of the alleged assailants were identified as black. Omaha's other newspapers also reported the attacks, but none matched the *Bee* in the amount of copy and details. The *Bee* consistently identified the race of

---

[45] Age, "Omaha Riot," 6; Larsen and Cottrell, *Gate City*, 166–8; Lawson, "Omaha, a City," 412–13.

[46] Age, "Omaha Riot," 31–2 (quote); Lawson, "Omaha, a City," 398.

[47] Lawson, "Omaha, a City," 412.

[48] Age, "Omaha Riot," 21.

[49] "Unknown Negro Assaults Miss Bessie Kroupa," *Omaha Bee*, July 8, 1919, 4; "Negro Burglar Gags and Binds Margaret Larson," *Omaha Bee*, August 9, 1919, 1; "Attacks Child After Trying to Assault Woman," *Omaha Bee*, August 17, 1919, 1.

the attackers and victims, for example, while the *Omaha World-Herald* only did so in some articles.[50]

Tom Dennison had seen his opportunity and taken it. The *Bee*, with an estimated circulation of 63,000, was Omaha's Republican paper, and its publisher was close to Dennison.[51] After the war, a newly hired reporter learned the significance of this relationship when his editor assigned him to take a statement from Frank Johnson, a local Republican leader, and publish it as an article. "Mr. Dennison is interested in this story," instructed the editor, "and it is the policy of this paper to print whatever Mr. Dennison and Mr. Johnson want."[52] In order to discredit his political opponents, Mayor Smith and the police commissioner, Dennison now wanted a narrative in the *Bee* about black men slipping through windows like incubi to assault white women and girls while the police did nothing to stop the attacks.

The fictional content of the *Bee*'s "serial" is evident from several sources. Omaha's NAACP branch found attorneys for the accused rapists, investigated the alleged attacks, and attended court hearings. Branch secretary Jessie Hale-Moss soon detected a troubling pattern: "the victims do not in many cases know who their assailants are," yet the police were quick to arrest black men. Take the case of Anna Glassman, purportedly assaulted by the man missing a hand. The police presented numerous suspects to her – how many tall, one-handed black men lived in Omaha? – but Glassman did not identify any of them. Days later, she claimed to have seen her attacker on the street. The suspect, a railroad worker, had a rock-solid alibi: he had been repairing track 100 miles from Omaha when the alleged assault occurred. After a foreman presented stamped time books, the court released the man.[53] In another case, the police charged a black man with attacking four young white girls, none of whom identified the suspect.[54]

Who, then, was guilty of the assaults? In some instances, Dennison's men – in blackface. Years later, Tom Crawford, a Dennison operative,

---

[50] For comparison of the *Bee*'s and the *World-Herald*'s coverage of the alleged attacks, see Menard, "Tom Dennison," 157–8.

[51] For the *Bee*'s circulation figures, see Lawson, "Omaha, a City," 415 n. 1; for Dennison's friendship with the Rosewaters, see Menard, "Tom Dennison," 152–7.

[52] Menard, "Tom Dennison," 157.

[53] Jessie Hale-Moss to John Shillady, August 21, 1919, box G-113, folder "Omaha, Nebraska 1913–1922," NAACP Records (quote); "Race Strife in Omaha," *Branch Bulletin* vol. III, no. 10 (October 1919), 93.

[54] Age, "Omaha Riot," 29.

admitted that "most cases of attacks were blackened faces – by Dennison hoodlums – to cause a panic among the women for political purposes," that is, to cause trouble for Mayor Smith.[55] Hale-Moss and the NAACP branch suspected as much at the time. As early as April, an NAACP delegation met with Chief of Police Marshall Eberstein to protest his recent public statement that the city's "better class of Negroes" needed to expel criminals from the black community. Such comments exacerbated racial tensions, the delegation noted, adding that if the police did their job, then blacks would not need to "hunt down their criminals" anymore than whites would. And was it "not improbable that these crimes might have been committed by the members of either race, with black or blackened faces"?[56] Eberstein thought not, but that summer, the police arrested a young white man who had blackened his face before committing a crime. The *Omaha Monitor* rebuked the city's daily papers for failing to write about this racial subterfuge.[57]

The NAACP's and the *Monitor*'s observations gained no traction, and the *Bee* continued to churn out assault stories. The release of suspects due to the lack of evidence received scant coverage. "Since the Washington and Chicago riots we are having to fight a propaganda to discredit the Negro in this community," Hale-Moss informed the NAACP's national office. Repeated requests to Omaha's newspapers for balanced, factual coverage went unheeded. Still, Hale-Moss refused to give up. In August she asked the Chamber of Commerce to arrange a meeting with the newspapers' editors so she could present the evidence disproving the rape accusations. The Chamber of Commerce ignored her, too.[58]

As had happened in Washington, D.C., white veterans mobilized to "protect" white women. In mid-September, after another report of a black man sexually assaulting a white woman, Colonel Don Macrae, of Council Bluffs, Iowa (on the eastern side of the Missouri River, across from Omaha), organized a citizens' nighttime patrol; many of the fifty male volunteers had served under his command in France. Armed with shotguns, they had orders to "halt night prowlers." Days later, the *Bee* reported yet another assault: Mrs. Homer Hamey was attacked in her

---

55 Murphy (Tom Crawford's alias) to Roy N. Towl, August 16, 1932, box 2, folder "1932, August, City Hall," Roy Towl Papers, Nebraska State Historical Society Library/Archives.
56 *Branch Bulletin* vol. III, no. 4 (April 1919), 36.
57 Age, "Omaha Riot," 32–3.
58 Lawson, "Omaha, a City," 412–13; Hale-Moss to Shillady, August 21, 1919.

home, allegedly by the same black man who had tried to assault her six weeks earlier.[59]

Even with the *Bee*'s obliging coverage, Tom Dennison had not as yet succeeded in ruining the reformers. A series of *Bee* editorials demanded the firing of Police Commissioner J. Dean Ringer, but he remained on the job. Recall petitions for Mayor Smith had petered out.[60] So Dennison masterminded his most brazen frame-up. His recklessness almost ruined him, but, as he had so often done, the Gray Wolf emerged a winner. Others were not so lucky.

Sacrificing Will Brown

Thursday, September 25, just before midnight. Agnes Loebeck, nineteen, strolls with her twenty-two-year-old beau, Millard Hoffman, who, because of a crippled leg, uses a cane. Two blocks from Loebeck's home, in the South Omaha neighborhood of Gibson, a black man leaps from the road and presses a revolver into Hoffman's back. He empties Hoffman's pockets and demands Loebeck's ruby-studded ring. Then he prods them into a vacant lot. Sit down, he orders Hoffman. With his revolver trained on the young man, he drags Loebeck by her hair to a ravine fifty feet away, where he rapes her. While keeping his weapon pointed at Hoffman and covering Loebeck's mouth with his left hand. When he is finished, he carries Loebeck, sobbing, back to Hoffman. Stay here for ten minutes, he commands. Terrified, Loebeck and Hoffman remain still as ordered, then rush home.

Such were the *Bee*'s and the *World-Herald*'s details of a reported assault on a young white couple, Agnes Loebeck and Millard Hoffman, by the "Black Beast," as the *Bee* called the alleged assailant.[61] At word of the attack, armed white men scoured the streets and police searched freight cars in nearby rail yards. Loebeck described her attacker as a small man who might be hunchbacked, but no one fitting that description was found. On Friday, a neighbor of a white woman named Virginia Jones told police about "two suspicious-looking negroes" (Will Brown and Henry

---

[59] "Returned Army Men to Protect Bluffs' Women," *Omaha Bee*, September 15, 1919, 3; "After Six Weeks Negro Again Tries to Assault Woman," *Omaha Bee*, September 20, 1919, 1.

[60] Lawson, "Omaha, a City," 396.

[61] "Negro Assaults Young Girl While Male Escort Stands by Powerless to Aid Her," *Omaha Bee*, September 26, 1919, 1–2; "Escort Held at Bay as Girl Assaulted," *MOWH*, September 26, 1919, 1; "Take 45 Negroes in Roundup After Attack on Girl," *Evening Omaha World-Herald* (hereafter *EOWH*), September 26, 1919, 1.

Johnson) who lived with Jones. When police entered the house, they claimed to find Will Brown huddled beneath his bed, a gun in hand. Brown was not hunchbacked, but the two officers presented him to Loebeck. "Yes, he is the man!" she reportedly exclaimed. "Take him away. The sight of him has been haunting me since he stopped me on the street and dragged me into the clump of weeds." Hoffman responded with similarly stilted language: "There is not the least bit of doubt but what he is the negro that assaulted Agnes."[62] Outside the Loebeck residence, hundreds of white men and women demanded rough justice. "We'll take care of this one!" cried one woman. "The courts won't punish him – we will!" shouted a man. Two hundred white railroad workers, wielding picks and clubs, hurried from the Union Pacific shops to join the mob, but a patrol car had already whisked Brown to jail. Members of the mob continued to declare their intent to use vigilantism to stop the wave of assaults.[63]

Will Brown asserted his innocence, but his housemates – whom the police had also arrested – declined to provide him with an alibi. Virginia Jones and Henry Johnson claimed that they were at the movies on Thursday night, and that Brown, who was not home until after midnight, seemed agitated when he came in. After booking Brown, police transported him to the jail in the Douglas County Courthouse in downtown Omaha, and the county attorney, Abel Shotwell, charged him with criminal assault.[64] Because the next day was Saturday, Shotwell had to wait until Monday to put Brown before a grand jury. That gave Millard Hoffman and his benefactor ample opportunity to hold Will Brown accountable in their own way.

From the start, certain details of the attack on Hoffman and Loebeck seemed improbable. How could a hunchbacked man carry out the assault with one hand clamped over his victim's mouth and the other aiming a revolver at her boyfriend fifty feet away?[65] Did the weapon not waver *once*; why did Hoffman not do *something*? Loebeck addressed these

---

[62] "Negro Assaults"; "Officers Keep Mob" ("suspicious-looking" quote); Age, "Omaha Riot," 38; "Forty Vagrants Shipped Out of Omaha on Train," *EOWH*, September 27, 1919, 1 (Loebeck's and Hoffman's quotes).

[63] "Officers Keep Mob"; "Negro Identified by Agnes Lobeck Nearly Lynched," *MOWH*, September 27, 1919, 1.

[64] "Negro Identified"; "Officers Keep Mob"; Age, "Omaha Riot," 41.

[65] According to the Military Intelligence Division, the attack on Loebeck lasted about fifteen minutes. See Intelligence Officer, Fort Omaha, to Department Intelligence Officer, Chicago, October 27, 1919, Case File 10218–371–11, RG 165, copy in box 1, reel 6, Kornweibel Papers.

questions in a statement to reporters. "I know Millard wanted to help me," she said, but he could not move for fear of getting shot. Also, "I did not want him to lose his life, for he is a cripple."[66] Hoffman's handicap was the key to making the alleged attack sound plausible. If the young man used a cane, how could he have rushed to Loebeck's rescue? Yet Hoffman was not quite as impaired as the newspapers implied. Indeed, he resented being described as a cripple. In his own telling, he fell as a toddler and broke one leg, which grew shorter than the other limb. He wore a leg brace and a shoe with a lift, causing a limp, but he did not need a cane.[67] Misrepresentation of his condition may have rankled Hoffman, but not Tom Dennison – it only made the story better.

For Dennison and Hoffman knew each other well. Aided by his cousin, a ward heeler, Hoffman had obtained work as Dennison's secretary a few years earlier. He also had pitched in during political campaigns and had voted illegally (he was not then of age) for Dennison candidates.[68] Although Hoffman now worked as a clerk for the Otis Elevator Company, he remained loyal to Dennison. His disability, if exaggerated – recall the *Bee*'s policy to "print whatever Mr. Dennison" wanted – made Hoffman an ideal figure around whom to fabricate a sexual assault. In an apparent attempt to conceal his connections to Dennison, Hoffman gave his first name as Millard and his address as 1923 S. 13th Street. The city directory listed no "Millard Hoffman," however, and the address was either a vacant lot or an abandoned home. But "Milton Hoffman" resided at 1952 S. 13th Street and worked for the Otis Company.[69] The different names are not attributable to a reporter's error, for "Millard," who was quoted in several articles printed after the alleged attack, never offered a correction, and Loebeck called him Millard, as noted. Although Will Brown had no alibi, there were no other witnesses to the attack – only the word of Loebeck and Hoffman put him at the scene.[70]

Hoffman's word was sufficient bond for white residents of South Omaha. On Saturday, September 27, police broke up an incipient mob

[66] "Escort Held."

[67] Hoffman told this story to Orville D. Menard in a 1979 interview. See Menard, "Tom Dennison," 165 n. 54.

[68] Menard, "Tom Dennison," 161.

[69] Davis, "Gray Wolf," 51–2 n. 109.

[70] Orville D. Menard, the leading scholar on Tom Dennison and Omaha politics during this era, concludes that Brown's innocence or guilt "remains unknown." See Menard, "Lest We Forget," 163. It is my belief, however, that the evidence strongly indicates Brown's innocence.

PART OF MOB ON SOUTH SIDE OF COURT HOUSE ABOUT 5:30 P. M.

FIGURE 5.4. Mob outside the Douglas County Courthouse. On September 28, 1919, part of this mob stormed the courthouse in downtown Omaha where Will Brown was being held. The dangling ropes were used to scale the building and break through windows. The mob also lit fires before seizing Brown to lynch him. *Source:* RG2467–5. Courtesy of the Nebraska State Historical Society.

outside of a school. Undeterred, young white men spread the word to assemble the next day to lynch Brown.[71] Around 1 P.M. on Sunday, fifty or so men and boys began amassing on the school grounds. Excited and boisterous, the mob set out toward the courthouse, one mile north. Passers-by, male and female, joined them, swelling the mob to 300. And at the head of the mob marched Milton Hoffman, who reputedly waved a revolver and shouted, "follow me." By four o'clock, the mob had arrived at the south side of the stone courthouse, at 17th and Harney Streets (Figure 5.4).[72] Just seven years old, the Douglas County Courthouse was a formidable structure to besiege. Atop a hill, it occupied a square block,

[71] Grand Jury Final Report, November 19, 1919, District Court Journal 176, Douglas County Courthouse, Omaha, Nebraska, 286–7.
[72] Colonel A. L. Dade to Commanding General, Central Department, October 15, 1919, box 5, folder "Omaha, Neb. (Race Riots)," RG 60, Glasser File; Grand Jury Final Report, 287; Case File 10218–371–11; "Frenzied Thousands Join in Orgy of Blood and Fire," *MOWH*, September 29, 1919, 1; "Colored Assailant of Agnes Loebeck Pays for His Crime," *Omaha Bee*, September 29, 1919, 2 (quote).

and the jail that Brown was held in was on the fourth floor, the building's highest.

Thirty policemen stood guard. Initially, there was no confrontation; some members of the mob even bantered with the policemen. Then auto mechanic J. L. Thomas began berating the officers for being part of a broken justice system. "When a negro does get arrested for assaulting a woman, all he gets is sixty days. Take off your badges, you cops," Thomas demanded, calling on them to join the mob. His pointed challenge pierced the fragile racial affinity keeping the peace. Forced to choose between rough justice and their sworn duty, the officers opted for the latter. "You are not judge and jury," responded a sergeant, and that was all the answer the vigilantes needed.[73]

The mob rushed forward, punching and kicking two policemen, who managed to escape into the courthouse. Bricks hurtled through windows, raining down broken glass. Police on an upper floor trained fire hoses on the mob, forcing a temporary retreat, but the volley of bricks and stones continued, aided by two young women who collected projectiles from a vacant lot. Two boys used a ladder to reach the third floor – "Hang the nigger!" one of the boys yelled repeatedly from his perch. On the courthouse's north side, another mob used a battering ram to break through doors. Police opened fire, but a vanguard of dozens was already inside the building. As twilight approached, a contingent of forty policemen, Sheriff Michael Clark, and several of his deputies prepared to defend the jail, which held Will Brown and 125 other prisoners. Chief Eberstein, Police Commissioner Ringer, and Mayor Smith were also inside the building. A gun battle forced the defenders to retreat to the third and fourth floors. Although only about 200 people were actively taking part in the siege, a crowd estimated at between 15,000 and 20,000 had filled the surrounding streets. Overwhelmed, the police did not attempt to disperse the onlookers. As the mob set fire to the first floor, the crowd roared its approval.[74]

The spreading fire compelled the defenders to seek shelter. Sheriff Clark took much-needed charge. Instructing his deputies to protect Brown, he unlocked cells and ordered everyone, including the prisoners, to the roof. Swirling smoke and bullets fired from neighboring buildings made the

---

[73] "Mob in Omaha Lynches Negro," *MOWH*, September 29, 1919, 2.

[74] "Mob in Omaha"; Case File 10218–371–11, 2; "Mob Jeers as County Structure Is Burning," *Omaha Bee*, September 29, 1919, 1; "Boy, 12, Denies Was Member of the Mob," *MOWH*, October 2, 1919, 11; "55 Held by Police as Mob Heads," *Omaha Bee*, October 1, 1919, 1 (quote).

roof just as dangerous as the interior. "We didn't ever expect to get out of there alive," Chief Eberstein recalled.[75] Mayor Smith returned to the first floor, intending to ask the mob to allow firemen inside, but rioters seized him. When he warned that federal troops would be called in, a peddler named George Davis knocked him unconscious. His attackers almost lynched him – a noose around his neck, Smith was hoisted to a streetcar signal tower – but a man named Russell Norgaard was credited with saving the mayor by loosening the rope and rushing him to a police car.[76]

Will Brown was not so fortunate. Just as his biography is mostly a mystery, so, too, are the details of his last moments, told only by others, whose recollections vary widely. Sheriff Clark described Brown as hysterical, crying out, "I am innocent, I never did it, my God, I never did it"; according to another account, Brown was calm and quiet, even helping to rescue five men trapped in the jail's laundry. The capture of Brown was also disputed. Eberstein said that a mob came up to the roof to seize Brown, while an unnamed rioter claimed that he hurled Brown out of a window. In the *Omaha World-Herald*'s telling, rioters took Brown out of his cell.[77]

A. J. Rhodes described what next happened as "the most terrible sight in my life." The young white man was returning from the movies with friends when they came across the riot. They watched a mob drag Will Brown to a light pole at 18th and Harney Streets, then "saw the negroe's body slowly rise through the air, while the mob poured bullets into his lifeless body. His arms hung grotesquely at his side and his limbs dangled in a most inhuman way."[78] After cutting Brown down, the lynchers dragged his corpse to a kerosene-soaked pyre of railroad ties and scrap lumber. The rope was cut into pieces sold for a dime each. After the fire died out, a news photographer captured an image of dozens of white men,

---

[75] "Sheriff Clark Tells Story of How Negro Prisoner Is Turned Loose to Lynchers," *Omaha Bee*, September 29, 1919, 2; "Mob Rushed by in Dense Smoke," *MOWH*, September 29, 1919, 2 (quote).

[76] "Mayor Caught by Mob and Hanged to Traffic Tower," *MOWH*, September 29, 1919, 1; "Lynching Committee of 30 Receives Will Brown from Other Court House Prisoners," *Omaha Bee*, September 29, 1919, 1; "Dramatic Story of Attack at Riot," *Omaha Bee*, December 16, 1919, 1; Menard, "Tom Dennison," 159–60.

[77] "Brown Frantic as Mob Congregates" (quote) and "Negroes Shoved Brown Into Mob," *MOWH*, September 29, 1; "Negro Calm as Mob Leaders Dragged Him Out to Death," *EOWH*, September 29, 1919, 1; "Mob Rushed by"; "Says Note from Jail Called Mob Upstairs," *EOWH*, September 29, 1919, 11.

[78] A. J. "Jack" Rhodes, diary entry, September 28, 1919, copy provided by Jean Crane to the Douglas County Historical Society, June 25, 2005. I am grateful to Orville D. Menard for sharing his research notes, which included information on this diary.

BURNING of BROWN'S BODY   RIOT OF SEPT. 28, 1919

FIGURE 5.5. Burning of Will Brown's body. Members of the mob burned and des-ecrated the body of Will Brown after he was lynched. These onlookers' expressions project defiance, pride, and excitement. Gordon X. Richmond was just fourteen when he pushed forward through the crowd (background right). More than a half-century later, he said, "I was nauseated by the sight and had nightmares for years afterward." *Source:* RG2281–69. Courtesy of the Nebraska State Historical Society.

several women, and a boy named Gordon X. Richmond crowded around Will Brown's charred body (Figure 5.5). Their faces project defiance, pride, curiosity, excitement. More than fifty years later, Richmond, only fourteen when he was photographed peering between the shoulders of two men, said, "I was nauseated by the sight and had nightmares for years afterward."[79] For Omaha's black residents, the nightmare had already started.

[79] "Colored Assailant of Agnes Loebeck Pays for His Crime," *Omaha Bee*, September 29, 1919, 2; "Mob in Omaha"; James Fogarty, "Face in a Photograph Sparks Mob Memory," *MOWH*, May 24, 1972 (quote).

Defending against the Mob

Emboldened by the courthouse siege, white men had begun assaulting African Americans downtown hours before the lynching. Around 5 P.M., a group of boys and men attacked a black man walking a few blocks from the courthouse. "I ain't done nothing," he protested as the rioters shoved and punched him. A uniformed white soldier and a boxer named Johnny Lee pulled the man to safety. "You don't want to hang an innocent man, do you?" Lee berated the rioters. A white youth jumped aboard a streetcar to beat a black passenger, one of several such attacks.[80] One mob almost lynched a black man outside the Omaha National Bank at 7 P.M., but police, aided by a few onlookers, rescued him. Two hours later, another mob chased a black man into an abandoned foundry. Armed with a revolver, he managed to keep the mob at bay until police arrived and rescued him.[81]

For their safety, Omaha's African American residents did not merely rely on the protection of police and white onlookers. Some blacks drove to Council Bluffs to shelter with its black community.[82] Many African Americans who remained in Omaha armed themselves. As had happened throughout 1919, the police treated these self-defensive measures as crimes. A taxi driver carrying a gun was jailed for possessing a concealed weapon.[83] When a teenager named Lester Price drew a gun aboard a streetcar to fend off attackers, the police arrested him.[84] At least four other black men faced concealed weapons charges. When a local white leader asked Reverend John Williams, the NAACP branch president, to urge black residents to stay home, Williams responded that they had no intention of hiding from mobs and were ready to defend themselves.[85] Will Brown's lynchers received this message, too. Some planned to drag

---

[80] "Frenzied Thousands Join in Orgy of Blood and Fire," *EOWH*, September 29, 1919, 2 (quotes); "Colored Assailant"; "Mob in Omaha"; "Omaha Scene of Latest Mob Exploit," *New York Age*, October 4, 1919, 1.

[81] "Lynching from Start to Finish," *EOWH*, September 29, 1919, 3; "Mob Enters Gun Stores to Secure Firearms," *Omaha Bee*, September 29, 1919, 2.

[82] "Bluffs Police Held Ready for Quick Call," *MOWH*, September 29, 1919, 3.

[83] M. Andreasen to Samuel McKelvie, November 19, 1919, box 1, folder 6, Samuel R. McKelvie Papers, Nebraska State Historical Society Library/Archives.

[84] "Nine More Rioters Indicted," *Omaha Bee*, October 24, 1919, 1; "Nine More Indicted by Special Grand Jury," *MOWH*, October 24, 1919, 1.

[85] "Seventy Five Men Held on Riot Charge," *MOWH*, October 2, 1919, 2; "55 Held by Police as Mob Heads"; "Negroes Urge Own Race to Stay Home," *EOWH*, September 29, 1919, 11.

Brown's body to 24th and Lake Streets, the center of Omaha's black community, but a young white man dissuaded them. "Those negroes there are all armed," he shouted.[86] According to the *Chicago Whip*, another mob abandoned its aim of storming the home of Police Commissioner Ringer when its leaders realized that they would need to march through a black neighborhood. Rumors of a counterattack by blacks, however, proved false. In fact, some black men were calling police precincts to ask if they could volunteer to help restore order. "Not on your life," a police captain told them. Undeterred, twenty-eight black veterans patrolled predominantly black residential areas on the north and south sides of Omaha that night.[87]

As Omaha's black residents did what they could to protect themselves, city officials implored Lieutenant Colonel Jacob Wuest, the commanding officer of nearby Fort Omaha, to intervene. Wuest responded in a plodding, legalistic manner, telling callers to contact the War Department in Washington. According to the 1878 Posse Comitatus Act, federal troops could not be used in domestic disturbances unless the president first received a formal request for their deployment, but the War Department had since granted commanding officers the discretion to act if delay might result in deaths and property destruction. Wuest thus had the power to dispatch troops, but he was either unaware of this authority or did not want to use it.[88]

Wuest did order his forces to prepare for riot duty, and he instructed two officers already at the courthouse to round up all uniformed soldiers and bring them back to Fort Omaha. This action stopped active-duty servicemen from joining the mob, but it also removed potential peacekeepers from the riot zone.[89] Meanwhile, Lieutenant Governor P. T. Barrows – Governor Samuel McKelvie was not in Lincoln, the capital, that day – frantically cabled Secretary of War Newton Baker: "RACE RIOT IN OMAHA COURT HOUSE BEING TORN DOWN POLICE FORCE INADEQUATE

---

[86] "Omaha Mob Hangs and Burns Negro Who Assaulted Girl," *Omaha Bee*, September 29, 1919, 1.

[87] "Mob Rule in Omaha – Mayor Hung," *Chicago Whip*, October 4, 1919, 1; "Mob in Omaha"; "Many Volunteer to Help Police," *MOWH*, September 29, 1919, 1 (quote); "Colored Members of Legion Pledge Selves to Aid Law Enforcement," *MOWH*, October 11, 1919, 7.

[88] Laurie, "U.S. Army," 135–8; Dade to Commanding General, October 15, 1919, 3; Lt. Col. Jacob Wuest to Commanding General, Central Department (Leonard Wood), October 2, 1919, Case File 10218–371–4, RG 165, copy in box 1, reel 6, Kornweibel Papers.

[89] Case File 10218–371–4.

NO STATE TROOPS GOVERNOR CANNOT BE REACHED." At 10:45 P.M., after the mob had almost killed Mayor Smith, Baker ordered Wuest to move in.[90]

The troops had a salutary effect. Major H. C. White, commanding the Twenty-seventh Balloon Company (an observation unit that used hot-air balloons), had no trouble breaking up the lingering crowds, though he did report sporadic shots and roving groups of looters. After hearing rumors that a mob intended to invade Omaha's black neighborhood, Wuest ordered the Seventeenth Balloon Company and 100 additional troops to the area. Other than occasional gun shots, the neighborhood was peaceful. By 2 A.M., Wuest reported, the mob was "well dispersed" and "the city was generally quiet."[91]

The next day, Monday, September 29, Wuest declared that the riot had ended and asked city residents to turn in their weapons to the police or his troops. At noon the city's acting mayor, W. G. Ure, ordered residents to stay off the streets. "There is danger in congregating in crowds at this time," he advised. "Avoid it." To prevent additional lynchings, deputy sheriffs and plainclothes police spirited twenty-two black prisoners out of Omaha in two army trucks. Most of the prisoners had been on the courthouse roof during the riot; two had minor wounds. By dusk, Wuest had 800 troops patrolling four zones throughout the city. The soldiers had the authority to stop and search vehicles and pedestrians.[92]

Although authorities had rebuffed black men's offer to help restore order, Wuest asked the city's white veterans to volunteer for peace-keeping duty. Hundreds, many in uniform, rushed to city hall. They were deputized, armed, and sent downtown to patrol and to guard the gutted, smoldering courthouse. "Our training may make us particularly valuable and we will do our part," said American Legion chapter president Allan Tukey.[93] Like the use of Bisbee's Citizen's Protective League

---

[90] Laurie, "U.S. Army," 138–40; Case File 10218–371–4; P. A. Barrows to the Secretary of War, September 28, 1919, box 5, folder "Omaha, Neb. (Race Riots)," RG 60, Glasser File (quote).

[91] Case File 10218–371–4, 3. For details of the troops' deployment, see Laurie, "U.S. Army," 139.

[92] "Proclamation by Colonel Wuest" and "Orders People Off the Street," *MOWH*, September 30, 1919, 6 (quote); "Negroes in Jail Taken to State Penitentiary," *MOWH*, September 30, 1919, 7; "Omaha Prisoners Silent in Penitentiary," *EOWH*, September 30, 1919, 5; "Omaha Quiet with Troops on Guard," *MOWH*, September 30, 1919, 1.

[93] "Enrolling Former Soldiers for Duty," *MOWH*, September 30, 1919, 1; "City Seeks 500 Men for Special Service," *EOWH*, September 29, 1919, 15 (quote); Wood to War Department, October 5, 1919, Wood to Commanding General, Headquarters General

to deport striking miners in 1917 and the deployment of Washington's Home Defense League in July 1919, the deputization of white members of Omaha's American Legion demonstrated yet again the readiness of government officials to erase the line between law enforcement and voluntary organizations.

And just as in Knoxville, black residents bore the brunt of disarmament and riot prevention as police and troops treated black self-defenders as criminals. "It was well known that the negroes of Omaha were thoroughly armed and prepared to meet any attacks that might be made upon them," asserted an army officer. "They were much excited by the lynching of Brown and were anticipating demonstrations by the mob in the quarter of the city in which most of them lived."[94] On Monday afternoon, police arrested George Harris for exhorting fellow blacks to arm themselves. That evening, soldiers detained twenty-five armed black men in plainclothes. The men, who wore special police badges, protested that Police Commissioner Ringer had sworn them in, but the soldiers disarmed them anyway.[95] A similar incident occurred when two black veterans picketed white-owned stores in the black neighborhood. They were disarmed and forced to give up their uniforms. The soldiers also took the weapons of two other black veterans involved in an argument with several white pedestrians.[96]

Black Omahans had a mixed response to the white troops. Some initially believed that the soldiers had orders to kill them, but others expressed gratitude for the protection. One man even slept at the garage where he worked because it was close to the soldiers' quarters.[97] Jessie Hale-Moss reported that tensions were high, but "our people thus far have held themselves in leash."[98] Reverend John Williams welcomed the troops but pointedly reminded everyone why soldiers now patrolled the city's streets: "The colored citizens of Omaha took no part in Sunday night's orgy. They wisely remained at home, prepared to defend their homes and loved ones to the last ditch. They will be found on the side of law and

Department, October 23, 1919, box 5, folder "Omaha, Neb. (Race Riots)," RG 60, Glasser File.

94 Dade to Commanding General, October 15, 1919, 4.
95 "Negro Specials Lose their Guns," *MOWH*, September 30, 1919, 1; "55 Held by Police."
96 Lt. O. W. Neidert to Director of Military Intelligence, October 16, 1919, Case File 10218–371–10, RG 165, copy in box 1, reel 6, Kornweibel Papers, 2; "Mayor Recovering from Riot Injuries," *Omaha Bee*, September 30, 1919, 1.
97 Case File 10218–371–10, 1.
98 Hale-Moss to Mary White Ovington, October 2, 1919, Waskow Notes, tab "Omaha Result."

SOLDIERS ON GUARD AT TWENTY-FOURTH AND LAKE STREETS
(Machine gun at left and one-pound cannon at right)

FIGURE 5.6. Soldiers on guard duty in North Omaha. Army troops quelled Omaha's race riot and prevented further violence, but, like the soldiers mobilized in Knoxville, they also disarmed African Americans who carried weapons to defend themselves. In one instance, they seized weapons from two black veterans and forced them to give up their uniforms. *Source:* RG2467–17. Courtesy of the Nebraska State Historical Society.

order and only ask that they be protected."[99] The presence of troops (Figure 5.6), combined with the cooperation of black residents, made additional rioting unlikely, but Major General Leonard Wood thought that he should see for himself.

As commander of the U.S. Army's Central Department, Wood presided over a fifteen-state zone stretching from West Virginia to Colorado. A physician and a lifelong army man, Wood was self-assured and ambitious. Hoping to secure the Republican nomination for president in 1920, Wood had been lining up supporters and currying favor with powerful Republicans since the war's end. He was on a speaking tour of the Dakotas that weekend but rushed to Omaha after learning about the riot. The general arrived exuding the omnipotence of a czar and the opportunism of a candidate. In a proclamation "To the Citizens of Omaha," he

[99] "Asserts Police Did Not Try to Disperse Mob," *Omaha Bee*, September 30, 1919, 8.

banned public gatherings and the carrying of weapons. He authorized the forces from Fort Omaha, now bolstered by troops from camps in Iowa, Illinois, and Kansas, to assist the police in making arrests. With order already restored, this imposition of partial martial law was both unnecessary and legally dubious. Wood also endorsed Wuest's use of deputized, armed white veterans, telling them that their "orders were to be carried out regardless of consequences in case of any disturbance."[100]

When additional disturbances did not occur, Wood ordered the troops and veterans to track down Sunday night's rioters. Using newspaper photographs, including the picture of the men and women crowded around Will Brown's corpse, soldiers and legion members detained scores of rioters. Although Wood lacked the explicit authority to use his soldiers and volunteers as a police force, Douglas County Attorney Shotwell welcomed the arrests: because the military had custody of the suspects, they could be held without bail while he prepared to bring the cases before a grand jury.[101] In effect, Wood and Shotwell had suspended habeas corpus.

By Thursday, October 2, the general had expanded his authority and influence even further. As if he had been appointed police commissioner, he advised the city council to add 100 new police officers and promised to procure military weapons for the force.[102] In a campaign-like address, Wood blamed Omaha's troubles on radical forces: "We've got to stamp out bolshevism and anarchy like we would a snake." Wood knew well that racial hatred, rough justice, and inflammatory press coverage of alleged black crime had led to the riot. Although he criticized "sensational newspapers," he hinted that he meant the radical press, not papers like the *Bee*: "Free speech, yes, but not free treason."[103] Blaming labor activists and anarchists for Omaha's riot did not fit the facts, but, as historian Clayton Laurie notes, "combating anti-radicalism was more popular and politically expedient than charging whites with the lynching murders of

---

[100] "Military Proclamation to the People of Omaha," *MOWH*, October 1, 1919, 1; Laurie, "U.S. Army," 139–40; Leonard Wood Diary, entries for September 28 to October 1, 1919, box 12, folder "Diary Jan. 1 – Dec. 31, 1919," Leonard Wood Papers, Library of Congress (quote).

[101] "Officials Tighten Coils of Law Around Those Who Were Implicated in Riots," *Omaha Bee*, October 4, 1919, 2; Laurie, "U.S. Army," 141; Dade to Commanding General, October 15, 1919.

[102] "City to Reorganize Police Department," *MOWH*, October 3, 1919, 6.

[103] "General Wood Tells of Bolshevism Peril," *MOWH*, October 4, 1919, 4 (quotes); "Seventy-Five Men Held on Riot Charges," *MOWH*, October 2, 1919, 2; Wood Diary, entries for October 2–3, 1919.

blacks and the destruction of public property."[104] Shifting the blame to radicals also helped Wood expound upon the central theme of his campaign, 100 percent Americanism.[105]

Wood left Omaha on Sunday, October 5; most of the troops soon followed. All told, more than 1,200 soldiers and almost 70 officers had served on riot duty. Before his departure, Wood thanked white veterans. "The work done by you and your associates has been a very real service in the maintenance of law and order," he told Allan Tukey. Expressing support for continued paramilitary voluntarism, Wood declared that every American Legion chapter should organize "platoons" to help civil authorities maintain the peace.[106] His praise demonstrated just how commonplace use of white volunteers had become. In Bisbee and Knoxville, armed white men had essentially deputized themselves, falling in with deputies (in Bisbee) and troops (in Knoxville) who did not turn them away. In Washington, the chief of police had deputized the Home Defense League, but General William Haan had made no effort to use these volunteers. Now Wood, one of the army's highest ranking officers, was actively calling for the *expansion* of paramilitary voluntarism – but only for whites.

The crowds who stormed courthouses in Knoxville and Omaha were lynch mobs. Riots resulting from mobs attempting to carry out rough justice were not uncommon before or after 1919, but three features make the Knoxville and Omaha riots notable. One, the mobs expanded the riots to target *all* blacks; two, black residents responded with armed resistance, even if that meant, as it did in Knoxville, confronting infantry troops; and three, black defenders were treated as criminals. This was, as seen in the previous sites of racial violence and black armed resistance, a prominent pattern throughout the year. In Omaha, the deployment of armed white veterans and the harassment of black veterans who attempted to serve as peacekeepers demonstrated another pattern: racial segregation of

---

[104] Laurie, "U.S. Army," 142.

[105] Wood defined "100 percent Americanism" as exclusive use of the English language, rejection of communism, devotion to law and order, and civic duty. See Leonard Wood, "Americanism," n.d., from "American Leaders Speak: Recordings from World War I and the 1920 Election, 1918–1920," Library of Congress, American Memory, accessed August 10, 2011 <http://memory.loc.gov/ammem/nfhtml/nfhome.html>.

[106] Laurie, "U.S. Army," 142; Wood to the Adjutant General, Army, October 6, 1919, Case Files 10218–371–6 and 10218–371–7, RG 165, copies in box 1, reel 6, Kornweibel Papers; Wood to Alan Tukey, October 4, 1919, box 118, folder "1919," Leonard Wood Papers (quote).

paramilitary voluntarism. Fortunately for Omaha's black residents, the armed volunteers did not turn their weapons on them.

That was not the case in the final three outbreaks of antiblack collective violence in 1919. These riots, which are treated in the next chapter, starkly exposed the dangers of allowing armed, deputized volunteers to carry out law enforcement duties. In all three places – Phillips County, Arkansas; Gary, Indiana; and Bogalusa, Louisiana – white vigilantes helped law officers and federal or state troops arrest or attack blacks. Consistent with the year's armed resistance, African Americans in all three places defended themselves in a multitude of ways. But the price paid was high, especially in Arkansas.

6

Armed Resistance to Economic Exploitation in Arkansas, Indiana, and Louisiana

Three riots closed out the year of racial violence. Two occurred in the South, the other in the upper Midwest. The riots shared a significant trait: the violence directed against African Americans originated in the exploitation of agricultural or industrial laborers. To be precise, the violence was a response to black-led or biracial resistance to economic exploitation. In late September, a coalition of white businessmen and planters moved to destroy a newly formed black sharecroppers' union in Phillips County, Arkansas. The sharecroppers' armed resistance resulted in a pogrom with a death toll that rivaled – most likely even exceeded – that of Chicago's. In October, black workers in Gary, Indiana, refused to be scapegoated during a massive strike that idled the city's steel mills and factories. Meanwhile, in Bogalusa, Louisiana, black lumber workers joined forces with their white co-workers to fight for improved conditions and wages.

In all three places, corporate and municipal authorities used armed vigilantes to suppress laborers' efforts to improve their economic standing. In Arkansas, U.S. Army troops joined force with these vigilantes. In Gary, federal troops were deployed under the command of General Leonard Wood. True to his statement in Omaha, Wood enthusiastically accepted the help of Gary's paramilitary voluntary associations to quell the civic disorder brought by the strikes. In Bogalusa, similar organizations worked with corporate guards (in effect, a company police force) to threaten, beat up, and, eventually, murder black and white union organizers.

African Americans fought back against these combined forces. In each of the preceding sites of the year's racial violence, black defenders could claim some victories. In Longview, Texas, a lynch mob had been deterred, for example; in Washington, mob incursions into the Uptown neighborhood had been halted. Such successes proved elusive in the final riots of 1919, not because of a lack of courage or effort, but because the defenders were so vastly outnumbered and outgunned.

Resisting Debt Peonage in the Arkansas Delta

In the fall of 1918, a white attorney named Ulysses S. Bratton agreed to represent black tenant farmers from the Arkansas Delta (Figure 6.1). Traveling to Bratton's Little Rock office, the sharecroppers recounted how their landlords cheated them. Overseers and owners refused to show their books, overcharged for supplies, and sometimes claimed the entire crop. As one sharecropper told Bratton, "they ain't allowing us down there room to move our feet except to go to the field."[1] The stories did not surprise the attorney, who was already familiar with the chicanery of the Delta's white planters. He knew that each fall the landowners or their managers estimated a tenant's cotton yield, totted up charges for seeds and tools – and then added whatever sum was needed to mire him in debt. In one case, a sharecropper's cotton sold for $500, but his landlord insisted he owed $697 for supplies. To prevent tenants from leaving, planters colluded to never take on a debt-burdened man. If a tenant fled, the planter pressed criminal charges.[2]

Known as debt peonage, the practice had a long history in the Arkansas Delta. A legacy of the antebellum plantation system, peonage guarded the fortunes of white landowners against fluctuations in cotton prices. Lumber companies embraced peonage when they began harvesting the Delta's rich pine forests, relying on sheriffs and courts to provide cheap labor through manipulation of vagrancy laws. Perversely, debt peonage required the victim's own expertise. One white planter admitted, "a nigger is able better than anybody else to tell just exactly how much cotton he is going to make. When 'laying by' time comes, I go down into his

---

[1] U. S. Bratton to Frank Burke, November 6, 1919, Waskow Notes, tab "Arkansas Riot."

[2] Bratton to Burke, November 6, 1919; "Typed Statement of Mr. E. C. Reed of Pine Bluff, Ark.," December 31, 1919, Waskow Notes, tab "Arkansas Army"; "Excerpts of the statement of an Arkansas lawyer in 'The Story of Southern White Man [sic],'" n.d., Waskow Notes, tab "Arkansas Riot."

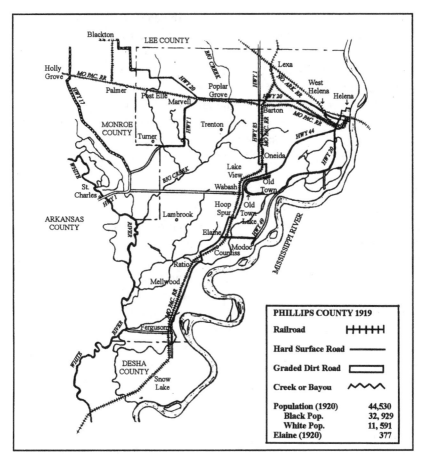

FIGURE 6.1. Map of Phillips County, Arkansas, circa 1919. Phillips County was an important producer of cotton and lumber in 1919. When black sharecroppers organized to obtain fair settlements for that year's cotton harvest, white landowners responded harshly, starting with an armed attack on a sharecroppers' union meeting at Hoop Spur on the night of September 30. *Source:* Butler Center for Arkansas Studies. Courtesy of the Butler Center for Arkansas Studies and the Central Arkansas Library System.

field, ask him how much he is going to make and 'doctor' his account accordingly."[3]

---

[3] For an overview of southern peonage, see Daniel, *Shadow of Slavery*, 19–42. For peonage in the Arkansas Delta, see Graves, "Protectors or Perpetrators?"; Woodruff, "African-American Struggles"; and Woodruff, *American Congo*. For the white planter's quote, see "Economic Conditions in Arkansas," *Branch Bulletin* vol. III, no. 11 (November 1919), 101–2.

Delta blacks tried many times to break the chains of peonage. Share-cropping itself was forged out of black resistance to planters' attempts to reinstitute the antebellum gang labor system. After the Civil War, an ex-slave named Bryant Singfield organized freedmen and women in Phillips County. Some of his fellow black residents briefly set up a farming collective on unclaimed land. In the fall of 1891, the Colored Farmers' Alliance called on its 20,000 members in Arkansas to stay out of the cotton fields until owners doubled their pay. Efforts to organize, however, brought retribution. Singfield disappeared and was presumed killed; the planters broke the 1891 strike.[4]

Yet black resistance to peonage increased during and after World War I. The Great Migration took blacks north just as planters wanted to cash in on the wartime demand for cotton, giving remaining sharecroppers a bit of leverage. Some demanded – and got – weekly cash payments. In Phillips County, the number of black landowners expanded 40 percent between 1910 and 1920. Conscripted young black men who had never left the Delta absorbed the New Negro identity spreading throughout the army. White leaders in Arkansas and Mississippi, anticipating challenges, resolved that returning veterans would not upset the prewar system of peonage and subservience. "We have all the room in the world for what we know as N-i-g-g-e-r-s," declared Mississippi governor Theodore Bilbo, but not for anyone committed to "Northern social and political dreams of equality."[5]

Enter Robert Hill, who believed it was time for those "dreams" to come true. Hill was born and raised in the Arkansas Delta, where he eked out a living doing agricultural labor. Wilsonian rhetoric and New Negro ideology greatly impressed him, as did the self-help and entrepreneurial lessons of Booker T. Washington. In 1918, Hill, then in his late twenties, incorporated a tenant farmers union, paying a white law firm to file the papers. He had no money, no organizing experience, no allies. For credentials and resources he substituted ambition, charm, and no small measure of courage. "The union wants to know why it is that the laborers can not control their just earnings which they work for," Hill announced. Calling on individual blacks to each recruit twenty-five prospective members, Hill promised to set up union lodges for modest fees.[6]

---

[4] Biegert, "Legacy of Resistance," 76–83; Woodruff, "African-American," 35–6.
[5] Woodruff, "African-American," 36–40 (quote on 40); Taylor, "We have just begun," 269–75.
[6] Rogers, "Elaine Race Riots of 1919," 144–5; McCool, *Union, Reaction, and Riot*, 12–13 (quote).

In May 1919, Hill traveled across the Delta to recruit. In his frock coat, he resembled a preacher, an association he encouraged by sprinkling his speeches with biblical allusions.[7] Some of his documents implied that the federal government had formed the union. The Examination Certificate, for example, bore the heading "Orders of Washington, D.C." and declared members "fit to sit in the Congress" set up by the union. Another document identified a union officer as "employed in the United States Service."[8] By the summer's end, several hundred black tenant farmers and laborers had joined lodges of the Progressive Farmers and Household Union of America, as it was formally known. Membership was strongest in Phillips County, where lodges formed in seven towns.[9]

The formation of the union led to the planned legal action against the planters, with U. S. Bratton agreeing to seek fair settlements for sixty-eight union members in Phillips County.[10] The plaintiffs included the Hicks brothers, Ed and Frank, who worked 100 acres of cotton and corn; Frank Moore, who tended nineteen acres of cotton and corn; and John Martin, who had recently moved to the county. Not all were sharecroppers. Ed Ware, secretary of the Hoop Spur lodge, owned his land and drove his Ford as a taxi.[11] On September 26, Hill met with the Hoop Spur lodge, telling its members that he would help their attorney gather evidence for the anticipated lawsuit. For his part, Bratton planned to present the landlords with an expected payment based on the market price for cotton. If the landlords refused to pay, Bratton would file suit in the Phillips County Circuit Court.[12]

A settlement was unlikely. The white planters, merchants, and entrepreneurs of Phillips County were close-knit and zealously guarded

[7] Claire Kennemore, "11 Negroes to Pay with Their Lives for Greed of One," *New York World*, November 16, 1919, Waskow Notes, tab "Arkansas Army."

[8] "Examination Certificate," July 10, 1919, and "The Great Torch of Liberty," n.d., box 18, folder 13, Charles Brough Papers, University of Arkansas, Special Collections.

[9] Taylor, "We have just begun," 274–5.

[10] Waskow, *From Race Riot,* 122–5; Rogers, "Elaine Race Riots," 144; Robert Church to Walter White, October 6, 1919, Waskow Notes, tab "Arkansas NAACP Probe."

[11] For details about the Hicks Brothers and Frank Moore, see Wells-Barnett, *Arkansas Race Riot,* 14–17; for John Martin, see *State of Arkansas v. John Martin and Alf Banks, Jr.,* #4482, November 4, 1919, copy in box 1, file 12, Grif Stockley Papers, Butler Center for Arkansas Studies, 44; for Ed Ware, see Stockley, *Blood in Their Eyes,* 131.

[12] McCool, *Union, Reaction, and Riot,* 21; U. S. Bratton to David Y. Thomas, March 1, 1920, box 19, folder "Civil Rights Resource Material – Helena, Ark. 1919," Arthur Waskow Papers, Wisconsin Historical Society. (The Waskow Papers are a separate collection from Waskow's transcriptions of the NAACP's 1919 mob violence file; see bibliography.)

their economic interests. Among them, few were as important as E. M. "Mort" Allen. A northerner, Allen had arrived in Phillips County in 1906 and quickly established himself. Marriage into a planter's family assured his social status; partnership with a wealthy man named Harry Kelley provided capital. In one of their first ventures, Allen and Kelley developed the town of Elaine to serve the lumber companies. Allen also opened a real estate office and insurance agency in Helena. Gerard Lambert, scion of the St. Louis-based pharmaceutical company that bore his family's name, hired Allen as the treasurer of Lambrook, his 21,000-acre logging and sharecropping operation near Elaine. Despite all these enterprises, Allen still found time to help establish the Business Men's League, serve as the president of the National Association of Insurance Agents, and raise a family.[13]

Allen and the white planters, many of whom belonged to the Business Men's League, knew that their continued prosperity depended on quiescent blacks, who comprised more than 75 percent of Phillips County's population (the 1910 census recorded 26,354 blacks, 7,181 whites).[14] Anticipating a postwar drop in demand for cotton, planters colluded in February 1919 to shrink the number of acres in cultivation. The decision gave the planters yet another reason to deny a fair settlement to their tenants. Allen spoke for many when he declared that "the old Southern methods are much the best" and that the "Southern men can handle the negroes all right and peaceably."[15] News of Robert Hill's unionizing thus greatly alarmed Allen and his peers.[16]

An opportunity to disrupt the union presented itself that fall. The Hoop Spur union lodge scheduled a meeting for the night of September 30, in an unpainted, one-room church. Three miles north of Elaine, Hoop Spur was little more than an unpaved road, a few houses, and a rail siding.[17] The meeting went late, past 10 P.M., but the church was full – U. S. Bratton's son Ocier was arriving the next morning to collect evidence for the settlement. Many of the sharecroppers carried shotguns and rifles. John Jefferson, who had just joined the lodge, remembered well Robert

---

[13] Stockley, *Blood in Their Eyes*, 19–27.

[14] "The Real Causes of Two Race Riots," *Crisis* 19, no. 2 (December 1919), 56.

[15] Stockley, *Blood in Their Eyes*, 27; E. M. Allen to David Y. Thomas, January 4, 1920, box 19, folder "Civil Rights Resource Material – Helena, Ark. 1919," Waskow Papers (quotes).

[16] For detailed treatment of planters' efforts to control workers in Phillips County after the war, see Woodruff, *American Congo*, 74–84.

[17] McCool, *Union, Reaction, and Riot*, 21.

Hill's instructions to come armed because the planters were likely to try to "break the meeting up." That night, a half-dozen men were put on security duty. Will Brown and others guarded the church, while John Martin and Will Wordlow patrolled the surrounding area. Wordlow later remembered being instructed to open fire "if anybody came up there bothering us." Hoop Spur had no streetlights so the guards were, literally, in the dark.[18]

Around 11 P.M., a vehicle came down the road and stopped close to the church, cutting its lights and engine. Lodge members fell silent and listened. According to one of the sharecroppers, John Ratliff, several union men went outside. From inside the car, a flashlight probed the darkness as a voice ordered, "you all get on away from here." And then, gunfire from all sides.[19] There were three men in the car. W. A. Adkins, a special agent for the Missouri Pacific Railroad, was the driver; Charley Pratt, a Phillips County deputy sheriff, rode in the passenger seat; and Kid Collins, a black trusty (a prisoner who helps officers in return for privileges) was in the backseat. According to Pratt, the men had simply stopped to "take a leak" when they noticed a group of armed black men. Words were exchanged – about what, Pratt did not say – and then the black men "commenced shooting." By Pratt's estimate, as many as 100 shots were fired. Adkins, hit in the abdomen, died almost immediately. Pratt suffered a wound in the knee as he ducked behind the car. Collins reportedly fired his gun, then fled the scene.[20]

The question of who fired first will likely never be answered, but the true purpose of Adkins and Pratt's drive is known. After the shooting, another Missouri Pacific special agent, T. K. Jones, overheard several planters discussing what the two men, along with Kid Collins, had been sent to do: break up the union meeting. Collins later confirmed that the car had stopped in Hoop Spur to ambush the sharecroppers.[21]

The union men scattered after the shooting, but not for long. Several criss-crossed the fields and woods between Elaine and Hoop Spur, pulling

---

[18] *State of Arkansas v. Frank Hicks* #4509, November 3, 1919, copy in box 1, file 11, Grif Stockley Papers, 41 (Jefferson quote); *State of Arkansas v. John Martin and Alf Banks, Jr.*, 34–8, 44; Wells, *Arkansas Race Riot*, 29–30 (Wordlow quote).

[19] *State of Arkansas v. John Martin and Alf Banks, Jr.*, 18–21 (quote on 21).

[20] *State of Arkansas v. John Martin and Alf Banks, Jr.*, 9–12 (quote on 9); McCool, *Union, Reaction, and Riot*, 24. See also Whitaker, *On the Laps of Gods*, 80–5.

[21] *Frank Moore et al. vs. the State of Arkansas*, Supreme Court of the United States, No. 955, October Term, 1919, transcript of record, box D-101, NAACP Records, 103–4, 110.

fellow sharecroppers from chores or out of bed. When one man protested that he was sick, Paul Hall told him, "you got to go, you will have to crawl." George Green went willingly, taking his shotgun. Within hours, more than forty armed men had assembled at Frank Moore's place, just north of Elaine. Moore organized the sharecroppers into a military-like formation in preparation for returning to Hoop Spur. "He didn't say for what purpose," one man later recalled, "but he says let's go, he says if a man breaks ranks he was going to turn loose on him."[22] Whether or not he recognized the similarity, Moore – who had not served in the military – was emulating the black men who had used their army training to fend off white mobs in Bisbee, Washington, Chicago, and Knoxville.

Meanwhile Phillips County Sheriff Frank Kitchens, who believed that the sharecroppers were intent on killing whites, was assembling his own force. As had happened in Longview, news of a gun fight between blacks and whites brought out armed white men. Kitchens even set up a head-quarters at the county courthouse to organize these volunteers. Hundreds of white veterans joined the posse, which divided into small groups before heading into the countryside to search for the sharecroppers.[23] The posse reached Elaine and Hoop Spur by mid-morning on October 1. T. K. Jones and another white man were already patrolling the Hoop Spur road. In another example of the blending of civil and corporate authority, Jones had orders to detain armed blacks who passed by. Only once did Jones see a band of black men, none of whom carried weapons. As he later attested, "I did not see a single negro with a gun or weapon of any kind during the whole day I was in the country."[24] It is difficult to imagine how an insurrection of black sharecroppers could have broken out around him unseen and unheard. For Kitchens and his posse, however, Adkins's death was proof enough that a black uprising was underway. On foot or riding in cars and trucks, the deputies scoured the roads and fields around Hoop Spur (Figure 6.2). Well-armed, they had *carte blanche* to disarm, detain, and subdue Phillips County's African Americans. This mission resulted in numerous armed confrontations with bands of sharecroppers, who knew well why they were being targeted: the planters wanted to destroy the union and protect debt peonage.

Herbert Thompson commanded a group of white veterans searching a bayou east of Hoop Spur. Around noon, he and his men fired on a band

---

[22] Wells-Barnett, *Arkansas Race Riot*, 38–9; *Frank Moore et al. vs. the State of Arkansas*, 38–40, 46–49 (quotes on 48–9).

[23] McCool, *Union, Reaction, and Riot*, 26; Stockley, *Blood in Their Eyes*, 48–9.

[24] *Frank Moore et al. vs. the State of Arkansas*, 104–5.

FIGURE 6.2. Posse searching for blacks. Deputized by Phillips County Sheriff Frank Kitchens, this posse scoured the roads and fields around Hoop Spur in a campaign to disarm, detain, and even kill black sharecroppers and their families. *Source:* AHC 1595.2, from the Collections of the Arkansas History Commission. Courtesy of the Arkansas History Commission.

of sharecroppers and a uniformed black veteran hiding in a thicket. The black men returned the fire. The exchange killed James Tappan, a white veteran, and two sharecroppers; the surviving blacks escaped.[25] The men commanded by sharecropper Frank Moore were close enough to hear the gunfire. "Let's go help them people out," Moore exclaimed. He led his band to the Hoop Spur road, where they saw several cars of deputies to the north. The union men dispersed, some moving alongside the railroad tracks, others staying on the road shoulder. One man allegedly fired his rifle at the deputies, fatally wounding a white man named Clinton Lee.[26]

As word of the deaths of Lee and Tappan spread, the posse embarked on a murderous rampage against African Americans. The four Johnston Brothers numbered among the victims. Dr. David A. E. Johnston was a prosperous Helena dentist and businessman. His brother Louis was a

[25] *State of Arkansas vs. Albert Giles and Joe Fox* #4481, November 4, 1919, copy in box 1, file 10, Grif Stockley Papers, 8–13, 16–19, 26–34.
[26] *State of Arkansas vs. Frank Hicks*, 22–5, 37–43 (quote on 37); *Frank Moore et al. vs. the State of Arkansas*, 32–6.

physician in Oklahoma, home for a reunion. The other two brothers, who owned an automobile dealership, were both veterans. Early on the morning of October 1, the brothers went squirrel hunting in the woods south of Elaine. After the merchant who had sold them shotgun shells told a deputy sheriff that the Johnstons were armed, the posse set out to find them.[27]

When the brothers learned of the disturbances, they left their guns and game inside their car and boarded a train to return home. Deputies arrested them before the train reached Helena. The men were shackled and put into the back seat of O. R. Lilly's Oldsmobile. A realtor and Helena alderman, Lilly apparently had a grudge against David Johnston. A friend of Lilly's had attempted to whip the dentist in an altercation a week earlier, but Johnston had instead beaten up his attacker. In the front seat with Lilly were two white men – one, Amos Jarmon, was the Phillips County treasurer – and Lilly's black driver Jim Carruthers. According to Jarmon, the car had stopped to help a disabled vehicle and its white occupants when David Johnston lunged over the seat, seized Lilly's gun, and killed him. Jarmon claimed that he and his partner then fatally shot Johnston while the white men from the other car killed Johnston's three brothers.[28]

Jarmon's story raises several questions. Who were the armed white men Lilly had allegedly stopped to aid? Where were the deputies who had arrested the Johnstons? If, in fact, David Johnston shot Lilly, would his brothers sit helplessly in the back seat or would they try to escape? The murders may have been premeditated, vengeance for David Johnston's prior beating of a white man as well as a move to eliminate Phillips County's most prosperous black men. Earlier in the year, white mobs in Charleston and Washington had attacked blacks and black-owned businesses to punish African Americans for their economic gains. Likewise, Sheriff Kitchens's posse was serving the planters' purposes by crushing the sharecroppers' union. Although the Johnstons were not affiliated with the union, their own entrepreneurial success made them targets. (After the shooting, the posse falsely claimed to find rifles and ammunition in David Johnston's office, supposedly proof that the brothers were secret leaders of the sharecroppers' insurrection.)[29] As for the death of Lilly, it is notable

---

27 Wells-Barnett, *Arkansas Race Riot*, 25; Stockley, *Blood in Their Eyes*, 82–3; "Report to the *Crisis*," attributed to Walter White, n.d., Waskow Notes, tab "Arkansas Army."

28 Stockley, *Blood in Their Eyes*, 82–5; "Report to the *Crisis*."

29 "Six More Are Killed in Arkansas Riots," *New York Times*, October 3, 1919; "Trace Plot to Stir Negroes to Rise," *New York Times*, October 4, 1919.

that whoever killed the Johnstons fired so many shots that the men were "sowed with bullets, so much so that their faces had to be covered at the funeral, and parts of their bodies were in shreds."[30] Is it possible Lilly himself was an accidental victim, shot by his own mob in the frenzy to murder the Johnstons? The questions that attend Jarmon's account undermine the claim that whites killed the Johnstons in self-defense.[31]

The Johnston Brothers were not the only black victims of the deputized white men. One band killed Charley Robinson, an elderly sharecropper, and arrested his wife. H. F. Smiddy, a special officer for the Missouri Pacific, commanded fifty to sixty men who rounded up blacks near Hoop Spur on the morning of October 1. None were armed, Smiddy said, but the posse shot many of the African Americans they encountered. According to Smiddy, vigilantes from Mississippi also joined the posse and "shot and killed men, women and children without regard to whether they were guilty or innocent of any connection with the killing of anybody, or whether members of the union or not."[32] John E. Miller, the Phillips County prosecutor at the time, repeated this story in a 1976 interview: "that damn Mississippi contingent came over ... [and] started the marauding."[33] Frances Hall was one victim. The Mississippi mob killed her, pulled her dress over her head, and left her body on a road.[34] The desecration of Hall's body highlighted the mob's ire: blacks who forgot their "place" would not just lose their lives; their bodies would be displayed as warnings about the dangers of defying white supremacy.

By nightfall, the black self-defenders of Phillips County faced a perilous situation. They were vastly outnumbered by the combined posse of the Phillips County and Mississippi vigilantes. Constant patrolling of the roads forced blacks to stay hidden or to move furtively through ditches and along railroad tracks. Their families were being attacked, their homes

[30] "Report to the *Crisis*."
[31] Ida Wells-Barnett believed the murder of the Johnston Brothers to be punishment for their prosperity; see *Arkansas Race Riot*, 25–6. Phillips County already had a record of killing successful black businessmen. In 1916, author Richard Wright, then a boy, was living in Elaine when white men killed his uncle because he rejected their offers to buy his thriving tavern. See Stockley, *Blood in Their Eyes*, 20; Taylor, "We have just begun," 268.
[32] *Frank Moore et al. vs. State of Arkansas*, 108–13 (quote on 113).
[33] John E. Miller interview with Walter Brown, Fort Smith, Arkansas, March 18, 1976, box 1, folder 1, University of Arkansas, Special Collections, 21.
[34] Wells-Barnett, *Arkansas Race Riot*, 20–1.

and cotton seized.[35] Darkness offered an opportunity to regroup, but only if they could find one another – the union men had no headquarters, no telephones, no cars. Many had been killed. But the worst was yet to come.

Arkansas governor Charles Brough had cabled Secretary of War Newton Baker as soon as he learned of the trouble in Phillips County. Claiming that blacks were "massing for attack," Brough requested army troops from Camp Pike. As had happened in Omaha, confusion over authority delayed action.[36] A train carrying almost 600 men and officers from the army's Third Division and Fifty-seventh Infantry did not arrive in Elaine until 8:30 A.M. on October 2. Colonel Isaac Jenks was the commanding officer. Jenks and his men, accompanied by the governor, disembarked believing that white residents were under siege. "We would see at the small stations along the route, small groups of white people armed with shot-guns, pistols, and rifles," reported Jenks's adjutant Captain Edward Passailaigue. Although hundreds of armed white men were patrolling Elaine, the officers were told that blacks had surrounded the town.[37]

Guided by local white men, four companies marched to a woods approximately three miles northwest of Elaine while two more companies remained in town. According to Passailaigue and Jenks, the troops in the field saw heavy action. Pressing into a dense thicket, they drew fire from "colored outlaws," who wounded one soldier and killed another. The troops cornered fifty armed blacks and seized their weapons. Soldiers rescued sixty or so white women and children from a remote cabin. Patrols forced the remaining armed blacks into a shrinking area, resulting in their capture and the alleged discovery of several hundred weapons, thousands of ammunition rounds, and incriminating records. "The negroes had thoroughly prepared themselves and with a little more leadership the whites . . . would have been massacred."[38] The cavalry – infantry and

[35] Ibid., 19–24.

[36] Stockley, *Blood in Their Eyes*, 3–5; Charles Brough to Newton Baker, October 1, 1919 (quote), and Senator W. F. Kirby to Army Chief of Staff, October 2, 1919, box 3, folder "Arkansas (Race Riots)," RG 60, Glasser File.

[37] Captain Edward P. Passailaigue to Assistant Chief of Staff, 3rd Division, October 7, 1919, box 3, folder "Arkansas (Race Riots)," RG 60, Glasser File; Colonel Isaac Jenks to Commanding General, Camp Pike, October 14, 1919, box 1229, folder "Racial Relations at Camp Pike, Arkansas," Record Group 407, Records of the Adjutant General's Office, U.S. Army, Central Decimal File, 1917–1925, U.S. National Archives and Records Administration, College Park, Md.

[38] Jenks to Commanding General, October 14, 1919 (first quote); Passailaigue to Assistant Chief of Staff, October 7, 1919, 3 (second quote).

artillery, to be precise – had arrived in the nick of time (Figure 6.3, Figure 6.4).

These After Action Reports are inaccurate and blatantly one-sided. Emphasizing the helplessness of stranded whites, the narratives do not even mention the posse. Passailaigue claimed that the soldiers killed approximately twenty armed blacks "for refusing to halt when so ordered or for resisting arrest" but many of these victims were unarmed or had not been given a chance to surrender.[39] Gerard Lambert, owner of the Lambrook plantation, watched soldiers mow down a black man who bolted from a building in which other African Americans were hiding. The troops told the witnesses that "this should be a lesson to them."[40] Like the Tennessee Fourth Infantry in Knoxville, the Camp Pike soldiers were acting in concert with the mobs that preceded them.[41]

Comparison of white and black casualties reveals further the lopsided conflict. Prior to the troops' arrival, four whites had been killed: W. A. Adkins, Clinton Lee, James Tappan, and O. R. Lilly. All four had attacked blacks. Another white, Corporal Luther Earles, was killed during gunfire between the troops and armed blacks.[42] In contrast, whites killed at least twenty blacks. In a year of intense racial violence, Phillips County stands out for the number of black deaths and the wide range of estimates for the final toll. Passailaigue estimated the number of dead blacks at twenty; the Bureau of Investigation, fifty to eighty; the NAACP, twenty-five to fifty. A white writer named Louis Dunaway later claimed that the troops killed more than 850 blacks, but he offered no proof.[43] As Walter White, who briefly visited Phillips County to investigate the killings, observed, the "number of Negroes killed during the riot is unknown and probably never will be known."[44] A coroner's inquest was never

---

[39] Passailaigue to Assistant Chief of Staff, October 7, 1919, 3 (quote); Jenks to Commanding General, October 14, 1919.

[40] Stockley, *Blood in Their Eyes*, 34–44 (quote on 43).

[41] For evidence of the troops targeting blacks, see Woodruff, "African-American," 41–2; Taylor, "We have just begun," 266; Miller interview, 13; "Here's Story of Way Rioting Was Handled in Arkansas," *Memphis Press*, October 4, 1919, in Waskow Notes, tab "Arkansas Army."

[42] Jenks to Commanding General, October 14, 1919.

[43] Passailaigue to Assistant Chief of Staff, October 7, 1919, 3; Agent McElveen, "In Re: Race Riot at Helena, Arkansas," October 4, 1919, RG 65, OGF 373,159, reel 820; "The Real Causes," 60; Walter F. White, "The Race Conflict in Arkansas," *Survey* 43, no. 7 (December 13, 1919), 233–4. For a critical evaluation of Dunaway's claim, see Stockley, *Blood in Their Eyes*, 35–9.

[44] Walter White to Thomas Mufson, December 9, 1921, Waskow Notes, tab "Arkansas Riot." For more on White's visit to Phillips County, see Schneider, *We Return Fighting*, 64–8.

FIGURE 6.3. Troops leading captured sharecroppers. In their After Action Reports, the officers who commanded these troops from Camp Pike, Arkansas, claimed that they had just prevented these sharecroppers from carrying out a conspiracy to murder whites. In fact, the troops had joined forces with a posse (see Figure 6.2) to attack and arrest blacks. *Source:* AHC 1595.8, from the Collections of the Arkansas History Commission. Courtesy of the Arkansas History Commission.

FIGURE 6.4. Troops leading captured sharecroppers. *Source:* AHC 1595.9, from the Collections of the Arkansas History Commission. Courtesy of the Arkansas History Commission.

held; newspapers did not identify black victims by name. Grif Stockley, noting that Phillips County's blacks have long spoken of a mass grave of victims, suggested that a search for the burial site be undertaken to provide a more accurate death toll, while Robert Whitaker, who identified twenty-two separate killing sites of African Americans during the pogrom, estimated that the death toll was more than 100.[45]

The massacre of blacks by the posse and troops from Camp Pike did not satisfy E. M. Allen and the planters, who wanted to ensure that their sharecroppers would never again challenge their power. The unions' leaders were charged with carrying out a conspiracy to murder whites. These trials had just begun when racial conflict with economic sources broke out elsewhere in the country, this time in northwest Indiana. Facing an array of hostile forces during a tempestuous strike, black workers again undertook self-defensive measures. Unlike Phillips County's sharecroppers, these workers had not organized a union, and the violence they faced did not reach the frightening levels of the Arkansas pogrom. Black self-defense in Indiana was scattered rather than organized, an instinctive reaction to physical intimidation and violence. Yet the influence of the New Negro movement gave added purpose to the resistance: black workers had resolved not to be blamed for the strike.

Resisting Scapegoating in Gary

Gary, Indiana, appeared to have little in common with the Arkansas Delta. Gary, founded by U.S. Steel in 1906 on the shores of Lake Michigan, was a booming industrial town with a large immigrant population. But like the Delta, Gary was a key battleground for the rights of laborers in the fall of 1919. The American Federation of Labor (AFL) wanted to unionize the steel industry. U.S. Steel produced half of the country's steel, and its chairman, Judge Elbert Gary, loathed unions. If the AFL could beat Gary and U.S. Steel, the union might force the remaining steel bosses to accept collective bargaining.

A big *if*, that. Judge Gary was obdurate and powerful. He peremptorily rejected the AFL's first two requests to negotiate contracts. The union responded with specific demands, including collective bargaining rights and an eight hour workday, but Gary and his board refused to budge. In August, the AFL turned down an offer from President Wilson to hold

---

[45] For Stockley's statement, see "Filling the Gaps: The Need for Additional Research"; for Whitaker's evidence, see *On the Laps of Gods*, 123–6, 325–9.

a summit to iron out the differences between the union and U.S. Steel. Shortly after a strike vote on September 22, more than 350,000 steel workers in fifty cities in ten states had walked out of their plants.[46] The rate of participation in Gary (named in honor of the judge) was especially high; of 18,000 laborers, more than 15,000, or 85 percent, struck.[47] Close to 80 percent of the city's population was foreign-born or black when the strike began.[48] Clearly the AFL could not win without the support of immigrants and African Americans, as L. H. Caldwell recognized.

A black attorney and Gary resident, Caldwell addressed a crowd of strikers at a city park on September 23. The union had asked him to speak about the strike, but Caldwell opted to also talk about other topics. History, for one. Civilization. Oppression. And race relations – he had much to say about race relations. "It is the weaker race that should be protected by the stronger as we have taken the stand of protecting the smaller nations against oppression," Caldwell declared in a flourish of Wilsonian rhetoric. For centuries, whites have branded blacks as their racial inferiors, Caldwell explained, and the results have hurt both races. Then the eloquent attorney drove home his point. "I defy any man or body or corporation that will use my people for a cause to create a race riot, by pitting one race against another. We represent the younger set of negroes who have in a body marched for this country in its struggle for democracy." The men – so many of them foreign-born – cheered in approval as Caldwell called for racial amity during the difficult days ahead. The *Gary Daily Tribune*, impressed with the speech and its reception, lauded the attorney for delivering "one of the most forcible speeches ever heard on the race question in this locality."[49]

The "race question," actually several questions, preoccupied the people of Gary. How would black workers react to the strike? Would U.S. Steel heighten racial tensions to weaken the strikers' unity? Would the company hire black replacement workers? Would white workers, native- and foreign-born, accept blacks into their union? Caldwell's speech was as much a warning to the AFL as it was to U.S. Steel, cautioning both parties not to exploit blacks for their own gains nor to take their allegiance for granted. "Colored people will not and dare not be made the goats of this strike," Caldwell said. Although he appeared to side with the strikers,

---

[46] Laurie and Cole, *Role of Federal Military Forces*, 264–6.

[47] Mohl, "Great Steel Strike of 1919," 38.

[48] Mohl and Betten, "Ethnic Adjustment," 364–5.

[49] "Possibility of Race Riot Denied Here," *Gary Daily Tribune*, September 24, 1919, 3.

Caldwell admonished the union for its exclusionary racial policies.[50] For the attentive listener, the attorney's remarks offered a clear signal that the black residents of Gary were going to stand up for themselves during the strike.

Due to wartime prosperity and opportunity, Gary's African American community was thriving. Migration from the South and elsewhere in the Midwest had increased the city's black population, and more than ten percent of the mills' workforce was black. Positions for skilled workers such as machinists and electricians had opened up. A black business district emerged on a five-block stretch of Broadway Avenue, Gary's main thoroughfare, offering the services of doctors, lawyers, tailors, and barbers. Black entrepreneurs had recently announced plans to open a bank. The *National Defender and Sun*, a black newspaper, began publishing in 1919. New members flocked to churches and fraternal lodges.[51]

The war was more than a source of prosperity for Gary's black residents; it also encouraged civil rights activism and spread the rhetoric of the New Negro movement. The Gary branch of the NAACP received its charter in 1915 and had 171 members by March 1919. Among other actions, the branch investigated the alleged mistreatment of convalescing black servicemen at a nearby hospital. On July 4, 1918, the black journalist Roscoe Conkling Simmons urged a Gary audience to use America's wartime mission to advance equality for blacks.[52] Approximately 500 black men from Gary (10 percent of the black population) served in the military during the war and returned to mill jobs. One week after the strike began, these veterans organized one of the nation's largest black American Legion posts.[53] The timing was not coincidental. The veterans knew that protecting their interests and rights – as workers and Americans – required unity and vigilance.

Both comity and prejudice shaped race relations in Gary. In the summer of 1917, Gary's police expelled some blacks who had just moved to Gary from East St. Louis in the wake of that city's riot. The police claimed

[50] Ibid.
[51] "First Colored Bank in Gary to be Established," *Gary Daily Tribune*, October 3, 1919, 1; Betten and Mohl, "Evolution of Racism," 52; Balanoff, "History of the Black Community of Gary, Indiana," 8–66.
[52] *Branch Bulletin* vol. III, no. 3 (March 1919), 25; Louis Campbell to Mary White Ovington, July 26, 1919, box G-62, folder "Gary, Indiana, 1917–1920," NAACP Records; Balanoff, "History," 122–6, 135–6.
[53] "Colored Men to Organize Local Post," *Gary Daily Tribune*, September 29, 1919, 8; "Largest Colored Post in Country Organized Here," *Gary Daily Tribune*, October 13, 1919, 8.

that they were simply trying to prevent a race riot from breaking out in Gary. Relations between black and foreign-born residents were sometimes volatile. During Chicago's race riot, a brawl broke out in Gary between the sons of Polish immigrants and black residents. One white resident, the son of Austrian immigrants, recalled that the "foreigners did not make friends with the colored people." However, historians Neil Betten and Raymond Mohl have concluded that "there is no evidence of significant conflict between white working class immigrants and their black neighbors on the south side [of Gary] until the mid 1920s."[54] Whatever the precise level of Gary's racial tensions, the strike was bound to affect them.

From the start, foreign-born workers were enthusiastic supporters of the strike. The National Committee for Organizing Iron and Steel Workers had enrolled approximately 7,000 Gary steelworkers in the union, the majority of them foreign-born.[55] While immigrants led the walk-out on Monday, September 22, a "great percentage of the American employees, including the colored men" remained on the job, reported the *Gary Daily Tribune*.[56] The strikers, wearing large ribbons emblazoned with the phrase "Union Picket," gathered near the plant gates and implored their co-workers to join them. Policemen hovered nearby, but no trouble broke out that day or the next. The strikers moved up and down Broadway Avenue – "a continuous stream of humanity all during the day and night," remarked one witness. They congregated on street corners, confidently predicting victory (Figure 6.5).[57]

Blacks who declined to join the strike began to attract attention. As it had done in Washington and Chicago, the Military Intelligence Division (MID) was monitoring the upheaval in Gary. According to one officer, strikers were "expressing themselves in no uncertain terms concerning the negro residents of the town" and the mixed response to the strike. Rumors of race rioting were spreading; so, too, "threats to kill all the negroes and wreck their homes."[58] The strikers also reviled and menaced

---

[54] Balanoff, "History," 23–4, 128–9; Paul Dremeley, "The Great Strike," n.d., box 1, folder 17, Paul Dremeley Papers, Indiana University Northwest Library, Calumet Regional Archives, 8 (first quote); Betten and Mohl, "Evolution of Racism," 52–3 (second quote).

[55] Foster, *Great Steel Strike*, 65. For a full-length treatment of the strike, see Brody, *Labor in Crisis*.

[56] "Conflicting Claims Made by the Strike," *Gary Daily Tribune*, September 22, 1919 (extra ed.), 1.

[57] Campbell, Janovsky, and Rowens report, September 23, 1919, MID Case File 10634–670–2, box 4, folder "Gary, Indiana #3," RG 60, Glasser File.

[58] Ibid.

FIGURE 6.5. The 1919 steel strike in Gary, Indiana. Already regarded with suspicion, black workers who refused to join this walkout found themselves the
target of angry strikers. In response, blacks defended themselves. *Source:* Photographer Chicago Daily News, Inc., DN-0071494. Courtesy of the Chicago History
Museum.

whites who crossed the picket line, but these men could, in effect, "pass"
when they were not leaving or entering the plants. African Americans did
not have this option; their race made them conspicuous targets wherever
they were.

Attacks on blacks broke out in Gary and nearby cities one week after
the strike began. On Monday, September 29, a dozen or so strikers
swarmed round a vehicle carrying four men – two black, two white – to
their jobs at the Aetna plant. When John Houston, one of the black men,
complied slowly with an order to exit the car, the strikers threw him to
the ground. Police rushed to the scene and arrested six strikers.[59] At Indiana Harbor, a crowd of 300 strikers attacked two black drivers, Clyde

[59] "6 Strikers Facing Riot Charges Now," *Gary Daily Tribune*, September 29, 1919, 1.

Bracken and Sam Blair, as they exited the Universal Portland Cement plant on Friday, October 3. Both men were veterans and had served in France. Indiana Harbor police did not intervene, and a deputy sheriff who witnessed the incident suggested that the police sided with the strikers. Bracken and Blair managed to escape, but, determined to complete their delivery, they returned to ask the deputy for protection. When strikers pelted them with bricks, Bracken fired several shots from a revolver, wounding one man. Rather than aid the drivers, the deputy took their weapons and allowed the Indiana Harbor police to arrest them. Afterward, the workers picketing the cement plant began "openly threatening attacks on all negroes." Although Bracken and Blair appeared to be crossing a picket line, the cement was slated for construction projects in Gary, where contractors were starting to lay off union tradesmen because of the strike's disruption of deliveries.[60]

A race riot appeared imminent.[61] A rumor that the Indiana Steel Company had hired hundreds of blacks as strikebreakers brought several hundred strikers to the plant gate. According to a MID report, strikers were "prowling through the colored residential district of Gary every night."[62] Overwhelmed, the police welcomed the help of Gary's Loyal American League. Like Bisbee's Citizen's Protective League and the Workman's Loyalty League, Gary's organization devoted itself to "100 percent Americanism," patriotism, and unwavering support for local law enforcement and U.S. Steel. Native-born businessmen – "little shopkeepers dependent upon the smile of the steel companies," labor activist Mother Jones derided them – dominated the league. Just like in Bisbee, Gary's volunteers believed communist agitators were masterminding their city's labor troubles. Gary's chief of police and the county sheriff quickly deputized the Loyal Leaguers, who formed police auxiliaries and went out on the streets.[63]

The second weekend of the strike was especially dangerous for blacks. On Saturday, October 4, strikers held mass meetings throughout Gary.

---

[60] "Striker Is Shot as He Interferes," *Gary Daily Tribune*, October 4, 1919, 2; Campbell, Janovsky, and Rowens report, October 3, 1919, MID Case File 10634–670–24, box 4, folder "Gary, Indiana #3," RG 60, Glasser File (quote).

[61] In its strike coverage, for example, the *Chicago Tribune* stressed racial conflict as a cause of the violence. See O'Hara, *Gary*, 77–83.

[62] Case File 10634–670–24.

[63] Donald Van Buren to Colonel A. L. Dade, November 12, 1919, box 4, folder "Gary, Indiana #2," and Campbell and Van Buren report, October 5, 1919, MID Case File 10634–670–34, box 4, folder "Gary, Indiana #2," RG 60, Glasser File; Mohl, "Great Steel Strike," 41 (Jones quote).

Several hundred strikers brandishing clubs and bricks gathered at plant gates to confront laborers ending their shifts. Some of the scabs were white, but a black worker suffered the worst injuries. Roaming the streets of the black neighborhood, two MID officers offered a pessimistic appraisal: "the feeling in this territory between the union pickets and the negro workers is exceedingly tense. It is our opinion that this will inevitably lead to a race riot."[64] For one of these officers, Lieutenant Donald Van Buren, the situation had an aura of *déjà vu* – he had patrolled Chicago during its riot.

At nightfall, crowds of strikers fanned out across the black neighborhood. Fights broke out as they attacked residents. The police, joined by Loyal Leaguers, rushed to break up the brawls. "Time and time again," reported a MID agent, "the police and the volunteer citizens organization were forced to charge the crowds." Although the authorities made arrests, they were no match for the strikers. On Sunday, Gary's mayor asked the Indiana State Militia to send four companies to stop the attacks on blacks, but he worried that even the militia could not handle the deteriorating situation.[65] Once again in 1919, blacks had to rely on themselves for protection.

Self-defense efforts, though uncoordinated, occurred throughout Gary. On Saturday night, a black laborer called for a taxi to pick him up before his shift ended – he feared the strikers would kill his family and burn his house if he was not there to protect them. Early on Sunday morning, strikers tried to stop six black men from walking to the mills. When one of the black men drew a knife, police arrested him.[66] When another group of picketers walked up to a streetcar carrying workers to the mill, the black men aboard "showed fight," reported a MID agent, prompting the strikers "to jump into the car and the trouble was on." The fracas spread to several adjoining blocks. Although the crowds attacked everyone suspected of being a strikebreaker, littering the streets with unconscious victims, reports of a race riot at one site brought hundreds of blacks to the scene.[67] As L. H. Caldwell had predicted, blacks were not allowing themselves to be scapegoats or victims.

Why did so many black workers refuse to join the strike? As organizer William Foster later admitted, the unions hurt themselves by

---

[64] Case File 10634–670–34.
[65] W. E. Rowens report, October 5–6, 1919, MID Case File 10634–670–33, box 4, folder "Gary, Indiana #2," RG 60, Glasser File.
[66] Case File 10634–670–34.
[67] Mohl, "Great Steel Strike," 39 (quote); Brown, "Role of Employers," 670.

discriminating against black laborers.[68] The organizing drive in the steel industry had begun in April 1918, which meant black laborers had experienced union racism or, at the very least, indifference, for seventeen months prior to the strike. Recent migrants from the South had little affinity with their foreign-born co-workers. Finally, black workers worried about losing their jobs if they joined the strike.[69]

The strikers' collective anger at black workers was not the only source of conflict, however; the mill owners themselves encouraged racial tensions by bringing in black strikebreakers and by hiring operatives to stir up trouble. According to Foster, the mills in Gary and neighboring cities hired and transported between 30,000 and 40,000 black replacement workers during the strike.[70] In Gary, a MID agent interviewed some of these men. They were sleeping in "old tourist cars" and, at great personal risk, rode the streetcars to work. Many told stories of being attacked on the trolleys by strikers.[71] Meanwhile, the Illinois Steel Company (a U.S. Steel subsidiary) hired the Sherman Detective Service to foment racial and ethnic tensions.[72]

For Gary's black residents, the deployment of troops to Gary was a mixed blessing. (Army units were mobilized in place of the state militia Gary's mayor had originally requested.) Under the command of Major General Leonard Wood, 18 officers and 512 enlisted men from the Sixth Division of the U.S. Army's Central Department arrived in the strike-torn city straight from Omaha, where they had just finished riot duty. Another 105 officers and 916 enlisted men from the Fourth Provisional Regiment joined these troops. Wood, who had blamed Bolsheviks for Omaha's antiblack collective violence, was sure that the same type of radicals were behind Gary's troubles. As he had done in Omaha, the general worked from a very expansive understanding of his authority, declaring martial law hours after his arrival. (The general joked in a letter, "I am still, in a way, Mayor of Omaha and Gary.")[73] The troops

---

[68] Foster, *Great Steel Strike*, 209–10.

[69] Brown, "Role of Employers," 668–70.

[70] Foster, *Great Steel Strike*, 207–8.

[71] Case File 10634–670–33.

[72] Commission of Inquiry, *Report on the Steel Strike of 1919*, 229–32; MID, Weekly Intelligence Summary for the Week Ending November 1, 1919, No. 127, in *United States Military Intelligence* vol. 10, 2168.

[73] Laurie and Cole, *Role of Federal Military*, 266–71; "Wood Declares Martial Law in Three Big Cities," *Morning Omaha World-Herald*, October 7, 1919, 1; General Leonard Wood to the Adjutant General, October 7, 1919 (two telegrams), box 4, folder "Gary, Indiana #2," RG 60, Glasser File; Wood to Moses, October 11, 1919, box 115, folder "1919 [2nd folder]," Leonard Wood Papers, Library of Congress (quote).

carried out foot patrols during the morning and evening shift changes and strictly enforced Wood's ban on public assemblies.[74] These actions stopped attacks on black workers, but the MID stepped up its surveillance of African Americans. In December 1919, the MID reported that the Wobblies were inciting blacks to attack whites once the troops were withdrawn and that a black radical was urging Gary workers to use bombs and firearms to start a revolution.[75] The surveillance was yet another irony of 1919. Targeted during the strike as scabs, blacks in Gary were now perversely labeled pawns of labor radicals.

The patrols and martial law drained the strikers' resolve and resources. (Aided by the troops and the MID, Gary police arrested hundreds of strike leaders and supporters, targeting especially Russian-born immigrants.)[76] Fearful of arrest, their financial situations deteriorating, strikers filtered back to the mills. The strike was a ghost of itself by early November; the union officially ended it two months later. Judge Gary was pleased and let General Wood know. The two men needed no introduction – Gary was already a staunch supporter of Wood's bid for the Republican nomination for president in 1920. "I paid a good deal of attention to your management of affairs at Gary during the strike," the judge wrote Wood. "It was splendid. The country, and particularly our people, owe you a debt of gratitude."[77]

Resistance to Economic Exploitation in Bogalusa

Gary was not the only company town riven by labor troubles in late 1919. Bogalusa, Louisiana, located sixty miles north of New Orleans, was, coincidentally, also founded in 1906. The Great Southern Lumber Company built the world's largest mill at Bogalusa, employing thousands of workers. The company put up rental homes and parks; it owned and operated all major city services, including the schools. Approximately 60 percent of Bogalusa's residents were black, and they lived in a

---

[74] Mapes to Wood, October 19, 1919, box 4, folder "Gary, Indiana #2," RG 60, Glasser File.

[75] MID, Weekly Intelligence Summary for the Week Ending December 6, 1919, No. 132, and Weekly Intelligence Summary for the Week Ending December 13, 1919, No. 133, in *United States Military Intelligence* vol. 10, 2425, 2474–5.

[76] For details of a typical raid, see D. H. Campbell and O. R. Janovsky report, October 11, 1919, MID Case File 10634–670–63, box 4, folder "Gary, Indiana #4," RG 60, Glasser File. For arrest figures, see Mohl, "Great Steel Strike," 45.

[77] Mohl, "Great Steel Strike," 40, 46.

segregated neighborhood. Bogalusa was, even more so than Gary, a twentieth century fiefdom, firmly under the control of Great Southern's general manager, W. H. Sullivan. (Despite its name, Great Southern was the creation of Buffalo, New York, investors, including Sullivan, who had depleted their forest holdings in New York and Pennsylvania.) Sullivan served as Bogalusa's mayor from 1914 to 1929. He handpicked city commission members for election and told the sheriff who to hire as deputies. Intent on keeping unions out of Bogalusa, Sullivan hired a private army. Nevertheless, the United Brotherhood of Carpenters and Joiners and the International Union of Timber Workers, both AFL affiliates, began organizing in Bogalusa after the war.[78]

Reprisals were harsh and swift. In April 1919, leaders of the black community – pastors, a school principal, a doctor – crossed Sullivan by inviting Los Angeles resident Bernice Anderson to Bogalusa to lecture on suffrage and workers' rights. A black organizer, Anderson encouraged workers to unionize and stated that blacks, having fought alongside of white soldiers, had earned the right to vote. Sullivan ordered the expulsion of the eight black men responsible for Anderson's visit. The *Chicago Defender*, which investigated the incident, suggested an additional motive for the exile: the targeted men had become too prosperous and progressive. "This parish will not stand for such sassy actions on the part of kitchen-smoked darkies; we own this town and will run it," a white barber tartly told the *Defender*'s representative. As had happened in Washington, D.C., African Americans' success had aroused the resentment of white residents, an animosity Sullivan was happy to exploit in order to obstruct unionization.[79]

But Sullivan had underestimated his opposition, especially black organizers Lem Williams and Sol Dacus. Williams was president of Bogalusa's Central Trades and Labor Council, headquartered at the automobile garage he owned. Williams also edited the *Press*, a union newspaper. By openly conducting union business on his property, Williams put it and himself at risk for retaliation from Sullivan's army, but the garage remained the union's base. Sol Dacus, president of the black timber workers' union, was just as resolute as Williams. Born in northern Alabama during the Civil War, Dacus, as a boy, had watched newly

---

[78] Norwood, "Bogalusa Burning."

[79] Norwood, "Bogalusa Burning," 614; "Drive Caucus from Small Town," *Chicago Defender*, May 3, 1919, 1 (quote); "Appeal to Mayor Is Turned Down," *Chicago Defender*, May 10, 1919, 1; Report from E. W. White, New Orleans, *Branch Bulletin*, vol. III, no. 7 (July 1919), 73.

enfranchised blacks vote and resist the Ku Klux Klan's terrorism. During the 1890s and 1900s, Dacus worked in Mobile, Alabama, and Gulfport, Mississippi, two cities with unionized black workers. He arrived in Bogalusa not long after the town's founding. His leadership of the black timber workers' union made him a prominent target, but he continued to organize Great Southern's black workers.[80] Although neither Williams nor Dacus took up arms to defend themselves during Bogalusa's labor strife, their refusal to yield to Great Southern's pressures represented a major form of black resistance, one reinforced by fellow white unionists.[81]

Great Southern tried many measures to stymie Williams and Dacus. It hired black workers to replace whites who joined the unions and spread propaganda among landowners that the unions were also organizing black agricultural laborers. When the organizers persisted, Sullivan tried a soft approach: if the unions stopped recruiting black workers, the company would stop firing white men. That tactic also failed, so Great Southern began firing whites *and* blacks who joined the locals.[82] Sullivan added thirteen new men to the police force and sent agents to Chicago to hire black strikebreakers. When the recruitment drive fizzled, Sullivan ordered the police and sheriff's deputies to bribe, beat, or exile the organizers. In mid-June, the company threatened to disrupt a meeting to enroll black workers in the timber union, but the move backfired. Led by fifteen uniformed veterans, 100 or so armed white men marched to Bogalusa's black neighborhood to escort workers to the meeting. Company gunmen and local law enforcement decided not to confront the union's defenders, and that night, more than 450 black men signed union cards. Hundreds more

---

[80] For details about Lem Williams, see Norwood, "Bogalusa Burning," 591; James Weldon Johnson, "Views and Reviews," *New York Age*, November 29, 1919, 4. For Sol Dacus, see Norwood, "Bogalusa Burning," 591, 618; T. J. Greer, "Report on Situation at Bogalusa, Louisiana," February 8, 1920, box C-319, folder "Subject File – Labor General January-July 1920," NAACP Records, 3.

[81] Black and white dockworkers in Galveston, Texas, also cooperated with one another, joining together to elect labor-friendly candidates to city offices in 1919 and to organize a strike in March 1920. In this case, the local chapters of the International Longshoremen's Association were racially segregated, but this did not prevent black workers from fighting for both workplace and racial equality. See Andrews, "Black Working-Class Political Activism," especially 638–46. For in-depth treatment of black workers' struggles for economic justice in a variety of occupations and places, see the introduction and essays in Arnesen, *Black Worker*.

[82] According to T. J. Greer, president of the Louisiana State Federation of Labor, the unions agreed to the deal but the company began firing whites and blacks less than one month later. See Greer, "Report on Situation," 1–2.

enrolled over the next two weeks.[83] To Sullivan's ire, the union showed no signs of quitting.

On August 31, a Bogalusa mob lynched black veteran Lucius McCarty. A married white woman claimed that McCarty had sexually assaulted her the night before. By one account, she "beat her assailant off at her home, seized a gun and fired several shots as he fled." Law officers used bloodhounds to find McCarty, also arresting six other black men. The woman quickly identified McCarty, and a mob shot him and dragged his body behind a car.[84] The murder might well have been a set-up aimed at deterring the biracial workers' parade planned for Monday, September 1 – Labor Day. The hounds had reportedly tracked McCarty through a pair of shoes left at the house. If McCarty had left his shoes at the alleged victim's house, then how had he escaped? The response of Bogalusa's city commission, which answered to Sullivan, is even more suggestive. Immediately after the lynching, the commission announced that the parade promoted miscegenation and must be cancelled. The unions ignored the veiled threat. Some 2,500 workers, a third of them black, marched through town to the all-white park.[85]

On September 23, Great Southern locked out all its workers. By this date, 95 percent of the workforce had enrolled in the unions. According to the company, an accident had crippled a mill steam engine and repairs would take up to three months. The explosion was no accident, however; Great Southern had intentionally damaged the engine in an effort to weaken the unions. During the lockout, Great Southern augmented its already formidable troops (armed guards, police, sheriff's deputies) by orchestrating the formation of the Self-Preservation and Loyalty League, yet another white vigilante organization. Drawn from Bogalusa's white mercantile and professional class, the Loyalty League equated biracial unions with "race-mixing" and Russia. (One rumor claimed that "a million rubles [came] into the Southland every month" for the use of "scheming and cunning" black organizers.) African Americans' wartime service further alarmed these whites: in France black soldiers had learned to use weapons and had allegedly consorted with white women. Great Southern thus had no trouble enlisting white, middle-class men in the

---

[83] Greer, "Report on Situation," 2; Norwood, "Bogalusa Burning," 614.

[84] Stephen Norwood identified the lynching victim as Placide Butler; see "Bogalusa Burning," 615. Newspapers gave his name as Lucius McCarty; see "Alleged Negro Assailant of White Woman Lynched by Mob," *Galveston News*, September 1, 1919, clipping in *NAACP Papers*, Part 7, Series A, reel 12, frame 19.

[85] "Alleged Negro"; Norwood, "Bogalusa Burning," 615.

Loyalty League. Well-armed, deputized, and having taken an oath to uphold white supremacy, the Loyalty Leaguers were ready to answer the company's call to arms.[86]

Great Southern deployed its army in mid-November. Loyalty Leaguers, law enforcement, and the company's guards carried out a series of kidnappings and assaults against union leaders. Seven gunmen from Great Southern lured Ed O'Bryan, the white president of the sawyers' union, into a car and drove him out of town. After severely beating O'Bryan, the attackers painted "I am an I.W.W." on his shirt and put him under armed guard on the New Orleans train. Sol Dacus was first offered a bribe: $2,000 for a home and livestock appraised at $3,500. After he rebuffed the offer, a mob shot up his house, but Dacus escaped.[87]

The next morning, November 22, Dacus returned to Bogalusa. Making no attempt to hide, he strode down Bogalusa's main street to Lem Williams's garage. Two fellow union men, white carpenters J. P. Bouchillon and Stanley O'Rourke, flanked Dacus, shotguns cradled in their arms. With passers-by staring, the carpenters declared their intention to safeguard Dacus. Word of the organizer's appearance quickly reached the Loyalty League and Wiley Magee, head of Great Southern's private army. Bearing arrest warrants for Dacus (for being suspicious) and Bouchillon and O'Rourke (for disturbing the peace), a posse of 150 armed white men from the league and the company headed to the repair garage. In addition to Dacus and his bodyguards, three or four other men were inside. For the vigilantes, the moment to crush the unions had arrived. By one account, the first vigilantes to arrive opened fire without warning after Williams, who had stepped to the threshold, demanded, "what do you fellows want?" He fell dead without uttering another word. A fusillade riddled the garage, killing Bouchillon and another carpenter. O'Rourke, who apparently tried to surrender, suffered fatal wounds. Williams's younger brother James scrambled to defend the garage. He managed to fire his twenty-two caliber rifle a few times, wounding posse leader Jules LeBlanc, a veteran, before surrendering. The twice-lucky Dacus managed to escape.[88]

The killing of the four union leaders crippled the biracial organizing campaign in Bogalusa. Taking no chances, the Bogalusa police arrested James Williams and charged him with murder. The thirteen vigilantes,

---

[86] Norwood, "Bogalusa Burning," 615–17 (quote on 617).
[87] Greer, "Report on Situation," 2–3.
[88] Greer, "Report on Situation," 3; Norwood, "Bogalusa Burning," 591–2, 619 (quote).

however, faced no charges for three weeks, until a special grand jury bound them over to await a hearing in May 1920. After Great Southern paid their bond, they came back to Bogalusa, where, reported a union man, "they are still armed and defying the law of the state." Sullivan's forces quashed what remained of the organization drive by arresting blacks for vagrancy. The city court judge dutifully fined each man and turned him over to Great Southern to work off the fee. Dacus never went back to Bogalusa. He relocated to New Orleans, where his family joined him. Like S. L. Jones and C. P. Davis of Longview, Texas, Dacus was forced to forfeit his life's assets – home, land, livestock, and more than $1,000 in war savings stamps.[89]

Despite enjoying near-absolute control of Bogalusa, William Sullivan asked Louisiana's governor to send for federal troops. (Louisiana had demobilized its militia after the war.) The request went to Major General Henry G. Sharpe, who had dealt with Charleston's first outbreak of racial conflict in December 1918. Sharpe, relying on the information provided by the governor, believed the trouble to be much greater than it was. Five officers and 100 troops arrived four days after the attack on Lem Williams's garage, but thanks to Great Southern's occupying forces, there was nothing for them to do. "Indications are that this call for United States troops was unnecessary," Sharpe reported on November 28. Nevertheless, the troops remained for another month. Sullivan was delighted – federal intervention buttressed Great Southern and the Loyalty League's claims that the unions and their alleged Red supporters had gravely threatened Bogalusa's civil order. On the day the troops departed, Sullivan (as Bogalusa's mayor) thanked their commanding officer for the "splendid way" he and his men "handled a very delicate situation."[90] And for Great Southern, a favorable situation: the company never recognized a union and no sustained attempts to organize workers were again made.[91]

Yet Bogalusa's unionists, including Dacus, made one last stand. The United Brotherhood of Carpenters and Joiners hired attorneys to defend James Williams and undertook an ambitious fundraising

[89] Greer, "Report on Situation," 4 (quote); Norwood, "Bogalusa Burning," 620–1; United Brotherhood of Carpenters & Joiners to Mary White Ovington, February 9, 1920, box C-319, folder "Subject File – Labor General Jan.-July 1920," NAACP Records.

[90] Sharpe to the Adjutant General, November 25 and 28, 1919 (Sharpe quote); Sullivan to Colonel James A. Shipton, December 23, 1919 (Sullivan quote), box 3, folder "Bogalusa, La.," RG 60, Glasser File; Laurie and Cole, *Role of Federal Military*, 256.

[91] Norwood, "Bogalusa Burning," 625.

campaign to support an investigation of the murders of Lem Williams, Stanley O'Rourke, J. P. Bouchillon, and Thomas Gaines, the fourth victim. To no avail, the AFL strenuously lobbied the Department of Justice to investigate. Although the grand jury did not indict James Williams for shooting Jules LeBlanc, it also declined to charge the thirteen vigilantes. Rebuffed in criminal court, the widows of the slain men and Sol Dacus sued Great Southern for damages. The cases dragged on for years. Despite Dacus's and witnesses' testimony detailing the destruction wreaked by Great Southern's gunmen, a federal jury in New Orleans ruled for the company. Lena Williams's case also ended in disappointment. Rather than accept an out-of-court payment of $2,500, as each of the other widows did, Lena advanced her civil suit to the U.S. Supreme Court. The case hinged on the legal status of the mob that had attacked Lem Williams's auto repair garage: were its members vigilantes or duly authorized officers of the law? In its 1928 decision, the Supreme Court singled out O'Rourke and Bouchillon's public announcement of their intent to protect Dacus. Such "threatening language," the justices ruled, permitted the sending of the posse. The court ruled for the defendants, and Lena Williams received no reparations.[92]

The upheavals in Arkansas, Gary, and Bogalusa had many similarities. In all three locales, powerful economic conglomerates quashed union organization and activity. Responding to requests from local or state officials, the War Department deployed federal troops, whose actions decisively aided landowners and corporations to the detriment of workers. (Though it should be noted that army patrols in Gary helped stop attacks on black workers by white strikers.) Vigilantes served as auxiliary police forces, as they had throughout the year. The actions of these vigilantes were especially violent in Arkansas, where they helped carry out a pogrom against black sharecroppers to uphold white supremacy and debt peonage. Although Bogalusa's vigilantes turned their weapons on both white and black organizers, protection of white supremacy was also intertwined with protection of the economic status quo.

Armed resistance is another notable feature of these three events. Despite being outnumbered, African Americans in the Arkansas Delta,

---

[92] Brotherhood to White, February 9, 1920; Frank Morrison to Mary White Ovington, February 4, 1920, box C-319, folder "Subject File – Labor General Jan.–July 1920," NAACP Records; Greer, "Report on Situation," 4–5. For details of Dacus's and the widows' cases, see Norwood, "Bogalusa Burning," 620–4 (quote on 624).

Gary, and Bogalusa fought to protect their interests and, in many instances, their lives. The danger faced by blacks was lowest in Gary. Still, roving bands of strikers and strike sympathizers menaced black residents and workers, who often used knives and guns to fend off attackers. In Bogalusa, where the danger was higher than in Gary, a small but highly visible group of black and white men joined together to defend themselves and their union organizing. This biracial unionization effort recalls the *esprit de corps* that briefly brought black and white servicemen together to resist police abuse in Charleston in late 1918. As volatile and violent as the backlash in Bogalusa was, it did not match the reprisal carried out by white elites in Phillips County, Arkansas. Confronting hundreds of armed troops and vigilantes, black sharecroppers nevertheless banded together to attempt to halt a massacre. The dynamic response of African Americans in all three places demonstrated the readiness of blacks to assert and protect their rights, not just as citizens, but also as workers.

7

"It Is My Only Protection"

Federal and State Efforts to Disarm African Americans

On July 31, 1919, Major Walter H. Loving of the army's Military Intelligence Division (MID) went to 135th Street and Lenox Avenue in Harlem to watch people buy newspapers at the corner's four newsstands. Washington's riot had ended ten days earlier, while Chicago's still raged, and Loving wanted to know how closely New Yorkers were following the events. What he saw greatly impressed him. Eager readers snapped up new editions as soon as they arrived, thousands of copies selling within ten minutes. "People, white and black, actually scramble to get these papers," he marveled, and the "bigger and more sensational the headlines, the quicker the paper is sold." Loving worried that New York was on the brink of its own race riot. "Never before have the Negroes of Harlem been so worked up over anything as they are at present over the recent race riot in Washington and the present one in Chicago," he remarked ominously.[1]

Loving was not exaggerating New York's racial tensions. Late on the night of July 19, an argument between two men – one black, the other white – almost led to a riot in Harlem. According to the *New York Times*, when the white man disputed something the black man said, the latter drew a handgun and fired five shots, wounding two bystanders. By the time a police captain and fifteen officers arrived, "several thousand excited negroes" had filled 127th Street between Second and Third Avenues. When the police dispersed the crowd and began searching houses for "persons believed to have been concerned in the riot," someone opened

---

[1] Loving to the MID Director, July 31, 1919, Case File 10218–345–3, RG 165, copy in box 1, reel 6, Kornweibel Papers.

fire on them.² On July 22, a black man stabbed a white man who had slapped a black woman in a subway car. That same day, a white soldier ordered a black man to give up his seat aboard an elevated train. When he refused, the soldier tried to pull him to his feet, and only the conductor's intervention prevented a fight from breaking out. Another white soldier stood outside a Harlem theater, spewing racist invective, until the police made him stop. "The least little cause is likely to start a riot," Loving warned.³

As the major recognized, "the least little" causes had roots in the now-flourishing New Negro movement. "Soap-box orators on street corners constantly remind their hearers that they went to fight for democracy abroad, and they now may be called upon to fight for that same democracy at home."⁴ The black press's exultation of the New Negro fighting for his rights, coupled with national outrage at the continuing depredations of white mobs, had encouraged forceful, swift resistance against even the slightest offenses of white supremacy. How soon, then, until the next riot, and where would it be?

This question preoccupied officers in the MID and officials in the Bureau of Investigation (BI), Department of Justice, and the Post Office. During and after the war, the MID and the BI carried out a massive program of surveillance of African Americans and suppression of black publications such as the *Messenger*, fixating on links between communists, socialists, and advocates of racial equality.⁵ The postwar cascade of racial violence convinced national security officials that a national uprising of blacks, inspired and led by socialists and communists, was now underway. Consider some of the report titles. *In re: Bolsheviki Activities, possible vio[lation] Espionage Act in propaganda among negroes. Attention Mr. Hoover in re: Negro Radical Activities. In re: William Monroe Trotter (Colored) (I. W. W. Agitator).*⁶ The fact that relatively few

---

² "War Talk Starts Riot in Harlem," *New York Times*, July 20, 1919.
³ Case File 10218–345–3.
⁴ Ibid.
⁵ For in-depth treatment of the federal government's surveillance of African Americans during the World War I era, see Kornweibel, *Seeing Red* and *Investigate Everything*; Ellis, *Race, War, and Surveillance*. Jeanette Keith provides additional evidence of the BI's efforts to compel black (and white) conscription and to suppress dissent in the rural South. See *Rich Man's War, Poor Man's Fight*, 135–61. For Loving's part in the surveillance, see Johnson, "Black American Radicalism."
⁶ The report titles come, respectively, from William C. Sausele, "In re: Bolsheviki Activities, possible vio [*sic*] Espionage act in propaganda among negroes," October 18, 1919, RG 65, OGF 375,446, reel 824; Joseph Baker to Frank Burke, October 29, 1919, RG 65,

"agitators" had connections to communist and socialist organizations did not dislodge this *idée fixe*. Indeed, the absence of evidence merely convinced officials, especially the young J. Edgar Hoover – who, on August 1, 1919, was named head of the Department of Justice's Radical Division – that they were not looking hard enough. Driven by Hoover, agents redoubled their efforts to uncover Red roots for what they dubbed "Radical Activities."[7]

The federal campaign to link the Red Scare to 1919's racial conflict is thoroughly documented.[8] Less well known, however, is the sustained drive undertaken in 1919 to disarm African Americans because of fears that they were plotting violent uprisings. With the cooperation of state and local officials as well as white gun dealers, federal and military officials seized weapons from individual black gunowners, monitored weapons sales to blacks, and asked gun dealers not to sell weapons and ammunition to African Americans. In many cases, gun dealers needed no prompting; on their own initiative, they turned away black customers. This attempted disarming of African Americans represented a national expansion of the practice already being carried out by riot troops and police during outbreaks of antiblack collective violence: the seizure of weapons from black self-defenders, who were then often charged with carrying concealed weapons.

Given the extent of black armed resistance during 1919, it is not surprising that African Americans found ways to evade efforts to strip them of their weapons. Determined to secure all of their constitutional rights, they resisted infringement of their right to bear arms. This was no abstraction. African Americans needed these weapons to defend themselves because, for the most part, local police and federal riot troops had failed to protect them against white mobs. A cartoon published in the *Washington Bee*, a black weekly, during that city's riot poignantly

---

OGF 3057, reel 304; Horace A. Lewis, "In re: William Monroe Trotter (Colored) (I.W.W. Agitator)," September 18, 1919, RG 65, OGF 49,899, reel 403.

[7] In May 1920, the BI admitted, "to date the Department [of Justice] has not found any concerted movement on the part of the negroes to cause a general uprising throughout the country." Instead, the primary causes of "negro difficulties" in Washington, Chicago, and elsewhere were "purely local." Nevertheless, the BI insisted that "propaganda of a radical nature" was a secondary cause. See "Negro Agitation," May 14, 1920, RG 65, OGF 3057, reel 304. For J. Edgar Hoover's role in directing the BI's search for radical sources of black activism, see Ellis, "J. Edgar Hoover."

[8] Kornweibel, *Seeing Red*, 19–25, 36–53, 84–99; Ellis, *Race, War, and Surveillance*, 183–227; Ellis, "J. Edgar Hoover."

FIGURE 7.1. Mob Law. This cartoon aptly captures the dilemma of African Americans during the year of racial violence: law enforcement officers failed to stop white mob violence, yet they demanded that blacks surrender weapons they needed to defend themselves. *Source:* The *Washington Bee*, August 2, 1919, p. 1. Courtesy of the Washingtoniana Division, D.C. Public Library.

captured this dilemma (Figure 7.1). The drawing depicts a policeman standing between a hulking white man wielding a pistol and a club and a much smaller black man bearing a pistol. "Wait until I disarm him," the policeman confides to the white figure (labeled Mob Law) as he orders the black figure to surrender his weapon. "It is my only protection," the black man answers.[9]

White Fears of Black Uprisings

The telegram arrived at the MID's office in Washington on the morning of July 31. According to the commanding officer of Camp Johnston, "race riots would be on in Jacksonville, Florida" on August 1. Or so military police at the camp believed, based on statements from local blacks. The officer reported that he was "taking all possible precautions" and had

[9] *Washington Bee*, August 2, 1919, 1.

apprised local officials.[10] With Chicago still embroiled in its bloody riot, was Jacksonville next?

No. The "reports" of an uprising proved nothing more than vague rumors that some black residents planned to shoot up the town, which never happened.[11] In the summer of 1919, Jacksonville was just one of several cities where nervous white citizens and officials, civilian and military, reported planned uprisings by African Americans. None of the "plots" were authentic, but they unsettled whites in the affected communities and set off alarms in the Post Office, Department of Justice, BI, and MID. Not since Nat Turner's revolt, in 1831, and John Brown's raid on the Harpers Ferry arsenal, in 1859, had fears of black uprisings so transfixed and troubled white Americans.[12] "Should the negro become fairly well organized and demand social equality, there is no doubt but that serious trouble would ensue throughout the entire southern belt of the United States," a white attorney from South Carolina warned the BI on July 3, 1919.[13] Major J. E. Cutler, a MID officer who had closely monitored the Washington and Chicago riots, believed "more bloodshed is very probable."[14] In mid-August, social events organized in Philadelphia for black servicemen attracted the attention of the BI.[15] In Newport News, a Labor Day speech by Matt Lewis, the black editor of the *Newport News Star*, enraged several white listeners, who claimed that Lewis said, "we colored people must hang together to protect ourselves against the whites . . . if a white man abuses you, knock him down." A local BI agent dutifully began abstracting the content of the *News Star*.[16]

An incipient yet warped awareness of the New Negro movement reveals itself in these fears. Anxiety over purported uprisings stemmed in part from an understanding that the riots in Washington, Chicago, and elsewhere were not aberrations. But few whites grasped that mass

[10] Telegram, Merillat (Camp Johnston, Fla.) to MID, July 30, 1919, Case File 10218–354–1, RG 165, copy in box 1, reel 6, Kornweibel Papers.

[11] MID, Weekly Intelligence Summary for the Week Ending August 16, 1919, No. 116, in *United States Military Intelligence* vol. 9, 1561.

[12] For white paranoia about black uprisings to help Germany during World War I, see Kornweibel, *No Crystal Stair*, 4ff.

[13] W. A. Blackwood to William J. Flynn, July 3, 1919, RG 65, OGF 3057, reel 304.

[14] J. E. Cutler to Robert Moton, August 13, 1919, box 113–1, folder 12, Walter H. Loving Papers, Moorland-Spingarn Research Center.

[15] J. F. McDevitt, "Re: Colored Activities," August 14, 1919, RG 65, OGF 373,160, reel 820.

[16] J. G. Shuey, "In re: Matt N. Lewis (Colored), Alleged Inflammatory Utterances," September 16, 1919, RG 65, OGF 373,701, reel 821.

resistance to antiblack collective violence linked these episodes. Instead, whites interpreted acts of resistance and rumors of uprisings as evidence that blacks themselves were responsible for the national outbreak of racial violence, and were plotting more attacks on whites.

Federal officials also grossly misunderstood the sources of black resistance: they believed a communist revolution was being mounted in the United States. Robert Bowen, a postal official, succinctly expressed this viewpoint in an essay entitled "Radicalism and Sedition Among the Negroes As Reflected in Their Publications," distributed less than three weeks before Washington's riot. He accused the *New York Age*, the *Crisis*, and especially the *Messenger* of arousing class consciousness among African Americans in order to establish communist rule. In Bowen's telling, "the negro masses may be made to assume a very dangerous power" through these publications. Bowen keenly appreciated that African Americans took their military service during the war as evidence of equality and had returned fighting for their rights: "As far back as the first movement of the American troops to France the negro publicists began to avail themselves of the argument that since the negro was fit to wear the uniform he was, therefore, fit for everything else." Although he excerpted statement after statement in which New Negro authors and publications hailed militancy in pursuit of democracy, he fixated on Chandler Owen and A. Philip Randolph's promotion of socialism and their support of the IWW. A simplistic and inaccurate syllogism dominated the essay: all New Negroes advocate equality; communists seek classless equality through revolution; therefore, all New Negroes are revolutionary communists.[17] The New Negroes were already outnumbered and outgunned. To judge by the rumors of black uprisings that inundated Washington in July and August, and the federal response to the rumors, New Negroes were now also misunderstood, maligned, and feared.

On July 24, 1919, the War Department received a request from the chief of police in New Orleans: what help would he receive from troops at the Newton Jackson Barracks should race riots break out? The chief also contacted the BI. He had been told blacks "were contemplating an uprising against the whites," so he was taking "all precautions to prevent any casualties in the event the negro population became hostile." These preparations included authorization of the city's Home Guard to patrol with police, if needed. A scheduled address by Milton J. Marshall, an

---

[17] Robert Bowen, "Radicalism and Sedition Among the Negroes As Reflected in Their Publications," July 2, 1919, RG 65, OGF 359,561, reel 793 (quotes on 1).

agent of Marcus Garvey's Black Star Line, was the cause for alarm. A poster promised Marshall would speak about blacks' wartime contributions and the need to make the United States safe for blacks. A BI agent, declaring the advertisement "inflammatory in the extreme," persuaded the mayor and police to halt the meeting and to force Marshall to leave town.[18]

Just days later, the MID filed a report about a secret black society called the Boule. Formed in Dahomey, West Africa, the Boule allegedly required members to swear "to die defending their brothers and to exterminate white rulers" and had helped start Washington's riot. A "printed slip which has fallen into the hands of investigators" revealed, the MID believed, a Boule plot to transport and stockpile weapons across the country: "One city at a time . . . / Send ammunition by the following way / By Parcel Post / By Express / By porters on Pullman." Light-skinned blacks, passing as whites, were supposedly buying the ammunition with the explanation that they needed it to protect themselves from blacks. The MID offered no corroborating evidence for the plot, however, or even for the Boule's existence.[19]

On August 6, BI chief Frank Burke summarized a pessimistic prognostication from a BI special employee named McCaleb, who lived in Texas: "It would appear that no way seems practicable to prevent [race riots], as they are apt to break out on the slightest provocation at any point in [Texas]." McCaleb had attended a meeting convened by the governor to discuss Longview's riot and the possible influence of communism, and he equated the New Negro movement with specific forms of radicalism, even if the evidence was lacking. "Nothing tangible was brought out in the conference regarding the Bolsheviki propaganda, but from the general and specific information obtained by the State authorities, it is certain that the negroes are being urged to defend their rights." According to McCaleb, whites believed that black veterans were responsible for

---

[18] Telegram, Newton Jackson Barracks, New Orleans, to Adjutant General, July 24, 1919, box 5, folder "New Orleans, Louisiana," RG 60, Glasser File; F. O. Pendleton, "In re: alleged negro uprising in New Orleans," July 28, 1919, RG 65, OGF 369,912, reel 812 (first and second quotes); F. O. Pendleton, "In re: Milton J. Marshall (Colored) alias Black Moses: possible treason," August 1, 1919, RG 65, OGF, in *Federal Surveillance of Afro-Americans*, reel 12, frames 161–2, 164 (third quote).

[19] Office of MID, New York, to Director of Military Intelligence, Case File 10218–364–2, July 1, 1919, box 9, folder "1919," RG 60, Glasser File (first quote on 4); MID, Weekly Intelligence Summary for the Week Ending September 13, 1919, No. 120, in *United States Military Intelligence* vol. 9, 1789 (second and third quotes).

raising tensions.[20] Another BI agent was blunter: "One of the principal elements causing concern [in Texas] is the RETURNED NEGRO SOLDIER who is not readily fitting back into his prior status of pre-war times." In other words, black veterans were insisting on their equality with whites.[21]

Rumors from Texas continued to preoccupy federal intelligence officials. In Waco, word spread that black residents were signing a declaration that the Great War had made equals of blacks and whites. BI agent R. W. Tinsley went straight to an "absolutely reliable" source: Mrs. Sarah Morris, a black janitor in Waco's federal building. She assured Tinsley that the rumor was unfounded. As a precaution, Tinsley consulted with the city's postmaster, who began monitoring the mail of a local black pharmacist, Dr. J. W. Fridia. Like Longview's S. L. Jones, Fridia was the local sales agent for the *Defender*, which, in Tinsley's view, "contained some rather radical articles." Also like Jones, Fridia was harassed by white men who demanded that he stop selling the paper. The pharmacist immediately asked for police protection. Rather than question the men who had menaced Fridia, the chief of police "warned him in no uncertain terms that if there was any trouble with the negroes that the agitators would be summarily dealt with." Fridia got the message; he promised to stop selling the *Defender*.[22]

By late August 1919, the BI was chasing the foggiest of rumors, yet the fact that no "uprisings" occurred did not abate its concern and that of other national security agencies.[23] The MID, in its last weekly intelligence digest for August, declared that although there had been no outbreaks of racial violence, the national atmosphere was like that of "an armed truce" and that agitators continued to stir black resentment by talking and writing about racial injustices.[24]

---

[20] "Special news of the day in brief," August 6, 1919, RG 65, OGF 129,548, reel 518.

[21] Gus T. Jones, "In re Negro Organizations Suspected of Radical or I.W.W. Tendencies," September 16, 1919, RG 65, OGF 371,751, in *Federal Surveillance of Afro-Americans*, reel 12, frame 445 (emphasis in original). For more on white fears of a black uprising in Texas, see Reich, "Soldiers of Democracy," 1498–1500.

[22] R. W. Tinsley, "In re: Negro Activities, Waco, Texas; Alleged Agitation for Racial Equality," August 26 (first quote), August 29, September 3, September 8 (second and third quotes), September 27, 1919, RG 65, OGF 379,422, reel 831.

[23] See, for example, the report "In re: Atlantic City, N.J., alleged prospective negro uprising," August 27, 1919, RG 65, OGF 374,236, reel 822. In this case, a BI agent asked a Richmond, Virginia, woman if she had heard a rumor about a black uprising while on vacation in Atlantic City.

[24] MID, Weekly Intelligence Summary for the Week Ending August 30, 1919, No. 118, in *United States Military Intelligence* vol. 9, 1664–5.

"Armed truce" was an apt phrase. The belief that African Americans were stockpiling arms and ammunition was a major source for white fears of black uprisings. The belief originated in the military. In April 1919, Colonel John Dunn, citing unnamed but supposedly reliable sources, warned MID director Marlborough Churchill that almost every service-man in the colored labor battalions returning from France has "secreted somewhere about their person or in their baggage, an army revolver obtained before they left the other side." Dunn urged Churchill to launch an immediate investigation:

The importance of this matter can hardly be over-estimated, since it is a well known fact that there is a great deal of social and labor unrest among the Negro population of the United States, who are demanding social equality as well as other changes from their pre-war status. Negro publications now openly advocate race war and violence, and if there be any truth in this report about the revolvers, this would seem to indicate one of the sources from which they are obtaining, or could obtain, fire arms for illegal purposes.[25]

Churchill agreed, but he ordered that servicemen of both races be searched upon disembarkation.[26] The results proved Dunn's "sources" to be far less than reliable. During May, 9,000 men arriving at Newport News were searched – just thirty-one pistols were discovered.[27]

Having failed to find guns, the MID looked for communist propa-ganda aboard the troop transports. One after another, investigating offi-cers reported no evidence of radical literature or proselytizing. Instead, they observed black soldiers discussing the need to fight for equality.[28] An officer aboard the USS *Orizaba* reported hearing two black soldiers agreeing that "the negro would have to stand for his rights as a citizen or be deprived of them." The officer remarked sourly, "this seems to throw some light as to what we may expect of the Negro in the near future."[29] Another officer overheard a black enlisted man say, "things

---

[25] John M. Dunn to Director of Military Intelligence, April 25, 1919, Case File 10218–329–1, RG 165, copy in box 1, reel 5, Kornweibel Papers.

[26] Churchill to Military Attaché, American Embassy, Paris, April 26, 1919, Case File 10218–329–2 (see also files 10218–329–3 and 10218–329–4), RG 165, copies in box 1, reel 5, Kornweibel Papers.

[27] John D. Austin to Commanding General, Port of Embarkation, Newport News, Va., June 10, 1919, Case File 10218–329–9, RG 165, copy in box 1, reel 5, Kornweibel Papers. See also Ellis, *Race, War, and Surveillance*, 211–12.

[28] J. E. Cutler to the Chief, Morale Branch, June 18, 1919, Case File 80–163–88, RG 165, box 132.

[29] Transport Personnel Adjutant, USS *Orizaba* to Intelligence Officer, Port of Embarkation, Newport News, July 3, 1919, Case File 80–163–117, RG 165, box 132.

would be different in the States now."[30] The personnel adjutant of one transport reported that black soldiers from the South were receiving letters from their families warning them not to wear their uniforms when they returned home because of attacks on black veterans.[31] Concern over the assertiveness of black soldiers reached the highest levels; in mid-July, Secretary of War Newton Baker ordered that the "mixing of white and colored troops" on transports should be avoided as much as possible.[32]

The fact that so many black veterans used legally purchased arms for self-defense during the Washington and Chicago riots stoked the smoldering fears of uprisings. A report forwarded to the BI in late August claimed that the troubles in those cities augured uprisings against whites in other cities. According to the unnamed author, who cited a so-called reliable source, African Americans were using express rail, parcel post, and even coffins to ship arms and ammunition. Blacks who could pass as whites were purchasing the weapons to avoid attracting attention. Quoting a secretive message allegedly circulating in New York, the author surmised that Philadelphia and Cleveland were the next targets. The twenty-six page report was strident, alarmist, and lacked corroboration; but it was also typical of the intelligence received by the BI and MID that summer.[33] BI agent William Sausele, who investigated a prediction that blacks would ambush whites during a St. Louis parade, determined that "most of these rumors, when traced, ended in some such blind alley, as 'heard it on a street car' . . . or 'talking to two men in a saloon,' etc."[34]

Yet BI agents and MID officers dutifully passed on the received information to their superiors, who did the same; copies swiftly arrived at the offices of other government intelligence offices. The chain of command thus became de facto verification of the reports' content. Consider the following cover letter, signed by MID director Marlborough Churchill and addressed to BI chief Frank Burke: "Enclosed herewith for your information find copy of 3rd Endorsement, dated St. Louis, Mo., August 4, 1919,

[30] Personnel Adjutant USS *Amphion* to Port Intelligence Officer, July 25, 1919, Case File 80–163–148, RG 165, box 132.

[31] J. E. Cutler to Chief, Morale Branch, July 17, 1919, Case File 80–164, RG 165, box 132; Churchill to the Army Chief of Staff, July 16, 1919, Case File 80–163, RG 165, box 132.

[32] Memorandum for the Adjutant General of the Army, n.d., Case File 80–163, RG 165, box 132.

[33] Joseph Baker to Frank Burke, August 21, 1919, RG 65, OGF 3057, reel 304.

[34] William C. Sausele, "In re: Bolsheviki activities, general investigations," October 14, 1919, RG 65, OGF 105,390, reel 484; Sausele, "In re: Bolsheviki Activities," October 18, 1919, RG 65, OGF 375,446, reel 824 (quote).

and addressed to Headquarters, Central Department, Chicago, Ill., and signed 'T. S. Maffitt, Captain, U.S.A., Intelligence Officer,' same being a report of an investigation made by the Intelligence Officer, St. Louis, of certain rumors that negroes were purchasing fire arms in St. Louis and East St. Louis, Mo."[35] Churchill offered not a word about the rumors' veracity (note the noncommittal phrase "for your information"), but the lengthy provenance of what was, essentially, a report about rumors suggested the information was of the utmost significance.

Like the rumors about racial uprisings, stories of rampant arms purchases and stockpiling proved exaggerated, inaccurate, or uncorroborated. For his report, Captain Maffitt had interviewed St. Louis's chief of police and chief of detectives. Both men stated that "their reports show that a large number of high-powered rifles and pistols and a large amount of ammunition have been purchased" by blacks in St. Louis and East St. Louis. When asked, however, neither man could estimate that "large number."[36] Concern that black employees were stealing gun parts to assemble weapons led the Remington Arms Company of Connecticut to place watchers on the factory floor.[37] In Denver, an intrepid BI agent, hearing rumors of increased arms sales, visited pawn brokers and gun shops in October. One pawn shop had sold a single handgun to an African American during the previous six weeks. Another broker had sold twenty-five pistols to blacks in July and eleven in August. The reason for the modest increase in sales was no mystery to the agent: "the Chicago trouble."[38] In Newport News, fears of a black uprising led the city council to require permits from a city official to purchase firearms, and the police prohibited the sale of weapons to African Americans. But there was an uptick in arms sales – to whites.[39]

Newport News was not the only community that restricted or prohibited arms purchases by African Americans. City authorities and local gun shops stopped weapons sales to blacks in Washington and Chicago during those cities' riots. Throughout Texas, gun dealers worked with

---

[35] Churchill to Burke, August 14, 1919, RG 65, OGF 375,446, reel 824.

[36] T. S. Maffitt, August 4, 1919, RG 65, OGF 375,446, reel 824.

[37] William P. Hazen, "Re: Larceny of Guns and Gun Parts from the Remington Arms Company," October 1, 1919, RG 65, OGF 901, in *Federal Surveillance of Afro-Americans*, reel 8, frame 90.

[38] Charles H. Heighton, "In re: sale of guns and ammunition," October 9, 1919, RG 65, OGF 375,462, reel 824.

[39] J. G. Shuey, "In re: Alleged preparation for uprising by negroes at Newport News, Virginia," August 11, 1919, RG 65, OGF 374,223 and 374,237, reel 822.

local, state, and federal officials to prohibit gun sales to blacks after those riots as well. On August 5, a Beaumont hardware store manager reported to the BI that five black men had tried to purchase rifles that day, but he had refused them. The manager was not alone. All of the hardware stores in Port Arthur and two other large hardware stores in Beaumont had agreed not to sell rifles to blacks, an embargo that continued until at least October. Indeed, all dealers "in the larger cities have been instructed by the Sheriff's Department not to sell any more ammunition or fire arms to the negroes," reported a special agent with the U.S. Railroad Administration.[40] An El Paso, Texas, gun dealer informed the MID that Pullman porters were trying to buy weapons and ammunition – he feared the porters were smuggling the guns to Chicago.[41] The sheriff of Harrison County, Texas, recorded all shipments of weapons and ammunition to black residents; he also stopped blacks from selling the *Defender*.[42]

African Americans who sent or sought weapons through the mail also risked the intervention of federal authorities. C. K. Jackson, a hotel porter in Washington, D.C., asked his brother to send him a revolver and cartridges from Scranton, Pennsylvania, during the capital's riot. After a postal inspector intercepted the package, the BI sent an agent to interview C. K. Jackson and his employer. The agent decided the "subject" was "a quiet, good man, very peaceful" and would not "use the revolver even if he had one." The BI closed the investigation without further action.[43] Also in Washington, a prominent black physician, fearing that more antiblack collective violence might break out, asked an attorney in New York to mail him six revolvers and ammunition. The request came to the attention of Major Loving, who implored the lawyer not to send the weapons.[44] Loving's request, as well as the BI agent's belief that it was his duty to assess C. K. Jackson's right to own a firearm,

---

[40] V. I. Snyder, "In re: Negro Race Riots," August 8, 1919, RG 65, OGF 369,955, reel 812; Fuller Williamson to R. S. Mitchell, August 23, 1919, RG 65, OGF 17,011, reel 347 (quote); H. W. Perkins, "In re: Purchase of Arms by Negroes," October 18, 1919, RG 65, OGF 287,223, reel 704.

[41] District Intelligence Officer to Department Intelligence Officer, August 30, 1919, Case File 10218–366–1, RG 165, copy in box 1, reel 6, Kornweibel Papers.

[42] C. L. Breniman, "In re: Negro race riot propaganda in Texas," August 28, 1919, RG 65, OGF 105,390, reel 484; Perkins, "In re: Purchase of Arms"; Snyder, "In re: Negro Race Riots."

[43] Roy McHenry to Frank Burke, August 9, 1919; George L. Wallace, "In re: C. K. Jackson, negro, New Cochran Hotel, Washington, D.C.," August 13, 1919, RG 65, OGF 372,680, in *Federal Surveillance of Afro-Americans*, reel 12, frames 540–2.

[44] W. H. Loving to M. Churchill, August 10, 1919, Case File 10218–350–7, RG 165, copy in box 1, reel 6, Kornweibel Papers.

illustrate the extent of the government's campaign to impede black gun ownership.

Armed by All Means

State and federal efforts to disarm African Americans only partially succeeded. By the fall of 1919, blacks across the nation had redoubled their efforts to obtain weapons for protection. The year's antiblack collective violence had not ended, while the armed resistance mounted during the race riots to date demonstrated the necessity of owning weapons. By all means possible, African Americans obtained firearms, which only reinforced government officials' belief that African Americans were plotting uprisings against whites.

In August 1919, a union-led strike at the Tatum Lumber Company of Hattiesburg, Mississippi, prompted black workers to obtain and carry weapons. BI agent D. G. McGilvray, who interviewed local gun dealers, determined that "numbers of negroes in this vicinity are unusually well armed with new guns and revolvers" because one hardware store owner continued to sell to blacks. Though he had no evidence, McGilvray accused the black union of wanting to start a race riot. (Unlike in Bogalusa, the unions in Hattiesburg were segregated.) The agent apparently did not consider the possibility that black laborers, fearful of meeting the same fate as the sharecroppers who had unionized in Phillips County, Arkansas, were arming to protect themselves. (McGilvray admitted that he never interviewed black union members because he did not want to.)[45]

Black residents of Hattiesburg were not alone in seeking out gun dealers eager to make sales. In Waco, Texas, a merchant who had sold several .30–30 rifles to blacks came to the attention of the BI after he told another Waco resident that he was receiving additional requests from blacks for the weapons. The BI shared this information with the local sheriff for "such investigation as the facts warrant."[46] In Newport News, Virginia, residents rushed to buy arms and ammunition before police began enforcing the ban on sales to blacks. One hardware store sold 2,700 pistol cartridges in the month before the ban took effect. Another dealer estimated

[45] D. G. McGilvray, "In re: Labor Trouble (Strike) at Tatum Lbr. Co's. Saw Mill," September 13, 1919, RG 65, OGF 374,239, reel 822; D. G. McGilvray, "In re – Alleged Race Trouble in Hattiesburg," October 26, 1919, RG 65, OGF 376,879, reel 826 (quote).

[46] F. M. Spencer to Sheriff John R. Currington, October 15, 1919, RG 65, OGF 361,396, reel 796.

that had he not obeyed the police order, he would have sold $5,000 of cartridges in five weeks. Perhaps because of the ban, rumors spread that blacks were plotting to loot the army's Pig Point General Ordnance Depot, located near Norfolk, prompting the depot's commanding officer to request an entire company of additional guard troops.[47] In Detroit, black gun buyers flocked to the shop of W. E. Wandersee, who welcomed their business. During a two month period in 1919, for example, the shop sold approximately 270 guns to African Americans. When a BI agent "under cover" asked if the guns were used for hunting, a clerk, himself an avid hunter, replied that he had "never observed a negro in the woods." Noting that many customers were southern migrants, the clerk surmised that they bought guns because they were not allowed to own them in the South. Or perhaps these purchasers simply wanted rifles to use at a nearby shooting gallery, which the agent also visited. (His "cover" did not fool the gallery's patrons, who apparently vandalized the agent's vehicle: "a very embarrassing incident of the boldness of negroes was illustrated on the car," the agent reported.)[48]

New Negro writers and their supporters reported and lauded weapons purchases by blacks. The *New York Call* listed Norfolk, Atlanta, New Orleans, Memphis, and East St. Louis as cities where black residents were arming and organizing themselves. The *Commoner*, also of New York, offered a rallying cry: "Let every Negro arm himself and swear to die fighting in defense of his home, his rights and his person."[49] In the *Cleveland Gazette*, Harry Clay Smith warned readers that because Cleveland might well be the next city to suffer white mob attacks, they should "have a U.S. Army Riot Gun" in their home. The blunt editorial attracted the attention of Cleveland's chief of police, who called upon Smith. The *Cleveland News* claimed that the chief confronted Smith and accused him of trying to incite a riot, but both men denied that a heated exchange took place. The chief "just asked me what my intentions were in printing the editorial and I assured him my intentions were good," reported

[47] Shuey, "In re: Alleged preparation," (August 11, 1919); Commanding Officer, Pig Point, Va., November 2, 1919, box 1, folder "Pig Point – Disturbances," Record Group 159, Records of the Inspector General Army, Reports of Annual Inspectors and Special Investigations, 1917–1920, U.S. National Archives and Records Administration, College Park, Md.

[48] John A. Dowd, "In re: I.W.W. Activities Revolutionary Matter," October 28, 1919, RG 65, OGF 376,429, reel 826.

[49] Transcribed note of clippings from the *New York Call*, July 25, 1919, and *New York Commoner*, July 23, 1919, Waskow Notes, tab "U.S. Reaction."

Smith, who pointedly reminded readers that advising citizens to take legal measures to protect themselves and their homes was no crime.[50] Other New Negroes took care to call for the use of arms only if attacked. William Byrd, Smith's colleague at the *Gazette*, plainly stated, "we believe in order and law. We desire all men to live up to this standard. But we demand of the colored race to protect themselves at all hazards! Gentlemen, you are not rioting, but are doing your duty." Or, as a Norfolk black newspaper put it with more flair, "white folks don't like cold steel any more than black folks."[51] Although it is difficult to measure the precise effects of these editorials – did arms sales tick up after publication? – these veritable calls to arms offered a forceful and public response to the clandestine campaign to disarm African Americans.

Concern over restrictions on black gun ownership prompted Archibald Grimké, president of the Washington, D.C., NAACP branch, to write directly to Secretary of War Newton Baker. The pogrom in Phillips County, Arkansas, had recently ended, and Grimké was troubled by Associated Press reports suggesting that federal troops had only disarmed African Americans during the upheaval. Was this true? Grimké wanted to know. "It must readily occur to you," he told Baker, "that any use of Federal forces in such a way as to convey the impression to the minds of Negroes and of the public in general, that the general government regarded the right of Negroes to bear and keep arms as not being protected as freely and completely by the Federal and State Constitutions relating to that subject, as the same right is protected in the case of other citizens, is a matter of the very deepest concern." Baker assured Grimké that the War Department made "no differentiation on the basis of race" when it authorized troops to disarm citizens during riots. Although Baker acknowledged that blacks were disarmed in Arkansas, he did not add that the troops did not similarly take guns away from whites.[52]

Whatever the War Department's policy, federal agents continued to record weapons sales to blacks in 1920. In April, clerks at a major

---

[50] "The Mob! A Warning," *Cleveland Gazette*, August 2, 1919, 2 (first quote); "Chief of Police Smith Refuses to Be 'Used' by a 'Cracker' Reporter," *Cleveland Gazette*, August 9, 1919, 1 (second quote).

[51] William A. Byrd, "The Militia in Race Riots," *Cleveland Gazette*, n.d., and "The National Disgrace and Shame," *Journal and Guide* (Norfolk, Va.), August 2, 1919, excerpted in Kerlin, *Voice of the Negro*, 15–18.

[52] Archibald Grimké to Newton Baker, October 27, 1919; Baker to Grimké, October 31, 1919, box 39–28, folder, "October 1919," Archibald Grimké Papers, Moorland-Spingarn Research Center.

Chicago sporting goods store expressed "amazement at the large sales of shot guns and ammunition to negroes during the past few weeks." A BI agent attributed this spike to fears of another race riot breaking out.[53] After a double lynching near Houston in June, black residents stocked up on rifle and revolver ammunition, prompting one hardware store owner to require black customers to obtain written permission from a white man for future purchases.[54] In Miami, blacks armed themselves as racial tensions rose during a dispute over the boundaries of segregated neighborhoods. In one case, a home being built by a black family in the white enclave of Highland Park was dynamited. The explosion immediately brought forth African Americans wielding "a furious assortment of weapons," in the words of a BI agent. Arriving at the scene, Miami's chief of police persuaded them to disperse peacefully.[55] Although several months had passed since the last major race riot in the United States, African Americans in Chicago, Houston, and Miami were taking no chances, finding ways to arm themselves.

During 1919, African Americans' procurement and use of arms to repel mobs forged the crux of resistance to antiblack collective violence. Even an avowal or exhortation to carry weapons was an exercise of resistance because it challenged white supremacists to first consider the personal risks of attacking blacks. The bearing of arms had another purpose. By carefully linking armed self-defense to the failure of authorities to prevent white mob attacks, New Negro writers challenged local, state, and federal governments to uphold the law, fully and fairly. The BI and MID, however, ignored this connection and perceived the postwar freedom struggle as nothing more than an appendage of socialism and communism. Recurrent, histrionic rumors of black uprisings consumed the attention and resources of the BI and MID, stoked the Red Scare, and brought a national initiative to deny African Americans' access to legal firearms and ammunition.

Despite this campaign, blacks continued to obtain weapons and demonstrated their willingness to mount armed resistance toward white supremacy. Federal agents narrowly viewed these episodes as added proof

[53] A. H. Loula, "Weekly Summary of Radical Activities," May 1, 1920, RG 65, Bureau Section File 202.600–14, reel 922.
[54] R. W. Tinsley, "Race Riot Situation, Wharton, Texas," July 2, 1920, RG 65, OGF 387,830, reel 846.
[55] Leon F. Howe, "Dynamiting of negro houses in Miami," July 7, 1920, RG 65, OGF 387,852, reel 846.

of an imminent black uprising. In contrast, African Americans saw the bigger picture: what, in the end, was the purpose of organizing and resisting? In an editorial entitled "Negro Fraternalism and the New Era," a black monthly, the *People's Pilot* (Richmond), offered a subtle answer to that question. With reference to the popularity of black lodges and secret societies, the *Pilot* noted growing fears that blacks might use the power of these organizations to do "dangerous things." Yes, we should put these organizations to use, the *Pilot* argued – to uplift the race, promote civics, provide education, and advance voting rights. We must "teach our organized people how to fight, to the finish, the battles of LIBERTY and livelihood." With a Wilsonian flourish, the editorial inverted white fears of black uprisings to offer both a rebuttal to the Red Scare and a reminder of what African Americans were trying to accomplish "during these trying times."[56]

---

[56] *People's Pilot*, "Negro Fraternalism and the New Era," October 1919, in Kerlin, *Voice of the Negro*, 174–5.

8

The Fight for Justice

The Arrests and Trials of Black and White Rioters

Throughout 1919, African Americans recognized that resistance to antiblack collective violence required sustained legal action to achieve three related goals: first, to ensure that blacks arrested for riot-related crimes received unbiased adjudication of the charges against them; second, to pressure authorities to charge and try white rioters; and third, to win financial compensation for the victims of mob assaults. This chapter focuses on this threefold fight for justice in the aftermath of the riots in Charleston, Longview, Washington, Chicago, Knoxville, and Omaha, all of which occurred between May and September 1919.

African Americans' legal initiatives in these communities shared several features. The national office and branches of the NAACP hired lawyers and raised defense funds for scores of black defendants. Black lawyers offered their services to jailed men and women. Black leaders in Charleston, Washington, and Chicago expanded their post-riot legal defense efforts into campaigns to end problems such as police and military mistreatment of African Americans. The collection of affidavits from victims of mob violence yielded substantial evidence of crimes against blacks and helped pressure authorities to file charges against white rioters. In Knoxville and Omaha, white authorities needed no prodding – they were eager to prosecute white rioters because of the extensive damage they had caused to the courthouses in both cities. Convictions proved elusive, however, as all-white juries acquitted almost every defendant. Supportive of the rioters' rough justice motives, jurors appeared willing to excuse crimes committed in the act of lynching (or of trying to lynch) black men. Similar difficulties in obtaining convictions attended the legal proceedings in Charleston and Longview.

New Negro writers added their voices to the legal struggle, frequently invoking the wartime contributions of African Americans and the purpose of the nation's entry into the world war. The United States could not serve as a model democracy as long as local, state, and federal authorities failed to protect all citizens, regardless of race, and let lawbreakers go unpunished. Washington's riot, because of its scope and location, drew special attention. Commentators emphasized the importance of upholding law and order at the seat of government in order to set an example for the rest of the nation. New Negroes also recognized the necessity of countering the slanted coverage of all the riots. As James Weldon Johnson wrote in the *New York Age*, "lying propaganda is being spread all over the country."[1] Documenting the actual causes of mob violence would, hopefully, inhibit or even prevent the prosecution of black self-defenders, who, in city after city, were being blamed for causing the riots. The rhetoric of the New Negroes was eloquent, their reasoning elegant; but, like the initiative to put white rioters in court, their ability to shape judicial outcomes proved limited.

Seeking Justice in Charleston

In the wake of Charleston's May 1919 riot, local black leaders mobilized on behalf of the victims of white mob attacks. Edward C. Mickey, an undertaker and secretary of the Charleston NAACP branch, organized a grievance committee that interviewed sixteen African Americans caught in the riot. The committee presented these affidavits, which offered harrowing, first person accounts of the mob assaults, to the navy and the New York office of the NAACP.[2] Mickey and the committee also asked Secretary of the Navy Josephus Daniels to order a comprehensive investigation, both of the riot and of the mistreatment of black residents by patrolling marines, and to punish the guilty parties. Observing that Charleston's "large and orderly" black population had long lived and worked peacefully with the Navy Yard, the committee petitioned "the Navy Department, through you, to see that such authority and power as may be necessary will be used that the Negro citizens of Charleston may

---

[1] James W. Johnson, "Act at Once!," *New York Age*, October 11, 1919, 4.

[2] *Record of Proceedings of a Court of Inquiry Convened at the Navy Yard, Charleston, S.C.*, May 27–June 19, 1919, File 9535, RG 125, box 203, folder 2, 122–3 (hereafter *Court of Inquiry*); Edward C. Mickey to Archibald Grimké, May 29, 1919, box 39–27, folder "May 1919," Archibald Grimké Papers, Moorland-Spingarn Research Center.

not again be made to suffer in person or in property by the presence of the uniformed representatives of the Navy."[3]

Mickey worried that Daniels and the navy would not take the riot seriously because its victims were black. As he reminded Archibald Grimké, a member of the Washington, D.C., branch of the NAACP, the army had hanged black soldiers for attacking white police and citizens in Houston in 1917 – why should this riot be handled any differently? Mickey also pointed out that "in Texas the Negroes were goaded by the white citizens to their action; here the Negroes never interfere, nor even cast insinuating remarks about uniformed white men."[4] Grimké, who, less than two months later, saw his own city engulfed in a race riot started by white servicemen, agreed. He called on the office of the secretary of the navy to check personally on the status of the grievance committee's petition. To Grimké's dismay, Daniels's own secretary knew nothing about it, nor even about the riot. "What, a case like this and you don't know what has happened in Charleston?" Grimké exclaimed. "Exactly the same sort of thing that happened in Houston, when you people hung nineteen of our men and put forty of them in prison for life, and you never heard anything of it?" Daniels's secretary sent him to the office of the judge advocate general, where Grimké pressed the matter further.[5] Mickey and Grimké were not the only ones to compare Charleston's riot to Houston's. "The case is so similar," commented the *Chicago Defender*, "that efforts will be made to have the war department take immediate action."[6]

The navy did, in fact, carry out a lengthy investigation of the riot. A court of inquiry, composed of three officers, held nineteen days of hearings and called dozens of witnesses, black and white, military and civilian, to the receiving ship at the Navy Yard. In its finding of facts, the court determined that the sidewalk encounter between an unidentified black man and two sailors, Roscoe Coleman and Robert Morton, precipitated the riot. It also concluded that "wild rumors and stories of a sailor having been shot by a negro" led to widespread attacks on blacks by servicemen

---

[3] "Resolutions presented by the Negro citizens of Charleston, S.C., to the Honorable Josephus Daniels, Sec. of the U.S. Navy, Wash. D.C., concerning a riot by enlisted men in Charleston, May 10, 1919," n.d., Waskow Notes, tab "Charleston Riot."

[4] Mickey to Grimké, May 29, 1919.

[5] Archibald Grimké statement, n.d., box B-2, folder "Annual Conferences – Reports of Branches 1919, #1," NAACP Records.

[6] "Sailors Stage Bloody Battles in Streets of Charleston," *Chicago Defender*, May 17, 1919, 1.

and civilians, with sailors forming the majority of the mobs. The court identified Coleman, Morton, and two other sailors, George W. Biggs and Ralph Stone, as the riot inciters and recommended that they be charged with conduct to the prejudice of good order and discipline. Though the court had no jurisdiction over Alexander Lanneau, the white salesman who had joined in the attacks on blacks, it urged Charleston authorities to charge him. The investigating officers cleared two marine privates for shooting the young black man William Brown, declaring his death to be the "result of his own misconduct in running when ordered to halt." Sailors Jacob Cohen and George Holliday faced the most serious charge, manslaughter, for shooting a black man named Isaac Doctor.[7]

The navy held courts martial for the six charged sailors, but the "justice for our people" sought by Edward Mickey was, for the most part, denied. Many of the accused men solicited the help of their Congressional representatives in an attempt to expedite their courts martial. "I have been confined almost six months," George Holliday wrote to Senator William Kirby (D-Ark.) in October, and "would like very much to be restored to duty as soon as possible."[8] In the case of Robert Morton, Senator Morris Sheppard (D-Texas) asked Secretary Daniels to explain "this unusual procedure where a man is held in confinement for nearly half a year without being given a hearing."[9] In November 1919, the judge advocate general attributed the delays to the "searching investigation" that preceded formal charges.[10] However, since the court of inquiry had completed its work in June and the navy had ordered the courts martial in September, the more likely cause for the delay was the judge advocate's difficulty in locating witnesses. Water Tender Andrew Ohla was the only known witness to Ralph Stone's attack on a black man during the first hours of the riot, but Ohla had left the navy in August. Unable to compel Ohla's appearance before the court, the judge advocate withdrew the charges against Stone in December. Another witness had "practically the only testimony connecting Biggs with any active part" in the riot; he,

---

[7] *Court of Inquiry*, box 203, folder 4, 265 (first quote), 268–272 (second quote on 268); Lt. William H. Reardon to Commanding Officer, Receiving Ship, Navy Yard, Charleston, S.C., May 10, 1919, in *Record of Proceedings of a Board of Investigation Convened on Board the U.S.S. Hartford*, May 17–19, 1919, File 9535, RG 125, box 203, folder 4 (hereafter *Record of Proceedings*).

[8] George Holliday to Senator William F. Kirby, October 29, 1919, File 26251–21674, RG 80, box 1289.

[9] Senator Morris Sheppard to Josephus Daniels, October 27, 1919, File 26251–21674, RG 80, box 1289.

[10] Judge Advocate General to Senator George Chamberlain, November 11, 1919, File 26251–21674, RG 80, box 1289.

too, had been discharged. Neither Biggs nor Morton appear to have been convicted at their courts martial.[11]

Roscoe Coleman tried to avoid a court martial by requesting a discharge from the navy because of his age. The Mansfield, Ohio, native sought the help of his congressman, Democrat William Ashbrook, admitting he had enlisted in the navy without his parents' consent when he was just fifteen. "My Mother is trying to get me discharged on the grounds of being under age, but she is making no headway," he wrote. Ashbrook and other members of the Ohio delegation lobbied the navy to discharge Coleman, even providing a copy of his birth certificate showing he was born in 1903. The judge advocate proceeded with the court martial anyway but acquitted Coleman in December. The navy released him from the brig and restored him to duty.[12]

Holliday and Cohen also went to trial. The judge advocate found them guilty of rioting (conduct to the prejudice of good order and discipline) but acquitted them of the manslaughter charges, sentencing each man to one year in prison and a dishonorable discharge. Although the court of inquiry had produced numerous witness statements placing Cohen and Holliday at the site of the shooting with weapons in hand, the exact details of these statements varied. The defendants had also reconsidered the wisdom of boasting about killing Isaac Doctor, as they had done on the night of the shooting. Holliday, for example, asserted that he was innocent of even the charge of rioting. Unable to meet the burden of proof for manslaughter, the judge advocate, to his apparent dissatisfaction, settled for the lesser convictions. In March 1920, to explain why he would not recommend clemency for Cohen, the judge advocate pointedly commented on "the very moderate sentence of the court for the serious offense committed."[13] Hundreds of white sailors had rioted in Charleston, three black men had died and seven had suffered gunshot wounds; and yet only two rioters

[11] Memoranda to the Judge Advocate General, September 13 and December 1, 1919 (quote on December 1 memorandum); Captain R. W. Peard to the Judge Advocate General, December 16, 1919, File 26251-21674, RG 80, box 1289. Unfortunately, the records do not indicate the outcomes of the courts martial of Biggs and Morton.

[12] William Ashbrook to General George Barnett, October 13, 1919; Roscoe Coleman to Ashbrook, October 10, 1919 (quote); Sen. Atlee Pomerene to Admiral Clark, October 20, 1919; Judge Advocate General to Ashbrook, January 3, 1920; Ashbrook to Judge Advocate General, November 3, 1919; Certificate of Birth for Roscoe O. Coleman, File 26251-21674, RG 80, box 1289.

[13] Judge Advocate General to Charles Coady, January 16, 1920; Judge Advocate General to Kenneth McKellar, January 16, 1920; Judge Advocate General to Nathan Cohen, March 19, 1920 (quote); George Holliday to the Secretary of the Navy, March 30, 1920, File 26251-21674, RG 80, box 1289.

went to jail for brief sentences, the very outcome Edward Mickey and Archibald Grimké had feared.

Victims of the riot also sought redress through civil action. Richard Mickey, Edward's brother, asked the national office of the NAACP to help with a request to the navy for payment for injuries and damages to black-owned property.[14] F. W. Morton, of the NAACP, proposed working with South Carolina's Congressional delegation to procure compensation to the city of Charleston, in hopes that some of the funds would go to deserving black residents. "I do not know how [Secretary of the Navy] Daniels stands with [the] S.C. delegation," Morton wondered, "but if any of them like him none too well, they might at least howl some, and that would not hurt at all."[15] Charleston mayor Tristam Hyde showed his support by personally presenting injured parties' claims to navy officials.[16] Moses Gladden, a gunshot victim of the mob, hired an attorney to file a claim, while Emma Dawson, whose son Peter Irving was paralyzed in a mob attack, appealed directly to the secretary of the navy. "My son is disabled," Dawson wrote, and the "cause is a gun shot wound inflicted by a sailor in the employ of the United States Government." The navy denied both requests. "This is not a matter within the jurisdiction of the navy department to consider," Franklin D. Roosevelt, then the acting secretary of the navy, told Moses Gladden's lawyer in November 1919. Only Congress, Roosevelt advised, could pay damages "if it should see fit to give it."[17] But Congress did not see fit; South Carolina's legislators showed no interest in sponsoring the bill proposed by the NAACP. As a result, black residents of Charleston did not receive compensation for injuries or property damage. (The navy also rejected the claims of the two white owners of the shooting galleries looted by sailors and marines.)

[14] For biographical details of the Mickey brothers, see the finding aid for the Mickey Funeral Home Papers (1906–1934), Manuscript Collection No. 1021, Avery Research Center for African American History and Culture, College of Charleston, Charleston, S.C., accessed June 6, 2011, at http://www.cofc.edu/avery/mickeyFuneral.htm.

[15] F. Morton to Richard H. Mickey, June 23, 1919, Waskow Notes, tab "NAACP Probes"; Morton to John Shillady, June 9, 1919; Mickey to Shillady, May 29, 1919, Waskow Notes, tab "U.S. Reaction – Worldview."

[16] Anthony J. McKevlin to William Roach, British Vice-Consul, Charleston, S.C., November 30, 1920, File 26283–2588, RG 80, box 1775, 2.

[17] E. F. Smith to the Secretary of the Sixth Naval District, October 29, 1919; Franklin D. Roosevelt to E. F. Smith, November 6, 1919 (Roosevelt quote); Emma Dawson to the Secretary of the Navy, September 18, 1920 (Dawson quote); Office of the Solicitor, Navy Department to Commandant, Sixth Naval District, October 7, 1920, File 26283–2588, RG 80, box 1775.

The navy did pay modest damages to one individual. Cyril Burton, a thirty-five-year-old bricklayer, was walking home on the night of the riot when several sailors robbed him and attacked him with pipes and clubs, slashing his scalp and almost severing the tip of a finger. Burton, who had lived in Charleston less than a year, was a native of Antigua and a British subject. The British vice consul in Charleston took up Burton's case, lobbying both the Departments of State and Navy to compensate Burton for his injuries, lost wages, and the robbery. In 1921, the navy paid him twenty-five dollars and recommended that Congress enact a special bill to give Burton another $200. By accepting the smaller payment, however, Burton apparently ceded his claim to additional damages, and Congress never passed the compensatory legislation.[18]

The fight for justice in Charleston extended beyond legal efforts to win damages and to see that white rioters were charged and tried. A committee of local black ministers offered several recommendations for the city of Charleston to prevent future mob attacks on blacks. The clergy urged the city to hire black police officers and to form an interracial committee. They called for the improvement of housing, sanitary, and education conditions for black residents. "The negroes were not the aggressors [in the riot]," the ministers noted. After reviewing the harm done by the mobs, they declared that black Charlestonians wanted "social justice and a square deal."[19] The riot, the clergy suggested, was a symptom of the racial inequities that the war – and blacks' wartime contributions – had exposed. Punishment of rioting whites and compensation of injured blacks was important; so, too, the social, political, and economic remedies sought by African Americans. It was a call taken up by black leaders in many of the cities and locales that experienced antiblack collective violence in 1919.

Seeking Justice in Longview, Texas

As detailed in Chapter 2, the armed resistance of Longview's black residents to white mob attacks in early July 1919 resulted in the declaration of

---

[18] Statement of Albert C. Wilkinson, M.D., Superintendent of Roper Hospital, May 14, 1919; Cyril Burton to Tristam T. Hyde, May 14, 1919; Office of the Solicitor, Navy Department, to James Roach, March 25, 1921; Theodore Roosevelt, Jr., to the Secretary of State, March 16 and May 28, 1921; Roosevelt to Speaker of the House Frederick Gillett, June 1, 1921, File 26283–2588, RG 80, box 1775; Waskow, *From Race Riot*, 15–16.

[19] Newby, *Black Carolinians*, 192–3.

martial law and the deployment of state troops and rangers. As the guardsmen collected weapons from white and black residents and enforced a
curfew, the rangers arrested the black men who had defended S. L. Jones,
the teacher who had challenged white supremacy by allegedly reporting
the lynching of Lemuel Walters to the *Chicago Defender*. (Jones and his
friend Dr. C. P. Davis, who had organized Jones's protective guard, had
both escaped to Chicago.) The guardsmen also rounded up sixteen white
men who had been part of the mob that had attempted to lynch Jones and
a dozen or so whites suspected of arson. All of the prisoners were detained
in a stockade erected on the courthouse lawn. Fearing the formation of
another lynch mob, authorities soon transferred the black prisoners to a
jail in Austin. The possibility of prosecution did not appear to distress
the white prisoners. As Texas Ranger Captain W. M. Hanson read out
arrest warrants, the men cracked jokes. "You didn't call my name," one
of them piped up – "don't play any favorites." All of the white prisoners
posted the $1,000 bond.[20]

The criminal proceedings against white rioters soon petered out. Two
men charged with arson convinced Hanson they were innocent and they
were released.[21] The others awaited the decision of an all-white grand
jury, but it appeared unlikely to recommend charges. Although a committee of white merchants, bankers, farmers, and lawyers drafted a resolution denouncing the "white men and boys [who set] fire to the houses"
of S. L. Jones and C. P. Davis, the committee reserved most of its opprobrium for Jones, his friends, and the *Chicago Defender*, accusing all of
them of slander and of inciting the riot. The committee appointed three
men to help the rangers and guardsmen: Judge Erskine Bramlette, Sheriff
D. S. Meredith, and Mayor G. A. Bodenheim. In other words, the very
men who had abetted the mob that carried out Lemuel Walters's lynching
and who had planned the attack on Jones's home were now helping to
dispense justice.[22]

Coverage in the black press of the Longview riot noted the connection
between the lynching of Lemuel Walters and the attack on S. L. Jones,
presenting both incidents as evidence of widespread contempt for the law

[20] "16 White Men Under Arrest at Longview," *Dallas Morning News*, July 15, 1919, 1,
Longview Riot File, Longview Public Library (quote); Tuttle, "Violence in a 'Heathen'
Land," 330; Waskow, *From Race Riot*, 18.
[21] "State Troops Are Leaving Longview," *Dallas Morning News*, July 17, 1919, transcription in the Longview Riot File.
[22] "Citizens of Longview Adopt Resolutions," *Dallas Morning News*, July 15, 1919, 2,
Longview Riot File.

among white southerners. Though it contained several factual errors, an article in the *Chicago Whip* correctly stated that Jones was the target of a mob because he had (allegedly) told the *Defender* about "the utter disregard of the law by the whites in this section."[23] The *Cleveland Gazette* provided a more detailed and accurate account, also expressing outrage that "armed white brutes" had set out to "lynch-murder" a black man in retaliation for the reporting of a lynching.[24] Longview "is a fair sample of the lawlessness which at present is stalking restlessly through the nation," commented the *Crisis*.[25] The collusion of Longview's white elites and the Texas Rangers suggested, however, that this "lawlessness" would continue.

Longview's black residents and their allies did win one important legal victory: the release of blacks who had taken up arms in self-defense. The transfer of black prisoners to Austin removed them from the oversight of Longview's white elites. While the prisoners awaited their court appearances, the Austin and San Antonio branches of the NAACP brought them food and the branches' legal committees lobbied to get the charges dropped. This effort earned the release of eleven men on the grounds of self-defense. The men who had defended Jones's home were also freed but warned not to return to Longview.[26] This Solomonic decision served as a warning to the town's black residents: resistance to white supremacy would incur, at the very least, exile. It also assuaged white residents that Longview was now rid of its black "troublemakers."

The NAACP paid a high price for its advocacy of the Longview defendants. Texas officials, including the adjutant general of the national guard, the attorney general, and judges, demanded to see the Austin branch's records and interrogated the branch president and secretary. On August 20, NAACP national secretary John Shillady, who had just interviewed S. L. Jones and C. P. Davis in Chicago, arrived in Austin to inquire about the investigation. Shillady quickly realized how much Longview had impressed state authorities, who insisted that they had proof of an imminent uprising by blacks. They also complained to Shillady that certain black publications (i.e., the *Defender*) had "evil effects" and were "inciting" Texas's black residents. A constable served Shillady with a

---

[23] "Martial Law in Texas," *Chicago Whip*, July 19, 1919, 1.
[24] "Lynch-Murder in North Texas and Many Homes Are Burned," *Cleveland Gazette*, July 19, 1919, 1.
[25] "The Riot at Longview, Texas," *Crisis* 18, no. 6 (October 1919), 297–8.
[26] "The Austin Branch" and "Reports of the Branches," *Branch Bulletin* vol. III, no. 9 (September 1919), 88, 91; Waskow, *From Race Riot*, 19.

subpoena to appear before a secret session of a court of inquiry and he was followed wherever he went in Austin. On August 22, several white men, including the constable and Judge Dave Pickle (who presided over the court of inquiry) accosted Shillady on the sidewalk, beat him up, and forced him to buy a train ticket to leave town.[27]

Jones and Davis also suffered for standing up to mob justice and white supremacy. In Chicago, the Olivet Baptist Church provided both men with temporary accommodations and arranged for them to tell their stories to the NAACP. Longview authorities soon seized what remained of their property. Realizing they could never return home, the two friends brought their families north to live with them. In 1920, Davis tried to seek compensation for the loss of his home and medical office in Longview. Two Chicago lawyers argued that Davis, because he was now an Illinois resident, could sue in federal court. Davis appealed to the national office of the NAACP for financial aid to pay the $500 retainer, but the Legal Committee turned him down, citing its belief that the suit had to be filed in a Texas court, where the possibility of winning the case with lawyers from Chicago was highly unlikely.[28] Although Dr. Davis never got his day in court, many of the African Americans who defended themselves against mob violence in the nation's capital just one week after Longview's riot did – and they won.

Winning Justice in Washington, D.C.

James Weldon Johnson, who had traveled from New York to witness Washington's riot, astutely recognized why African Americans and their allies must mount an all-out legal response to the mob attacks: if justice could not be won at the capital, then what hope was there for the rest of the nation? As a contributing editor to the *New York Age*, Johnson wrote a series of eloquent, forceful editorials that framed the legal and political issues. "An armed mob of lynchers wearing the uniform of the United States Government should not be allowed to wreak vengeance indiscriminately, or even to take the law in their own hands. This exhibition of savagery at the seat of government only shows how deep the spirit of race hatred and contempt for law has eaten into the nation's

---

[27] "The National Secretary in Texas," *Branch Bulletin* vol. III, no. 9 (September 1919), 85–9 (quotes on 86); Schneider, *We Return Fighting*, 29–32.

[28] Tuttle, "Violence in a 'Heathen' Land," 333; Dr. C. P. Davis to John Shillady, June 14, 1920; Field Secretary to Davis, June 25, 1920; Arthur Spingarn to Walter White, June 21, 1920, in *NAACP Papers*, Part 7, Series A, reel 19.

vitals."[29] Referring to the recently concluded peace proceedings in Paris, Johnson pointedly asked how the United States could show concern for the rights of other nationalities while abandoning its black citizens. "Let President Wilson realize that there is as much at stake for democracy and humanity in the United States as in any other spot on the globe."[30]

Johnson was not the only New Negro eager to open a legal front after Washington's riot. William Monroe Trotter's National Equal Rights League organized the Vigilance Committee to raise money to pay for the defense of African Americans who had been arrested. The National Race Congress formed a similar committee.[31] Chandler Owen and A. Philip Randolph called for biracial juries and the hiring of more black police officers in cities such as Washington.[32] In the *Cleveland Gazette*, William Byrd linked the mob violence in Washington to the failure of the nation to enforce the Fourteenth and Fifteenth Amendments. "This nation should hide its face when it forces the colored men in America to fight to maintain their franchise," Byrd wrote. He urged black men to pledge their votes to the Republican Party, which must promise to "restore a democratic government in the south as well as in the entire nation."[33] These calls for action did not go unheeded.

Washington's NAACP branch put itself at the vanguard of the legal battle. The branch was one of the association's largest and most active. Even as the riot was occurring, three branch officials – Swan Kendrick, Horace Anderson, and George E. C. Hayes – pressed for an end to police bias and brutality. In a conference with Louis Brownlow, president of the D.C. Board of Commissioners, they told him about the beatings of black men that were occurring at police station houses. The men asked to be deputized, so they could freely visit the stations, but Brownlow dodged the request and stated that he had ordered the police to start arresting white rioters. He added that most of the "gun play" was being done by African Americans. Anderson firmly corrected him. Any use of firearms by blacks "was occasioned by the feeling that they had to protect themselves as for the preceding two nights no protection had been given

[29] "Mob Law at Capital," *New York Age*, July 26, 1919, 4.
[30] "In the Shadow of the Dome of the Capitol," *New York Age*, July 26, 1919, p. 4.
[31] "Vigilance Committee Has $343 for Defense," *New York Age*, August 30, 1919, 1.
[32] "The Cause of and Remedy for Race Riots," *Messenger* vol. II, no. 9 (September 1919), 14–21.
[33] William A. Byrd, "Amendments Must Be Forced!," *Cleveland Gazette*, August 30, 1919, 1.

them against the whites." The distinction seemed lost on Brownlow. He assured the men they could call on him again, but they left the meeting doubting his commitment to fairness.[34]

Meanwhile the local NAACP branch initiated legal efforts to aid black self-defenders, as its counterparts in Texas had done. Three talented black lawyers served on the branch's Legal Committee: James Cobb, William Houston, and Royal Hughes. Cobb, a native of Louisiana, had moved to Washington to attend Howard University Law School and would later serve as a Municipal Court judge in Washington. Houston, also a graduate of Howard, had his own practice and taught night classes at the law school. His son, Charles Hamilton Houston, had just completed his service as an infantry officer stationed at Fort Meade, Maryland. (As a Howard law professor during the 1930s and 1940s, Charles educated a generation of lawyers, including Thurgood Marshall, who helped the NAACP win landmark civil rights cases after World War II.) Branch secretary Swan Kendrick described Hughes as "enthusiastic and eager," praising him for his willingness to represent anyone who lacked counsel.[35] All three men were in Washington during the riot, which had particularly unsettled Cobb; he had warned James Weldon Johnson that if authorities did not act immediately, "the city will be drenched with blood."[36]

The Legal Committee's biggest task was to defend the dozens of black men jailed during the riot for carrying weapons. In addition, several blacks who had used force to protect themselves faced felony charges in the Supreme Court of the District of Columbia. These defendants included the teenager Carrie Johnson and her father, accused of killing a police detective during a mob attack on their home; George Dent, charged with assault with a dangerous weapon; and Theodore Micah Walker and

---

[34] "Additional Notes," *Branch Bulletin* vol. III, no. 8 (August 1919), no page number given; Swan M. Kendrick, Horace G. Anderson, and George E. C. Hayes, "In re a Conversation with Commissioner Brownlow," July 22, 1919, box G-34, folder "DC Branch 1919 March–July," NAACP Records.

[35] For biographical details of William and Charles Houston, see finding aid, William LePre Houston Family Papers, Library of Congress, http://memory.loc.gov/service/mss/ eadxmlmss/eadpdfmss/2010/ms010216.pdf, accessed July 15, 2013; for Cobb, see finding aid, James Adlai Cobb Papers, Moorland-Spingarn Research Center, Howard University, http://www.howard.edu/library/moorland-spingarn/Colla-c.htm, accessed July 15, 2013; for Kendrick's appraisal of Hughes, see S. M. Kendrick to Archibald Grimké, July 25, 1919, box 39–28, folder "July 1919," Archibald Grimké Papers (quote).

[36] James A. Cobb to James W. Johnson, July 21, 1919, box D-49, folder "Cases Supported: Caldwell July-October 1919," NAACP Records.

William Laney, charged with the separate shooting deaths of two white men after they fired at mobs chasing them.[37]

The cases of individuals charged with lesser crimes went to Police Court, where two white judges, Hardison and McMahon, presided on Tuesday, July 22, 1919, the riot's third day. Arrested black men far outnumbered white men: only six of the fifty-two men charged with carrying concealed weapons were white. The justices, eager to restore civil order, swiftly imposed the maximum penalty or bond on one man after another. Sixty-five men had to pay twenty-five dollar fines or serve twenty-five days in jail for disorderly conduct, while five men found guilty of carrying firearms received sentences of a year in jail and a $500 fine. Defendants who requested jury trials for deadly weapons charges had to post bonds of $2,000 rather than the customary $500. This "additional blow to the gun-toters" evoked cries of outrage from the black observers who filled the courtrooms.[38]

Cobb, Houston, and Hughes also protested – they had come to court that morning ready to defend the arrested black men. One of the judges agreed to confer in chambers with the lawyers, who observed that "while these men were technically guilty of carrying concealed weapons the greater portion of them had done so in self defense and from that standpoint they should be judged." Robert Terrell, the city's only black judge, made the same point in open court to Judge McMahon. The Police Court justices apparently agreed. The next day, they ordered investigations of the concealed weapons cases to distinguish between self-defenders and troublemakers. As a result, the justices placed nineteen black men convicted of carrying weapons on probation, and only one man received a year's jail sentence and $500 fine. (In that case, "the sentence was deserved," commented Cobb.)[39]

Milton Waldron, pastor of Washington's Shiloh Baptist Church, appealed directly to U.S. Attorney General A. Mitchell Palmer on behalf

[37] Case numbers 35310 (Johnson), 35350 (Walker), and 35540 (Dent), Criminal Docket vol. 35 (1919), Record Group 21, Records of the Supreme Court of D.C., U.S. National Archives and Records Administration, Washington, D.C., (hereafter CD 35, RG 21).

[38] "Rioters in Courts," *Washington Post*, July 23, 1919, 1 (quote); James A. Cobb to Mary White Ovington, December 3, 1919, box G-34, folder "DC Branch 1919 August–December," NAACP Records.

[39] D.C. Branch of the NAACP, letter to members, July 23, 1919, box G-34, folder "DC Branch 1919 March–July," NAACP Records; Cobb to Ovington, December 3, 1919 (first quote); Cobb to Ovington, December 2, 1919 (second quote), box G-34, folder "DC Branch 1919 August-December," NAACP Records; "Negroes of Washington Were Forced to Defend Themselves," *New York Age*, August 2, 1919, 1.

of black self-defenders, pointing out "the indiscriminate arrests of colored people in connection with the Race riots and the extreme penalty imposed upon them." At Palmer's request, Waldron provided a list of more than thirty black defendants. In an August 8 letter to U.S. District Attorney John E. Laskey, Palmer noted the exorbitant bonds levied against numerous individuals. "Of course, it goes without saying there ought to be no discrimination of that character and I am wondering if you could not find a way to impress our views in that regard upon the authorities who have to deal with the question."[40] Although Cobb, Houston, and Hughes had already remedied the problem, persuading the nation's top law enforcement official to intervene was no small accomplishment. Furthermore, Laskey's office was responsible for prosecuting the black defendants remanded to the Supreme Court of the District of Columbia, so the district attorney now knew that Palmer expected them to receive unbiased treatment.

The Legal Committee of the Washington NAACP branch also offered its services to the defendants remanded to the Supreme Court of the District of Columbia: Carrie Johnson, Theodore Micah Walker, William Laney, and George Dent. Johnson and Walker politely declined, as they both already had legal counsel and said they did not want "help in the sense of charity at all."[41] William Walker, of Newport News, Virginia, had already come to Washington to help his brother, whose three attorneys secured his release on bond pending a grand jury hearing. William Laney accepted the offer, so Cobb, Houston, and Hughes served as his attorneys.[42] All of the defendants would wait months – in two cases, years – before the courts decided their fates.

Theodore Micah Walker appeared before the grand jury in February 1920. Louis Havlicek, the marine wounded in the shoot-out between Walker and a white mob, had died on July 23, 1919, so Walker now faced the possibility of a murder charge. But had a bullet from his revolver killed Havlicek? The grand jury apparently did not believe so; on February 10, 1920, it chose not to indict Walker. George Dent, charged with firing shots into a mob attacking the streetcar that he was riding on, pled not guilty after being indicted on January 30, 1920. His trial lasted all of

[40] Milton Waldron to A. Mitchell Palmer, August 1, 1919 (first quote); Palmer to Waldron, August 8, 1919; Palmer to John E. Laskey, August 8, 1919 (second quote), transcriptions in Waskow Notes, tab "D.C. Riot."

[41] Kendrick to Grimké, July 25, 1919.

[42] "Washington Letter," *New York Age*, August 2, 1919, 4; Case numbers 35310, 35350, 35540, and 35360, CD 35, RG 21.

one day: the jury returned a verdict of not guilty.[43] Carrie Johnson's trial for the first degree murder of Detective Sergeant Harry Wilson did not begin until January 1921. U.S. Attorney Laskey hoped the jury would accept police claims that Carrie was the only armed person in the room when Wilson was shot. Carrie's father also faced a first degree murder charge, but the judge barred the defense from introducing this crucial fact to the jury. He also prohibited Carrie's attorneys, B. L. Gaskins and T. M. Watson, from claiming that Carrie acted in self-defense. Still, the two lawyers hammered at the prosecutor's contention – in a pitch-dark bedroom, several detectives wielding revolvers, who could know beyond a reasonable doubt whose shots had killed Wilson, let alone that Carrie had planned to kill Wilson? Laskey, sensing the jury wavering, reduced the charge to manslaughter. The jury found Carrie guilty, but her attorneys immediately requested a new trial, arguing that she had feared for her life and had defended herself. When a different judge, Frederick L. Siddons, accepted the motion, Laskey decided to discontinue the prosecution (*nolle prosequi*). Almost two years after the shooting in her home, Carrie Johnson was a free woman.[44]

William Laney waited even longer than Johnson for a verdict. Seven white witnesses insisted that Laney shot Kenneth Crall, a member of the mob that had chased Laney, but several hours of police interrogation failed to budge Laney from his claim of innocence. The coroner did not help Laney's case. After extracting the bullet from Crall's body, the coroner peremptorily concluded that Crall "came to his death by being shot with a pistol in hand of [Laney]."[45] The first attempt to convict Laney of first degree murder ended in a mistrial in March 1920, after the judge granted a defense motion that recent publicity regarding letters allegedly written by Laney had prejudiced the jury. Determined to secure a conviction, the prosecution retried Laney in June 1921 in Siddons's court. Although Siddons had allowed Carrie Johnson another trial on the basis of her state of mind, he did not allow Laney's

[43] Case numbers 35540, 36169, and 35350, CD 35, RG 21; "Jury Convicts Two of Assault," *Washington Post*, March 4, 1920, 4; "$1 Hold-Up Booty; 3 Placed on Trial," *Washington Post*, March 5, 1920, 2.

[44] "Girl Faces Murder Charge," *Washington Post*, January 9, 1921, 21; "Girl Is Convicted in Wilson's Death," *Washington Post*, January 14, 1921, 14; "Girl Gets New Trial," *Washington Post*, June 4, 1921, 9; "Released in Riot Killing," *Washington Post*, June 21, 1921, 5.

[45] Case number 35360, CD 35, RG 21 (quote); "Negro Held for Death of Youth Shot During Riot," *Washington Times*, July 27, 1919, 1.

attorneys to refer to the mobs on Massachusetts Avenue the night of Crall's death, or even the rioting that had engulfed the city. This forced Cobb, Houston, and Hughes to defend Laney as if he and Crall were the only ones present at the shooting. The prosecution wrestled with its own challenge: the police had arrested Laney based on the claims of eyewitnesses, but at trial none of them – and more than two dozen took the stand – attested that they actually saw Laney fire his weapon at Crall. Despite Siddons's decision to separate Crall's shooting from the riot, several witnesses recounted a tumultuous, confusing scene, with gunfire "flying in the streets and everywhere." To buttress its case, the prosecution relied on a self-described ballistics expert, who offered the dubious assertion that the deadly bullet, though wadded and misshapen, matched unique markings in Laney's revolver.

On June 30, 1921, the jury convicted Laney of manslaughter, and Siddons sentenced him to eight years in prison. His attorneys successfully appealed the verdict and secured his release on bond. Houston, Cobb, and Hughes asked the appellate justices to discard the pretext that the rioting was irrelevant. The white mobs were "not on a Sunday-school expedition" and, with murderous intent, had chased Laney, who rightly feared for his life. But the appellate court accepted the prosecution's contention that Laney had found sanctuary in his friends' backyard and should not have ventured out onto the street. On February 7, 1924, William Laney was transported to the federal penitentiary in Leavenworth, Kansas. He left behind a wife and child.[46]

The outcome disappointed Houston and his colleagues, but they and the other black attorneys handling riot cases could still take pride in a job well done. They had convinced the police court magistrates to reduce punishments or even dismiss charges against dozens of black men who had carried weapons for their own protection. In the Supreme Court of the District of Columbia, dogged, resilient defenses of Walker, Dent, and Johnson led to freedom for all three through grand jury action, acquittal, or *nolle prosequi*. The U.S. attorney also abandoned the prosecution of four black men charged with a July 21, 1919, shooting at the Naval Hospital, although two of the defendants waited until October 15, 1923,

[46] "Race Riot Murder Trial," *Washington Post*, March 11, 1920, 2; "Mistrial in Laney Case," *Washington Post*, March 24, 1920, 18; "Indictments Found for Theater Crash Quashed on Appeal," *Washington Post*, December 4, 1923, 2; Case number 35360, CD 35, RG 21. For detailed treatment of Laney's trial, see O'Donnell, "Courting Science, Binding Truth," 297–309 ("Sunday-school" and "flying in the streets" quotes are on 300 and 303, respectively).

before their cases were finally dropped.[47] These legal victories did not remedy the authorities' failure to bring charges against white rioters, but they at least prevented further inequity.

Winning Justice in Chicago

Like the Metropolitan Police Department in Washington, Chicago's police had treated black victims and self-defenders as criminals, had refused to arrest mobbing whites, and had shrugged off black pleas for protection. As a result, unjustly arrested black men filled jail cells when Chicago's riot ended on August 2, 1919. The "arrests made for rioting by the police of colored rioters were far in excess of the arrests made of white rioters," the Coroner's Jury noted reprovingly.[48] State's Attorney Maclay Hoyne later freely acknowledged the discrimination. "There is no doubt that a great many police officers were grossly unfair in making arrests," he said publicly. "They shut their eyes to offenses committed by white men while they were very vigorous in getting all the colored men they could get."[49]

Victims of police antagonism included Kin Lumpkin, attacked by a white mob at an elevated station on July 28. Rather than arrest his assailants, the police charged Lumpkin with rioting and jailed him for four days. William Thornton, searching for his mother in the riot zone, asked a police officer to escort him home. Instead, the officer arrested him. Another black man's request for police protection resulted in a clubbing; when the man fled, an officer shot and arrested him.[50] For firing on a white mob throwing bricks at his home, A. Clement MacNeal, executive secretary of the Chicago branch of the NAACP, was charged with deadly assault and his bail set at $5,000, twice the average bond.[51] In one instance, police arrested several white and black men for carrying concealed weapons. One of the blacks could pass and was jailed with the white prisoners. The police quickly released these men and returned their

---

[47] Case number 35315, CD 35, RG 21; "Rioters in Court Required to Give Bonds for $2,000," *Washington Evening Star*, July 23, 1919, 1.

[48] Peter Hoffman, Coroner, *Report of the Coroner's Jury on the Race Riots*, November 3, 1919, box 38, folder 1980, Graham Taylor Papers, Newberry Library, 7.

[49] Chicago Commission, *Negro in Chicago*, 34.

[50] Ibid., 34–5.

[51] "The Chicago Race Riots," *Branch Bulletin* vol. III, no. 8 (August 1919), no page number given; "'Death for Rioters,' Court Says," *Chicago Defender*, August 9, 1919, 1; Walter White to Mary White Ovington, August 7, 1919, box C-75, folder "1919," NAACP Records.

weapons, commenting, "you'll probably need [these]."[52] Comparison of the riot's injuries and arrests by race further highlights police bias. The injury rate of blacks was twice that of whites; so, too, the arrest rate. Of 520 injured persons whose race was recorded, 342 were black, 178 white; of 229 indictments, 154 were black, 75 white.[53]

On August 4, 1919, State's Attorney Hoyne convened a twenty-four member grand jury to review riot-related charges. The all-white panel included prominent Chicago businessmen such as Albert Pick, a restaurant equipment wholesaler, and piano manufacturer George Bent. Judge Robert E. Crowe exhorted the jurors to make examples of the rioters, white and black. "Anarchy exists in Chicago at the present time," he declaimed, "and it is the duty of you men to stamp it out through the most effective means known to the law and that is by the indictment of those guilty." Hoyne had already joined forces with Attorney General Edward J. Brundage and Coroner Peter Hoffman to compile and present evidence. Brundage assigned thirty assistants to riot cases; subpoenas were issued for more than 1,000 witnesses. Obliging justices in the Municipal Court bound many defendants charged with carrying concealed weapons over to the grand jury. Hoyne and his assistants helped police interrogate prisoners and "several confessions were wrung" from the 250 blacks and dozens of white men in jail.[54]

Walter Colvin and Charles Johnson, two black teenagers charged with the murder of a white peddler, had their putative confessions "wrung out" during one such interrogation. When Colvin insisted he was at home when the man was killed, an assistant state's attorney angrily called him a liar. "If you don't say you cut him [the victim] I will beat hell out of you," the attorney threatened. Even after being clubbed and kicked, Colvin asserted his innocence. One of his assailants, a police lieutenant, said, "you killed that man [and] if you say you didn't, you are a damned liar and I am going to kill you." Charles Johnson, too, was beaten until he confessed – the fact that his brother was a police officer did not spare him the brutality.[55]

52 Walter White to Mary White Ovington, August 13, 1919, box C-75, folder "1919," NAACP Records.
53 Chicago Commission, *Negro in Chicago*, 35.
54 "Hang Rioters, Judge Urges Grand Jury," *Chicago Daily News*, August 4, 1919 (home edition), 1 (first quote); "First Rioter's Confession Obtained," *Chicago Evening American*, August 2, 1919, 1; "250 Negroes, Many Whites Held in Riots," *Chicago Daily News*, August 2, 1919 (home edition), 1 (second quote); "August Grand Jury Which Indicted 17 Rioters in First Day's Work," *Chicago Tribune*, August 5, 1919, 2.
55 "Brief and Argument for Plaintiffs in Error," Supreme Court of Illinois, April term, 1920, Waskow Notes, tab "Chicago NAACP & Defense."

The state's attorney's office also pressured numerous black self-defenders to incriminate themselves. Lieutenant Louis Washington, who had defended himself during a white mob attack on July 28, "finally broke down" after "hours of severe examination," the *Evening American* reported, though he "persists in his statements that he stabbed the man to protect himself."[56] Samuel Johnson, who had been arrested after repelling a mob from his front yard, reputedly confessed that "he might have" shot one of the attacking whites.[57] Emma Jackson, accused of killing a white man stoning her house, was interrogated at length, but she continued to deny she fired the fatal shot.[58]

Hoyne's intent to indict and convict black defendants was abundantly evident as the grand jury began its work – not one white appeared before the panel during its first two days of deliberations. Instead, Hoyne produced one black defendant after another, including Emma Jackson and her four housemates. Many in the first wave of defendants were charged with firing on police officers. At first the grand jury obliged Hoyne; by August 6, it had delivered seventeen indictments.[59] But when Assistant State's Attorney Robert Rollo presented yet another bill against a black defendant, a juror spoke up. "Is there none but colored cases for consideration of this body today?" Rollo replied that cases against both races were being prepared, but for now "there are only colored cases to consider." After a brief conference, the jury asked to adjourn, insisting that cases against white offenders be presented. Hoyne bristled at the demand, archly using the third person to dismiss the jury's concern. "The state's attorney is doing his duty, expects the grand jury to do its duty, and he needs no suggestions from any one as to how he should do his duty." Unimpressed with Hoyne's bluster, the jury refused to review the murder bill against Emma Jackson until white cases were presented (Figure 8.1).[60]

The grand jury's "strike," as the press dubbed it, could not have come at a better time for the NAACP's Walter White, who arrived in Chicago the same day. He quickly recognized that time was running out to gather evidence that could be used to indict white rioters. White hoped to prove

---

[56] "Negro War Vet Admits Riot Slaying, Charge by Hoyne Assistant," *Chicago Evening American*, August 5, 1919, 2.

[57] "Seven Indictments in Riots Returned," *Chicago Daily News*, August 5, 1919 (home edition), 1.

[58] "Indict 42 in Day, Is Plan of Jury," *Chicago Evening American*, August 6, 1919, 1.

[59] Ibid.

[60] "Grand Jury Asks Facts About White Rioters Be Offered," *Chicago Daily News*, August 6, 1919 (box score edition), 1 (all quotes); "Strike for Hearing on New Cases," *Chicago Evening American*, August 7, 1919, 1.

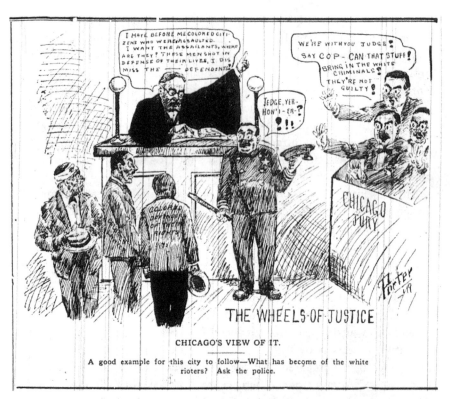

FIGURE 8.1. Wheels of Justice. In the wake of Chicago's riot, the state's attorney only presented charges against black defendants. Chicago's all-white grand jury questioned the absence of white defendants and went on "strike," refusing to review a murder charge brought against black self-defender Emma Jackson until the state's attorney also presented white cases for the jury's review. *Source:* The *Washington Bee*, August 23, 1919, p. 1. Courtesy of the Washingtoniana Division, D.C. Public Library.

that police had refused to arrest whites who had killed blacks; he also wanted to establish the link between the riot and the springtime bombings targeting black-occupied homes in white neighborhoods.[61] For the next four weeks, he scoured the city, interviewing witnesses to mob attacks and collecting dozens of affidavits. Told of the drive-by shooting involving an off-duty police officer named John Cunningham, White tracked down several witnesses, including the black man wounded in the shooting, and personally delivered the statements to the grand jury. As a result, Cunningham and his cohorts were brought before the grand jury and

[61] White to Ovington, August 7, 1919.

indicted. By early September, White had collected substantial evidence of the culpability of thirty-two whites (thirty men and two women) in crimes against blacks.[62]

White also met with local black leaders to discuss legal defense strategies. He came away convinced that the NAACP would have to act independently, especially after speaking with Ida B. Wells, the Tennessee schoolteacher-turned-journalist who now lived in Chicago. "She launched into a tirade against every organization in Chicago because they have not come into her organization and allowed her to dictate to them," White reported. "She is a troublemaker and is causing complications by starting a fund of her own to defend riot victims." White's judgment about Wells was unduly harsh, but his worries had other sources. At a conference with the newly formed Joint Emergency Committee, representing the NAACP Chicago branch, the Urban League, and the Ministers-Social Workers-Citizens Committee, White "found a total lack of realization among the so-called leaders here of the seriousness of the situation and the future of the Negro in Chicago as well as definite, tangible plans for doing the work that needs to be done."[63] Heeding White's advice, the national office of the NAACP began preparing its own legal defense initiative.

Meanwhile, State's Attorney Hoyne relented and began presenting bills against whites. In addition to indicting four white drive-by shooters, the grand jury approved bills against four white men for assaulting and shooting a black man named Everet Martin.[64] The jury also indicted four whites for attacking a Mexican citizen, Fidencio Gonzalez. (In this case, pressure from the Mexican embassy helped bring action.)[65] Still, the number of indicted blacks far outnumbered whites, especially in the most serious cases; by late August, the jury had indicted eleven blacks but no whites for murder. Twenty-five blacks and fifteen whites faced trial for deadly assault, and concealed weapons charges had been approved against fourteen blacks and nine whites.[66]

On September 8, the national NAACP committed $5,000 to its legal defense fund for black defendants in Chicago. It also hired two

---

[62] "The Chicago Riots," *Branch Bulletin* vol. III, no. 10 (October 1919), 94.

[63] White to Ovington, August 11 (first and second quotes) and August 13, 1919 (third quote), box C-75, folder "1919," NAACP Records.

[64] "500 Whites Quit Yards in Protest," *Chicago Evening American*, August 8, 1919, 1.

[65] "Indict 3 Whites, 41 Blacks in Riot Quiz," *Chicago Daily News*, August 8, 1919 (home edition), 3; File 311.121g58/1, Record Group 59, Records of the U.S. Department of State, Central Decimal File, 1910–29, box 3571, U.S. National Archives and Records Administration, College Park, Md.

[66] "Lull After the Storm," *Survey* 42, no. 22 (August 30, 1919), 782.

prominent Illinois attorneys, S. S. Gregory and James J. Barbour, and dispatched board member Arthur Spingarn and national secretary John Shillady to Chicago. Spingarn immediately took charge, seeking to ease tensions between the NAACP and local organizations, especially the Ministers-Social Workers-Citizens Committee (renamed the Chicago Peace and Protective Association). He prodded the Chicago branch to raise more funds – at least sixty black defendants could not pay for their defenses – and to sign up more lawyers, white and black. Among those recruited was Clarence Darrow. The Cook County Lawyers Association, comprised of black attorneys, certainly welcomed the help. By this point, one of its members, James Scott, had already handled – and won – dozens of criminal cases. Victories included the dropping of charges against Louis Washington, the army veteran who had stabbed a white attacker in self-defense.[67]

More success followed. On September 6, the Coroner's Jury exonerated William Henderson, charged with the stabbing death of a street car conductor who had attacked him. Emma Jackson and her four co-defendants went on trial on September 20; the jury took less than two hours to acquit them all. In mid-October, Clarence Darrow, James Scott, and another lawyer quickly picked apart the state's case against A. Clement MacNeal, who had defended his home against a mob. The judge dismissed all charges and rebuked the state's attorney for even trying the case. Of seventy-five indicted black defendants, fifty-eight went to trial – forty-three were acquitted and three cases were dropped. Just six men were convicted. In two cases, the court merely fined the guilty men one dollar each. Two other convictions led to prison sentences of less than one year.[68]

These court victories offered no consolation to Walter Colvin and Charles Johnson. On September 19, a jury found both teenagers guilty of manslaughter; the judge handed down life sentences. Refusing to give up,

---

[67] John Shillady to Mary White Ovington, September 17, 1919, Waskow Notes, tab "Chicago NAACP & Defense,"; NAACP statement, n.d., Waskow Notes, tab "U.S. Reaction – World View"; "Memorandum re Conference in Chicago," n.d., box 28, folder "Chicago Riots 1919," Arthur Spingarn Papers, Library of Congress. For Washington's release, see "'Death for Rioters,' Court Says."

[68] "2 Negroes and Mexican Exonerated," *Chicago Evening American*, September 6, 1919, 1; "Verdicts Refute Charge of State's Attorney Hoyne," *Chicago Defender*, September 27, 1919, 1; Report from A. Clement MacNeal, December 31, 1919, Waskow Notes, tab "Chicago NAACP & Defense"; "Reports of the Branches," *Branch Bulletin*, vol. III, no. 11 (November 1919), 104; "Reports of the Branches," *Branch Bulletin* vol. IV, no. 2 (February 1920), 17.

their attorneys, with help from James Barbour, appealed the conviction to the Illinois Supreme Court. The defense presented evidence of the torture the boys had suffered and pointed out glaring inconsistencies in the eyewitness testimony used to convict them. The state's high court denied the motion for a new trial, however, ruling that additional witness statements (which identified older men as the victim's killers) obtained after the first trial were insufficient grounds to grant a new trial.[69]

Another disappointment: the indictments of white rioters resulted in few convictions. By August 13, 1919, only seventeen white men had been indicted. Although a total of forty-one whites were eventually indicted, only seven had stood trial by January 1920. Notable white defendants included George Stauber, whose rock-throwing had caused Eugene Williams to drown, sparking the riot; but he was acquitted in June 1920. A jury delivered a guilty verdict against the four white men who had assaulted Fidencio Gonzalez, but the longest prison sentence was one year. In another case, a white soldier named Clarence Jones was tried for attacking a black janitor, William King. Fleeing a mob, King had sought protection from the uniformed Jones, who had instead joined in the attack. After deliberating for twenty hours, the jury could not agree on a verdict. (Facing a second trial, Jones pled guilty and was sentenced to twenty-three days in jail.)[70] The athletic clubs that had carried out coordinated attacks on blacks were also conspicuously absent from court. Although Chief of Police John Garrity had ordered the clubhouses closed until further notice, and a raid on the Sparklers club on August 13, 1919, brought seven arrests for arson, the gangs received only token punishment. Ragen's Colts, among other gangs, blatantly ignored Garrity's order – a police raid in September found thirty members present at its clubhouse. None was arrested after they promised to leave.[71]

[69] "Verdicts Refute Charge"; "Brief and Argument for Plaintiffs"; "2 Negro Boys Get 'Life' for Riot Killing," *Chicago Tribune*, September 20, 1919, 17; Supreme Court of Illinois, *People v. Colvin et al.*, No. 13367, June 16, 1920, accessed September 25, 2013, http://homicide.northwestern.edu/docs_fk/homicide/4225/PeopleVColvin.pdf.
[70] "Give to the Anti-Lynching Fund," *Branch Bulletin* vol. III, no. 11 (November 1919), 102; "Verdicts Refute Charge"; "Reports of the Branches" (February 1920); "Riot Grand Jury Votes to Indict 13 White Men," *Chicago Tribune*, August 13, 1919, 5; J. Wesley Jones, "West Side News," *Chicago Defender*, June 5, 1920, 13; Nettie George Speedy, "Cites Record to Prove Judge Crowe's Fairness," *Chicago Defender*, October 30, 1920, 8.
[71] "Seek Injunction to Force Garrity to Let Athletic Clubs Open," *Chicago Evening American*, August 28, 1919, 3; "Clubs Accused in Riot Arson Plots," *Chicago Daily News*,

Although the vast majority of white rioters never answered for their crimes, the NAACP and its allies in Chicago had still scored significant judicial victories. They had won almost fifty acquittals, dismissals, and dropped prosecutions (*nolle prosequi*). They had proven that a well-organized legal team, supported by donations, could take on judges and prosecutors intent on throwing the book at black defendants. Furthermore, black attorney Augustus Williams – the great uncle of Eugene Williams – undertook a one-man campaign to win damages for blacks, following the example of attorneys who had represented black victims of Charleston's riot. Citing an Illinois law that assigned liability to cities in which a mob of twelve or more damaged a person's home or property, Williams and the Joint Emergency Committee filed suits on behalf of blacks expelled from their homes. Williams also sued to obtain $5,000 for each family of blacks killed by mobs. After Williams won his first case, the city's attorney made him an offer: if he won three of any five cases of his choice, the city would settle the remainder. Williams won, and the city paid out $4,500 to the other families.[72]

The Trials of White Rioters in Knoxville

Unlike the antiblack collective violence in Chicago and Washington, Knoxville's late August 1919 riot resulted in an immediate effort to prosecute white rioters. In its failed bid to lynch a black prisoner, Maurice Mays, the Knoxville mob had caused an estimated $15,000 of damage to the county jail and enabled the escape of several felons. Consequently, authorities resolved to make an example of the mob's leaders. Three days after Knoxville's riot ended, Sheriff William Cate had arrested thirty men on charges such as house-breaking, larceny, and aiding prisoners to escape. Identifying the suspects was easy – Cate's deputies and city police officers had had ample opportunity to watch the rioters commit crimes after the jail had been breached. Cate was in no mood for mercy, denying bond to the accused men unless it was "unquestionably solvent." Due to the damage, all prisoners, black and white, were held in the first floor cells. When some white men complained about being housed with blacks,

August 14, 1919 (home edition), 1; transcription of article, *Chicago Herald-Examiner*, September 12, 1919, Waskow Notes, tab "Chicago NAACP & Defense."

[72] "Victims to Sue City," *Chicago Whip*, August 15, 1919, 1; "Negroes Will File Suits for Damages," *Chicago Daily News*, August 2, 1919, 15; Arthur Waskow notes on interview with Augustus L. Williams, July 1959, Waskow Notes, tab "Chicago NAACP & Defense."

jailer Earl Hall – who, like Sheriff Cate, had lost most of his possessions during the riot – retorted that they should have thought about that before they tore the jail apart. Attorney General R. A. Mynatt had already empaneled a grand jury, which listened to an impassioned address from Judge Thomas Nelson. "The crimes committed by the mob are most damnable," Nelson declared. "They strike at the very root of civilization and decent society." More arrests followed, and, on September 12, 1919, Mynatt's office presented the charges to the all-white jury, which delivered bills against thirty-six defendants. Twenty-three men were each indicted on three felony counts: theft of Sheriff Cate's possessions, intent to commit murder (of Maurice Mays), and abetting escape. Thirteen more white men faced misdemeanor charges of rioting; another eight were released.[73]

Meanwhile, most of the escaped prisoners, including a convicted murderer, remained at large. Cate vowed to do everything possible to recapture the convicts, but a large posse and the help of sheriffs and deputies from neighboring counties failed to track them down. "It is believed the men went to the mountains and will remain in hiding until the search is checked," reported the *Knoxville Journal and Tribune*. As a final insult, Cate and Judge Nelson received a crude letter threatening another jail break, this time to free the accused rioters. "Be shure to have all those Prisoners spoken of turned loose before satirday night ... [or] we'll get you sooner or later." As a precaution, a machine gun detachment from the Tennessee Fourth Infantry took up position outside the county jail, and the irate sheriff authorized his deputies to "shoot, and shoot to kill" if another mob stormed the jail.[74]

Authorities were much less concerned with arresting the men, black and white, who had clashed in the streets after the courthouse riot. Rioters who had looted arms were not arrested. Most of the eyewitnesses to

---

[73] "Damage to Jail May Be $15,000," *Knoxville Sentinel*, September 1, 1919, 11; "30 Arrests Made by Sheriff," *Knoxville Journal and Tribune*, September 4, 1919, 3; "Maurice F. Mays Is Indicted for Murder in the First Degree," *Knoxville Sentinel*, September 3, 1919, 1 (quotes); "36 Indicted on Charges of Rioting and Jail Breaking," *Knoxville Journal and Tribune*, September 13, 1919, 7.

[74] "Bonds for Men Held on Rioting," *Knoxville Journal and Tribune*, September 5, 1919, 11 (first quote); "Two of Fifteen Prisoners Who Escaped from County Jail Saturday Night Voluntarily Return," *Knoxville Sentinel*, September 1, 1919, 10; "To Shoot Any Attempting," *Knoxville Sentinel*, September 9, 1919, 18 (second quote); "Shoot, and Shoot to Kill! Is Order Given to Jail Guards," *Knoxville Sentinel*, September 13, 1918, 1 (third quote); "Prisoners May Have Gone West," *Knoxville Journal and Tribune*, September 11, 1919, 7.

the break-ins were other looters, and the affected businesses were only interested in retrieving the stolen weapons. In a newspaper advertisement, four stores promised not to press charges if guns were brought back within three days. By September 6, the stores had collected more than 250 weapons.[75] Gunmen in the shoot-out at Vine and Central also escaped prosecution. Again, identification of shooters, white and black, was difficult, if not impossible. Only two fatalities had occurred that night. The first, Lieutenant James Payne of the Fourth Infantry, was the victim of friendly fire. At the coroner's inquest into the death of black veteran Joe Etter, numerous witnesses testified that Etter had fired first at the guardsmen; no charges were filed. The undertaker also urged the Etter family to bury Joe quickly to avoid trouble.[76]

Prosecution of the white rioters was scheduled to begin on October 13, but only nine of 500 potential jurors passed voir dire. A flurry of additional summons soon produced a complete and all-white, male jury. Most of the jurors worked as farmers or miners. The trial proceeded quickly; Mynatt opted to hold a single trial for the nineteen rioters charged with felonies (he had dropped the charges against four defendants). Mynatt was so certain that he had won that he skipped his summary, but his optimism was misplaced. After deliberating for a day, the jury acquitted fourteen defendants and could not agree on verdicts for the remaining five. The outcome dismayed Mynatt, who declared, "there was never a more guilty set of men turned loose."[77] Judge Nelson issued a statement describing the jurors' decisions as "wholly unwarranted by the evidence" and announced that he would never again allow any of the men to serve on a jury in his courtroom.[78] Mynatt retried two of the five deadlocked cases. In 1920, he prosecuted ironworker Martin Mays (no relation to Maurice Mays) for prying open a jail cell lock during the riot. This time, the jury found Mays guilty, but he received a pardon after serving a year of his sentence. A jury also convicted Charles Cash, who had

[75] "Notice," *Knoxville Journal and Tribune*, September 2, 1919, 14; "265 Guns Sent Back to Stores," *Knoxville Sentinel*, September 6, 1919, 10.

[76] "30 Arrests Made by Sheriff"; Mary Etter interview with Ann Wilson, May 19–23, 1979, Beck Cultural Exchange Center.

[77] "36 Defendants on Trial Today," *Knoxville Journal and Tribune*, October 13, 1919, 7; "Get 9 Jurors Out of 500," *Knoxville Journal and Tribune*, October 14, 1919, 7; Lakin, "Dark Night," 28 (quote).

[78] Transcribed article from *East Tennessee News*, November 13, 1919, Waskow Notes, tab "Knoxville Riot."

held a flashlight for Mays during the riot; he, too, only spent a year in jail.[79]

The Knoxville juries were reluctant to convict fellow white men of crimes committed in the name of rough justice, that is, the attempt to lynch Maurice Mays for allegedly killing a white woman. Mynatt did not appreciate that the *purpose* of the courthouse siege was more important than the *proof* he presented of each rioter's guilt. A black resident recognized this fact in a letter published in the *Knoxville Journal and Tribune*. "The jury must have been either prejudiced or intoxicated to render the verdict that it did... the men of which [the jury] was composed are not a bit better than the worst men in the mob."[80] The same challenge – white jurors' sympathy for rough justice – awaited Omaha's district attorney, who, like Mynatt, was determined to prosecute the white rioters who had severely damaged that city's courthouse during the lynching of Will Brown.

The Trials of White Rioters in Omaha

Major General Leonard Wood, who had arrived in Omaha at the end of its outbreak of antiblack collective violence in September 1919, pursued white rioters as doggedly as Sheriff Cate did in Knoxville. Waves of arrests made by Wood's troops swelled the city and county jails. (As noted in Chapter 5, Wood lacked the legal authority to execute these police functions.) By October 1, 1919, seventy-five suspected rioters were in custody; by October 18, that number had doubled. The typical prisoner was white, male, young, and working class. About a dozen suspects were from out of town. Twelve black men numbered among the prisoners; at least five were arrested for carrying weapons.[81] Authorities were most interested in prosecuting the riot's inciters, arsonists, and looters; the lynchers of Will Brown; and the assailants of Mayor Edward Smith (who had almost been lynched). Obtaining convictions, however, proved arduous and frustrating.

[79] Lakin, "Dark Night," 28 n. 77; *State vs. Martin Mays*, No. 509 (Supreme Court of Tennessee, Eastern Division, June 7, 1920), Transcript of Record, Knox County Archives, 34–5, 75.
[80] Quoted in Lamon, "Tennessee Race Relations," 83.
[81] "Seventy-Five Men Held on Riot Charges," *Morning Omaha World-Herald*, October 2, 1919, 2 (hereafter *MOWH*); "55 Held by Police as Mob Heads," *Omaha Bee*, October 1, 1919, 1.

Arrests for arson and looting included twenty-six-year-old Leonard Johnson, charged with burning a police patrol car and robbing a pawn shop. Louis Weaver, a twenty-one-year-old cook, was accused of torching the courthouse – his hands and head were burned and bandaged when the police found him hiding in his basement.[82] Two young men who pled guilty to charges of unlawful assembly and rioting named an *Omaha Bee* reporter, John Moore, as a rioter and arsonist, leading to his arrest and a bout of indignant *Bee* articles alleging a police frame-up.[83]

James Shields was among the first to be arrested for Will Brown's murder. Police found the suspect, who had a gunshot wound in his leg, hiding beneath his bed covers.[84] C. P. Gernant was arrested after telling people he took part in the lynching.[85] Based on the statements of several witnesses, police charged Ralph Snyder with conspiracy to commit murder, unlawful assembly, and rioting.[86] A total of eleven men faced charges of killing Will Brown or murder conspiracy; all eleven pled not guilty.[87] The boasting of L. J. Behrings, a railroad brakeman, landed him in jail; he told four people how he had cinched the noose around Mayor Smith's neck.[88] Two other men were charged with assaulting Smith: George Davis, a peddler who had allegedly knocked the mayor unconscious; and Leonard Weber, an artist accused of hitting Smith so hard over the head with a revolver that he broke the weapon.[89]

Identification of the riot's inciters revealed the culpability of teenage and preteen white youth. Outside the courthouse, excited boys had become mob apprentices. Sol Francis, age twelve, had clambered up a firemen's ladder and shouted, "hang the nigger!" Despite his age, he was held without bail. He denied being on the ladder, claiming that he had only "walked around awhile [inside the courthouse] trying to get the other

---

[82] "Seven More Arrested for Sunday Night Riot," *MOWH*, October 6, 1919, 1; "Claims Put Rope Around Mayor's Neck, Police Say," *MOWH*, October 5, 1919, 1; "Alleged Hangman in Custody," *Omaha Bee*, October 5, 1919, 1.

[83] Age, "Omaha Riot," 97–101.

[84] "Claims Put Rope Around Mayor's Neck."

[85] "Grand Jury Frees Alleged Rioters," *MOWH*, October 18, 1919, 5.

[86] "16 Indictments Are Returned by the Grand Jury," *Omaha Bee*, October 26, 1919, 10; Age, "Omaha Riot," 108–9.

[87] Age, "Omaha Riot," 116.

[88] "Claims Put Rope Around Mayor's Neck."

[89] "Man Charged With Conspiracy to Murder Negro Placed on Trial," *Omaha Bee*, December 8, 1919, unfiled clipping held at the Douglas County Historical Society; "Charge Artist Hit Mayor Smith," *MOWH*, October 15, 1919, 9.

fellows to quit breaking things and to let the nigger alone."⁹⁰ William
Francis (no relation), age seventeen, had allegedly mounted a horse and
shouted encouragement to the mob. He, too, asserted his innocence: "I
did not get inside the court house, either on horseback or on foot."
General Wood, who interviewed him, judged him "a simple high school
boy" who, pressed by his worried father, would "tell all he knows."⁹¹
William Francis remained in jail, though, waiting an appearance in
court.

Douglas County Attorney Abel Shotwell convened a grand jury composed of white men. Most of the sixteen jurors had working or lower
middle class backgrounds. They repaired railroad cars and sold automobiles; they farmed, clerked, or drove trucks. But two men were company
presidents, including jury foreman John W. Towle, who ran a steel works.
Judge William A. Redick instructed the jurors to carry out their duties
"with calm and unbiased minds, but with a stern determination to uphold
the laws of the state and bring all offenders to justice."⁹² For his part,
Shotwell was determined to give the jury plenty of opportunities to deliver
that justice.

The jury began hearing witnesses on October 10. By mid-November, it
had received the testimony of 535 observers and handed down 120 indictments. Those charged included William Francis, the young horse rider;
Louis Weaver, the arsonist who had severely burned himself; and James
Shields, one of Brown's lynchers. However, most of the indictments were
for minor crimes. "We have been unable to learn of any eye-witnesses
who could identify the persons who killed William Brown," the jurors
reported. Likewise, they could not determine all the names of the arsonists and the rioters who broke down the courthouse doors. "We have
sadly lacked the willing testimony of eye-witnesses who are supposed to
be on the side of Law and Order, but have remained strangely silent, and
have not volunteered their knowledge to assist in bringing the probably
guilty to justice by trial." The code of silence enabled many suspects to

⁹⁰ "Boy, 12, Denies Was Member of the Mob," *MOWH*, October 2, 1919, 11; "55 Held
by Police."
⁹¹ "True Bills Against 8 of Rioters," *Omaha Bee*, October 22, 1919, 1; "'Boy on Horseback'
Denies Leading Mob; Just Hollered," *MOWH*, October 5, 1919 (William Francis quote);
Leonard Wood Diary, entry for October 3, 1919, box 12, folder "Diary Jan. 1st–Dec.
31, 1919," Leonard Wood Papers, Library of Congress (Wood quote).
⁹² "Sixteen Grand Jurors Pledged to Riot Probe," *MOWH*, October 9, 1919, 6; "Judge
Redick's Charge to Jury," *MOWH*, October 9, 1919, 2 (quote).

claim that they were merely observers, resulting in almost daily releases. For example, the charges against James Shields and Leonard Weber were dismissed.[93]

Shotwell was confident he could convict three prominent suspects: George Davis (Mayor Smith's assailant), Ralph Snyder (one of Will Brown's lynchers), and arsonist Louis Weaver. Called in his own defense, Davis denied he was at the courthouse, even though Smith had pointed at him from the stand and declared, "I would say before God that Davis is the man." Despite thirty-six hours of deliberation, the jury failed to reach a verdict. Undeterred, Shotwell retried Davis in January 1920. The district attorney now had evidence refuting Davis's alibi, but the second jury also remained hung.[94] At his trial, Snyder proudly claimed to be the man who had warned the mob not to drag Will Brown's corpse to the city's black neighborhood. This, Snyder's attorney contended, was the act of a brave individual trying to keep the peace after the police's failure to stop the riot. This sly presentation helped win an acquittal for Snyder.[95] Only Weaver's trial ended with a conviction and prison sentence.[96]

Shotwell won a few other convictions, but juries proved reluctant to punish rioters and lynchers for carrying out rough justice. Indeed, "the more serious the charge, the more likely an acquittal." Of the eleven men charged with murdering Will Brown, only one, seventeen-year-old newsboy Sam Novak, was found guilty; the judge committed him to a reformatory until adulthood. The eight assault cases ended with dismissals, a hung jury (Davis's case), or minor punishments in exchange for guilty pleas. Of the thirty-two men who faced rioting and unlawful assembly charges, more than half pled guilty and paid fines or went to jail

---

93 For the jury's difficulties, see Grand Jury Final Report, November 19, 1919, District Court Journal 176, Douglas County Courthouse, 279–82 (quotes). For Leonard Johnson's release, see "Jury Indicts Ten for Complicity and Lynching," *MOWH*, October 22, 1919, 1. For releases due to lack of evidence, see "Grand Jury Frees Alleged Rioters"; "Boys Released by Grand Jury, Lack Evidence," *Omaha Bee*, October 25, 1919, 11. James Shields did plead guilty to conspiracy to commit murder but was only fined court costs and $200; he served no time. See Age, "Omaha Riot," 116 n. 56.
94 "Dramatic Story of Attack at Riot," *Omaha Bee*, December 16, 1919 (quote); "Swears He Was Home on Night of Riot," *Omaha Bee*, December 18, 1919, unfiled clippings held at the Douglas County Historical Society; Age, "Omaha Riot," 109–13.
95 "Jury Ponders on Case of Man Held for Riot," *Omaha Bee*, December 11, 1919, unfiled clipping held at the Douglas County Historical Society; Age, "Omaha Riot," 108.
96 "Jury Asks New Instructions in Arson Case," *Omaha Bee*, December 3, 1919; "Man Convicted of Arson Gets One to 20 years," *Omaha Bee*, December 13, 1919, unfiled clippings held at Douglas County Historical Society.

for no more than three months. The remainder asserted their innocence. Only one was convicted and sentenced to ninety days in jail.[97]

The outcomes of judicial proceedings against five blacks charged with carrying concealed weapons during the riot – and only blacks had been arrested for having weapons – were mixed. Lester Price, a young black man attacked aboard a streetcar, pled guilty. The fact that he had tried to defend himself did not impress Judge Redick, who sentenced him to thirty days in jail. Two men were fined; charges against the other two were dropped.[98]

Perhaps the greatest injustice involved the three people who had made the riot possible. Political boss Tom Dennison had orchestrated the framing of Will Brown by having his young loyalist Milton "Millard" Hoffman and Agnes Loebeck fabricate a claim of sexual assault. Hoffman had even helped organize the mob in South Omaha that had marched on the courthouse where Will Brown was being held. Eager to question Hoffman, police officers searched South Omaha but could not find him – Dennison had sent Hoffman to Denver, where he lived for seven years before moving back to Omaha, unnoticed. In the meantime, he and Loebeck married. Hoffman was never charged with a crime. Nor was Dennison, whose machinations were not detailed until the late 1980s by political scientist Orville D. Menard. The courthouse riot fulfilled Dennison's goal of ousting the reformers from office during the next election, and, throughout the 1920s and early 1930s, he once again reigned as the political and vice boss of Omaha's Third Ward, living to the age of seventy-five.[99]

The threefold fight for justice during the year of racial violence – defense of black rioters, prosecution of white rioters, and compensation for victims – brought mixed results. Charleston's NAACP branch, aided by the branch in Washington, D.C., successfully pressured the navy to investigate the May 1919 riot. The ensuing courts martial of sailors who had rioted did not, however, deliver punishments commensurate with the crimes committed, and the navy and Congress rejected all but one lawsuit seeking damages for the riot's victims. Longview's targets of mob violence also received no compensation, but two of the NAACP's branches in Texas secured the release of the men who had taken up arms to defend S. L. Jones from a lynch mob. The greatest court victories came in

---

[97] Age, "Omaha Riot," 116–18 (quote on 116); "True Bills Against 8 of Rioters."
[98] "Boys Released by Grand Jury"; Age, "Omaha Riot," 117.
[99] "Seventy-Five Men Held"; Menard, "Tom Dennison," 161; Davis, "Gray Wolf," 44–8.

Washington and Chicago, where sustained defense efforts – some lasting years – resulted in acquittals, dismissals, or *nolle prosequi* actions in the cases of dozens of African Americans who had carried or used weapons to defend themselves. In Chicago as well, a black attorney brought and won several civil lawsuits on behalf of riot victims. All of these victories off-set the recurrent failure of authorities to convict white rioters, including in Knoxville and Omaha, where prosecutors had actively pursued cases against mob leaders. For jury after jury, however, rough justice trumped the evidence. As New Negro writers pointedly observed, the failings of the courts to hold white rioters accountable condoned, even encouraged, more mob violence.

The flaws of the judicial system went far beyond the favorable treat-ment accorded to white rioters, as Maurice Mays, the young Knoxville resident accused of murdering a white woman, and twelve black share-croppers jailed for resisting mob violence in Phillips County, Arkansas, knew all too well. Charged with capital crimes, they faced the death penalty if convicted. Would any of these defendants receive a fair trial? As demonstrated by the efforts of the NAACP and others on behalf of these men, the fight for justice was not over.

9

The Fight for Justice

The Death Penalty Cases

The Knoxville riot and the Arkansas pogrom both produced death penalty cases that vividly highlighted the consequences of racially biased court proceedings in 1919. In Knoxville, Maurice Mays was charged with killing a young white woman named Bertie Lindsey. A mob's pursuit of rough justice – the attempted lynching of Mays – had expanded into widespread attacks on black residents. Armed resistance and the deployment of state militia to restore order did not delay Mays's trial. Knox County Attorney General R. A. Mynatt presented the case against Mays to an all-white grand jury, which indicted Mays for murder just a few days after the riot ended. The rush to judgment was just as swift in Phillips County, Arkansas. Acting in concert with a massive posse, U.S. infantry troops had killed or captured most of the black sharecroppers who had resisted the violent campaign against their fledgling union. At the behest of white elites, special agents of the Missouri Pacific Railroad tortured the prisoners to extract "confessions" that the union men had plotted an uprising to murder whites. Brought to court in chains, these men did not even have a chance to speak to their attorneys before their trials began.

The cases bore many similarities. All-white juries in Knoxville and Phillips County speedily convicted the defendants and white judges promptly handed down death sentences. Mays and the sharecroppers were framed – let there be no doubt that every man was innocent of the charges against him. Prosecutors used unreliable eyewitnesses, corrupt forensics, and forced confessions to win over juries, which were already eager to deliver guilty verdicts. Authorities refused to give the defendants adequate time to prepare their defenses and flouted their

245

respective states' laws governing trial processes. By the end of 1919, execution loomed for Mays and the Elaine Twelve, as the condemned sharecroppers were called.[1] But sustained legal efforts brought stay after stay as attorneys for all thirteen men fought to overturn the convictions and secure new – and fair – trials. In the case of Mays, the battle began with his adoptive parents, whose dogged efforts eventually gained support from the NAACP's Tennessee branches. The Elaine Twelve received immediate legal aid from the NAACP's national office, although it concealed its role to prevent reprisals against the men for accepting assistance from an organization much hated in the South. The fight for justice in the death penalty cases was a resounding success: all but one of the thirteen condemned men were saved.

The Fight to Save Maurice Mays

Sheriff William Cate had likely saved Maurice Mays's life by smuggling the prisoner out of Knoxville and taking him to Chattanooga at the start of the riot. From his Chattanooga jail cell, Mays (Figure 9.1) asserted his innocence of the murder of Bertie Lindsey. In a public letter addressed to the *Knoxville Sentinel*, Mays detailed his alibi and recounted police officer Andy White's vendetta against him. "The affair and arrest of me is one of real prejudice and oppression. I deny any connection with the killing in any way. If the officers had a desire to treat fair and give me justice why didn't they make more than one arrest and keep the arrests secret and allow the woman [Ora Smyth, who witnessed the killing] to come and identify all the prisoners at the same time and pick out the guilty one?"[2] These were credible protestations. Mays had a solid alibi, there was no physical evidence linking him to the crime, and he was the only suspect shown to Ora Smyth, who was so distraught that a policeman had to support her while she looked at Mays (see Chapter 5). The weakness of the case against Mays did not, however, trouble Attorney General R. A. Mynatt. On Wednesday, September 3, he presented the case to a grand jury, which indicted Mays for murder. Mynatt promised a "speedy" but "fair" trial.[3]

---

[1] The Elaine Twelve were: Alf Banks, Ed Coleman, Albert Giles, Joe Fox, Paul Hall, Ed and Frank Hicks, Joe Knox, John Martin, Frank Moore, Ed Ware, and Will Wordlow.
[2] "Mays Denies He Is Guilty Negro," *Knoxville Sentinel*, September 1, 1919, 11.
[3] "Knox Grand Jury Begins Probe Today," *Knoxville Journal and Tribune*, September 3, 1919, 1 (quotes); "Maurice F. Mays Is Indicted for Murder in the First Degree," *Knoxville Sentinel*, September 3, 1919, 1.

FIGURE 9.1. Portrait of Maurice Mays. Sentenced to death for a crime he did not commit, Maurice Mays and his adoptive parents exhausted their savings and enlisted the help of Tennessee's NAACP branches in an effort to secure a new, and fair, trial. *Source:* Beck Cultural Exchange Center, Inc. Courtesy of the Beck Cultural Exchange Center, Inc.

Sheriff Cate brought Mays back from Chattanooga on September 25; his trial began a week later. Mayor John McMillan – Mays's birth father – said little publicly about the trial. William and Frances Mays, the adoptive parents, hired former Knox County prosecutor Reuben Cates and William Yardley, a black lawyer, to defend their son, but the two attorneys could not present the strongest part of their case. The night before Mays's return to Knoxville, a swarthy white man or light-skinned black man sexually assaulted and shot a white woman, Mrs. Dacie Ward. The circumstances eerily resembled the murder of Bertie Lindsey: a bedroom window pried open at 3 A.M.; a woman asleep, her husband away, working; a flashlight shone in her face. "Lay still or I'll kill you," the rapist had warned, brandishing a handgun. When Ward resisted, he shot her in the chest but did not kill her.[4] Ward was one of three white women attacked while Mays was in jail. One victim even said the assailant "told me to lay still or he would shoot me like he did Bertie Lindsey." But Judge Thomas Nelson turned down Cates's request to call the three women as witnesses, denying the defense an opportunity to raise considerable doubts about the case against Mays.[5]

So Cates and Yardley hammered at the evidence. They exhaustively detailed Mays's campaign work for McMillan (who had just lost the election) and called witnesses who had seen Mays close to the time of the murder. How could he have stealthily made his way to the Lindsey home, almost two miles from his own, committed the crime, and returned to his room so quickly? His shoes were not muddy; his gun, cold and unused. The two attorneys tactfully raised doubts about Smyth's identification and dwelled on Andy White's loathing of Mays. Finally, Mays took the stand to establish his alibi and to declare his innocence.[6]

The prosecution spared no effort to secure a guilty verdict. Mynatt and Assistant Attorney General Fred Houk built their case around Smyth's identification and buttressed it with circumstantial evidence: Mays owned a thirty-eight revolver, the same type of weapon used to shoot Lindsey; his shoes were muddy (or so said Sheriff Cate, who had examined them nine hours after the crime occurred); the soles were supposedly similar to footprints found outside the Lindsey home (though no casts were made of the footprints). Tennessee governor Albert Roberts appointed a well-known local attorney, Samuel Heiskell, to aid Mynatt and Houk. Heiskell's tight-lipped countenance masked a flair for the dramatic – at one point, he tried to present as evidence photographs of white women allegedly discovered in Mays's room. (Judge Nelson rejected the motion.) Heiskell had grown up in Tennessee during Reconstruction, and he used that historical period as a touchstone. In a grandiloquent, seventy-five minute summation, Heiskell announced that respect for law, order, and justice was at its lowest point since the end of the bloody Civil War. Will you turn back the tide of crime sweeping the nation, he challenged the enrapt jury, or will you abandon civilization to rapists, thieves, and

---

[4] "Another Woman Is Victim of Attack," *Knoxville Sentinel*, September 25, 1919, 1.
[5] Lakin, "Dark Night," 27.
[6] "Mayes [sic] Case Goes to Jury Today," *Knoxville Journal and Tribune*, October 4, 1919, 3; "Maurice Mayes [sic] Guilty of Murder; Jury Was Only Out Eight Minutes," *Knoxville Journal and Tribune*, October 5, 1919, 7.

degeneracy? Using an old prosecutor's trick, he declared that *just* Ora Smyth's identification *or* the evidence about the gun and shoes was enough to convict; together, they proved Mays's guilt beyond all doubt.[7]

For most of the four day trial Mays remained calm and confident, smiling frequently and snacking on fruit his parents brought him. After adjournment on the third day, he joined his parents and black spectators in a prayer service in the courtroom. The next morning, however, a worried expression replaced his smile as he listened to the closing arguments and Judge Nelson's jury instructions. It was almost 5 P.M. on Saturday, October 4, but Nelson had no intention of adjourning until Monday. The jurors deliberated for eight minutes: Maurice Mays was guilty of murdering Bertie Lindsey. Mays stoically received the verdict while his attorneys assured him that they would file a motion for a new trial.[8]

Judge Nelson denied the motion and sentenced Mays to death. On October 20, 1919, Mays braced himself for transport to the state prison in Nashville. His black cellmates in the now-repaired Knox County jail sang hymns and prayed with him before his departure. "Don't give up hopes," Mays told his parents. "I believe the good Lord will save me from death, for I am innocent." His father William trusted in God as well, but he resolved not to leave his son's fate to divine power alone.[9]

From the moment Maurice was arrested, William and Frances Mays fought to clear his name. The obstacles were formidable. The attenuated pretrial period left little time to prepare a defense. John McMillan continued to stay silent about the case. Knoxville's black residents, including members of the NAACP branch, believed Mays was guilty and devoted their attention to publicizing the mistreatment they had endured during the Tennessee Fourth Infantry's occupation of the riot zone.[10] The NAACP's national office issued a press release about these abuses but said nothing about the charges against Mays.[11] Although Chattanooga's

[7] Lucy Templeton, "Portrait of Sam Heiskell," *Knoxville News-Sentinel*, August 17, 1958, clipping in Subject File, "Knoxville, Tenn. Mayors Through 1939," McClung Historical Collection; Lakin, "Dark Night," 27; "Mayes Case Goes"; "Maurice Mayes Guilty."

[8] "Maurice Mayes Guilty."

[9] Lakin, "Dark Night," 27; "Mayes [sic] Is Taken to State Prison," *Knoxville Journal and Tribune*, October 20, 1919, 7 (quote).

[10] James Cary to John Shillady, September 18, 1919, box G-198, folder "Knoxville, Tenn., 1915–1935," NAACP Records; James Cary to John Shillady, May 8, 1920, box D-61, folder "Case Supported – Maurice Mays, Jan.–Dec. 1920," NAACP Records.

[11] Press release of the NAACP, September 24, 1919, Waskow Notes, tab "NAACP Speeches." For an example of the black press's use of the release, see Kerlin, *Voice of the Negro*, 83–4.

NAACP branch tried to raise legal funds for Mays, it did not send out solicitations until late September, less than two weeks before the trial's start.[12] Undeterred, the Mays dipped into their savings and raised funds on their own so that Cates and Yardley could prepare for the Tennessee Supreme Court's mandatory review of the verdict. By mid-November, the Mays had paid their son's attorneys more than $500.[13]

Cates was confident the court would overturn the guilty verdict. A new state law required juries to determine the punishment in capital cases, but Judge Nelson had handed down the death sentence himself. This glaring judicial error reinvigorated defense efforts. L. D. Smith, a white Knoxville attorney, promised to donate up to $100 if other supporters raised $500. William Mays introduced M. W. Dent, secretary of Chattanooga's NAACP branch, to black residents of Knoxville who had changed their minds about the case. Mays "is innocent without the shadow of a doubt," Dent concluded in a request for help from the NAACP's national office. The Knoxville branch made a similar appeal. "Confidentially, I must say that the accused did not bear a wholesome reputation in the community," one member wrote to John Shillady, "but we believe him innocent of the crime charged. If you can do anything do it NOW!" Just days before the state supreme court review, Maurice himself sent a handwritten note to Shillady asking him "to help me raise funds to employ a private investigator to help me establish my innocence." But the national office regretfully declined to help – Knoxville was one riot too many for the association's limited resources. "All our funds have been heavily tied up with expenses growing out of the Chicago [and other] riots," Shillady told Dent.[14]

On November 24, the state's highest court offered Mays a glimmer of hope. It vacated his guilty verdict and death sentence due to Judge Nelson's mistake and ordered a new trial.[15] Mays continued to entreat the national NAACP for help and wrote a fund-raising poem *Help Me Please*: "Doomed to die without a crime / My hope is Public Aid / Who

---

[12] R. R. Wright to John Shillady, September 25, 1919, box D-61, folder "Case Supported –
    Maurice Mays 1919 – Sept.–Dec.," NAACP Records.
[13] Maurice Mays timeline, n.d., box D-61, folder "Case Supported – Maurice Mays Jan.–
    Dec. 1920," NAACP Records.
[14] M. W. Dent to Mary White Ovington, November 11, 1919 (first quote); J. G. Beck
    to Shillady, November 5, 1919 (second quote; emphasis in original); Mays to Shillady,
    received November 24, 1919 (third quote); Shillady to Dent, November 21, 1919 (fourth
    quote), box D-61, folder "Case Supported – Maurice Mays 1919 – Sept.–Dec.," NAACP
    Records.
[15] Lakin, "Dark Night," 27.

will volunteer, and help / To save me from the Grave?"[16] In January 1920, his parents staged a benefit at a Knoxville theatre, asking attendees to "give $1.00 to save a life."[17] William Mays also contacted William Pickens, the NAACP's branch organizer, who wrote about the case in the *Crisis*. The pleas for help caught the attention of Walter White, who told Shillady, "the Maurice Mays case impresses me as being one in which we ought to take action." Shillady again said that the NAACP's legal defense funds were stretched to the breaking point. Forgetting that Mays's arrest had sparked white mob violence against the black residents of Knoxville, Shillady added, "there is no issue involved that makes this a NAACP case, other than the general contention that Mays is a colored man who cannot pay for his own defense."[18]

Mays's parents shrugged off the rejection and forged ahead with the Knoxville branch's support. Together they published an article detailing Maurice's alibi for the night of Bertie Lindsey's murder, the lack of reliable evidence, and the continuing sexual assaults of white women.[19] J. H. Henderson, pastor of Knoxville's leading black church, Mount Zion Baptist, led fundraising efforts. When the NAACP rebuked him for soliciting funds from out-of-state branches, a violation of national rules, he turned to Tennessee's four other branches. In a flier entitled "An Appeal to the Public for a Worthy Cause," Henderson pointed out William Mays's considerable sacrifices: he "has spent all of his savings during a life time, on his boy, and must face the cold world the remaining years of his life, empty-handed: but oh!, if he can get his boy back, he would care nothing for the lost fortune." By November 1920, the Knoxville branch had raised more than $600. Although this was considerably less than the goal of $3,000, the Mays were able to retain Reuben Cates as their son's attorney and to hire a private detective to gather evidence.[20]

---

[16] Mays to Shillady, received December 10, 1919; Mays to Du Bois, received December 15, 1919; "Help Me Please," n.d., box D-61, folders "Case Supported – Maurice Mays 1919 – Sept.–Dec." and "Case Supported – Maurice Mays – Jan.–Dec. 1920," NAACP Records.

[17] Handbill, n.d., box G-198, folder, "Knoxville, Tenn. 1915–1935," NAACP Records.

[18] William Mays to William Pickens, February 24, 1920, and March 12, 1920; Pickens to Mays, March 3, 1920; Walter White to Shillady, March 16, 1920 (first quote); Shillady to White, May 10, 1920 (second quote), box D-61, folder, "Case Supported – Maurice Mays – Jan.–Dec. 1920," NAACP Records.

[19] "Maurice Mays and the Lindsey Murder Mystery," n.d., box D-61, folder "Case Supported – Maurice Mays – Jan.–Dec. 1920," NAACP Records.

[20] J. H. Henderson, September 6, 1920; Acting Secretary, Knoxville Branch, to J. W. Lane, September 23, 1920; J. H. Henderson to Catherine Lealtad, November 11, 1920, box

Maurice Mays's second trial commenced on April 18, 1921. Spectators filled the Knox County courtroom, watching as Maurice leaned to kiss his mother and accept a sheaf of letters and a bag of fruit from his father. The prosecution, again aided by Samuel Heiskell, reprised its strategy from the October 1919 trial, relying on witness testimony and the circumstantial evidence. A tearful Ora Smyth, her voice quavering but clear, identified Mays, who shook his head. Gertrude Dyer, the neighbor who had aided Smyth on the night of the murder, insisted she had seen Mays, a flashlight in his hand, running down an alley, even though at the time she was unable to identify the race of the man. Chief of Police E. M. Haynes confidently asserted that Mays's pistol had been recently fired because some of the cartridges had lint on them, proof, the chief claimed, that Mays had been carrying the pistol in his pocket. Policeman Andy White strained to describe Mays's behavior as suspicious and shifty; a deputy sheriff declared Mays's shoes had red clay mud on them.[21]

Cates and co-defense attorney William Yardley did their best to raise doubts about this testimony. They touted Mays's alibi and again called him to the stand. "You didn't shoot Bertie Lindsey?" Cates asked him directly. "No, sir," Mays replied. While he was on the stand, the prosecution provocatively asked, "how many pictures of white women did you have in your room over there?" Although Judge Xen Hicks, substituting for Judge Thomas Nelson, supported Cates's vigorous objection, the question came up again later. This time Mays answered: the only picture of a white person in his room was of John McMillan. After Mays stepped down, his attorneys called many of the white women who had been sexually assaulted before and after Mays's arrest. One after another, the women described an armed intruder surprising them while they slept, shining a light in their faces, and threatening to shoot if they resisted. No less than twelve attacks were detailed but jurors heard not a word – at the prosecution's request, Hicks had dismissed the jury from the courtroom.[22]

D-61, folder "Case Supported – Maurice Mays – Jan.–Dec. 1920"; Henderson to Walter White, March 25, 1921; "An Appeal to the Public for a Worthy Cause," n.d. (quote), box D-61, folder "Case Supported – Maurice Mays – Mar.–Oct. 1921," NAACP Records.

[21] "Maurice Mays Again Identified as Mrs. Bertie Lindsey's Slayer,' *Knoxville Sentinel*, April 19, 1921, clipping in box E-9, Maurice Mays Papers, Beck Cultural Exchange Center; *State vs. Mays* 145 Tenn. 118 (1921), Transcript of Record, Knox County Archives, 84–86, 160–93, 213–20.

[22] *State vs. Mays*, 252–452, 459–506 (quotes on 280 and 432).

On the morning of April 23, 1921, the all-white, male jury filed into the courtroom after deliberating for a total of sixteen minutes, split between the previous afternoon and that morning. "Gentlemen of the jury, have you reached your verdict?" asked Hicks. The courtroom was crowded, as it had been all week, but no one stirred. "We find the defendant guilty of murder in the first degree, and fix the penalty at death in the electric chair," answered the foreman. Mays again received the decision calmly, turning to look at his father and kiss his mother. "Don't worry, Maurice," his attorney Cates told him. "Be the same good prisoner you have been all along."[23]

And he was, right up to March 15, 1922. Judge Hicks rejected the defense's motion for a new trial. In August 1921, the NAACP sent the Knoxville branch $100 to support an appeal, but the money was too little, too late. In October, the Tennessee Supreme Court upheld the verdict and the U.S. Supreme Court declined to hear the case. John McMillan, among others, entreated Tennessee governor Alfred Taylor to commute the death sentence but he declined, fearing leniency might hurt him politically. Mays himself appealed to Ora Smyth, asking her to retract her identification of him. "Your mistaken words alone will be the cause of my death. Won't you please consider the seriousness of causing an innocent person's death by mistake." Smyth refused, declaring her conscience clear. Just before he was strapped into the electric chair on March 15, 1922, Maurice embraced his father and prayed. With his last words, Mays declared, "I am as innocent as the sun that shines."[24]

Maurice Mays was not the only victim of the wrongful verdicts resulting from his two trials. William and Frances Mays had lost their son and their savings. Knoxville's sexual predator continued to stalk and rape women. By late 1924, more than thirty-two assaults had occurred and eight women had been murdered; the perpetrator was never caught.[25]

---

[23] "Maurice Mays Found Guilty of First Degree Murder," *Knoxville Sentinel*, April 23, 1921, clipping in box E-9, Maurice Mays Papers.

[24] James Weldon Johnson to J. H. Henderson, August 20, 1921; Henderson to Walter White, October 9, 1921, box D-61, folder "Case Supported – Maurice Mays – Mar.–Oct. 1921," NAACP Records; "Mayes' [sic] Body Due to Arrive in Knoxville," *Knoxville Journal and Tribune*, March 16, 1922 ("mistaken" quote); "Supreme Court Judges Intercede with Governor in Behalf of Mays," *East Tennessee News*, March 23, 1922, clippings in box E-9, Maurice Mays Papers; Lakin, "Dark Night," 27–8 ("innocent" quote).

[25] Egerton, "A Case of Prejudice."

In 1926, John McMillan committed suicide at the age of 57. After coming home from work one afternoon, he asked his wife to get him some ice cream; while she was gone, he shot himself in the head.[26] Seven years after it ended, Knoxville's riot was, it appeared, still claiming victims.

The Trials and Convictions of the Elaine Twelve

In late September 1919, white planters in Phillips County, Arkansas, had ordered the destruction of their sharecroppers' union, leading to one of the year's worst episodes of antiblack collective violence: at least twenty-five African Americans, likely many more, were killed. Even as the pogrom was underway, authorities and vigilantes stamped out the Progressive Farmers and Household Union of America and harassed its legal counsel. Ocier Bratton, the son of the union's attorney U. S. Bratton, arrived by train on the morning of October 1 to take statements from black sharecroppers who were being cheated by their white landlords. Dozens of men were already waiting at the train station. Around 10 A.M., as Bratton was recording their claims, half a dozen white men strode up. The sharecroppers scattered at their sight. "I guess you will have to adjourn your little meeting," one of the white men announced. Bratton was shoved into a car and driven to the town of Elaine, where an angry crowd threatened to hang him. Many in the mob "appeared to be the leading citizens," Bratton later noted. His guards kept the would-be lynchers at bay and locked him inside a storeroom that already held two black men in chains. Bratton remain imprisoned for more than thirty days.[27]

Robert Hill, the founder of the union, was more fortunate than Bratton – Hill escaped with the sharecroppers when the armed whites arrived. Eluding capture throughout the day, he slipped out of Phillips County undetected. He surfaced in Kansas, a marked man, indicted in Arkansas for murder and "nightriding" for allegedly leading a conspiracy to massacre whites. "Please get up at once for my help," Hill wrote the NAACP, "because if they get me, they will kill me."[28] A lengthy extradition struggle

[26] *Knoxville Journal*, July 1, 1926, 1, and July 2, 1926, 1.
[27] Extract of a letter from O. S. Bratton to U. S. Bratton, November 5, 1919, Waskow Notes, tab "Arkansas Army."
[28] Robert Hill to U. S. Bratton, December 4, 1919, Waskow Notes, tab "Arkansas Riot"; Hill to the NAACP, November 26, 1919, box 32, folder "Elaine, Ark. riot 1919–23,"

ensued, but it was overshadowed by the trials of the union men captured by the posse and troops.

Phillips County's white elites played an integral part in the court proceedings by forming the Committee of Seven. Members included businessman E. M. "Mort" Allen; merchant Sebastian Straus; Helena's mayor J. G. Knight; and two county officials, Judge H. D. Moore and Sheriff Frank Kitchens.[29] The committee, seeking to reassert subjugation of black labor and to deter blacks from fighting for their economic and political rights, wanted to "prove" that a conspiracy to murder whites had barely been averted and that the leaders and participants had admitted their "guilt." Swift and harsh punishment, the committee hoped, would quickly restore the status quo.

The Committee of Seven was particularly interested in extracting confessions from union members Alf Banks and Will Wordlow. Both men had attended the union meeting on the night of September 30 that had ended in a shoot-out with a sheriff's deputy and a special agent of the Missouri Pacific Railroad. The posse had captured both men on October 1 and put them in the Helena jail, which soon held more than 100 other African Americans. Sheriff's deputies took Banks and Wordlow to a closed room where, in the words of a white witness, they were "whipped with a leather strap that would cut the blood at every lick." The deputies, aided by Missouri Pacific special agents, thrust formaldehyde up their prisoners' noses. They stripped the men naked and delivered electrical shocks. Banks described his experience: "I was frequently whipped with great severity, and was also put into an electric chair and shocked, and strangling drugs would be put to my nose to make me tell things against others that they had killed or shot at some of the white people and to force me to testify against them." Said Wordlow, "to escape from the torture, I finally said what they wanted me to say." Missouri Pacific special agent T. K. Jones whipped so many prisoners that he lost count. Prisoners who escaped whippings were forced to watch others being lashed. Jones explained that the terrified observers "were told if they did not give the testimony that was wanted that they would get the same thing that those that were whipped got." Beaten into submission, the prisoners were

Arthur Spingarn Papers, Library of Congress (quote); Cortner, *Mob Intent on Death*, 14–15, 55; C. M. Walser and C. R. Maxey, "In re – Negro Insurrection at Hoop Spur and Elaine," October 10, 1919, RG 65, OGF 373,159, reel 820, 4.

[29] "The Arkansas Peons," *Crisis* 23, no. 2 (December 1921), 72–6; Waskow, *From Race Riot*, 137.

then dragged before the Committee of Seven to offer up their so-called confessions.[30]

Regional newspapers obliged the Committee of Seven with supportive coverage. "The negroes at Hoop Spur have been under the influence of a few rascally white men and designing leaders of their own race who have been exploiting them for personal gain," reported the *Helena World* on October 3. The paper described sharecropper and union man Ed Hicks as a leader of the "Negro insurrection" and repeated the false claim that authorities had discovered rifles and ammunition in the office of black dentist David Johnston (who was killed by the posse during the pogrom). The *Daily Democrat-Times* (Greenville, Miss.) charged an unnamed white man, probably Ocier Bratton, with inciting blacks to "rise against the white residents" of Phillips County. Another Mississippi newspaper referred to the Committee of Seven as "authorized investigators" who had definitive proof of a plot to "slaughter" whites on October 6 while the *Helena World* characterized the absent Robert Hill as a schemer who had preyed upon the "ignorance and superstition of a race of children."[31]

Arkansas's newspapers also depicted white vigilantes as the victims of rampaging blacks. In the *Helena World*'s telling, O. R. Lilly, a member of the posse that murdered David Johnston and his brothers, fell from his car, uttering his last words "they've got me, boys," as his loyal black chauffeur Jim "knelt beside him, sobbing." Black "bandits" killed another posse member, James Tappan.[32] The *Arkansas Gazette* identified Missouri Pacific special agent W. A. Adkins, who had confronted the union men at their September 30 meeting, as the first victim of the conspiracy. According to the *Gazette*, that meeting was the final mobilization for the massacre, which allegedly featured "'Paul Revere' couriers rounding up armed blacks using the password "we've just begun."

[30] For Jones's testimony, see *Frank Moore et al. vs. the State of Arkansas*, Supreme Court of the United States, No. 955, October Term, 1919, transcript of record in box D-101, NAACP Records, 106–7 (first and fourth quotes); for Banks's and Wordlow's testimony, see *Albert Giles and Joe Fox vs. the State of Arkansas* #2412, January 9, 1920, copy in box 1, file 10, Grif Stockley Papers, Butler Center for Arkansas Studies, 97–9 (second and third quotes). See also Whitaker, *On the Laps of Gods*, 159–64.

[31] "Elaine Insurrection Is Over; Committee of 7 in Charge," *Helena World*, October 3, 1919, 1; "Race Riot in Phillips County, Ark.," *Daily Democrat-Times*, October 2, 1919, 1; "Negroes Planned Killing of Whites," *Tunica* (Miss.) *Times*, October 11, 1919, 1; "Inward Facts About Negro Insurrection," *Helena World*, October 7, 1919, 1, clippings in box 2, file 5, Grif Stockley Papers.

[32] "Elaine Insurrection Is Over."

Women were even – "it was said" – tucking automatic revolvers into their socks.[33]

Newspapers across the country echoed the local coverage. "Bands of negroes... had planned a general slaughter of white people tomorrow," reported the *Omaha Morning World-Herald*, which was still covering Omaha's courthouse riot.[34] According to the *Omaha Bee*, the death of Adkins resulted from an ambush by blacks.[35] After acknowledging that black tenant farmers had the right to organize, the *St. Louis Post-Dispatch* conjectured that a legitimate movement "might gradually be turned to sinister ends by unscrupulous leaders."[36] The *Gary Daily Tribune* (Ind.) claimed that two armed blacks had "paraded" the streets of Elaine, proclaiming their intention to attack whites.[37] In the *New York Times*'s telling, Ocier Bratton had been "preaching social equality among the negroes" who had armed themselves in advance of the "general uprising against the whites."[38] Yet again, newspapers across the country were blaming African Americans for the mob violence inflicted upon them.

The black press countered with articles identifying the actual reasons for the violence. White planters' efforts to cheat and control their tenants, "not any attempt at uprising or insurrection on the part of the Negroes," was the basic cause of the riot, reported the *New York Age*, which detailed the efforts of the sharecroppers' attorney, U. S. Bratton, to obtain honest settlements. James Weldon Johnson ridiculed claims that a vast conspiracy to kill whites had been uncovered: "A more malicious and unfounded lie was never spread." Such claims, he noted, are all too familiar, another example of the "propaganda" that legitimizes further oppression of African Americans.[39] The *California Eagle* published a pastor's sermon decrying the "race prejudice" motivating the mobs not just

---

[33] "Phillips County Blacks Planned Uprising Today," *Arkansas Gazette*, October 6, 1919, clipping in box 1229, folder "Racial Relations at Camp Pike, Arkansas," Record Group 407, Records of the Adjutant General's Office, Army, Central Decimal File, 1917–1925, U.S. National Archives and Records Administration, College Park, Md. (hereafter RG 407).

[34] "Find Alleged Negro Plot Against Whites," *Omaha Morning World-Herald*, October 6, 1919, 3.

[35] "9 Dead in Arkansas Race Riots," *Omaha Bee*, October 2, 1919, 1.

[36] Transcription of article, *St. Louis Post-Dispatch*, October 12, 1919, Waskow Notes, tab "Negroes Incited."

[37] "Race Riots Resumed in Arkansas," *Gary Daily Tribune*, October 2, 1919, 1.

[38] "Six More Are Killed in Arkansas Riots," *New York Times*, October 3, 1919.

[39] "Cotton Prices at Bottom of Trouble in State of Arkansas" (first quote) and "The Arkansas Hoax" (second quote), *New York Age*, October 18, 1919, 1, 4; "Arkansas Land Owners Defraud Tenants," *New York Age*, October 25, 1919, 1.

in Arkansas, but Omaha and Chicago as well.[40] The *Cleveland Advocate* offered a blunt and brief rebuttal: its headline for an article about the alleged uprising read, "This Story Sounds Like a Fairy Tale."[41]

As the fight to establish the truth about Arkansas's pogrom continued, the Committee of Seven announced its findings. Spokesman E. M. Allen vilified Robert Hill as both a con man, for fleecing sharecroppers, and a zealot, for plotting mass murder. The glaring contradiction of these conclusions – as Grif Stockley comments, when "one is profitably bilking others, one does not send them out to be killed" – did not faze Allen, who made much of Hill's insinuation to sharecroppers that the federal government had approved of the union. According to Allen, Hill "told the darkies that he was an agent of the government . . . [which] had called into existence this organization which would be supported by the Government in defense of the negroes against the white people." Allen also accused Hill of requiring "all members of the Union" to take up arms to someday attack whites. (Reference to the "Union" had the added effect of evoking the hated history of federal protection of black rights in the South after the Civil War.) Finally, Allen declared that he had personally questioned 100 black prisoners: "The stories they tell are almost identical as to the promises and representations made by Hill." Allen did not explain how he could know, exactly, what Hill had said since he was still at large.[42]

Accuracy and logic were not the report's aims, however; the Committee of Seven aimed to provide Phillips County prosecutor John E. Miller with "evidence" to secure convictions. Not that Miller required help. As Missouri Pacific special agent T. K. Jones later noted, public sentiment against the defendants "was so bitter and so strong and so universal that it was absolutely unanimous and no man could have sat upon a jury in any of these cases and have voted for an acquittal and remained in Helena afterwards."[43] Both the Committee of Seven and Miller resolved to hold the trials as quickly as possible – restoration of the status quo was imperative. (On October 7, the day the committee released its report, handbills ordering blacks to "STOP TALKING! Stay at home – Go to work – Don't worry!" appeared all over Elaine and Helena.)[44]

[40] J. Whitcomb Brougher, "Law and Lawlessness," *California Eagle*, October 18, 1919, 1.
[41] "This Story Sounds Like a Fairy Tale," *Cleveland Advocate*, October 11, 1919, 1.
[42] Stockley, *Blood in Their Eyes*, 87–9.
[43] *Frank Moore et al. vs. the State of Arkansas*, 107.
[44] Committee of Seven, "To the Negroes of Phillips County," October 7, 1919, box 1229, folder "Racial Relations at Camp Pike, Arkansas," RG 407.

In a three day period, an all-white grand jury delivered charges against 122 black men; seventy-three indictments came on just one day, October 30. Two grand jurors, Sebastian Straub and T. W. Keesee, also served on the Committee of Seven.[45] The trials began less than a week later. Union member Frank Hicks was the first to appear in court, on November 3, charged with the murder of posse member Clinton Lee. The presiding judge, J. M. Jackson, appointed a white Helena attorney named Jacob Fink to represent Hicks. John Miller, the prosecutor, called seven witnesses, including two black men, George Green and John Jefferson, who had been tortured. Under Miller's questioning, Green claimed he saw Hicks fire at the vehicle that Lee was riding in, adding that Hicks warned, "God damn it, I will shoot you" when Green told him not to fire. During cross examination, however, Green admitted he was not sure who actually made that threat. Neither of the two white men present when Lee was shot, R. L. Brooks and Tom Faulkner, could identify the shooter; Brooks did not even know from which direction the shots came. Sid Stokes, Elaine's mayor, testified that Frank Hicks had confessed to firing at the car. Stokes insisted that no one had abused Hicks: "when he got started [with his statement] he just told us the story right there, straight through." Hicks himself did not take the stand. His attorney did not call any witnesses on his behalf, nor did he make a closing statement. The all-white, male jury convicted Hicks in eight minutes.[46]

A similar rush to judgment and incompetent defense counsel marked the ensuing proceedings. Indeed, Judge Jackson opened the trial of Ed Hicks (Frank's brother) and sharecroppers Frank Moore, Joe Knox, Ed Coleman, and Paul Hall that very day. The state charged these five men with aiding in the murder of Clinton Lee and called the same witnesses who had just testified against Frank Hicks. Again, questioning failed to establish who had shot Lee. Miller queried black witnesses at length about the September 30 meeting, seeking to prove that the union had conspired to kill whites. When the defense objected, Judge Jackson ruled that such questions "will be admissible for the purpose of showing a conspiracy." Miller was only able to demonstrate that the men had been armed, and he did not rebut John Jefferson's statement that the union men carried weapons for self-defense. Yet the defense did not take advantage of this

---

[45] Waskow, *From Race Riot*, 137; Stockley, *Blood in Their Eyes*, 109.

[46] *State of Arkansas v. Frank Hicks* #4509, November 4, 1919, copy in box 1, file 11, Grif Stockley Papers, 10, 25–31, 46, 49–52 (first quote on 25, second on 50); "Frank Hicks Found Guilty of Lee's Murder," *Helena World*, November 3, 1919, copy in box 2, file 5, Grif Stockley Papers; Stockley, *Blood in Their Eyes*, 110–15.

opening to further contest Miller's claim of a conspiracy. None of the accused took the stand, their attorneys called no witnesses on their behalf. The jury delivered guilty verdicts against all five men in seven minutes. The next day, November 4, another jury took six minutes to convict John Martin and Alf Banks of the murder of railroad special agent W. H. Adkins; Will Wordlow's jury convicted him for the same crime in two minutes. Still another trial held on November 4 resulted in the convictions of Albert Giles and Joe Fox for the death of James Tappan, bringing the number of guilty verdicts to eleven. A twelfth conviction, of Ed Ware for Adkins's death, came on November 17 – Ware had eluded capture for several weeks. Judge Jackson sentenced all twelve men to death.[47]

In the *Cleveland Gazette*, William Byrd pointedly observed that the court delivering these verdicts and punishments "was composed of the murderers that began the riot."[48] Yet, as was so often the case during 1919, whites who had committed violence against blacks in Phillips County were not charged, let alone tried.[49] Another vocal black critic of the outcome, Ida B. Wells, traveled from Chicago to visit the condemned prisoners, wearing a disguise when she came to the jail. She found the men resigned to their fate, singing and praying but resolving to die like men. An impassioned Wells exhorted them to pray not for heaven but for their lives. As Will Wordlow later recalled, Wells's visit gave them new hope.[50] Wells soon published a pamphlet calling attention to the men's plight and the reasons why they had joined the sharecroppers' union – yet another example of the struggle to establish the facts about the pogrom.[51]

For his part, E. M. Allen welcomed the swift verdicts and expressed no doubt about the outcome. "We have absolutely no twinge of conscience as far as the trials are concerned," he stated. He even believed the courts had been merciful: "Under the law we could have convicted many more and could easily have sentenced fifteen or twenty more to death."[52] Under whose law, though? That was a question Scipio Jones resolved to answer in favor of the condemned men.

---

[47] *Frank Moore et al. vs. State of Arkansas*, 35–8 (quote on 38); Stockley, *Blood in Their Eyes*, 115–19; "Six Negroes Found Guilty" and "A Verdict in Six Minutes," *Helena World*, November 4, 1919, copies in box 2, file 5, Grif Stockley Papers.

[48] William A. Byrd, "New Form of Lynch-Murder," *Cleveland Gazette*, November 15, 1919, 1.

[49] Stockley, *Blood in Their Eyes*, 108.

[50] Patricia Boughton to the author, February 6, 2009, in author's possession. Boughton is Will Wordlow's granddaughter and generously shared this history.

[51] Wells-Barnett, *Arkansas Race Riot*.

[52] E. M. Allen to David Thomas, January 21, 1920, box 19, folder "Civil Rights – Resource Material – Helena, Ark. 1919," Arthur Waskow Papers, Wisconsin Historical Society.

The Fight to Save the Elaine Twelve

Scipio Jones was one of Arkansas's leading black attorneys. Born during the Civil War, Jones worked as a school teacher while he studied law. He passed the bar in 1889 and began practicing in Little Rock. Jones frequently represented black fraternal organizations such as the Mosaic Templars of America. A loyal Republican, Jones worked to end the party's exclusion of blacks. In 1902, he assembled a ticket of black independent Republicans after the party sponsored an all-white ballot. Although none of Jones's candidates won, the incident demonstrated the attorney's underlying determination. Jones was no firebrand, however; he had not joined Little Rock's NAACP branch because he disapproved of the NAACP's use of publicity to pressure white authorities.[53] Despite their differences, Jones and the civil rights organization became allies in the effort to defend the Elaine Twelve (Figures 9.2 and 9.3).

The NAACP, buoyed by its legal wins after Washington's and Chicago's riots, moved to help the imprisoned sharecroppers even before their trials. Walter White, bearing press credentials from the *Chicago Daily News*, traveled to Arkansas. His fair skin and blue eyes fooled Governor Charles Brough, who presented White with a letter of introduction to use in Phillips County. In Helena, White spoke with Sheriff Frank Kitchens (who had organized white vigilantes into a massive posse during the pogrom), but White was exposed before he could interview the prisoners. After a black resident told him that whites had discovered his true identity, White hurriedly boarded a Memphis-bound train. (The conductor told him he was about to miss the "fun": a search was just underway for "a damned yellow nigger down here passing for white." When White asked what would happen, the conductor answered, "when they get through with him he won't pass for white no more!")[54]

Jones feared Arkansas's blacks would ultimately pay the price for this northern intervention. On October 19, he and other leading black citizens of Little Rock publicly praised Brough, crediting the governor with saving lives and promising that "the best colored people of the state" stood behind him.[55] Yet Jones also met with Walter White and arranged a meeting with U. S. Bratton, who shared the evidence of debt peonage that his firm had collected. White realized that publication of this evidence was imperative – what better way to refute the Committee of

---

[53] Dillard, "Scipio A. Jones"; Stockley, *Blood in Their Eyes*, 92–9.
[54] White, *Man Called White*, 47–51 (quotes on 51).
[55] Stockley, *Blood in Their Eyes*, 99.

FIGURE 9.2. Attorney Scipio Jones with the Elaine Twelve. Arkansas native Scipio Jones raised money and served as the attorney for the twelve sharecroppers who were tortured to obtain false confessions then used to convict them of conspiring to murder whites in Phillips County, Arkansas, in 1919. Years of appeals and a Supreme Court decision freed the men and established the federal government's obligation to ensure due process and equal protection in state judicial proceedings. *Source:* Black History General Photograph Collection, PHO 4–77. Courtesy of the Butler Center for Arkansas Studies and the Central Arkansas Library System.

Seven's fictional sharecropper conspiracy?[56] Jones's timely introduction thus enabled the NAACP to rebut the prevailing white narrative about a black sharecropper conspiracy in Phillips County.

White soon published articles detailing the white planters' exploitation of black sharecroppers.[57] The NAACP's leadership understood, of course, that the truth was hardly enough to free the condemned men. Legal efforts to delay the men's execution and to overturn the convictions had to be

---

[56] White, *Man Called White*, 47.
[57] "Economic Conditions in Arkansas," *Branch Bulletin* vol. III, no. 11 (November 1919), 101–2; Walter White, "'Massacring Whites' in Arkansas," *Nation* 109, no. 2840 (December 6, 1919), 715–16.

FIGURE 9.3. Attorney Scipio Jones with the Elaine Twelve. *Source:* Black History General Photograph Collection, PHO 4–78. Courtesy of the Butler Center for Arkansas Studies and the Central Arkansas Library System.

carried out quickly. In light of White's troubles in Helena, the NAACP realized that it would have to conceal its involvement as much as possible. An experienced Arkansas attorney was needed – someone like Scipio Jones.

But the NAACP did not want to put a black attorney before white judges and juries, fearing that racial prejudice would doom the appeals. The organization also wanted to avoid the problem that had arisen in Chicago: local blacks competing with one another *and* the NAACP to raise defense funds. As James Weldon Johnson commented about Jones and his partner Thomas Price, "there is a possibility of . . . colored lawyers going . . . on a tangent to raise money and, of course, to figure in the cases, thereby messing up the whole matter." For their part, Jones and Price were not waiting for the NAACP's approval. During November, they began working with Little Rock's black community to raise money, and Jones visited Phillips County to gather evidence and information for appeals.[58]

[58] Stockley, *Blood in Their Eyes*, 142–4 (quote on 142).

Meanwhile the NAACP worked with the Brattons to find a white attorney. U. S. Bratton and his son Ocier had narrowly escaped prosecution themselves. The Committee of Seven's strongmen had not tortured Ocier, but the grand jury charged him and his father with barratry (filing nuisance lawsuits). While the trials of the Elaine Twelve were underway, John Miller admitted that he had only sought charges against the Brattons to appease local whites but that he would not prosecute them. Obviously, the Brattons themselves could not serve as defense counsel for the Elaine Twelve. (Death threats and social ostracism soon forced the family to move to Michigan.) The senior Bratton advised the NAACP to hire Colonel (C.S.A.) George Murphy of Little Rock. Age had not dulled the seventy-nine-year-old attorney's legal acumen, and, as a former attorney general for Arkansas, Murphy had the credentials the NAACP wanted for defense counsel. By late November, the colonel had agreed to represent the Elaine Twelve for a fee of $3,000.[59]

Murphy and Jones soon merged their efforts, with U. S. Bratton monitoring the partnership for the NAACP. Jones scored a crucial early victory by persuading Governor Brough to consider commuting the death sentences for all but one of the convicted men.[60] Together, Jones and Murphy drafted motions for new trials. Not only was Murphy confident that the motions would succeed, but he believed, according to Bratton, that "these motions will be revelations to the world in that they will show the true inwardness of the outrages that have been perpetrated on these people."[61] The defense had ample cause to seek retrials. Their motions first cited the prejudicial atmosphere in Helena. Second, the court had not allowed the men to consult with their attorneys, depriving them of due process – the men did not even see their court-appointed defense counsel until "they were carried from the jail into the court room and put upon trial." Third, the practice of convening all-white juries in Phillips County had violated the Fourteenth Amendment's guarantee of equal protection of the laws. The motions included affidavits from Alf Banks and Will Wordlow recounting their torture and the Committee of Seven's demands that they testify that they had seen their fellow union men shoot whites.[62]

[59] Cortner, *Mob Intent on Death*, 41–4; Stockley, *Blood in Their Eyes*, 140–2, 155.
[60] Stockley, *Blood in Their Eyes*, 144; Cortner, *Mob Intent on Death*, 48–51.
[61] Mary White Ovington to Archibald Grimké, December 4, 1919, box 39–28, folder "December 1919," Archibald Grimké Papers, Moorland-Spingarn Research Center.
[62] Cortner, *Mob Intent on Death*, 84–6; *State of Arkansas v. John Martin and Alf Banks, Jr.*, #4482, November 4, 1919, copy in box 1, file 12, Grif Stockley Papers, 62 (quote).

Judge Jackson denied the motions, but Brough stayed the executions on December 20, 1919, just seven days before they were to be carried out, to allow an appeal to the state supreme court. At this point, Murphy and Jones discovered an error in the trials of Ed Ware, Alf Banks, Will Wordlow, Albert Giles, Joe Fox, and John Martin (Ware et al.). Arkansas law required verdicts to specify the degree of murder, but the juries had only declared the defendants "guilty as charged in the indictment." The attorneys bundled these six cases together, while the remaining six cases (Frank Moore, Ed and Frank Hicks, Joe Knox, Ed Coleman, and Paul Hall; Moore et al.) were appealed using the original motion.[63]

As the Elaine Twelve and their attorneys awaited a decision, Robert Hill fought extradition to Arkansas to face the charges of murder and nightriding. He had relocated to Topeka, Kansas, where he enlisted the aid of the local NAACP branch. In turn, the branch secured the help of Hugh Fisher, a white Republican lawyer with political ambitions in a heavily Democratic state. Sensing an opportunity to court black votes, Fisher convinced Kansas governor Henry Allen that Hill could not receive a fair trial in Arkansas. Allen's decision on March 23, 1920, to refuse the extradition request provoked outrage in Phillips County and a backlash in Kansas against the governor, who nevertheless held firm.[64]

The Arkansas Supreme Court soon gave whites in Phillips County another reason to be angry. On March 29, 1920, the court overturned the convictions in Ware et al., ruling that a murder conviction that failed to stipulate degree "is so fatally defective, that no judgment can be entered upon it." However, the justices upheld the convictions of Moore et al. In rejecting the defense's contention that an all-white jury violated equal protection, the court ruled that the objection should have been raised at the trial's start. The court also turned down the claim that torture and a prejudicial atmosphere had denied due process. The evidence was legally adequate; the jury, correctly charged as to its duties.[65]

The reversal of the Ware et al. convictions proved only a temporary victory. Judge Jackson denied Jones and Murphy's request for a change of venue and for more time to prepare their defense. The defense succeeded in striking potential jurors for cause – ninety-nine total in Joe Fox and Albert Giles's trial – and in introducing evidence of torture, but the new trials,

[63] Stockley, *Blood in Their Eyes*, xxviii; Cortner, *Mob Intent on Death*, 86–7; *State of Arkansas v. John Martin and Alf Banks*, 56 (quote).

[64] For the Hill extradition battle, see Cortner, *Mob Intent on Death*, 55–83.

[65] Cortner, *Mob Intent on Death*, 86–9 (quote on 87).

held in early May 1920, were as one-sided as the first proceedings. All six men were again convicted of murder. This time, each jury made sure to specify first degree murder in their verdicts, and Jackson handed down death sentences on July 23, 1920. Governor Brough again stayed the executions to allow appeals. He also postponed scheduling the executions of Frank Moore and the other five men whose original convictions had been upheld. On May 24, the defense had filed a writ of certiorari with the U.S. Supreme Court, seeking a review of the trial proceedings. If denied, then the Moore defendants would have few legal options left.[66]

Jones and Colonel Murphy's partner, Edgar McHaney, traveled to New York to plan their next step with the NAACP. On the second day of the trials, Murphy had fallen ill and remained in Arkansas. U. S. Bratton expressed misgivings about McHaney, whom he accused of being compromised because he was "scared to death for fear of the local feeling."[67] After the meeting, McHaney requested a $25,000 fee to continue, deeming the sum "very moderate compensation" for the required work. The NAACP countered with an offer of $5,000. Although McHaney accepted and agreed to prepare an appeal for the U.S. Supreme Court, Scipio Jones, who had presented the defense by himself in the retrials of Ware et al., now appeared more important than ever to the NAACP and the Elaine Twelve.[68]

Several setbacks occurred that fall. On October 11, 1920, Murphy died in Little Rock. That same day, the U.S. Supreme Court denied the writ of certiorari. In November, Governor Brough, under pressure from whites in Phillips County, announced that he would not grant clemency to any of the Elaine Twelve. Brough claimed that the restraint shown by whites during the riot was a key factor in his decision: just as whites had "refrained from mob violence," he would not interfere with the course of justice. The "cause of law enforcement and maintenance of law and order," Brough said, can only be served by a strict compliance with the law." Jones countered with a statement that artfully questioned why the governor chose that moment to declare his commitment to justice, when the methods (i.e., torture) used to obtain evidence had not as yet been fully exposed. Jones even suggested that such a revelation might quiet the calls for immediate executions.[69]

---

[66] For the second set of trials, see Stockley, *Blood in Their Eyes*, 164–75.

[67] Stockley, *Blood in Their Eyes*, 169, 174–5; Bratton to Shillady, August 15, 1920, Waskow Notes, tab "Arkansas Army" (quote).

[68] Cortner, *Mob Intent on Death*, 94–7 (quote on 95).

[69] Whitaker, *On the Laps of Gods*, 233–5; Cortner, *Mob Intent on Death*, 97–100 (quotes on 100).

A twofold legal campaign ensued, with Jones, aided by McHaney, fighting to stay the executions and to secure new trials. The basis for new trials remained the same: due process, prejudicial atmosphere, and equal protection. Jones appealed the second set of Ware et al. convictions to the Arkansas Supreme Court, hoping that a second review might finally persuade the justices that a fair trial in Phillips County was impossible. Given the court's peremptory rejection of the first appeal, the chances of success appeared slim. Yet the Moore defendants faced an even more precarious situation. The U.S. Supreme Court's rejection of the writ of certiorari meant that the death sentences could be carried out after the state supreme court formally received the ruling. Though Brough was leaving office, he repeated his intention to deny clemency.[70]

Then, reprieve for the Ware defendants. In December 1920, the Arkansas Supreme Court again reversed those convictions. This time the justices accepted Jones's argument that the exclusion of African Americans from jury selection because of their race had denied the defendants due process and equal protection. In a significant finding, the court noted that the exclusion violated not just the Fourteenth Amendment but also state law, which permitted defendants to challenge the jury selection process even after the trial was underway. In the first trials, Ware and the other men's lawyers had not made such a challenge; Murphy and Jones had during the second trials. According to the court, Judge Jackson had erred by refusing to hear evidence that the jury selection violated the defendants' rights. The decision did not free the men, however; it meant that the state had to try them for the third time.[71]

Meanwhile, Arkansas's new governor, Thomas McRae, scheduled execution of the Moore defendants for June 10, 1921. Although the jury selection in those trials had also been tainted, the failure of the original defense to file a motion, as well as the Arkansas Supreme Court's upholding of those convictions, precluded an appeal. Only a writ of habeas corpus filed in a federal court, asking it to review Arkansas's detention of the men, could save the men's lives. On June 8, McRae announced he would not stop the executions. With just two days left, Jones and McHaney filed the writ of habeas corpus in Little Rock – unable to find a federal judge who could hear the petition, they had no choice but to turn to the state court. The hearings on the state writ delayed the executions and allowed the attorneys to prepare a writ for the federal district court.[72]

[70] Cortner, *Mob Intent on Death*, 101–5 (quote on 102).
[71] Ibid., 102–5.
[72] Whitaker, *On the Laps of Gods*, 237–50.

On September 27, 1921, a U.S. District Court judge, J. H. Cotteral, dismissed the federal petition. Yet he also declared there was probable cause for an appeal to the U.S. Supreme Court, based upon the defense's presentation of the torture used against Moore and the others, the all-white juries, and the prejudicial trial atmosphere. The ruling was a significant breakthrough, as was Judge J. M. Jackson's decision to grant a change of venue for the Ware defendants, with the third set of trials scheduled for October 1921 in Lee County, Arkansas. The prosecution, realizing that it could no longer take guilty verdicts for granted, asked for a continuance, which was granted. Another boost to the defense: McHaney persuaded Missouri Pacific special agents H. F. Smiddy and T. K. Jones to provide affidavits detailing the torture of the Elaine Twelve.[73]

When McHaney demanded more money, the NAACP refused, reminding him that he had agreed to represent the men for $5,000. McHaney quit. Scipio Jones was now responsible for defending the Ware defendants and for preparing the U.S. Supreme Court appeal for the Moore defendants. The NAACP authorized Jones to hire a white law firm in Lee County to aid in the Ware cases. No longer trying to conceal its role, the NAACP began referring to Jones as "the Association's attorney in Arkansas."[74] As Jones soon learned, however, the association still harbored doubts about his abilities.

Jones filed his notice of appeal in October 1921. His briefs contrasted the lawful, peaceful assembly at the September 1919 union meeting with the ambush by the Adkins party and the mob killings of African Americans. In plain prose, Jones described the torture, coercion, and trials that had sped these men to death sentences: "[everyone], Judge, jury and counsel, were dominated by the mob spirit that was universally present in court and out." Jones also emphasized the exclusion of blacks from all of the juries and the defendants' denial of counsel prior to their appearance in court. The NAACP was impressed enough with the briefs to publish them in the *Crisis* and to use them as a fundraising tool, but would they sway the U.S. Supreme Court?[75]

The Supreme Court scheduled a hearing for January 1923. In the meantime, the Ware defendants awaited retrial. The prosecution received a second continuance in April 1922, and another in October. In each

---

73 Cortner, *Mob Intent on Death*, 131–2; Whitaker, *On the Laps of Gods*, 261–7; Stockley, *Blood in Their Eyes*, xxx–xxxi.
74 Cortner, *Mob Intent on Death*, 132–3 (quote on 133).
75 "The Arkansas Peons," *Crisis* 23, nos. 2 and 3 (December 1921 and January 1922), 72–6, 115–17 (quote on 76).

instance the court rejected the defense's motions to dismiss the cases. Imprisoned since October 1919, the men remained in the penitentiary throughout 1922. Such delays, whatever they forecast about the prosecution's confidence, threatened to exhaust the defense's resources.

Fundraising was thus crucial. Just as black Tennesseans had mobilized to pay for Maurice Mays's appeal, black Arkansans continued to raise money for the Elaine Twelve. At times, the Citizens Defense Fund Commission (CDFC), formed in early 1920, expended more on legal costs than the NAACP did: as of early 1921, the CDFC had spent more than $10,000; the NAACP, approximately $8,000. Scipio Jones himself raised $7,000, much of which came from the Mosaic Templars.[76]

On January 11, 1923, the Supreme Court heard the case of *Moore v. Dempsey*. NAACP board member Moorfield Storey represented the condemned men, but Jones was not at his side, even though the NAACP had announced five days earlier that he would serve as co-counsel. At the last minute, Storey decided he wanted U. S. Bratton as co-counsel. As a final indignity, Storey used Jones's briefs to present his oral argument before the court.[77]

It was a very convincing argument, thanks to Jones. In a seven to two decision delivered February 19, the Supreme Court sent the Moore cases back to the U.S. District Court to determine if the evidence of torture and the Committee of Seven's conspiracy to frame the six men were true.[78] Although the men were not as yet free, the likelihood of their execution had dramatically diminished, and the Supreme Court had firmly established the federal government's power to ensure and require due process and equal protection in state judicial proceedings.[79]

The Arkansas Supreme Court soon provided a victory for the remaining half of the Elaine Twelve. In June the court ruled that the detention of the Ware defendants was unconstitutional because the men had been held for more than a year without trial. They were released later that month. The Moore defendants remained imprisoned for almost two more years, even though Arkansas did not seek to retry the men. The ever-reliable Scipio Jones was, yet again, the key figure in this final, protracted legal battle. Negotiations with Phillips County prosecutor John Miller and Governor Thomas McRae resulted in an agreement in November that Moore and

---

[76] Stockley, *Blood in Their Eyes*, xxxi; Cortner, *Mob Intent on Death*, 50–2, 106–8, 160–1.

[77] Whitaker, *On the Laps of Gods*, 277–85; Stockley, *Blood in Their Eyes*, 213–15; Dillard, "Scipio A. Jones," 207–8.

[78] Stockley, *Blood in Their Eyes*, 215–17; Cortner, *Mob Intent on Death*, 154–5.

[79] Whitaker, *On the Laps of Gods*, 286–93.

the other men's sentences would be commuted to twelve years imprisonment but that the governor would pardon the men within a year. Although McRae never pardoned them, he signed undated furloughs for the six men on his last day in office in January 1925, effectively freeing them.[80] Jones could celebrate the outcomes for his clients, but his rude ousting from the Supreme Court hearing was not easily forgotten – if not for the snub, Jones would have been the first black attorney to appear before the U.S. Supreme Court.

The release of the last of the Elaine Twelve brought a victorious close to the years-long struggle to rectify what was, arguably, the most egregious injustice occurring in 1919. The rush to judgment in Phillips County was, as Scipio Jones had repeatedly observed in his briefs, another manifestation of mob violence. The torture used to extract confessions was a continuation of the pogrom that had killed dozens of African Americans and had obliterated the sharecroppers' union. The fact that men who had participated in the pogrom served on the juries that convicted the Elaine Twelve demonstrated further continuity. The NAACP's national office and branches carried out the arduous legal work required to keep the men out of Arkansas's death chamber. Winning a case before the U.S. Supreme Court capped the organization's success in defending African Americans who had been wrongfully charged (and, in many cases, also subjected to physical abuse) in the Washington and Chicago riots. *Moore v. Dempsey* had added significance because it established the federal government's obligation to require states to uphold due process and equal protection. This precedent fulfilled a long-standing demand of the New Negroes: if the states cannot dispense justice fairly and constitutionally, then the federal government must force them to do so. Nothing less was worthy of a nation that had fought to make the world safe for democracy.

The NAACP's victory for the Elaine Twelve was not possible without the contributions of others. Scipio Jones, for one; the Mosaic Templars, who raised funds, for another. The donations of ordinary black Arkansans, who gave money to the CDFC, was just as important. Ida B. Wells, who had furtively visited the condemned men after their trials, boosted their spirits and, through her lengthy article, publicized their case. U. S. Bratton, the sharecroppers' original attorney, provided legal guidance to the NAACP, referring them to Colonel George Murphy, whose firm won the first round of appeals. No one could give back the years

---

[80] Stockley, *Blood in Their Eyes*, xxxi–xxxii; Whitaker, *On the Laps of Gods*, 294–308.

that the Elaine Twelve spent wrongfully imprisoned or take away the physical and psychological scars of torture, but this collective effort had saved their lives.

But Maurice Mays's life was not saved. It is not possible to know whether or not earlier intervention by the NAACP's national office would have made a difference. The Tennessee branches did all they could, as did Mays's parents and Knoxville's black residents. That their effort fell short in no way impugns the devotion shown, the sacrifices made. Mays's wrongful conviction and execution, usually presented as an addendum to the Knoxville riot, is, in fact, historically important. Mays's trials were, like those of the Elaine Twelve, rough justice masking as legitimate court proceedings. The struggle to save Mays's life was thus also a campaign to turn back rough justice, to halt "lynch-murder," to use the *Cleveland Gazette*'s phrase, in all its forms. And the fight in Knoxville was but one of many mounted against rough justice in 1919.

10

Fighting Judge Lynch

The killing of Will Brown on September 27, 1919, during Omaha's riot marked the fifty-fourth lynching of the year. All told, seventy-seven African Americans lost their lives to lynching in 1919.[1] The victims included another black man named Will Brown, burned alive alongside his friend Jack Gordon in Washington, Georgia, on October 5. Gordon had allegedly shot a white deputy; this Will Brown helped him escape from jail. The mob also killed a third man, Moses Freeman, who had allegedly lied about Gordon and Brown's whereabouts.[2]

By the standards of the era's white supremacy, Freeman had committed a serious crime: he had obstructed a mob during its pursuit of rough justice. Many other lynching victims in 1919 lost their lives for similar transgressions against white supremacy. In April, a mob in Blakely, Georgia, beat black veteran Wilbur Little to death for ignoring warnings to stop wearing his military uniform.[3] Another veteran and a female acquaintance lost their lives near Pickens, Mississippi, in May for allegedly writing an insulting note to a white woman.[4] On August 1, two different Georgia mobs carried out lynchings: the first killed veteran Charles

---

[1] "The Lynching Industry, 1919," *Crisis* 19, no. 4 (February 1920), 183–6. For additional lynching figures, see Kerlin, *Voice of the Negro*, 100–101; "The Lynching Record for the Year 1918," *Crisis* 17, no. 4 (February 1919), 180–1; "The Lynching Industry – 1920," *Crisis* 21, no. 4 (February 1921), 160–2.

[2] Kerlin, *Voice of the Negro*, 109.

[3] "Army Uniform Cost Soldier His Life," *Chicago Defender*, April 5, 1919, clipping in *NAACP Papers*, Part 7, Series A, reel 10, frame 321.

[4] "Dual Lynching Reported," May 9, 1919, and "Pickens Produces Lynching Mystery," May 10, 1919, *Memphis Commercial Appeal*, clippings in *NAACP Papers*, Part 7, Series A, reel 13, frame 1051.

Kelly for failing to yield to a white driver; the second lynched Argie Robinson for refusing to address a white man as "Mister." A mob in Tuscaloosa, Alabama, dismembered Cicero Cage for pulling a white woman off her horse.[5] Yet another Georgia mob hanged an inebriated man for praising blacks' armed resistance to mob attacks during Chicago's riot.[6]

To whites who joined or condoned the lynch mobs, the "crimes" of Wilbur Little and the others were hardly petty. Each victim had defied or insulted the rites and rules governing racial interactions. African Americans' wartime military service had strained the practice and ideology of white supremacy, the New Negro movement was rising. Whites had resolved to hold fast the lines of racial inequality at home as black soldiers returned from France. The slightest infraction – a uniform worn with pride, a right-of-way not recognized, an elided term of address – could, and did, incur brutal punishment at the hands of "persons unknown," as so many lynchers were labeled in coroners' reports.

Yet black Americans did not submit meekly to the mobs' nooses and rifles. Although armed resistance to lynching was not as widespread as the self-defense undertaken during the riots, African Americans deterred mobs on several occasions in the South and the North. African Americans and their allies also waged war against lynching on 1919's other two fronts: they worked to document and report the facts about individual lynchings, and they fought to bring the perpetrators to justice. The NAACP also publicized select episodes of black resistance in order to build support for antilynching legislation at the state and federal levels. Likewise, a legal effort to halt the execution of a black soldier, Sergeant Edgar Caldwell, who had killed a white man in self-defense in late 1918 highlighted the national significance of individual acts of resistance. The NAACP, as it would later do for each of the Elaine Twelve, successfully persuaded the U.S. Supreme Court to hear its appeal of Caldwell's conviction. The NAACP's antilynching initiative and its bid to save Caldwell's life are well documented, but both merit further examination as part of African Americans' three-front war against racial violence. Studies of the antilynching campaign emphasize that the NAACP was responding to the *national* frequency of white mob activity and the

---

[5] "Lynching Industry, 1919"; George Towns to John Shillady, August 8, 1919, *NAACP Papers*, Part 7, Series A, reel 10, frame 551.

[6] "Brags Chicago Riots Are Coming in State and Found Hanged," *Macon Telegraph*, August 6, 1919, clipping in *NAACP Papers*, Part 7, Series A, reel 10, frame 543.

victimization of blacks.[7] True, but *local* acts of resistance also influenced the organization's decisions and actions. Caldwell's case shares several features with the riots and pogroms examined in preceding chapters: black self-defense against violence, the actions of white vigilantes and posses, biased court proceedings, and a persistent legal battle to rectify the injustice. In this context, the case is a microcosm of black resistance during the year of racial violence.

The Antilynching Initiative from War to Peace

In July 1918, Woodrow Wilson delivered a statement black Americans had been waiting a long time to hear. Calling lynching "a disgraceful evil," Wilson implored his fellow Americans to renounce mob action and to adhere to the principles of "ordered law and humane justice." The president questioned the nation's ability to promote the spread of democracy "if we disgrace our own by proving that it is, after all, no protection to the weak." Mobs were no better than the enemy, Germany, whose war crimes had "made lynchers of her armies." Wilson's rhetoric was forceful and plaintive – "no man who loves America, no man who really cares for her fame and honor and character, or who is truly loyal to her institutions, can justify mob action" – but the address was also notable for its omissions. Wilson did not mention that mobs overwhelmingly took the lives of black Americans, nor did he refer to the frequency of southern lynchings. Most conspicuously, he said nothing about what the federal government might do to stop or punish mobs. Instead, the president called upon citizens, community law officers, and state governors "to see to it" that the rule of law was followed.[8] Still, the proclamation indicated an awareness of a problem that the president had long ignored.

Numerous black leaders and their allies had been urging Wilson to speak out against lynching. Robert Moton, the leader of the Tuskegee Institute, wrote to the president following a journey across Alabama, Georgia, and the Carolinas. "There is more genuine restlessness and dissatisfaction on the part of the colored people than I have ever before known," he warned on June 15, 1918. "It seems to me that something ought to be done pretty definitely to change the attitude of these millions

---

[7] See, for example, Zangrando, *NAACP Crusade*; Dray, *At the Hands of Persons Unknown*, 215–75; Schneider, *We Return Fighting*, 172–93.

[8] Woodrow Wilson, "A Statement to the American People," July 26, 1918, in Link, *Papers of Woodrow Wilson* vol. 49, 97–8.

of black people; and this attitude, which is anything but satisfactory, not to use a stronger word, is one very largely due to recent lynchings and burnings of colored people." A Baptist official, Reverend D. D. Crawford, was more pointed than Moton in a May letter to Emmett Scott. "We cannot fight in Europe and at home too," Crawford wrote; a people "disheartened" by lynchings "cannot give their best."[9] Scott joined Secretary of War Newton Baker and George Creel, director of the Committee on Public Information, in requesting a presidential antilynching statement. The three men were also responding to the recently held Washington Conference of Black Editors, which had made federal antilynching legislation a top priority.[10]

Not surprisingly, New Negroes in the black press lauded Wilson's statement. James Weldon Johnson reminded readers of the *New York Age* that the president had echoed points long made by the newspaper. The *Chicago Defender* proudly pointed to its recent publication of a black soldier's open letter to Wilson to take a stand against lynching. Harry Clay Smith, of the *Cleveland Gazette*, believed that the president was specifically denouncing the lynching of blacks; otherwise, his statement might have only referred to mob actions against opponents of the war (including the April lynching in Illinois of a German-American). The black press also noted that Wilson's statement had encouraged many prominent white newspapers to editorialize against lynching. Is the nation "on the eve of true democracy," the *Defender* asked, adding, perhaps pessimistically, "who knows?"[11]

Part of that question's answer lay in the fate of an antilynching bill introduced in April 1918 by Representative Leonidas Dyer (R-Mo.). Dyer's bill held mobs (defined as three or more individuals acting lawlessly) liable for federal prosecution. It also outlined stiff punishments, criminal and civil, for state officials who failed to act to stop or prosecute mobs. To facilitate passage of the bill, Dyer asked the NAACP to draft a list of witnesses for hearings and to comment on the bill's constitutionality. The latter request presented a problem for the NAACP. Although passage of antilynching legislation was a priority, the NAACP's legal expert, board member Moorfield Storey, did not at this time believe that

---

[9] Moton and Crawford are quoted in J. E. Spingarn to Marlborough Churchill, July 22, 1918, box 562, file 291.2, Record Group 407, Records of the Adjutant General's Office, U.S. Army, Central Decimal File, 1917–1925, U.S. National Archives and Records Administration, College Park, Md. (hereafter RG 407), 1.

[10] Jordan, *Black Newspapers*, 122–8.

[11] Jordan, *Black Newspapers*, 129–31 (quote on 131).

the Fourteenth Amendment's guarantee of equal protection of the law supported the federal actions prescribed in the bill. Fellow board member Joel Spingarn, then serving as a major in the Military Intelligence Division (MID), suggested that the federal government take antilynching action in the name of the war. Spingarn outlined his plan in a letter to MID director Marlborough Churchill, providing a lengthy digest of declining black support for the war because of lynching. Federal antilynching legislation can be passed "based on the war powers of the Constitution, in order to cope with the danger which the growth of unrest and dissatisfaction among colored people involves with respect to the successful prosecution of the war," Spingarn concluded.[12]

Secretary Baker and the NAACP both endorsed the Spingarn solution as a substitute for the Dyer Bill, and a supportive Congressman, Warren Gard (D-Ohio), brought the measure before the House Judiciary Committee. The bill never made it out of committee, however; the southern Democrats who still controlled Congress in 1918 had no intention of scheduling an antilynching bill for a vote. The war's end nullified the justification for the Gard bill, while Dyer's bill continued to languish in the House. A spate of lynchings in December 1918 – four on the same day in Shubuta, Mississippi – pushed 1918's lynching toll up to sixty-four.[13] Yet African Americans and their allies remained undaunted. As the new year began, they promised that if the federal and state governments failed to act, they would.

The promise came from many voices – newly returned soldiers, community leaders, NAACP board members – and hammered home two points: the time to stop lynching was *now*, and African Americans were ready to defend themselves against mobs. In January 1919, Sergeant Greenleaf B. Johnson, a veteran of the 372nd Regiment, linked Wilson's antilynching statement to the Paris peace proceedings, then just underway. Noting that the president had insisted a final peace settlement "must also include complete guarantee for the protection of minority races," Greenleaf urged his fellow African Americans to remind the U.S. delegates in Versailles that their own nation as yet failed to provide such guarantees within its borders. "They are our public servants. Why not tell them what we want, like others do?"[14] That same month, Moorfield

---

[12] Zangrando, *NAACP Crusade*, 42–6; Spingarn to Churchill, July 22, 1918, 8 (quote).

[13] Zangrando, *NAACP Crusade*, 44; Newton Baker to Rep. Edwin Webb, July 1918, box 562, file 291.2, RG 407; "Lynching Record for the Year 1918."

[14] Sergeant Greenleaf B. Johnson, "Continued Lynching of Negroes in Spite of President's Warning," *Washington Bee*, January 18, 1919, clipping in box C-374, folder "Military, General 1919, Jan. and Feb.," NAACP Records.

Storey warned of "a serious crisis" as southerners cracked down on blacks "who will come back [from military service] feeling like men, and not disposed to accept the treatment to which they have been subjected."[15] A trip across the South that spring by his colleague Herbert Seligmann validated the venerable attorney's prediction. In Memphis, Seligmann listened as Robert Church, a local black leader, told the mayor that blacks were ready to defend themselves if attacked. A black lawyer in Jackson, Mississippi, told Seligmann about a November 1918 incident in which armed black men prevented the arrest of a soldier who had defended his female companion against the insults of two white soldiers.[16] In Washington, D.C., Captain James Wormley Jones, a black veteran of the Western Front, roused an audience in March by ridiculing Robert Moton's recent advice that black soldiers be "calm and unassuming" upon their return to the United States. "I am not going around with a chip on my shoulder," Jones promised, "but when I am insulted and my rights denied me, I am here to tell you that I am ready to declare war any minute."[17]

The NAACP added to this groundswell of protest. Cofounder Mary White Ovington told a Washington audience that antilynching meetings needed to be held in cities across the country.[18] James Weldon Johnson and Walter White traveled frequently to investigate lynchings. National secretary John Shillady issued press releases aimed at prodding state officials to take action against lynching. For example, he wired Georgia governor Hugh Dorsey to ask him to demand "that legal authorities [in Georgia] proceed energetically to ascertain identity of lynchers, indict them and bring them to trial."[19] Board members Moorfield Storey and Joel Spingarn offered legal guidance; W. E. B. Du Bois, editor of the *Crisis* and director of research and publicity, provided or edited stories about individual lynchings and year-end summaries.

The NAACP pursued a two-pronged strategy: first, to document and publicize each instance of the crime; and second, to convict lynchers and

[15] Storey to Shillady, January 10, 1919, box C-75, folder "Storey, Moorfield, January–March 1919," NAACP Records, 1.

[16] "Report of Herbert J. Seligmann," May 1919, box C-74, folder "Seligmann, Herbert, 1919–22," NAACP Records.

[17] Jones is cited in W. H. Loving to Marlborough Churchill, March 18, 1919, box 113–1, folder 12, Walter H. Loving Papers, Moorland-Spingarn Research Center. When making his report, Loving did not know that Jones, a Washington, D.C., police detective, was grooming himself for undercover work. In November 1919, the Department of Justice made Jones an agent and assigned him to monitor black radicals. See Williams, *Torchbearers of Democracy*, 296–7.

[18] Loving to Churchill, March 17, 1919, box 113–1, folder 12, Walter H. Loving Papers.

[19] Shillady to Dorsey, May 3, 1919, box C-334, folder "National Conference on Lynching May 1–8, 1919," NAACP Records.

law enforcement officials who colluded with lynchers. If existing law inhibited convictions, then antilynching legislation, at the state and federal levels, must be enacted. The first National Conference on Lynching, organized by the NAACP and held in New York in May 1919, forcefully stated this strategy. Resolutions included obtaining Congressional passage of the federal antilynching bill, organizing committees to work for individual state laws, and raising funds for a national publicity effort against lynching. One of the speakers, NAACP field organizer William Pickens, pointed out the connections between lynching, resistance, and the breakdown of law enforcement: "If the black man were justified and supported by the law when he clearly and plainly acts in self-defense, the colored man himself would break up about one-half of the mob violence in this country."[20] As numerous incidents during 1919 in the South and the North showed, African Americans were already acting in self-defense, in most cases without the support of legal authorities.

Fighting Judge Lynch in the South

Blakely, Georgia, in southwestern Early County, had a reputation as the most hostile town in the state for African Americans – "some record," Walter White commented. Here not only did a black driver have to yield to whites, he had to stop his vehicle or team and ask permission to continue. "If he tries to go by without obtaining such permission or after the white man had refused it, he is beaten, and if he resists, he is lynched," White reported.[21] For black residents, use of violence to uphold these extreme forms of white supremacy sometimes proved too much to bear. In 1916, a white man's attempt to whip a young black man sparked a shooting that wounded several whites and killed four blacks. In retaliation for this resistance, mobs lynched two blacks by burning them alive.[22]

When a white mob pounded on the door of the Bryant home in late November 1918, the men of the family scrambled for their weapons. The Bryants were prosperous farmers who owned their land and had lived in Early County for several decades. One of the sons, Henry, had just mustered out of the army. He and his younger brother opened fire on the mob. According to the *Pittsburgh Courier*, a young white woman

---

[20] "The Anti-Lynching Conference," *Crisis* 18, no. 2 (June 1919), 92.
[21] White to Shillady, April 15, 1919, *NAACP Papers*, Part 7, Series A, reel 10, frame 1011.
[22] Grant, *Anti-Lynching Movement*, 106.

who lived nearby "was infatuated with Henry Bryant, but he refused to encourage the same." His avoidance of the woman was no protection against a mob, however – not when the "honor" of a white woman was involved. Henry and his brother reportedly held off the mob until their ammunition ran out. The younger Bryant was wounded but escaped; according to the *Courier*, Henry was lynched.[23]

In April 1919, a mob in Monroe, Louisiana, confronted unexpected resistance when it made repeated attempts to lynch George Holden, a man accused of writing an insulting note to a white woman. The note was a forgery; Holden could not write. (And, as the *Vindicator*, a black newspaper, pointedly asked, if Holden was literate would he have signed his name and delivered the note to the woman's doorstep?) The actual "crime" committed by Holden, a skilled laborer, was the competition he presented to white workers, which led a mob to shoot him at his home. Holden survived and was taken to the St. Francis sanitarium, Monroe's only hospital, where doctors amputated his badly wounded leg. The chagrined mob, wearing masks, came to the hospital on April 28, pushing aside two white nurses to finish the lynching in the black ward. They attacked a patient who had just returned from surgery – but the man was not Holden. (The unfortunate man died the next day.) The nurses called the police, who gave them a pistol but also advised them to give up Holden if the mob came back. Their humiliation and frustration mounting, mob members returned within the hour, but the nurses refused to let the men pass. One woman fired a warning shot; another ripped off a mask, exposing a man she knew. The mob fled as the nurses held the unmasked man for the police. He was taken into custody yet somehow got away once he was on the street. The mob finally completed its mission the next day, seizing Holden from a train and shooting him. (Prone on a stretcher in the baggage car, Holden was being moved to a Shreveport hospital for his putative safety.)[24]

As noted, the nurses were white. Devotion to the welfare of their patients rather than an aversion to rough justice motivated their stand against the mob. In a statement to the press, the nurses remarked, "we

---

[23] "American Huns Meet Stiff Opposition in Midnight Attack on Colored Men in Small Georgia Town," *Pittsburgh Courier*, January 18, 1919, clipping in *NAACP Papers*, Part 7, Series A, reel 10, frame 320. The NAACP did not collect additional documentation of Bryant's murder, however, and did not include it on its tally of 1918 lynchings.

[24] "Louisiana Mob Lynches Negro," *East Tennessee News*, May 1, 1919; "Monroe Hangs Head in Shame," *New Orleans Vindicator*, May 17, 1919, clippings in *NAACP Papers*, Part 7, Series A, reel 12, frames 388, 401.

think it a disgrace to Monroe for a mob to come to the sanitarium to carry out their vengeance, and to scare the nurses and patients, when they easily could have waited until the patient was carried home."[25] In other words, lynching George Holden was not abhorrent, but doing it in a hospital was. White residents of Monroe appeared to agree: "Many of the best citizens of the parish have made it clear, by their words and actions, that if the peace officers... fail in their duty hereafter, ways and means will be found to throw them out of office and men who will enforce the law will be put into their places." The *New Orleans Times Picayune*, a white newspaper, editorialized against lynching but also suggested that the Monroe mob had committed a serious crime by frightening white patients in the hospital. If such "outrages" continued, the *Times Picayune* wrote, "we can see the time coming when peaceable white persons will not be safe in that community."[26] By this reasoning, the episode's significant feature was that the nurses had stood up for law and order – for whites.

For the black press, however, the nurses' resistance to the lynch mob was itself noteworthy. "Mob Foiled at Hospital by Nurses," read the second part of the *New York Age*'s headline about the event, while the *Vindicator* caught attention with the lead-in, "Brave White Nurses Beat Back Mob Twice." Praise for the nurses' actions intimated that armed resistance was an effective deterrent – "a few little puny women could with one gun scare the cowardly mob away" – and pointed to the glaring absence of effective protection from sworn officers of the law. As the *Vindicator* asked, "where is your security in the land of the free and the home of the brave"? The NAACP posed a similar question in an open letter to Louisiana's governor.[27] The murder of George Holden thus highlighted the need to publicize armed self-defense and the failure of law enforcement to protect black citizens.

In July 1919, a band of armed black men in Dublin, Georgia, successively deterred a lynch mob. Like Blakely, which was approximately 170 miles southwest, Dublin was a dangerous place for African

[25] "Ouachita Parish Sternly Demands Law Enforcement," *New Orleans Times Picayune*, May 12, 1919, clipping in *NAACP Papers*, Part 7, Series A, reel 12, frame 394.

[26] "Louisianans Accused Over Acts of Lawlessness – Mob Foiled at Hospital by Nurses," *New York Age*, May 24, 1919 (first quote); "Lawlessness Advances," *New Orleans Times Picayune*, May 13, 1919 (second quote), clippings in *NAACP Papers*, Part 7, Series A, reel 12, frames 397, 403–4.

[27] "Louisianans Accused"; "Monroe Hangs Head in Shame" (quotes); NAACP press release, May 5, 1919, *NAACP Papers*, Part 7, Series A, reel 12, frames 359–60.

Americans. Dublin landowners, like planters in Phillips County, Arkansas, arbitrarily increased their cotton shares, forced renters to sign rigged contracts, and arranged two-year jail sentences for tenants who left the land. Overseers frequently raped farmers' wives. "When that overseer comes to your home and tells your wife to go out of that house, to go to the field, to his kitchen, or his wash tub, she must go," Dublin NAACP branch president G. W. Williams reported. "Lincoln declared long ago that we are free citizens, but the overseer is there yet." One farmer who refused to let the overseer take his wife had his entire crop seized as punishment. Williams intimated that the man was lucky – too often, black men "must reckon with the hang-rope and the torchlight."[28]

The armed resistance occurred during a volatile period in Dublin. In an effort to establish economic independence, several black farmers had begun organizing a cooperative to buy fertilizer and equipment.[29] On May 15, black farmhand James Walters was lynched after being accused of raping his white boss's eleven-year-old daughter.[30] In mid-June, a white driver drew a pistol on a black man named Herbert Cummings during a dispute over a car accident. Cummings, who was also armed, fired first and killed the driver. Fearing he would be lynched, Cummings fled Dublin. Two weeks later, four white men fatally wounded a man who they mistakenly believed was Cummings. In another incident, six white men ordered black storeowner Bob Ashley to open up at midnight to sell them sodas. When Ashley refused, the men blasted the store with gunfire, wounding him. Ashley managed to find his pistol and return fire, killing one of his attackers. These last two incidents were connected. Ashley was related to Cummings and one of the shooters was the brother of the white man Cummings had killed. As G. W. Williams observed, Dublin's white residents, "enraged over their failure to catch Cummings, then set upon Negroes in general." Members of the Dublin NAACP branch, determined to prevent Ashley's lynching, placed an armed guard around the boarding house where Ashley was recuperating. For three successive nights, a mob drove up "but, upon seeing the strong Negro guard, they retired." Worried that a riot might break out, the sheriff asked Georgia's governor to send state militia, which kept the armed groups apart until

---

[28] "The Delegates Speak," *Branch Bulletin* vol. III, no. 7 (July 1919), 72.

[29] "McAden's Impressions of Thriving Dublin," *Atlanta Independent*, February 1, 1919.

[30] Anonymous letter to the NAACP, August 11, 1919; NAACP cover letter, August 20, 1919; "Georgia Negro Lynched for Attack on Girl," *New York Globe*, May 16, 1919; "Lynching Evil on the Increase," *Vicksburg* (Miss.) *Herald*, May 16, 1919, *NAACP Papers*, Part 7, Series A, reel 10, frames 660–3, 666, 672.

Ashley recovered. Although he was forced to leave town, his defenders had almost certainly saved his life.[31]

Another instance of resistance occurred in Milan, Georgia. On the night of May 24, two white men, John Dowdy and Lewis Evans, pounded on the door of a widow named Emma McCollers, who had two young daughters. Dowdy and Evans – both drunk, both armed – demanded that she turn her daughters over to them. When she refused, Dowdy fired his pistol through the door. The girls fled and hid underneath the adjacent house. In their apparent quest to sexually assault the girls, Dowdy and Evans broke down the neighbor's door and began ripping up floorboards. The noise awoke another neighbor, seventy-two-year-old Berry Washington, who picked up his shotgun and rushed to the scene. When Dowdy challenged him, Washington answered that he had come to "see what was the matter with the women and children." Dowdy again drew his weapon and fired. His shot went wide; Washington's did not. Evans fled the house, leaving his dead friend on the floor.

Washington had defended himself and McCollers's daughters, but Dowdy's death created new dangers – in Georgia, white retaliation for black self-defense was swift and fierce. Would Evans return in an hour or so with an angry mob? Neighbors advised Washington to turn himself into the chief of police as soon as possible. The police moved Washington to the jail in the nearby town of McRae, but that precaution did not long remain secret. The next night, ten white men came to the jail. With the cooperation of the deputy sheriff, the men removed Washington and took him back to Milan. The mob hanged him from a post and killed him with a barrage of gunfire. Washington's pastor, the Reverend Judson Dinkins, noted bitterly that the victim "was lynched because he protected his own women, in his part of the town." To drive home the lesson that black self-defense was never justified, white men fanned out across Milan on the night of the lynching and ordered black residents to leave town. Many did not return for two days.[32]

The lynching of another black resister happened in August near Abbeville, Georgia. A black veteran named Jim Grant intervened when

---

[31] "Reports of the Branches," *Branch Bulletin* vol. III, no. 8 (August 1919), 80–1; "Reports of the Branches," *Branch Bulletin* vol. III, no. 9 (September 1919), 90 (quotes); Arthur Waskow, "Minor Riots in 'Mob Violence 1919' File NAACP Mss.," n.d., Waskow Notes, tab "U.S. Reaction."

[32] NAACP, "A Lynching Uncovered by the National Association for the Advancement of Colored People," July 1919, box 15, folder "Printed Matter 1919," Moorfield Storey Papers, Library of Congress (quotes on 4); Dinkins to Monroe Work, May 26, 1919, *NAACP Papers*, Part 7, Series A, reel 10, frames 928–30.

two white men, Lee Gammage and his son, apparent bounty hunters, seized a black man suspected of theft. Grant shot and wounded the Gammages. Although he had not tried to halt a lynching, Grant had used deadly force to interfere with enforcement of the law and, by extension, white supremacy – the Gammages may not have been sworn officers, but they were white. A mob nabbed Grant as he attempted to board a train and hanged him at the site of the shooting. The mob also brought in Grant's father, whipped him, and then exiled him from the area.[33]

The lynchings of Jim Grant and Berry Washington demonstrated the lethal hazards of resistance to southern white supremacy in 1919. The mobs executed the men on the sites of their transgressions to offer a chilling warning to the black community. The symbolic features of the killings did not end there. In the case of Jim Grant, his "sin" redounded upon his father: the elder Grant had to be punished because his son had harmed a white father. When considered alongside the other results of confronting mobs – the exile of Bob Ashley for one, the lynching of Henry Bryant for another – the resistance might appear futile. Yet for that very reason it is notable. Despite the knowledge that they might pay for their deeds with their lives, Henry Bryant, Bob Ashley, members of the Dublin NAACP branch, Berry Washington, and Jim Grant had taken up arms to deter lynchers or to prevent violent crimes such as rape and kidnapping. By their actions, they embodied the figurative male in Carita Owens Collins's poem, "Be a Man!": "Not a weak suppliant demand; But an eye for an eye, and a soul for a soul, Strike back, black man, strike!"[34]

It was no coincidence that two of these men, Bryant and Grant, were veterans. Throughout 1919, black veterans often intervened to aid fellow African Americans during confrontations with white supremacists. In Mississippi, a black veteran shot two white men who had rushed to help two white youths in their fight with two young blacks; in Miami, veterans defended a black driver from a group of attacking white drivers. Black soldiers' readiness to rush into such frays "reflected a spirit of camaraderie and boldness to challenge violence perpetrated upon black southerners and fellow former soldiers in particular," as historian Chad L. Williams has noted.[35] This boldness was not limited to the South.

---

[33] "Negro Is Lynched in Wilcox County," *Atlanta Constitution*, August 15, 1919; "Georgia Mob Hangs Negro Service Man," *Mobile* (Ala.) *Register*, August 15, 1919, clippings in *NAACP Papers*, Part 7, Series A, reel 10, frame 328.

[34] Carita Owens Collins, "Be a Man!," in Kerlin, *Voice of the Negro*, 185.

[35] Williams, *Torchbearers of Democracy*, 240–1.

Fighting Judge Lynch in Pennsylvania

In 1919, Coatesville, Pennsylvania, located in the southeastern county of Chester, was a city much like Gary, Indiana. Steel mills loomed over the town and dominated the economy; an influx of Eastern European immigrants and black southern migrants had swelled the population.[36] Racial tensions also simmered. On July 6, an ugly story flashed through Coatesville: a black man in an army uniform had sexually assaulted a fifteen-year-old white girl. The police had arrested the rapist, the rumor continued, and lynchers were on their way to the city jail. Black men and women quickly amassed in the northeast part of town and headed for the jail, some of them carrying baseball bats and pool cues. The police interdicted them and arrested nine men and women for inciting a riot. Determined to stop rough justice, black residents now faced charges rarely brought against white rioters.

The rumor that had precipitated the incident was false: the police had not arrested an alleged rapist, a white lynch mob had not formed. Had Coatesville's black residents overreacted? They did not think so; nor, it turned out, did the mayor and the Chester County court. Although the mayor had initially supported the arrests, he later asked the police to release most of the jailed women. Five other blacks, including a woman named Esther Green, posted bail. Two men who remained jailed pressed for habeas corpus hearings. The judge ruled that the assembly to prevent the anticipated lynching did not qualify as riot incitement and ordered the men's release. As a local newspaper reported, a black civic organization had assured the mayor and the people of Coatesville that black residents had "meant no harm" but "simply didn't propose to stand aside and have a repetition of what occurred here some years ago."[37]

That is, black residents did not want to witness another lynching. In August 1911, a Coatesville mob had killed Zachariah Walker, a black steel worker. While drunk, Walker had shot and killed a popular white police officer. Walker was wounded during his capture and put under guard at the local hospital. The mob drove his guard away, wrenched the prisoner from his bed, and roughly carried him to a nearby field. "Don't give me no crooked death because I'm not white!" cried Walker, but

---

[36] Downey and Hyser, *No Crooked Death*, 1–14.
[37] Waskow, "Minor Riots"; "Lynch Law and State Police," *Lancaster* (Pa.) *Examiner*, July 8, 1919; "Negroes Can Gather to Prevent Lynching," *Philadelphia North American*, July 14, 1919 (quote), clippings in *NAACP Papers*, Part 7, Series A, reel 6, frames 237, 247.

the mob hurled him into a roaring fire. Although the mob leaders were tried, none were convicted.[38] Many black residents remembered Walker's gruesome death, and they had resolved not to let history repeat itself.

Later that year, rioting almost broke out in Chester, another southeastern Pennsylvania city with a recent history of racial conflict. On the night of October 11, a young black man named William Neely returned to a saloon that had thrown him out twice that night. The bar, likely a speakeasy, was located in Chester's Black Belt but catered to white and black patrons. Neely opened fire with a pistol, killing one man and wounding four others; all of the victims were white. Police quickly arrested Neely and transferred him to a nearby town, where he was placed under heavy armed guard. Chester's mayor ordered all entertainment parlors closed but the town remained tense. Large, angry crowds of whites roamed the streets. So did crowds of blacks, who, like the black residents of Coatesville, wanted to prevent a recurrence of antiblack collective violence.[39]

In late July 1917, Chester, a booming industrial city that had attracted thousands of southern migrants, had experienced a race riot. In a foreshadowing of the 1919 Washington and Omaha riots, the local newspaper inflamed racial tensions with its coverage of black-on-white crime. On July 24, 1917, an altercation between four blacks and a white man named William McKinney escalated into a stabbing that fatally wounded McKinney. The next day, his friends gathered along the strip of black-owned businesses in Chester and started attacking black men going to or coming from their jobs. One mob boarded a streetcar to beat up black passengers. Local police, a posse of 150, and state troopers halted the attacks and almost fifty white rioters were arrested. Still, racial clashes continued for four more days. A state trooper reported seeing mobs of between 200 and 300 white men roaming the streets, assaulting blacks. A counterforce of 150 armed African Americans amassed near Market Square downtown and charged a crowd of armed white men. A black railroad laborer, chased by a mob of white shipyard workers, fired at his pursuers, killing one. Hundreds of blacks left Chester but most black residents remained, going to work with pistols tucked in pockets or packed in lunch pails. Sixty years later, a Chester resident recalled that black residents had kept shotguns by their doors for years afterward.[40]

---

[38] Downey and Hyser, *No Crooked Death*, 15–39, 70–92, 100–6, 109–16 (quote on 35).
[39] "Killing by Negro Enrages Chester," *New York Times*, October 12, 1919.
[40] Smith, "The 1917 Race Riot."

The October 1919 saloon shooting in Chester did not result in another race riot. Police, supported by deputized citizens, prevented clashes between the white and black crowds roaming the streets.[41] Nevertheless, the incident served as a reminder that racial tensions in Chester had lessened only slightly since 1917. The readiness of black residents to take to the streets also demonstrated that, just like two years earlier, they would not surrender quietly to white violence.

In an editorial about the near-riot in Coatesville in July 1919, the *Lancaster* (Pa.) *Examiner* commented that national condemnation of "Judge Lynch and mob law" in the South should not blind northerners to the problem of lynching in their own states. "We can surmise somewhat more justly the conditions prevailing throughout Mississippi, Alabama, Georgia and the other offending States by comparing them to the conditions in our only city that has to face similar problems," the *Examiner* advised, referring to Coatesville. Although the purpose of the editorial was to praise the Pennsylvania State Police (who were trying to find the alleged Coatesville rapist), it also offered an apt reminder that lynch mobs were not exclusively a southern problem – they were a national phenomenon.[42] By taking to the streets in Coatesville and Chester to avert, respectively, an anticipated lynching and a race riot, black Pennsylvanians likewise provided evidence that resistance to white mobs was not limited to the South.

Black Resistance and the Continuing Antilynching Campaign

Armed resistance to lynch mobs in 1919 aided the NAACP's ongoing campaign for state and federal action to extinguish rough justice. NAACP branches reported local occurrences of violence and resistance to the national office, which publicized some of the incidents in order to build support for legislation. If not for branch members such as G. W. Williams and the Reverend Judson Dinkins, the NAACP might never have learned about the attack on Bob Ashley, in Dublin, Georgia, or the murder of Berry Washington, in Milan, Georgia. The latter case offered the NAACP an opportunity to advance its antilynching cause in a dramatic fashion. The May 25, 1919, lynching of Washington had received almost no attention outside of Milan. On May 31, the *Daily Telegraph* (Macon, Ga.) reported the lynching of a black man named "Wash Horn" for killing

---

[41] "Killing by Negro Enrages Chester."
[42] "Lynch Law and State Police."

John Dowdy but also noted that "no one in the communities figuring in the case would admit knowing anything about it." Dinkins, Washington's pastor, detailed the shooting of Dowdy and Washington's lynching in a May 26 letter to the Tuskegee Institute's Monroe Work, who forwarded the letter to the NAACP several weeks later. Walter White immediately recognized the similarities between Dinkins's account and the *Daily Telegraph* story, which the NAACP had clipped. White also realized that the lynching of Berry Washington deserved special attention because Washington had been killed for his actions to protect black women and children and himself. Furthermore, although white residents of Milan appeared to be suppressing news about the murder, Dinkins's letter had attracted the attention of the *Atlanta Constitution*, which published an investigative report on July 25, 1919, entitled "Moonshine Whisky and Lynch Law Raise Tumult in Telfair County."[43]

The *Constitution*'s story, which the NAACP reprinted and distributed nationally, revealed the lynching's cover-up. The NAACP hoped that the publicity would aid passage of an antilynching bill recently introduced in the Georgia legislature and lead to the arrest of Washington's killers. Among other points, the bill authorized the dismissal of law officers who abetted lynchings and the payment of rewards for the identification of lynchers. "Give the state a law under which lynchers may be run down and brought to book and treated as the law treats other murderers!" the *Constitution* exhorted the legislature. The newspaper also warned that a failure to act might lead to federal intervention, a reference to the Dyer bill. After the *Constitution*'s story appeared in print, Governor Dorsey, a supporter of the state antilynching bill, offered a $1,000 reward for information leading to the arrest and conviction of Washington's killers. A prominent Atlanta physician added another $500.[44]

These efforts fell short. The Georgia legislature did not pass the antilynching bill. The Superior Court of Telfair County convened a special grand jury in late August, and presiding judge W. D. Graham enjoined it to determine who the lynchers were and how they had gained access to the McRae jail. "Whatever may be said about the race question," the judge remarked, "to my mind there is but one solution: Protect the negro in his absolute rights of life, liberty and property, and give him fair

[43] "A Lynching Uncovered"; Dinkins to Work, May 26, 1919; "Negro Is Lynched for Killing White," *Daily Telegraph*, May 31, 1919 (quotes), and Walter White to Monroe Work, July 18, 1919, *NAACP Papers*, Part 7, Series A, reel 10, frames 943, 965.

[44] "A Lynching Uncovered" (quote on 7); *Branch Bulletin* vol. III, no. 8 (August 1919), 79.

and impartial trials in the courts." After a week of hearings, the jurors reported "the deplorable fact" that a lack of evidence prevented identification of the lynchers. The jury did recommend that the court commence removal proceedings against the Telfair County sheriff for "gross negligence of duty in not protecting the prisoner in his charge." On the night of the lynching, the sheriff was conspicuously away from the jail, leaving his deputy Dave McRanie in charge. The jury concluded that McRanie actively helped the mob; indeed, "he was not only a sympathizer but a ring-leader of said mob." The proceedings against the sheriff, however, resulted in his acquittal. As for McRanie, the jury could not recommend his removal – he had been shot and killed not long after the lynching.[45]

Despite the sheriff's acquittal, the NAACP could point to three positive outcomes: it had exposed the lynching of a black self-defender; it had found an antilynching supporter in one of Georgia's most important newspapers, the *Atlanta Constitution*; and it had proved that law enforcement officials who colluded with mobs could be tried, even in Georgia, which led the nation in lynchings. Seeking to capitalize on these gains, the NAACP stepped up its lobbying of Congress. It already had an ally in Congressman Dyer, who resubmitted his antilynching bill, but Dyer was not a Capitol Hill power broker.

Senator Charles Curtis (R-Kans.) was. The November 1918 election gave Republicans commanding majorities in both houses of Congress. As majority whip, Curtis wielded considerable power to shape the Senate's legislative agenda and action. In September 1919, he introduced a resolution (S.R. 189) to investigate the causes of lynching and mob violence, including the race riots, and to propose preventive action.[46] James Weldon Johnson helped persuade Curtis to sponsor the resolution following the riots in Washington and Chicago. In a September 3 letter, Johnson noted that yet another riot, Knoxville's, had broken out since last they corresponded. "This Knoxville riot simply makes more important the matter which I have talked with you about on my two recent visits, namely, a Congressional investigation of lynching, and a printed report on same." Johnson also lined up the support of several other Republican senators, including Curtis's fellow Kansan Arthur Capper, and provided

---

[45] "Graham Charges Jury on Telfair Lynching," *Atlanta Constitution*, August 28, 1919 (Graham quote); "Sheriff's Removal Ordered by Court," *Birmingham Age-Herald*, September 9, 1919 (jury quotes), *NAACP Papers*, Part 7, Series A, reel 10, frames 991, 993; Schneider, *We Return Fighting*, 102.

[46] "Congressional Investigation of Mob Violence," *Branch Bulletin* vol. III, no. 10 (October 1919), 94.

a brief documenting the extent of lynching and the pressing reasons for an investigation. Armed resistance figured prominently in the report. In a section entitled "The Danger," the NAACP first listed "frequent clashes and bloody encounters between white men and Negroes and a condition of potential race war in many cities of the United States." Also noted was armed resistance to white supremacist organizations such as the Ku Klux Klan. Meanwhile, John Shillady and Herbert Seligmann (who now worked full time on publicity) directed a national effort to solicit letters and telegrams in support of the resolution.[47]

Hearings on S.R. 189 were deferred until mid-January 1920. As Curtis informed Johnson, the Judiciary Committee did not want to act until deliberations on the Versailles Treaty had finished. Some committee members also declared lynching and mob violence to be matters for the states to handle. In a sign of the Bureau of Investigation and the Military Intelligence Division's success in connecting the New Negro movement to communism, Curtis told Johnson that a "number of letters show that the I.W.W.'s have stirred up the whites and the colored people."[48] Johnson and Shillady, testifying before a Judiciary subcommittee, tried to dispel this association. They submitted additional documentation about lynching, emphasizing the growing number of victims seized from law enforcement officers and jails (thirteen in 1918; thirty-four in 1919) and the heinous forms of death (burnings, mutilations). Two individuals directly affected by racial violence addressed the subcommittee. U. S. Bratton spoke about the debt peonage that had led to the antiblack collective violence in Phillips County, Arkansas; Archibald Grimké, president of the Washington, D.C., branch of the NAACP and a witness to Washington's riot, endorsed the NAACP's goals.[49] (Both Johnson and Shillady, it should be noted, also knew firsthand the terror of mob or mob-like violence. Years earlier, provost guards in Jacksonville, Florida, had beaten and threatened to lynch Johnson for speaking with a fair-skinned black woman whom the soldiers had assumed was white.[50] In August 1919,

---

[47] Johnson to Curtis, September 3, 1919 (first quote); Johnson to Capper, September 3, 1919; NAACP, "Shall the Mob Govern," September 30, 1919; NAACP press release, October 8, 1919; Curtis to Johnson, October 13, 1919; NAACP, "Why a Congressional Investigation of Lynching in the United States?," n.d. (second quote), *NAACP Papers*, Part 7, Series A, reel 2, frames 318–19, 413–15, 436, 449, 454, 466–8.

[48] Curtis to Johnson, October 13, 1919 (quote); "Talk of Congress Inquiry," *New York Times*, September 30, 1919, *NAACP Papers*, Part 7, Series A, reel 6, frame 310.

[49] "The Curtis Resolution," *Branch Bulletin* vol. IV, no. 2 (February 1920), 13.

[50] Johnson, *Along This Way*, 165–70.

several white men had severely beaten Shillady in Austin, Texas, where he was trying to persuade state officials to end their interference with the NAACP's operations.[51])

Behind the scenes, Moorfield Storey tried to assuage subcommittee chair William Dillingham's (R-Ver.) doubts about the constitutionality of federal action to halt lynching. The attack on Shillady and Texas's refusal to charge his assailants had changed Storey's view on the legitimacy of superseding local and state courts. If Congress did not act and states continued to fail to prosecute lynchers, he told Dillingham, "so far as the colored people are concerned there is no republican government." An investigation must precede Congressional passage of a federal antilynching law, Storey further argued, both to justify the law and to turn public sentiment against lynchings.[52]

The NAACP's lobbying and Curtis's clout did not prevail; Congress declined to investigate the sources and prevention of lynching and race riots. Likewise, the Dyer bill remained stalled, despite the Republican majority in the House. With a presidential election coming later that year, Johnson and the NAACP turned their efforts toward likely candidates. A questionnaire drafted by W. E. B. Du Bois asked first if the respondent supported passage of federal antilynching legislation. At the Republican national convention, Johnson urged party leaders to include an antilynching plank in the party platform, but the lukewarm response suggested that the struggle to halt lynching was still in its early stages.[53]

Indeed it was. The NAACP's quest for federal antilynching legislation continued for decades. So, too, did efforts to defend African Americans who faced criminal charges for self-defensive or retaliatory actions against whites who had attacked them. One case in particular provided a foundation for this ongoing legal action and represented another front in the campaign to end lynching.

Black Resistance and the Struggle for Justice: The Case of Sergeant Edgar Caldwell

Like many of the racial altercations that occurred in 1919, the one involving Sergeant Edgar Caldwell began on a streetcar. On Sunday, December

[51] See Chapter 8.
[52] Schneider, *We Return Fighting*, 173; Zangrando, *NAACP Crusade*, 56 (quote).
[53] Zangrando, *NAACP Crusade*, 56.

15, 1918, Caldwell boarded an Alabama Power Company car outside his base, Camp McClellan, to travel to nearby Hobson City. His pass entitled him to a much-needed day of recreation. Caldwell, who had joined the army prior to World War I, had served in the Twenty-fourth Infantry but was now assigned to a labor battalion. The work was hard, the hours long, the barracks squalid. Caldwell and his fellow black soldiers hauled lumber and cleared roads from sunup to sundown, returning to sleep in tents. Hobson City, which adjoined the industrial city of Anniston, Alabama, was a thriving black town with soda fountains, restaurants, and theaters. But Caldwell, who was wearing his dress uniform, never got the chance to enjoy his leave.[54]

The streetcar's conductor was Cecil Linten, a young white man from a small town, new to the job. Motorman Kelsie Morrison was working with him that day. Both men vigorously enforced the rules of racial segregation governing ridership, and uniformed black servicemen posed a particular challenge to these rules and the streetcar employees' authority, even their manhood. After boarding, Caldwell refused to either move from the white section or pay an arbitrary surcharge. Angered by the sergeant's defiance, Linten punched him in the face, then he and Morrison ejected him from the rear exit. The two men jumped out and were kicking or about to kick Caldwell when he rolled over, pistol in hand, and fired twice. A head shot killed Linten; the other bullet gravely wounded Morrison. Caldwell fled, quickly outpacing the white passengers who rushed off the streetcar after him.

News of Caldwell's defiance and self-defense provoked retaliatory attacks on African Americans and the formation of a posse. In Anniston, a mob of angry white men attacked a passing black porter. Police, sheriff's deputies, and civilian volunteers scoured the countryside to find Caldwell. Military police from Camp McClellan joined the search. The *Anniston Star*'s rush copy depicted Linten's widow as paralyzed with grief and considered a fatherless future for Morrison's five children. As historian Adriane Lentz-Smith observes, the *Star* set Caldwell's deed against the tableaux of white supremacy: the soldier had "wrought havoc on the white family and in so doing, endangered one of the most fundamental institutions in Southern society."[55]

---

[54] For detailed treatment of the Caldwell case, see Schneider, *We Return Fighting*, 92–7; Lentz-Smith, *Freedom Struggles*, 169–205; Mikkelsen, "Fighting for Sergeant Caldwell."

[55] Lentz-Smith, *Freedom Struggles*, 169–205 (quote on 176).

Caldwell's arrest that night only heightened racial tensions. Discovered by a military policeman, Caldwell surrendered peacefully. His captor then made a crucial decision: he turned the sergeant over to the Anniston police, who put him in the county jail. As an active-duty serviceman who had allegedly committed a crime while in uniform, Caldwell was subject to military justice. As the racial clashes on Charleston's streetcars in December 1918 had demonstrated, however, civilian officials were anxious to assert their authority over black servicemen who transgressed local customs and laws during the transition from war to peace. A different sort of habeas corpus now prevailed. The state of Alabama had possession of Sergeant Caldwell, and, as subsequent judicial proceedings proved, the state was loathe to cede custody of Caldwell to the U.S. Army, even after a contingent of military policemen protected the jail from a lynch mob.

Within four days of his detention, Caldwell had been arraigned and indicted for first degree murder by a grand jury that deliberated for less than two hours. Hobson City pastor R. R. Williams and several other black clergy quickly recognized that a rush to convict Caldwell and sentence him to death was underway. Williams and his peers, aided by local black businessmen, formed a legal defense committee, hired attorneys for Caldwell, and started raising funds from area residents. These efforts failed to prevent a guilty verdict (delivered on January 17, 1919, by an all-white, male jury) and a sentence of death (with the execution scheduled for February 28), but Williams did convince the NAACP and the federal government to intervene in the case.[56]

Williams had contacted the national office of the NAACP less than a week after Caldwell's indictment. Uncertainty about Caldwell's status – if the sergeant had been discharged, he had no right to a military trial – gave the NAACP pause, as did the nature of the shooting.[57] At this point, the NAACP did not know that Linten and Morrison had been kicking Caldwell when he fired his pistol. Williams persisted, also writing to Emmett Scott, who persuaded Secretary of War Newton Baker to speak to the president. Wilson asked Alabama governor Thomas Kilby to stay the execution pending an investigation by the U.S. attorney general.

[56] Mr. Morton to Mr. White Re: Caldwell Case, June 14, 1919, box D-49, folder "Cases Supported: Caldwell, July–October 1919," NAACP Records; Schneider, *We Return Fighting*, 93–4; Lentz-Smith, *Freedom Struggles*, 183–5.
[57] Morton to White, June 14, 1919.

As Williams had hoped, key officials in Washington were recognizing the constitutional issue underlying Caldwell's trial: could a state claim jurisdiction in a case that, because of Caldwell's active-duty military service, necessarily involved the federal government?[58]

Governor Kilby stayed Caldwell's execution pending an appeal to the Alabama Supreme Court. In July 1919, the court rejected Caldwell's attorneys' claim that the sergeant had received an unfair trial.[59] Undeterred, his supporters – who now included Moorfield Storey, Archibald Grimké, and Washington attorney James Cobb – formulated a new legal strategy. Cobb observed that the circumstances of the shooting warranted a charge of manslaughter, not first degree murder. He also argued that the War Department, although it had given custody of Caldwell to Alabama, had the obligation "to see that he gets a fair and impartial trial." (Cobb, who provided crucial legal support to black self-defenders in Washington, made these points in a letter posted to James Weldon Johnson on July 21, the last day of the capital's riot.)[60] Cobb hoped for a rehearing before the Alabama Supreme Court. Joined by Emmett Scott, among other influential personages, Cobb persuaded Assistant U.S. Attorney General Robert Stewart to write a brief arguing that the U.S. government had a constitutional obligation to ensure that Caldwell received a fair trial.[61] However, Attorney General A. Mitchell Palmer declined to fully support the case, a decision that Cobb attributed to Palmer's presidential aspirations.[62]

The Alabama court agreed to rehear Caldwell's case in October, to no avail; the justices again upheld the conviction. But Cobb and his allies had paved the way for an appeal to the U.S. Supreme Court, which put the case on its docket. The NAACP expanded its coverage of the case in the *Crisis*, using it to highlight racial inequities in the courts.[63] Cobb enhanced his legal position by arguing that a state of war still technically existed between Germany and the United States. Thus Alabama, and all states, lacked the authority to try a soldier. On March 6, 1920, the day after he presented his case to the Supreme Court, Cobb expressed

[58] Lentz-Smith, *Freedom Struggles*, 188–91.
[59] Ibid., 192.
[60] Cobb to James W. Johnson, July 21, 1919, box D-49, folder "Cases Supported: Caldwell, July–October 1919," NAACP Records.
[61] Cobb to James W. Johnson, August 28, 1919, box D-49, folder "Cases Supported: Caldwell, July–October 1919," NAACP Records.
[62] Mikkelsen, "Fighting for Sergeant Caldwell," 474–5.
[63] Ibid., 475–9.

cautious hope to John Shillady about the outcome, based on the "very great interest taken in the case" by the justices. He added, "whatever the outcome may be we can be conscious of the fact that we have done our full duty."[64]

True, but the outcome still stung. Writing for the majority, Chief Justice Edward Douglass White – a Confederate veteran – ruled that because Caldwell's crime occurred in a jurisdiction in which actual conditions of war did not exist, Articles of War did not empower the military to supersede the state's prerogative. Congress never intended for military justice "to bring about, as the mere result of a declaration of war, the complete destruction of State authority and the extraordinary extension of military power upon which the argument rests," White concluded.[65] On July 30, 1920, the state of Alabama hanged Edgar Caldwell.

Yet the legal fight to save Caldwell was not a total defeat. The Reverend R. R. Williams, James Cobb, and the NAACP had successfully drafted the U.S. government as an ally. The Justice Department had, if only tentatively, accepted the constitutional argument that the federal government has specific obligations to ensure that states provide fair trials to the accused. That the Supreme Court did not agree in 1920 did not spell an end to the matter. The 1923 *Moore v. Dempsey* decision sprang from a similar rush to judgment in the unfair trials of the Elaine Twelve, but in this case the Supreme Court decided the matter in favor of the federal government's obligation to ensure fair trials, whether state or federal, for all citizens.

Antilynching efforts during 1918 and 1919 were an important part of African Americans' three-front fight against mob violence. Many times blacks took up arms to deter lynchers, particularly in Georgia, but this resistance was not limited to the South. In Coatesville, Pennsylvania, African Americans acted to halt mob violence they believed was imminent. Although the rumor of an imminent lynching was false, Coatesville's black residents remembered that a mob had burned a black prisoner to death in 1911, and they were determined to prevent another lynching. The NAACP's documentation of lynchings and, where applicable, armed resistance supported the organization's continuing campaign to enact a

[64] Cobb to Shillady, March 6, 1920, box D-49, folder "Cases Supported: Caldwell, January-March 1920," NAACP Records.

[65] U.S. Supreme Court, *Caldwell vs. Parker*, No. 636 (October Term, 1919), April 19, 1920, copy in box D-49, folder "Cases Supported: Caldwell, April-July 1920," NAACP Records (quote on 5); Lentz-Smith, *Freedom Struggles*, 202–4.

federal antilynching law, once again showing how important it was to establish and publicize the actual causes of antiblack collective violence. Such legislation also advanced the fight for justice because it provided punishments for lynchers and local and state authorities who colluded with or protected lynchers. The failure of Congress to pass a bill did not prevent the NAACP and black attorneys and ministers from using all available legal means to defend Sergeant Edgar Caldwell or to put the lynchers of Berry Washington on trial. That these efforts fell short offered yet more evidence that the struggle to eradicate rough justice was far from over.

Conclusion

1919's Aftermath and Importance in the Black Freedom Struggle

A. Mitchell Palmer wanted the new year to begin with a bang. For the attorney general, 1920 must be the year that he and the Department of Justice, aided by state and local law enforcement agencies, snuffed out the greatest cause of domestic upheaval during 1919.

Reds. Bolsheviks. Communists. Whatever the label used, Palmer was determined to detain and, if possible, deport the radicals blamed for the previous year's labor strife and bombings, including the one that had wrecked his home in Washington in June 1919. The so-called Palmer Raids began in November, when the Bureau of Investigation (BI) led a round-up of several hundred members and officers of the Union of Russian Workers in twelve cities, but the biggest action occurred on the night of Friday, January 2, 1920. In thirty-three cities spanning the country, Palmer's agents coordinated the arrests of more than 4,000 people, Americans and immigrants alike, by disrupting meeting halls, social venues, even restaurants. In many cases, BI infiltrators had arranged meetings at the designated zero hour, 9 P.M. local time, to maximize the number of arrests. Boston's Communist Party had eighteen branches; each was raided simultaneously. Cooperating police in New York had to call twenty-three trucks to transport all the prisoners in that city.[1]

Palmer and the Department of Justice's fixation with radicalism did not signal disinterest in the racial conflict that had claimed more than 150 lives during 1919. Sharing the long-held views of officials in the BI, Military Intelligence Division (MID), and Post Office, Palmer believed that the raids had the added effect of neutralizing the provocateurs who

---

[1] Ackerman, *Young J. Edgar*, 113–19, 180–5; Murray, *Red Scare*, 196–7, 210–22.

had urged blacks to fight for their rights. Indeed, a Department of Justice report submitted to the Senate in November 1919 appended the report of postal official Robert Bowen on "radicalism and sedition" in the black press.

New Negroes who were not socialists or communists were not impressed with this latest attempt to blame radical ideologies for the year's racial troubles. Blacks are not "joining the ranks of 'reds' to overthrow the government," William Byrd wrote in the *Cleveland Gazette*. Instead, blacks' refusal to "take what they once took," that is, oppression, violence, and denial of their rights, is "real Americanism."[2] In the *New York Age*, James Weldon Johnson turned upside down the Department of Justice report's claim that black leaders opposed law and order. If lynching, inequality in employment and educational opportunities, and disfranchisement were, in fact, part of the nation's "established rule of law and order," Johnson commented sardonically, then "radical Negro leaders are guilty of the charge of sedition made against them." As he had done throughout 1919, Johnson reminded readers that these so-called radicals actually wanted to save the Constitution, to see its rights and the laws derived from them enforced fairly, without regard to race.[3]

An outbreak of mob violence in February 1920 once again revealed the fundamental source of racial conflict in America: the extralegal enforcement of white supremacy. In Lexington, Kentucky, a black veteran named William Lockett had confessed to the rape and murder of a ten-year-old white girl.[4] Prosecutors promised swift action, but a collective desire to deliver rough justice spread through Lexington and Fayette County. Troops from the Kentucky National Guard surrounded the county courthouse to prevent a lynching.[5] Although Lockett pled guilty at his trial on February 9, a jury still had to determine his sentence. While deliberations were underway, a massive mob charged the guardsmen, who opened fire. The barrage killed five and wounded eighteen. Unfazed, the mob went on a looting rampage, breaking into pawn shops and hardware stores to steal weapons. Kentucky's governor wired a request for federal troops to Major General Leonard Wood, who dispatched a force of 1,000 soldiers from Camp Zachary Taylor. Their commander, Brigadier General

---

[2] William Byrd, "A Rank Insult to the Race!," *Cleveland Gazette*, December 6, 1919, 1.
[3] James Weldon Johnson, "Views and Reviews," *New York Age*, November 29, 1919, 4.
[4] "Negro Expresses Sorrow Over Casualties," *Louisville Courier-Journal*, February 10, 1920, 3.
[5] "Soldiers Will Protect Negro," *Louisville Courier-Journal*, February 6, 1920, 3; "Guns Bark to Warn," *Louisville Courier-Journal*, February 9, 1920, 1.

Francis C. Marshall, declared martial law; vigorous patrolling dispersed the mob. The jury sentenced Lockett to death, and he was taken to the state penitentiary without further incident.[6] For all the talk of black radicalism, white vigilantism remained a major problem.

The Lexington riot appeared to be evidence that another year of racial violence was underway, but a cascade of race riots did not occur in 1920. Still, occasional outbreaks of antiblack collective violence, and African Americans' armed resistance to it, reveal a lasting aftermath to 1919, the year of racial violence. These episodes included lynchings, mob attacks, collusion between law enforcement officials and private citizens, and specific acts of violence intended to prevent African Americans from exercising their constitutional rights – all hallmarks of 1919. Furthermore, in 1921, a devastating and horrific race riot erupted in Tulsa, Oklahoma, where black residents fought to halt a pogrom comparable to the one that had struck Phillips County, Arkansas, in 1919.

In June 1920, a posse of white deputies and private citizens lynched four black men in Wharton, Texas, near Houston. Two of the men, brothers Washington and Osborn Giles, were accused of killing a white constable; the other two victims had tried to help them flee. Worried that the lynchings might continue, black residents armed themselves. An alarmed hardware store owner contacted the BI, which sent an agent to investigate. Local gun dealers promised to contact the BI "in the event that any suspicious calls were made for ammunition." The agent also looked into the lynchings, but after city officials and leading white citizens assured him that "local parties" were responsible, he ended his inquiry. As had been the case throughout 1919, black self-defense – "agitation," in the agent's measure – was of greater concern than lynch mobs.[7]

Racial tensions surfaced again in Kentucky, this time in Louisville. White soldiers from Camp Zachary Taylor were harassing young black women who lived nearby. On July 18, 1920, two young black men intervened when two enlisted men insulted female passers-by. The black men won the fight, as the Louisville NAACP branch reported; fifty soldiers later returned to get their revenge. When a shot rang out, armed black men fired back, wounding three white soldiers. Police arrested several black men, but none of the servicemen were charged. The Louisville

---

[6] "Rioting Halts Negro's Trial," *Louisville Courier-Journal*, February 10, 1920, 3; Laurie and Cole, *Role of Federal Military Forces*, 297–301.

[7] R. W. Tinsley, "Race Riot Situation, Wharton, Texas," July 2, 1920, RG 65, OGF 387,830, reel 846.

branch hired a lawyer, who persuaded the court to drop charges against three defendants for lack of evidence. The branch also persuaded the Camp Taylor provost marshal to provide protection for the adjoining black community in order to prevent future altercations.[8] Though much smaller in scale, the Louisville conflict resembled Washington's 1919 riot in two ways: blacks had fought back against uniformed soldiers who had attacked them, and the local NAACP branch had undertaken legal action to protect black self-defenders from prosecution.

In late 1920, reports that blacks were stockpiling arms and ammunition across the South prompted the BI to again monitor arms sales and to look for evidence of insurrections.[9] Agents in New Orleans and Dallas, among other cities, reported that arms sales to blacks were at normal or lower than normal levels.[10] Arkansas's sharecroppers, hit hard by dropping cotton and rice prices, had no cash to buy weapons. As one agent concluded, an "uprising" was unlikely because blacks "are very hard pressed for money and depend on their white employers to tide them over the winter in reference to their food supply."[11] Following the example of Phillips County's planters, landlords had tightened the chains around their sharecroppers.

Yet signs of resistance still flickered in Arkansas. In Helena, a black preacher named E. B. Morris allegedly urged his congregation to quietly prepare for "some time in the future [when] they would have to arise and fight that they might obtain justice which they were entitled to." Helena's police chief reported that he was seizing at least one firearm a month from black residents. In DeValls Bluff, the sheriff told the BI that black tenant farmers believed white landowners were conspiring to cheat them. One sharecropper had even warned his landlord that if he did not receive at least forty-five cents per bale, "they would have to kill him to

---

[8] Louisville branch to the NAACP, July 27, 1920; Lee L. Brown to Walter White, August 9, 1920; W. H. Brown et al., to Lee L. Brown, August 11, 1920, box G-76, folder "Louisville, Kentucky, 1920," NAACP Records.

[9] Vincent W. Hughes to Chief, Bureau of Investigation, November 29, 1920, RG 65, Bureau Section File 203,677, reel 943.

[10] Frank J. Blake, "Negro Activities, Dallas, Texas," December 7, 1920; J. A. Condon, "Alleged Purchases of Arms & Ammunition by Negroes," December 7, 1920; J. V. Bell, "Alleged Up-Rising and Radical Movement on the Part of the Negroes in the South," December 10, 1920; Henry P. Alden, "Negro Radical Associations," December 13, 1920; Agent Bolanry, "Negro Activities in the St. Louis District," December 14, 1920, RG 65, Bureau Section File 203,677, reel 943.

[11] F. W. Lynch, "Negro Activities Throughout the South – Arkansas," December 31, 1920, RG 65, Bureau Section File 203,677, reel 943.

get the cotton." And in Pine Bluff, the strength of black fraternal lodges and unions raised the concerns of the BI and local law officers.[12]

In November, African Americans' attempts to vote incurred a massive backlash in Florida. As a result of the recently ratified Nineteenth Amendment, women were now eligible to vote. In Jacksonville, approximately 4,000 black men and women queued up to vote on November 2, 1920, holding registration certificates. Election officials turned them away, claiming that they needed additional documentation. West of Tallahassee, a resurgent Ku Klux Klan threatened to kill Dr. W. S. Stevens and several other leading black citizens for encouraging blacks to vote. When Stevens arrived at the polls, angry white men prevented him from voting and ordered him to leave town. Still defiant, Stevens refused to move. The Klan in another town beat up two brothers for registering black voters.[13]

The worst violence of 1920 – and the greatest instance of black resistance – occurred in Ocoee, Florida, near Orlando. Two black landowners, Julius Perry and Mose Norman, led a campaign to register the town's 500 black residents, drawing an ominous warning from the local Klan. Undeterred, both men, who had registered and paid the poll tax, arrived at the voting station, where they were told they were not eligible voters. Norman came back with a shotgun, only to be beaten and chased off. The Klan then dispersed throughout Ocoee, intent on lynching Norman and Perry and terrorizing black residents so that none would ever again try to vote. A mother and her baby were burned alive in their home. Perry and eight armed companions managed to hold a mob at bay, killing two, until the house was torched. Perry was arrested and jailed in Orlando, where a complicit sheriff allowed the Klan to lynch him. His desecrated corpse was dumped in Ocoee with a warning sign. By its end, the Klan's pogrom had killed as many as fifty blacks.[14] The death toll in Florida in 1920 was thus as high as Chicago's and Arkansas's in 1919. But an even greater outbreak of antiblack collective violence was yet to come.

On Memorial Day 1921, in Tulsa, Oklahoma, a black shoeshine named Dick Rowland tripped while entering an elevator operated by a seventeen-year-old white girl, Sarah Page. Did Rowland bump her?

---

[12] F. W. Lynch, "Negro Activities Throughout the South to Purchase Firearms," December 23, 1920, RG 65, Bureau Section File 203,677, reel 943 (quotes on 3 and 5).

[13] "Report of Walter F. White," n.d., box C-312, folder "Subject File – KKK 1920," NAACP Records.

[14] "Report of Walter F. White"; Williams, *Torchbearers of Democracy*, 257–8; Schneider, *We Return Fighting*, 120–4.

Reflexively grab her arm to steady himself? Or did he not touch her at all? Like the street encounter between Elsie Stephnick and two black men that sparked Washington's riot in 1919, details were hazy. Page apparently screamed, Rowland fled; police quickly arrested him. He only ran, he explained, because the girl's cry scared him. The next day, the *Tulsa Tribune* reported the incident as an assault and claimed that Rowland had ripped Page's clothes. The streets of Tulsa buzzed with calls for a lynching.[15]

Rough justice was common in Tulsa and throughout Oklahoma, which recorded four lynchings in 1920. All told, the territory and state experienced approximately one hundred lynchings between 1889 and 1921. During World War I, white vigilante groups such as the Knights of Liberty had violently expelled members of Tulsa's IWW chapter.[16] By the evening of May 31, 1921, several hundred white men and women had surrounded the courthouse where Rowland was jailed – a lynching seemed imminent.

Two dozen armed black men drove to the courthouse and declared their intention to protect Rowland. The sheriff and a black police officer convinced them to leave, but the authorities' failure to disperse the mob – one estimate put it at 2,000 – brought out another self-appointed protective force, this one seventy-five strong. Trouble broke out as soon as the armed black men left their vehicles. A brief burst of gunfire wounded or killed several black men, and their comrades retreated to Greenwood, Tulsa's prosperous black neighborhood, with armed whites in pursuit.[17]

The ensuing violence continued to follow familiar patterns from 1919: white rioters looted stores for weapons; overwhelmed law officers hastily deputized hundreds of white men, creating a mob with phantom badges; vigilantes joined forces with professional and deputized officers; and African Americans, led by veterans, defended themselves as best as they could. As approximately 200 Oklahoma National Guard troops secured their armory and the city's utilities, the police and sheriff deputized 500 white men – and the NAACP's Walter White. The intrepid White, who had rushed to Tulsa, was once again mistaken for white and himself deputized. "Now you can go out and shoot any nigger you see and the law'll be behind you," a white man told him. Meanwhile African Americans prepared to defend Greenwood. Many had military

[15] Halliburton, *Tulsa Race War*, 3–5.
[16] "The Lynching Industry – 1920," *Crisis* 21, no. 4 (February 1921), 160–2; "Lynching Map of the United States of America," *Crisis* 23, no. 4 (February 1922), 168–9; Hirsch, *Riot and Remembrance*, 61–5.
[17] Halliburton, *Tulsa Race War*, 5–6; Hirsch, *Riot and Remembrance*, 82–91.

experience. World War I veteran "Peg Leg" Taylor earned legendary status in Tulsa for his bravery during the riot, while another veteran used his service revolver to guard an intersection. Along the railroad tracks dividing Greenwood and white Tulsa, an enfilade deterred waiting attackers throughout the night. School teacher Mary E. Jones Parrish stayed up all night, marveling at "these brave boys of ours [who] fought gamely and held back the enemy for hours." At dawn, however, thousands of white men charged forward, overwhelming the defenders.[18]

In Chicago in 1919, white gangs had looted and burned selectively, seeking to drive out black residents in the disputed borderlands along the Black Belt. In Greenwood, all black homes and businesses were targets as marauding whites sought to destroy every sign of black prosperity and to kill as many blacks as possible – a pogrom. By noon on Tuesday, May 31, the mob had leveled Greenwood, killed dozens of blacks, and routed the remaining black defenders. More than 1,200 homes burned down in a fire that covered a thirty-six square block area. The value of the lost realty was estimated at between 1.5 and 1.8 million dollars. Reflecting on the cost of the pogrom more than seventy-five years later, black resident Mabel Little said, "at the time of the riot, we had ten different business places for rent. Today, I *pay* rent."[19]

As historian Chad L. Williams notes, Tulsa's riot "marked the climax of this bloody period."[20] Although episodes of antiblack collective violence did not cease altogether – in 1923, Rosewood, Florida, was destroyed in a race riot that killed several blacks – they never again reached the levels of 1919 and its 1920–21 aftermath. Use of violence to uphold the subjugation of blacks did not abate, however; white supremacists continued to use lynchings, arson, and murder against those who challenged the racial status quo. So African Americans continued to fight back.

The Long Reach of 1919's Resistance

As a significant part of the twentieth century freedom struggle, African Americans' three-front fight against racial violence yielded precedent, methods, and inspiration for continuing action. Black veterans remained

---

[18] Hirsch, *Riot and Remembrance*, 91–8 (first quote on 93); Mary E. Jones Parrish, "Events of the Tulsa Disaster," in Halliburton, *Tulsa Race War*, 43 (second quote).

[19] Hirsch, *Riot and Remembrance*, 6–8, 99–110 (quote on 8).

[20] Williams, *Torchbearers of Democracy*, 258.

potent symbols and agents of resistance. The outbreak of a second world war in 1939 highlighted the gap between the rhetoric and practice of democracy in the United States, the same problem that had attended U.S. entry into World War I. By using Wilsonian rhetoric to justify U.S. defense mobilization and aid to democratic allies, President Franklin D. Roosevelt unintentionally invited renewed efforts on the part of African Americans to secure equality. Drawing on the lessons he learned during and after World War I as a New Negro leader and writer, A. Philip Randolph used mass action to pressure the Roosevelt administration to give African Americans equal opportunities to work in defense plants. U.S. entry into the war, again predicated on making the world safe for democracy, produced a new generation of black veterans committed to halting the violent assertion of white supremacy. By the 1950s, armed resistance was, again, a prominent part of the freedom struggle, as it had been in 1919.

The three-front fight also shaped the contours of federal obstruction of the freedom struggle. Despite a lack of evidence, J. Edgar Hoover continued to equate black militancy with communism. As director of the FBI from 1924 until 1972, Hoover expanded the modes of surveillance and intelligence-gathering that the Bureau of Investigation and the Military Intelligence Division had utilized during the year of racial violence. After World War II, the FBI used its extensive surveillance apparatus to monitor and harrass civil rights activists.

The Harlem Renaissance of the 1920s is an early example of the three-front fight's lasting power. Centered in New York but national in scope, this flourishing of black culture produced many works of art and literature celebrating black veterans, armed resistance to mob violence, and the freedom struggle. In 1919, Claude McKay's poem "If We Must Die" had offered a clarion call for resistance. During the 1920s, McKay wrote two novels featuring worldly black veterans as protagonists. Disillusioned with racism in the military and in the postwar United States, the characters are restless, averse to settling down, discontent even with vibrant Harlem. Painter Edwin Harleston also depicted black veterans in his art. He was living in his hometown of Charleston, South Carolina, when it experienced the first major race riot of 1919. That same year, he worked with the city's NAACP branch to register voters and produced a painting entitled "The Soldier." The half-length portrait presents a uniformed black soldier, medals pinned to his chest, arms crossed. His expression is resolute, pensive, unyielding, the face of "a self-determined militant, prepared, if necessary, to fight again." In 1924, Walter White, who had traveled to Chicago and Phillips County, Arkansas, in the after-math of their antiblack collective violence, published a novel, *The Fire in the Flint*, that features a black physician (and veteran) who organizes sharecroppers. The doctor's struggle against white supremacy leads to a fatal confrontation with the Ku Klux Klan.[21] These and other literary and artistic renderings of black veterans sustained the self-proclaimed mission for which these men had fought – to make America safe for democracy.[22]

This mission continued as the United States prepared for another world war. In 1941, A. Philip Randolph dramatically framed African Americans' expectations by organizing the March on Washington Movement. Racial discrimination was rampant in the nation's defense plants and unions, the War and Navy Departments maintained racial segregation in the armed services. Roosevelt's unwillingness to address these problems led Randolph, who was now head of the Brotherhood of Sleeping Car Porters, to call for 100,000 African Americans to march in Washington, D.C., in July. Working with the NAACP and the National Urban League, Randolph set up recruiting stations in major cities to enlist marchers; buses and trains were chartered. The movement's slogan: "We loyal Negro American citizens demand the right to work and fight for our country." Randolph canceled the march after Roosevelt signed Executive Order 8802, which banned discrimination in defense industries and the government based on race, color, creed, and national origin. Randolph also insisted that the president support the Fair Employment Practices Committee (FEPC), created to enforce the order. In existence until 1946, the FEPC reduced, though it did not eradicate, racism in defense plants and government hiring and contracts.[23]

The March on Washington Movement represented the evolution of Randolph's decades-long struggle for racial and economic equality. As co-editor of the *Messenger* in 1919, Randolph had promoted socialism as a cure for the causes of race riots: exploitation of workers; segregated unions, schools, and neighborhoods; a biased justice system. Although Randolph had, by 1941, moved away from socialism, he was no less committed to breaking down racial barriers in the workplace. "He [the negro] wants to make the world safe for democracy, and is therefore

[21] Williams, *Torchbearers of Democracy*, 335–41 (quote on 336).
[22] For an in-depth study of African Americans' cultural responses to the war, see Whalan, *Great War*.
[23] Kersten, *A. Philip Randolph*, 53–65.

determined to make America safe for himself," Randolph had written in 1919.[24] By organizing the March on Washington Movement, he was seeking to do precisely that – provide black Americans with an unfettered opportunity to work for and serve their nation.

The Double V campaign reprised the dual mission of protecting democracy globally and domestically. Declared by the *Pittsburgh Courier* in early 1942, the campaign's slogan was "Democracy: Victory at Home, Victory Abroad." As they had done during World War I, African Americans made vital contributions to mobilization and military service, but the notion of "closing ranks" was roundly rejected. The number of NAACP branches tripled, membership soared. Founded in 1942, the Congress of Racial Equality (CORE) pioneered the use of nonviolent action to protest racial segregation in northern cities. Howard University students organized peaceful protests against segregated public establishments in Washington, D.C.[25] Osceola McKaine embodied the connection between World War I veterans' fight against white supremacy and the Double V campaign. An officer in the Ninety-second Division, McKaine had helped establish the League for Democracy in 1919 and had attracted the attention of the Military Intelligence Division for his forceful calls to fellow veterans to resist white supremacy. In 1940, McKaine revived the NAACP branch in Sumter, South Carolina, and took part in numerous political initiatives in the South during the war.[26]

The Double V campaign faced considerable resistance. As had happened during World War I, antiblack collective violence broke out frequently. Detroit experienced the worst riot, in 1943. Like East St. Louis in 1917, wartime Detroit's population had swelled with white and black southern migrants who found work in the city's proliferate factories. Competition for housing heightened racial tensions, the Ku Klux Klan staged "hate strikes" at factories that promoted black workers. On Sunday, June 20, a fight between black and white youth at a park grew into a citywide riot, spurred by false rumors of depredations against both whites and blacks. Roving groups of whites and blacks attacked one another throughout the night and the next day. By the time federal troops restored order, the rioting had killed thirty-four people (twenty-five black, nine white).[27] Detroit's riot was one of more than 200 wartime

---

[24] The Editors, "The Cause of and Remedy for Race Riots," *Messenger* vol. II, no. 9 (September 1919), 14–21 (quote on 20).

[25] Sitkoff, "Racial Militancy."

[26] Williams, *Torchbearers of Democracy*, 348.

[27] Collins, *All Hell*, 115–18.

racial clashes. Much of the conflict stemmed from white workers' opposition to the employment of blacks in defense plants, leading to strikes in Maryland, New York, Michigan, and Chester, Pennsylvania, which had experienced a race riot in 1917.[28]

Although major race riots did not break out after the war, black veterans again served on the front lines of the freedom struggle, as they had in 1919. Robert F. Williams is a prominent example. As a teenager, Williams moved from the South to Detroit, where he was caught in the city's riot and helped defend a black man being attacked by whites. Drafted just as the war ended, he spent eighteen months in the army, then returned to his hometown of Monroe, North Carolina. In 1947, Williams participated in an armed stand against Klansmen who planned to desecrate the body of a sharecropper and combat veteran executed by the state for killing his white landlord. Led by Booker T. Perry, a black veteran of World War I, forty men took up position at the funeral home and aimed their rifles when the Klan arrived in cars. Outnumbered, the Klansmen left. The episode proved to Williams "that we had to resist, and that resistance could be effective if we resisted in groups, and if we resisted with guns." Beginning in the mid-1950s, Williams became a leading advocate of what he called armed self-reliance. He revived Monroe's fading NAACP branch by recruiting fellow veterans and working class blacks. As the Klan resurged, he organized a self-defense unit, which repelled an armed attack in 1957. He used articles, speeches, and radio broadcasts to nationally project his message of self-help, black pride, political action, and armed resistance.[29]

In the 1960s, black veterans provided armed protection to civil rights workers in one of the cities that had experienced racial violence in 1919: Bogalusa, Louisiana. The Great Southern Lumber Company was long gone, replaced by a paper mill, but racism remained a problem. In 1965, CORE set up a field operation to end segregation and inequality. In echoes of Bogalusa's 1919 labor and racial strife, a white mob formed with the intention of attacking CORE organizers William Yates and Dave Miller. The two volunteers were staying with black resident Robert Hicks, who was determined to protect them. Hicks assembled an armed guard and the attack was averted. A second attempt to harm Yates and Miller came just two days later. When the Justice Department ignored requests to provide protection, Hicks and CORE asked for the help of the Deacons for Defense and Justice.

[28] Sitkoff, "Racial Militancy."
[29] Tyson, *Radio Free Dixie*, 38–50, 79–89, 189–219 (quote on 50).

The Deacons had formed in 1964 in Jonesboro, Louisiana, after the Klan began harassing CORE activists engaged in a desegregation campaign there. Aided by a white CORE worker, black residents of Jonesboro established a volunteer defensive force. The Deacons, who patrolled day and night, carried firearms and walkie-talkies. A majority were army veterans. On foot and in cars, they monitored whites passing through Jonesboro's black community. As a result, almost all Klan attacks on blacks and black homes stopped.

The Deacons were just as successful in Bogalusa. When Klansmen opened fire on Hicks's house in April 1965, the Deacons shot back. When whites ventured into the black neighborhood looking for a fight, Deacons quickly encircled them. With Deacons by their sides at all times, CORE volunteers kept up their work. Army veteran Charles Sims carried a veritable arsenal in his car trunk: boxes of ammunition, shotguns, a carbine, even hand grenades. For more than a year, the Deacons protected the civil rights workers and deterred attacks by white supremacists. Said Hicks, "if it hadn't been for these people [the Deacons], a setup, the idea of people willing to protect themselves – Negroes – I'd say we wouldn't be here today."[30]

The Deacons for Defense and Justice were but one example of black armed self-defense in the post-World War II era.[31] As civil rights campaigns intensified and spread during the late 1950s and early 1960s, black and white participants relied on armed defenders such as the Deacons for protection, even if the activists themselves practiced nonviolence. Black veterans organized a force to protect the Tuscaloosa (Ala.) Citizens for Action Committee, which carried out a nonviolent campaign against segregation in the summer of 1964. As historian Simon Wendt observes, "armed defense efforts became a significant auxiliary to voter registration drives and nonviolent protest as well" in Mississippi during the same time, the Freedom Summer.[32] As Klan violence increased in Lowndes County, Alabama, during a voter registration drive in 1966, black residents armed and carried out effective, if decentralized, self-defense.[33]

The Black Panther Party for Self-Defense, formed in 1966 in Oakland, California, also put armed self-defense at the forefront of its program of

[30] Wendt, "Roots of Black Power?," 145–50 (Hicks quote on 149). For more on the Deacons, see Hill, *Deacons for Defense*.

[31] Studies include Wendt, *Spirit and the Shotgun*; Strain, *Pure Fire*; Umoja, *We Will Shoot Back*.

[32] Wendt, "Roots of Black Power?," 150–65 (quote on 153). For civil rights activism among black veterans after World War II, see Parker, *Fighting For Democracy*.

[33] Jeffries, *Bloody Lowndes*, 100–6.

black nationalism. The Panthers carefully followed California law when they carried weapons during self-organized patrols to monitor police activity. Prominent display of arms became an indelible image of the Panthers, especially after they carried guns outside of the California state capitol in 1967 to protest a gun control bill. Media coverage of the event helped spread the view that the Panthers were violent and lawless, but as cofounder Bobby Seale explained, "we don't use our guns, we have never used our guns to go into the white community to shoot up white people. We only defend ourselves against anybody... who attacks us unjustly and tries to murder us and kill us for implementing our programs."[34] Although the Panthers did not use their arms to deter armed attacks by white supremacists, as Robert Williams and the Deacons for Defense and Justice had, police actions led to shoot-outs on several occasions. In December 1969, a raid in which police opened fire without warning killed Chicago Panthers Mark Clark and Fred Hampton, the latter while he was in bed.

There are many similarities between armed black resistance during 1919 and the 1960s. Like 1919's self-defenders, Robert Williams and the Black Panthers were subjected to intensive government surveillance and harassment. Indeed, FBI director J. Edgar Hoover, who had helped oversee the Justice Department's World War I-era monitoring of black activists, began using the secret COINTELPRO (counterintelligence program) for this same purpose during the 1960s. The FBI maintained an extensive file on Robert Williams and pursued him on trumped-up kidnapping charges, causing him to flee the country; COINTELPRO support clandestinely enabled the Chicago police raid that killed Mark Clark and Fred Hampton.[35]

California's gun control law was just one attempt to restrict African Americans' gun rights, recalling the disarming of blacks during 1919. The freedom movement in Lowndes County prompted area gun stores to turn away blacks trying to purchase ammunition. So residents found alternative sources. They bought ammunition in Georgia; kin and friends living elsewhere brought it with them on visits.[36] Just like 1919's self-defenders, residents circumvented coordinated efforts to obstruct their ability to protect themselves and to resist white supremacist violence.

As it did during 1919, armed resistance asserted black manhood against white supremacy's emasculating effects. As Simon Wendt argues,

[34] Seale, *Seize the Time*, 71.
[35] Tyson, *Radio Free Dixie*, 208–9, 262–86; Haas, *Assassination of Fred Hampton*.
[36] Jeffries, *Bloody Lowndes*, 103.

the Black Panthers' prominently displayed weapons served as "gendered symbols of defiance that served to affirm and nurture black masculinity."[37] Robert Williams sounded much like New Negro journalist William Byrd when he criticized those who counseled nonviolence in the face of mob attacks: "When we passively submit to these barbaric injustices, we most surely can be called the 'sissy race' of all mankind."[38] The adoption of a black panther as a logo in Lowndes County (prior to the Black Panther Party's use of the image) projected power, courage, and pride. Student organizer Stokely Carmichael evoked the image's gendered associations when he observed that a "man needs a black panther on his side when he and his family must endure – as hundreds of Alabamians have endured – loss of job, eviction, starvation, and sometimes death, for political activity."[39] For the Black Panthers, Robert Williams, and the men of Lowndes County, armed resistance to white supremacy was an integral part of both the freedom struggle and their manhood. The same was true of 1919's armed self-defenders.

Another parallel between 1919 and the post-World War II freedom struggle is the intertwined nature of the resistance. During 1919, African Americans followed up their armed struggles with associated efforts to establish the facts about the sources of antiblack collective violence and to secure justice for wrongfully accused self-defenders. These three fronts, as I have referred to them, were never discrete actions. Freeing wrongfully charged self-defenders required immediate legal action as well as correctives to the misleading narratives about the causes of the racial violence. In a similar way, the nonviolent side of the Freedom Movement and Black Power complemented and served one another. Scholars such as Peniel E. Joseph have questioned and revised the once-common view that civil rights and Black Power initiatives were separate movements.[40] As demonstrated by the examples of Robert Williams and the Deacons for Defense and Justice, among others, the two often worked hand-in-hand. So, too, did African Americans' three fronts during 1919.

These similarities should not surprise us. If we take the long view, recognizing that mob violence served to enforce and protect white supremacy since the end of the Civil War, then we must also acknowledge a long

---

[37] Wendt, "Roots of Black Power?," 158.

[38] Tyson, *Radio Free Dixie*, 141. Danielle L. McGuire argues that efforts to protect black women from sexual violence committed by white men were a significant source of post-WWII civil rights. See McGuire, *At the Dark End*.

[39] Jeffries, *Bloody Lowndes*, 153.

[40] Joseph, "Introduction: Toward a Historiography"; Joseph, *Neighborhood Rebels*; Joseph, "Rethinking the Black Power Era"; Joseph, "Black Power Movement."

tradition of armed resistance. The Union League. Ida B. Wells. The New Negroes. Veterans of the 370th Regiment, Ninety-third Division, fighting in the trenches of France, fighting in the streets of Chicago. Spanish-American War veteran Joe Etter, facing down barricaded troops in Knoxville. The residents of Tulsa, holding the line against a mob of thousands for as long as they could. In taking up arms in self-defense during the civil rights era, African Americans kept alive a practice that had thrived during 1919.

Bibliography

Manuscript Collections

Beck Cultural Exchange Center, Inc., Knox County Public Library System, Knoxville, Tenn.
  Liston Dantzler interview with Joe Crump, 1980
  Mary Etter interview with Ann Wilson, 1979
  Maurice Mays Papers
Butler Center for Arkansas Studies, Little Rock, Ark.
  Grif Stockley Papers, Series I, Elaine Massacre Research Materials, Subseries II, General Research
Chicago History Museum, Research Center
  "The Personal History of Robert Lucas Donigan," transcribed from eleven 90 minute cassette tapes in February 1980 and typed by his son, Robert William Donigan, August 1981, Honolulu, Hawaii
Douglas County Courthouse, Omaha, Nebraska
  Grand Jury Final Report, November 19, 1919, District Court Journal 176
Douglas County Historical Society, Omaha, Nebraska
  A.J. "Jack" Rhodes diary
  Unfiled newspaper clippings (1919 riot)
Indiana University Northwest Library, Calumet Regional Archives, Gary, Ind.
  Paul Dremeley Papers
Knox County Archives, Knoxville Tenn.
  State vs. Martin Mays, No. 509 (Supreme Court of Tennessee, Eastern Division, June 7, 1920)
  State vs. [Maurice] *Mays* 145 Tenn. 118 (1921)
Library of Congress, Manuscript Division, Washington, D.C.
  Newton Baker Papers
  Chicago Commission on Race Relations Records, Minutes 1919–1920
  National Association for the Advancement of Colored People Records, Group I
  Arthur Spingarn Papers

Mary Church Terrell Papers
Moorfield Storey Papers
Leonard Wood Papers
Longview Public Library, Longview, Texas
Longview Riot File
Marquette University, Department of Special Collections and University Archives, Milwaukee, Wisc.
Catholic Social Action Series, "Arthur G. Falls, Reminiscence, 1962" (typed ms.)
McClung Historical Collection, Knoxville, Tenn.
Subject File
Moorland-Spingarn Research Center, Howard University, Washington, D.C.
Archibald Grimké Papers
Walter H. Loving Papers
Vertical File
Nebraska State Historical Society Library/Archives, Lincoln, Nebraska.
Samuel R. McKelvie Papers, RG1 SG27
Roy Towl Papers, RG 1477AM
Newberry Library, Chicago, Ill.
Theodore Kornweibel Research Papers, 1910–1960
Victor Lawson Papers
Graham Taylor Papers
South Carolina Historical Society, Charleston, S.C.
Kirk Scrapbook
United States National Archives and Records Administration, College Park, Md.
Records of the Department of State, Central Decimal File, 1910–29, Record Group 59
Records of the Department of Justice, Glasser File, Record Group 60
Records of the Federal Bureau of Investigation, Record Group 65
Bureau Section File
Old German File
Records of the Secret Service, Daily Reports of Agents on White House Detail, 1902–1936, Record Group 87
Records of the Office of the Inspector General (Army), Record Group 159
Port Inspector, Newport News and Norfolk, 1918–1920
Reports of Annual Inspectors and Special Investigations, 1917–1920
Records of the War Department, General Staff, Military Intelligence Division, Record Group 165
Case Files 80–163, 80–164, 80–163–88, 80–163–117, 80–163–148 (box 132)
File 2198 (box 15)
Microfilm Publication 1440
Records of the Department of Labor, General Records, 1907–1942 (Chief Clerk's Files), Records of the Division of Negro Economics, Record Group 174
Records of Regular Army Mobile Units, World War I Organization Records Cavalry, 1916–1921, Record Group 391
Records of the Adjutant General's Office, U.S. Army, Central Decimal File, 1917–1925, Record Group 407

United States National Archives and Records Administration, Washington, D.C.
  Records of the Supreme Court of D.C., Record Group 21
  Records of the Navy, General Correspondence of the Secretary of the Navy,
  1916–1926, Record Group 80
  Records of the Office of the Judge Advocate, Navy, Records of Proceedings of
  Courts of Inquiry, Record Group 125
University of Arkansas, Special Collections, Little Rock, Ark.
  Charles Brough Papers, MS B79
  John E. Miller interview with Walter Brown, 1976, MC 279
Wisconsin Historical Society, Madison, Wisc.
  William G. Haan Papers, Mss. FP
  Arthur Waskow Notes on the NAACP 1919 Mob Violence File, Mss. M76–
  358. (Note: this collection contains Waskow's typed transcriptions of the
  NAACP's file, which consisted of newspaper clippings, memoranda, and affi-
  davits. It is a separate collection from the Arthur Waskow Papers.)
  Arthur Waskow Papers, Mss. 5

Published Collections, Reports, and Series

*Annual Report of the Commissioners of the District of Columbia Year Ended
  June 30, 1919* vol. I *Miscellaneous Reports.* U.S. House of Representatives,
  66th Cong., 2nd sess., Doc. 423.

*Biennial Report of the Adjutant General of Texas From January 1, 1919 to
  December 31, 1920.* Austin, Texas: Knape Printing, 1921. Texas State Library
  and Archives, Austin, Texas.

*Federal Surveillance of Afro-Americans (1917–1925): The First World War, the
  Red Scare, and the Garvey Movement.* Theodore Kornweibel, Jr., ed. Frederick,
  Md.: University Publications of America, 1986.

Papers of the NAACP, Part 7: *The Anti-Lynching Campaign, 1912–1955,* Series
  A: *Investigative Files, 1912–1955.* Frederick, Md.: University Publications of
  America, 1987.

Supreme Court of Illinois, *People v. Colvin et al.,* No. 13367, June 16, 1920.

United States Military Intelligence. Introd. by Richard D. Challener. New York:
  Garland Publishing, 1978.
  Volume 9: *Weekly Intelligence Summaries July 12–September 27, 1919*
  Volume 10: *Weekly Intelligence Summaries October 4–December 6, 1919*

Newspapers and Magazines

Atlanta Independent
Black Dispatch (Oklahoma City)
Branch Bulletin (NAACP)
Charleston American
Charleston News-Courier
Chicago Daily News
Chicago Defender
Chicago Evening American
Chicago Evening Post

Chicago Tribune
Chicago Whip
Cleveland Gazette
Crisis
Crusader
Gary Daily Tribune
Knoxville Journal and Tribune
Knoxville News-Sentinel
Knoxville Sentinel
Louisville (Ky.) Courier-Journal
Messenger
New York Age
Omaha Bee
Omaha World-Herald
Survey
Washington Bee
Washington Evening Star
Washington Herald
Washington Post
Washington Times
Wisconsin Weekly Blade

Dissertations and Theses

Age, Arthur V. "The Omaha Riot of 1919." M.A. thesis, Creighton University, 1964.

Balanoff, Elizabeth. "A History of the Black Community of Gary, Indiana, 1906–1940." Ph.D. diss., University of Chicago, 1974.

Mellis, Delia C. "'The monsters we defy': Washington, D.C., in the Red Summer of 1919." Ph.D. diss., City University of New York, 2008.

O'Donnell, Sean Tath. "Courting Science, Binding Truth: A Social History of *Frye v. United States*." Ph.D. diss., Harvard University, 2007.

Books and Articles

Abernethy, Lloyd M. "The Washington Race War of July, 1919." *Maryland Historical Magazine* 58, no. 4 (December 1963): 309–24.

Abu-Lughod, Janet L. *Race, Space, and Riots in Chicago, New York, and Los Angeles.* New York: Oxford University Press, 2007.

Ackerman, Kenneth D. *Young J. Edgar: Hoover, the Red Scare, and the Assault on Civil Liberties.* New York: Carroll and Graf, 2007.

Andrews, Gregg. "Black Working-Class Political Activism and Biracial Unionism: Galveston Longshoremen in Jim Crow Texas, 1919–1921." *Journal of Southern History* 74, no. 3 (August 2008): 627–68.

Arnesen, Eric. *Black Protest and the Great Migration: A Brief History with Documents.* The Bedford Series in History and Culture. Boston: Bedford/St. Martin's, 2003.

———, ed. *The Black Worker: Race, Labor, and Civil Rights since Emancipation.* Urbana: University of Illinois Press, 2007.

Bair, Barbara. "True Women, Real Men: Gender, Ideology, and Social Roles in the Garvey Movement." In *Gendered Domains: Rethinking Public and Private in Women's History*, edited by Dorothy O. Helly and Susan M. Reverby, 154–66. Essays from the Seventh Berkshire Conference on the History of Women. Ithaca, N.Y.: Cornell University Press, 1992.

Baldwin, Davarian L. *Chicago's New Negroes: Modernity, the Great Migration, and Black Urban Life.* Chapel Hill: University of North Carolina Press, 2007.

Barbeau, Arthur E. and Florette Henri, *The Unknown Soldiers: Black American Troops in World War I.* Philadelphia: Temple University Press, 1974.

Bauerlein, Mark. *Negrophobia: A Race Riot in Atlanta, 1906.* San Francisco, Calif.: Encounter Books, 2001.

Beaver, Daniel R. *Newton D. Baker and the American War Effort, 1917–1919.* Lincoln: University of Nebraska Press, 1966.

Bederman, Gail. *Manliness and Civilization: A Cultural History of Gender and Race in the United States, 1880–1917.* Chicago: University of Chicago Press, 1995.

Benton-Cohen, Katherine. "Docile Children and Dangerous Revolutionaries: The Racial Hierarchy of Manliness and the Bisbee Deportation of 1917." *Frontiers* 24, nos. 2 and 3 (2003): 30–50.

———. *Borderline Americans: Racial Division and Labor War in the Arizona Borderlands.* Cambridge, Mass.: Harvard University Press, 2009.

Betten, Neil and Raymond A. Mohl. "The Evolution of Racism in an Industrial City, 1906–1940: A Case Study of Gary, Indiana." *Journal of Negro History* 59, no. 1 (January 1974): 51–64.

Biegert, M. Langley. "Legacy of Resistance: Uncovering the History of Collective Action by Black Agricultural Workers in Central East Arkansas from the 1860s to the 1930s." *Journal of Social History* 32, no. 1 (Fall 1998): 73–99.

Brody, David. *Labor in Crisis: The Steel Strike of 1919.* Philadelphia: Lippincott, 1965; reprint, Westport, Conn.: Greenwood Press, 1982.

Brown, Cliff. "The Role of Employers in Split Labor Markets: An Event-Structure Analysis of Racial Conflict and AFL Organizing, 1917–1919." *Social Forces* 79, no. 2 (December 2000): 653–81.

Brown, Elsa Barkley. "To Catch the Vision of Freedom: Reconstructing Southern Black Women's Political History, 1865–1880." In *African American Women and the Vote, 1837–1965*, edited by Ann D. Gordon et al., 66–99. Amherst: University of Massachusetts Press, 1997.

Brown, Richard Maxwell. *Strain of Violence: Historical Studies of American Violence and Vigilantism.* New York: Oxford University Press, 1975.

Bruce, Dickson D., Jr. *Violence and Culture in the Antebellum South.* Austin: University of Texas Press, 1979.

Brundage, W. Fitzhugh. *Lynching in the New South: Georgia and Virginia, 1880–1930.* Urbana: University of Illinois Press, 1993.

Buchholz, Margaret Thomas, ed. "Josephine: The Washington Diary of a War Worker, 1918–1919." *Washington History* 10, no. 2 (Fall/Winter 1998–1999): 4–23.

Butler, Brian. *An Undergrowth of Folly: Public Order, Race Anxiety, and the 1903 Evansville, Indiana, Riot.* New York: Garland, 2000.

Capeci, Dominic J., Jr. and Jack C. Knight. "Reckoning with Violence: W.E.B. Du Bois and the 1906 Atlanta Race Riot." *Journal of Southern History* 62, no. 4 (November 1996): 727–66.

Capozzola, Christopher. *Uncle Sam Wants You: World War I and the Making of the Modern American Citizen.* New York: Oxford University Press, 2008.

Carter, Heath W. "Making Peace with Jim Crow: Religious Leaders and the Chicago Race Riot of 1919." *Journal of Illinois History* 11, no. 4 (Winter 2008): 261–76.

Cecelski, David S. and Timothy B. Tyson, eds. *Democracy Betrayed: The Wilmington Race Riot of 1898 and Its Legacy.* Chapel Hill: University of North Carolina Press, 1998.

Chicago Commission on Race Relations. *The Negro in Chicago: A Study of Race Relations and a Race Riot.* Chicago: University of Chicago Press, 1922.

Cohen, Adam and Elizabeth Taylor. *American Pharaoh: Mayor Richard J. Daley: His Battle for Chicago and the Nation.* Boston: Little, Brown, 2000.

Coit, Jonathan S. "'Our Changed Attitude': Armed Defense and the New Negro in the 1919 Chicago Race Riot." *Journal of the Gilded Age and Progressive Era* 11, no. 2 (April 2012): 225–56.

Collins, Ann V. *All Hell Broke Loose: American Race Riots from the Progressive Era through World War II.* Praeger Series on American Political Culture. Santa Barbara, Calif.: Praeger, 2012.

Commission of Inquiry, the Interchurch World Movement. *Report on the Steel Strike of 1919.* New York: Harcourt, Brace and Howe, 1920.

Contee, Clarence G. "Du Bois, the NAACP, and the Pan-African Congress of 1919." *Journal of Negro History* 57, no. 1 (January 1972): 13–28.

Cortner, Richard C. *A Mob Intent on Death: The NAACP and the Arkansas Riot Cases.* Middletown, Conn.: Wesleyan University Press, 1988.

Daniel, Pete. *The Shadow of Slavery: Peonage in the South, 1901–1969.* Urbana: University of Illinois Press, 1972.

Davis, John Kyle. "The Gray Wolf: Tom Dennison of Omaha." *Nebraska History* 58, no. 1 (Spring 1977): 25–52.

Dillard, Tom. "Scipio A. Jones." *Arkansas Historical Quarterly* 31, no. 3 (Autumn 1972): 201–19.

Doreski, C. K. "From News to History: Robert Abbott and Carl Sandburg Read the 1919 Chicago Riot." *African American Review* 26, no. 4 (Winter 1992): 637–50.

Downey, Dennis B. and Raymond M. Hyser. *No Crooked Death: Coatesville, Pennsylvania, and the Lynching of Zachariah Walker.* Urbana: University of Illinois Press, 1991.

Drake, St. Clair and Horace R. Cayton. *Black Metropolis: A Study of Negro Life in a Northern City.* Revised and Enlarged Edition. Chicago: University of Chicago Press, 1993.

Dray, Philip. *At the Hands of Persons Unknown: The Lynching of Black America.* New York: Modern Library, 2003.

Dubofsky, Melvyn. *We Shall Be All: A History of the Industrial Workers of the World.* Chicago: Quadrangle Books, 1969.

Duster, Alfreda M., ed. *Crusade for Justice: The Autobiography of Ida B. Wells.* Chicago: University of Chicago Press, 1970.

Egerton, John. "A Case of Prejudice: Maurice Mays and the Knoxville Race Riot of 1919." *Southern Exposure* 11 (July/August 1983): 56–65.

Ellis, Mark. "J. Edgar Hoover and the 'Red Summer' of 1919." *Journal of American Studies* 28, no. 1 (April 1994): 39–59.

———. "W. E. B. Du Bois and the Formation of Black Opinion in World War I: A Commentary on 'The Damnable Dilemma.'" *Journal of American History* 81, no. 4 (March 1995): 1584–90.

———. *Race, War, and Surveillance: African Americans and the United States Government during World War I.* Bloomington: Indiana University Press, 2001.

Emirbayer, Mustafa and Ann Mische. "What is Agency?" *American Journal of Sociology* 103, no. 4 (January 1998): 962–1023.

"Filling the Gaps: The Need for Additional Research – A Panel Discussion." *Arkansas Review: A Journal of Delta Studies* 32, no. 2 (August 2001): 155ff.

Fitzpatrick, Michael Andrew. "'A Great Agitation for Business': Black Economic Development in Shaw." *Washington History* 2, no. 2 (Fall/Winter 1990–91): 48–73.

Foley, Barbara. *Spectres of 1919: Class and Nation in the Making of the New Negro.* Urbana: University of Illinois Press, 2003.

Foster, William Z. *The Great Steel Strike and Its Lessons.* New York: B. W. Huebsch, 1920.

Fox, Stephen R. *The Guardian of Boston: William Monroe Trotter.* Studies in American Negro Life. New York: Atheneum, 1970.

Franklin, John Hope. *The Militant South: 1800–1861.* Cambridge, Mass.: Harvard University Press, 1956.

Frederickson, George M. *White Supremacy: A Comparative Study in American and South African History.* New York: Oxford University Press, 1981.

Gaines, Kevin K. *Uplifting the Race: Black Leadership, Politics, and Culture in the Twentieth Century.* Chapel Hill: University of North Carolina Press, 1996.

Gilje, Paul A. *Rioting in America.* Bloomington: Indiana University Press, 1996.

Gilmore, Glenda Elizabeth. *Gender and Jim Crow: Women and the Politics of White Supremacy in North Carolina, 1896–1920.* Chapel Hill: University of North Carolina Press, 1996.

Glass, Edward L. N., compiler. *The History of the Tenth Cavalry, 1866–1921.* Acme Printing Co., 1921; reprint, Fort Collins, Co.: Old Army Press, 1972.

Godshalk, David Fort. *Veiled Visions: The 1906 Atlanta Race Riot and the Reshaping of American Race Relations.* Chapel Hill: University of North Carolina Press, 2005.

Grant, Donald L. *The Anti-Lynching Movement: 1882–1932.* San Francisco, Calif.: R and E Research Associates, 1975.

Graves, John William. "Protectors or Perpetrators? White Leadership in the Elaine Race Riots." *Arkansas Review: A Journal of Delta Studies* 32, no. 2 (August 2001): 130ff.

Grossman, James R. et al., eds. *The Encyclopedia of Chicago*. Chicago: University of Chicago Press, 2004.

Grossman, James R. *Land of Hope: Chicago, Black Southerners, and the Great Migration*. Chicago: University of Chicago Press, 1989.

Haas, Jeffrey. *The Assassination of Fred Hampton: How the FBI and the Chicago Police Murdered a Black Panther*. Chicago: Lawrence Hill Books, 2010.

Hahn, Steven. *A Nation Under Our Feet: Black Political Struggles in the Rural South from Slavery to the Great Migration*. Cambridge, Mass.: Harvard University Press, 2003.

Hale, Grace Elizabeth. *Making Whiteness: The Culture of Segregation in the South, 1890–1940*. New York: Pantheon Books, 1998.

Halliburton, R., Jr. *The Tulsa Race War of 1921*. San Francisco, Calif.: R and E Research Associates, 1975.

Halpern, Rick. *Down on the Killing Floor: Black and White Workers in Chicago's Packinghouses, 1904–54*. The Working Class in American History. Urbana: University of Illinois Press, 1997.

Harrison, Hubert H. *A Hubert Harrison Reader*, edited with introduction and notes by Jeffrey B. Perry. Middletown, Conn.: Wesleyan University Press, 2001.

Hartfield, Ronne. *Another Way Home: The Tangled Roots of Race in One Chicago Family*. Chicago: University of Chicago Press, 2004.

Haynes, Robert V. *A Night of Violence: The Houston Riot of 1917*. Baton Rouge: Louisiana State University Press, 1976.

Haywood, Harry. *Black Bolshevik: Autobiography of an Afro-American Communist*. Chicago: Liberator Press, 1978.

Hemmingway, Theodore. "Prelude to Change: Black Carolinians in the War Years, 1914–1920." *Journal of Negro History* 65, no. 3 (Summer 1980): 212–27.

Hill, Lance E. *The Deacons for Defense: Armed Resistance and the Civil Rights Movement*. Chapel Hill: University of North Carolina Press, 2004.

Hill, Robert A. and Barbara Bair, eds. *Marcus Garvey, Life and Lessons: A Centennial Companion to the Marcus Garvey and Universal Negro Improvement Association Papers*. Berkeley: University of California Press, 1987.

Hirsch, James S. *Riot and Remembrance: The Tulsa Race War and Its Legacy*. Boston: Houghton Mifflin, 2002.

Holt, Glen E. and Dominic A. Pacyga. *Chicago, a Historical Guide to the Neighborhoods: The Loop and South Side*. Chicago: Chicago Historical Society, 1979.

Horne, Gerald. *Race War! White Supremacy and the Japanese Attack on the British Empire*. New York: New York University Press, 2004.

Hudson, Cheryl. "'The Negro in Chicago': Harmony in Conflict, 1919–22." *European Journal of American Culture* 29, no. 1 (2010): 53–68.

Jacobson, Matthew Frye. *Whiteness of a Different Color: European Immigrants and the Alchemy of Race*. Cambridge, Mass.: Harvard University Press, 1998.

Jeffries, Hasan Kwame. *Bloody Lowndes: Civil Rights and Black Power in Alabama's Black Belt*. New York: New York University Press, 2009.

Jensen, Joan M. *The Price of Vigilance*. Chicago: Rand McNally and Co., 1968.

Johnson, James Weldon. *Along This Way: The Autobiography of James Weldon Johnson*. New York: Viking Press, 1933.

Johnson, Walter. "On Agency." *Journal of Social History* 37, no. 1 (Fall 2003): 113–24.

Johnson, Wray R. "Black American Radicalism and the First World War: The Secret Files of the Military Intelligence Division." *Armed Forces and Society* 26, no. 1 (Fall 1999): 27–54.

Jordan, William G. "'The Damnable Dilemma': African-American Accommodation and Protest during World War I." *Journal of American History* 81, no. 4 (March 1995): 1562–83.

———. *Black Newspapers and America's War for Democracy, 1914–1920.* Chapel Hill: University of North Carolina Press, 2001.

Joseph, Peniel E. "Introduction: Toward a Historiography of the Black Power Movement." In Peniel E. Joseph, ed. *The Black Power Movement: Rethinking the Civil Rights – Black Power Era*. New York: Routledge, 2006, 1–25.

———. "The Black Power Movement: A State of the Field." *Journal of American History* 96, no. 3 (December 2009): 751–76.

———. "Rethinking the Black Power Era." *Journal of Southern History* 75, no. 3 (August 2009): 707–16.

———, ed. *Neighborhood Rebels: Black Power at the Local Level*. New York: Palgrave Macmillan, 2010.

Karpf, Juanita. "Get the Pageant Habit: E. Azalia Hackley's Festivals and Pageants during the First World War Years, 1914–1918." *Popular Music and Society* 34, no. 5 (December 2011): 517–56.

Keith, Jeanette. *Rich Man's War, Poor Man's Fight: Race, Class, and Power in the Rural South during the First World War*. Chapel Hill: University of North Carolina Press, 2004.

Kelley, Robin D. G. "'We Are Not What We Seem': Rethinking Black Working-Class Opposition in the Jim Crow South." *Journal of American History* 80, no. 1 (June 1993): 75–112.

Kerlin, Robert T. *The Voice of the Negro 1919*. New York: E. P. Dutton, 1920; reprint, New York: Arno Press, 1968.

Kersten, Andrew. *A. Philip Randolph: A Life in the Vanguard*. Lanham, Md.: Rowman and Littlefield, 2007.

Knock, Thomas J. *To End All Wars: Woodrow Wilson and the Quest for a New World Order*. Princeton, N.J.: Princeton University Press, 1995.

Kornweibel, Theodore, Jr. *No Crystal Stair: Black Life and the Messenger, 1917–1928*. Contributions in Afro-American and African Studies, Number 20. Westport, Conn.: Greenwood Press, 1975.

———. *"Seeing Red": Federal Campaigns Against Black Militancy, 1919–1925*. Bloomington: Indiana University Press, 1998.

———. *"Investigate Everything": Federal Efforts to Compel Black Loyalty During World War I*. Bloomington: Indiana University Press, 2002.

Lakin, Matthew. "'A Dark Night'; The Knoxville Race Riot of 1919." *Journal of East Tennessee History* 72 (2000): 1–29.

Lamon, Lester C. "Tennessee Race Relations and the Knoxville Riot of 1919." East Tennessee Historical Society's *Publications* 41 (1969): 67–85.

Larsen, Lawrence H. and Barbara J. Cottrell. *The Gate City: A History of Omaha.* Boulder, Co.: Pruett Publishing Co., 1982; reprint, Lincoln: University of Nebraska Press, 1997.

Laurie, Clayton D. "The U.S. Army and the Omaha Race Riot of 1919." *Nebraska History* 72, no. 3 (Fall 1991): 135–43.

Laurie, Clayton D. and Ronald H. Cole. *The Role of Federal Military Forces in Domestic Disorders, 1877–1945.* Washington, D.C.: Center of Military History, United States Army, 1997.

Lawson, Michael L. "Omaha, a City in Ferment: Summer of 1919." *Nebraska History* 58, no. 3 (Fall 1977): 395–417.

Lemann, Nicholas. *Redemption: The Last Battle of the Civil War.* New York: Farrar, Straus and Giroux, 2006.

Lentz-Smith, Adriane. *Freedom Struggles: African Americans and World War I.* Cambridge, Mass.: Harvard University Press, 2009.

Link, Arthur S. et al., eds. *The Papers of Woodrow Wilson. Vol. 49: July 18-September 13, 1918.* Princeton, N.J.: Princeton University Press, 1985.

Lumpkins, Charles L. *American Pogrom: The East St. Louis Race Riot and Black Politics.* Athens: Ohio University Press, 2008.

Manela, Erez. *The Wilsonian Moment: Self-Determination and the International Origins of Anticolonial Nationalism.* New York: Oxford University Press, 2007.

Marks, Carole. *Farewell – We're Good and Gone: The Great Black Migration.* Bloomington: Indiana University Press, 1989.

Maxwell, William J. *New Negro, Old Left: African-American Writing and Communism Between the Wars.* New York: Columbia University Press, 1999.

McBride, Genevieve G. "The Progress of 'Race Men' and 'Colored Women' in the Black Press in Wisconsin, 1892–1985." In *The Black Press in the Middle West, 1865–1985,* edited by Henry Lewis Suggs, 325-48. Contributions in Afro-American and African Studies, Number 177. Westport, Conn.: Greenwood Press, 1996.

McCool, B. Boren. *Union, Reaction, and Riot: A Biography of a Rural Race Riot.* Memphis, Tenn.: Bureau of Social Research, Division of Urban and Regional Studies, Memphis State University, 1970.

McGuire, Danielle L. *At the Dark End of the Street: Black Women, Rape, and Resistance – A New History of the Civil Rights Movement from Rosa Parks to the Rise of Black Power.* New York: Knopf, 2010.

McLaughlin, Malcolm. *Power, Community, and Racial Killing in East St. Louis.* New York: Palgrave Macmillan, 2005.

———. "Ghetto Formation and Armed Resistance in East St. Louis, Illinois." *Journal of American Studies* 41, no. 2 (August 2007): 435–67.

McWhirter, Cameron. *Red Summer: The Summer of 1919 and the Awakening of Black America.* New York: Henry Holt, 2011.

Mellis, Delia. "'Literally Devoured': Washington, D.C., 1919." *Studies in the Literary Imagination* 40, no. 2 (Fall 2007): 1–24.

Menard, Orville D. "Tom Dennison, the Omaha Bee, and the 1919 Omaha Race Riot." *Nebraska History* 68, no. 4 (Winter 1987): 152–65.

―――. "Lest We Forget: The Lynching of Will Brown, Omaha's 1919 Race Riot." *Nebraska History* 91, nos. 3 and 4 (Fall/Winter 2010): 152–65.

Mikkelsen, Vincent P. "Fighting for Sergeant Caldwell: The NAACP Campaign against 'Legal' Lynching after World War I." *Journal of African American History* 94, no. 4 (Fall 2009): 464–86.

Mixon, Gregory. *The Atlanta Riot: Race, Class, and Violence in a New South City.* Gainesville: University Press of Florida, 2005.

Mjagkij, Nina. *Loyalty in Time of Trial: The African American Experience during World War I.* The African American History Series. Lanham, Md.: Rowman and Littlefield, 2011.

Mohl, Raymond A. "The Great Steel Strike of 1919 in Gary, Indiana: Working-Class Radicalism or Trade Union Militancy?" *Mid-America* 63, no. 1 (January 1981): 36–52.

Mohl, Raymond A. and Neil Betten. "Ethnic Adjustment in the Industrial City: The International Institute of Gary, 1919–1940." *International Migration Review* 6, no. 4 (Winter 1972): 361–76.

Moore, John Hammond. "Charleston in World War I; Seeds of Change." *South Carolina Historical Magazine* 86, no. 1 (1985): 39–49.

Murray, Robert K. *Red Scare: A Study in National Hysteria, 1919–1920.* Minneapolis: University of Minnesota Press, 1955; reprint, New York: McGraw Hill, 1964.

Newby, I. A. *Black Carolinians: A History of Blacks in South Carolina from 1895 to 1968.* Columbia: University of South Carolina Press, 1973.

Norwood, Stephen H. "Bogalusa Burning: The War Against Biracial Unionism in the Deep South, 1919." *Journal of Southern History* 63, no. 3 (August 1997): 591–628.

O'Hara, S. Paul. *Gary, the Most American of All American Cities.* Bloomington: Indiana University Press, 2011.

Omaha's Riot in Story and Picture. Omaha, Neb.: Omaha Educational Publishing Company, 1919.

Onishi, Yuichiro. "The New Negro of the Pacific: How African Americans Forged Cross-Racial Solidarity with Japan, 1917–1922." *Journal of African American History* 92, no. 2 (Spring 2007): 191–213.

Pacyga, Dominic A. *Polish Immigrants and Industrial Chicago: Workers on the South Side, 1880–1922.* Columbus: Ohio State University Press, 1991.

Parker, Christopher S. *Fighting For Democracy: Black Veterans and the Struggle Against White Supremacy in the Postwar South.* Princeton, N.J.: Princeton University Press, 2009.

Patterson, Andrea. "Black Nurses in the Great War: Fighting for and with the American Military in the Struggle for Civil Rights." *Canadian Journal of History* 47, no. 3 (Winter 2012): 545–66.

Pfeifer, Michael J. *Rough Justice: Lynching and American Society, 1874–1947.* Urbana: University of Illinois Press, 2004.

_____. *The Roots of Rough Justice: Origins of American Lynching*. Urbana: University of Illinois Press, 2011.

Prather, H. Leon, Sr. "We Have Taken a City: A Centennial Essay," in Cecelski and Tyson, *Democracy*, 15–41.

Reich, Steven A. "Soldiers of Democracy: Black Texans and the Fight for Citizenship, 1917–1921." *Journal of American History* 82, no. 4 (March 1996): 1478–1504.

_____. "The Great War, Black Workers, and the Rise and Fall of the NAACP in the South." In *The Black Worker: Race, Labor, and Civil Rights since Emancipation*, edited by Eric Arnesen, 147–77. Urbana: University of Illinois Press, 2007.

Richards, Leonard L. *"Gentlemen of Property and Standing": Anti-Abolition Mobs in Jacksonian America*. New York: Oxford University Press, 1970.

Roediger, David R. *The Wages of Whiteness: Race and the Making of the American Working Class*. New York: Verso Press, 1991.

Rogers, O. A., Jr. "The Elaine Race Riots of 1919." *Arkansas Historical Quarterly* 19 (1960): 142–50.

Ross, Felicia G. Jones. "Democracy's Textbook: A History of the Black Press in Ohio, 1865–1985." In *The Black Press in the Middle West, 1865–1985*, edited by Henry Lewis Suggs, 246–51. Contributions in Afro-American and African Studies, Number 177. Westport, Conn.: Greenwood Press, 1996.

Ross, Marlon B. *Manning the Race: Reforming Black Men in the Jim Crow Era*. New York: New York University Press, 2004.

Royster, Jacqueline Jones, ed. *Southern Horrors and Other Writings: The Anti-Lynching Campaign of Ida B. Wells, 1892–1900*. The Bedford Series in History and Culture. Boston: Bedford/St. Martin's, 1997.

Rudwick, Elliott M. *Race Riot at East St. Louis, July 2, 1917*. Carbondale: Southern Illinois University Press, 1964.

Schneider, Mark Robert. *"We Return Fighting": The Civil Rights Movement in the Jazz Age*. Boston: Northeastern University Press, 2002.

Scott, Emmett J. *Scott's Official History of the American Negro in the World War*. Chicago: Homewood Press, 1919.

Seale, Bobby. *Seize the Time: The Story of the Black Panther Party and Huey P. Newton*. New York: Random House, 1970; reprint, Baltimore, Md.: Black Classic Press, 1991.

Senechal, Roberta. *The Sociogenesis of a Race Riot: Springfield, Illinois, in 1908*. Urbana: University of Illinois Press, 1990.

Shapiro, Herbert. *White Violence and Black Response: From Reconstruction to Montgomery*. Amherst: University of Massachusetts Press, 1988.

Shellum, Brian G. *Black Officer in a Buffalo Soldier Regiment: The Military Career of Charles Young*. Lincoln: University of Nebraska Press, 2010.

Sitkoff, Harvard. "Racial Militancy and Interracial Violence in the Second World War." *Journal of American History* 58, no. 3 (December 1971): 661–81.

Smith, Eric Ledell. "The 1917 Race Riot in Chester, Pennsylvania." *Pennsylvania History* 75, no. 2 (Spring 2008): 171–96.

Smith, J. Douglas. *Managing White Supremacy: Race, Politics, and Citizenship in Jim Crow Virginia*. Chapel Hill: University of North Carolina Press, 2002.

Stockley, Grif. *Blood in Their Eyes: The Elaine Race Massacres of 1919.* Fayetteville: University of Arkansas Press, 2001.

Strain, Christopher B. *Pure Fire: Self-Defense as Activism in the Civil Rights Era.* Athens: University of Georgia Press, 2005.

Summers, Martin. *Manliness and Its Discontents: The Black Middle Class and the Transformation of Masculinity, 1900–1930.* Chapel Hill: University of North Carolina Press, 2004.

Taft, Philip. "The Bisbee Deportation." *Labor History* 13, no. 1 (Winter 1972): 3–40.

Taylor, Kieran. "'We have just begun': Black Organizing and White Response in the Arkansas Delta, 1919." *Arkansas Historical Quarterly* 58, no. 3 (Autumn 1999): 264–84.

Tolnay, Stewart E. and E. M. Beck. *A Festival of Violence: An Analysis of Southern Lynchings, 1882–1930.* Urbana: University of Illinois Press, 1995.

Trotter, Joe William, Jr. *The Great Migration in Historical Perspective: New Dimensions of Race, Class, and Gender.* Bloomington: Indiana University Press, 1991.

Tuttle, William M., Jr. *Race Riot: Chicago in the Red Summer of 1919.* New York: Atheneum, 1970.

———. "Violence in a 'Heathen' Land: The Longview Race Riot of 1919." *Phylon* 33, no. 4 (Fourth Quarter 1972): 324–33.

Tylee, Claire M. "Womanist Propaganda, African-American Great War Experience, and Cultural Strategies of the Harlem Renaissance: Plays by Alice Dunbar-Nelson and Mary P. Burrill." *Women's Studies International Forum* 20, no. 1 (1997): 153–63.

Tyson, Timothy B. *Radio Free Dixie: Robert F. Williams and the Roots of Black Power.* Chapel Hill: University of North Carolina Press, 1999.

Umoja, Akinyele Omowale. *We Will Shoot Back: Armed Resistance in the Mississippi Freedom Movement.* New York: New York University Press, 2013.

Vaughn, Stephen. *Holding Fast the Inner Lines: Democracy, Nationalism, and the Committee on Public Information.* Chapel Hill: University of North Carolina Press, 1980.

Voogd, Jan. *Race Riots and Resistance: The Red Summer of 1919.* New York: Peter Lang, 2008.

Walker, Juliet E. K. "The Promised Land: The Chicago Defender and the Black Press in Illinois, 1862–1970." In *The Black Press in the Middle West, 1865–1985,* edited by Henry Lewis Suggs, 21–33. Contributions in Afro-American and African Studies, Number 177. Westport, Conn.: Greenwood Press, 1996.

Waskow, Arthur I. *From Race Riot to Sit-In, 1919 and the 1960s: A Study in the Connections between Conflict and Violence.* Garden City, N.Y.: Anchor Books, 1967.

Watson, Fred. "Still on Strike: Recollections of a Bisbee Deportee." *Journal of Arizona History* 18, no. 2 (Summer 1977): 171–84.

Wells-Barnett, Ida B. *The Arkansas Race Riot.* Chicago: Hume Job Print, 1920.

Wendt, Simon. "The Roots of Black Power? Armed Resistance and the Radicalization of the Civil Rights Movement." In *The Black Power Movement:*

Rethinking the Civil Rights – Black Power Era, edited by Peniel E. Joseph, 145–65. New York: Routledge, 2006.

_____. *The Spirit and the Shotgun: Armed Resistance and the Struggle for Civil Rights.* New Perspectives on the History of the South. Gainesville: University Press of Florida, 2007.

Whalan, Mark. *The Great War and the Culture of the New Negro.* Gainesville: University Press of Florida, 2008.

Whitaker, Robert. *On the Laps of Gods: The Red Summer of 1919 and the Struggle for Justice That Remade a Nation.* New York: Three Rivers Press, 2008.

White, Walter. *A Man Called White: The Autobiography of Walter White.* New York: Viking Press, 1948; reprint, New York: Arno Press, 1969.

Who's Who in Chicago. Chicago: A. N. Marquis Co., 1931.

Williams, Chad L. "Vanguards of the New Negro: African American Veterans and Post-World War I Racial Militancy." *Journal of African American History* 92, no. 3 (Summer 2007): 347–70.

_____. *Torchbearers of Democracy: African American Soldiers in the World War I Era.* The John Hope Franklin Series in African American History and Culture. Chapel Hill: University of North Carolina Press, 2010.

Williams, Kidada E. *They Left Great Marks on Me: African American Testimonies of Racial Violence from Emancipation to World War I.* New York: New York University Press, 2012.

Wolcott, Victoria W. *Remaking Respectability: African American Women in Interwar Detroit.* Chapel Hill: University of North Carolina Press, 2001.

Woodruff, Nan Elizabeth. "African-American Struggles for Citizenship in the Arkansas and Mississippi Deltas in the Age of Jim Crow." *Radical History Review* 55 (Winter 1993): 33–51.

_____. *American Congo: The African American Freedom Struggle in the Delta.* Cambridge, Mass.: Harvard University Press, 2003.

Woodson, Carter G. *The Negro in Our History.* Fifth ed. Washington, D.C.: Associated Publishers, 1928.

Work, David. "Their Life's Blood: The Tenth Cavalry in Arizona, 1914–1921." *Journal of Arizona History* 46 (Winter 2005): 349–374.

Wright, George C. *Racial Violence in Kentucky, 1865–1940: Lynchings, Mob Rule, and "Legal Lynchings."* Baton Rouge: Louisiana State University Press, 1990.

Yellin, Eric S. "'It Was Still No South to Us': African American Civil Servants at the Fin de Siècle." *Washington History* 21 (2009): 22–47.

_____. *Racism in the Nation's Service: Government Workers and the Color Line in Woodrow Wilson's America.* Chapel Hill: University of North Carolina Press, 2013.

Zangrando, Robert L. *The NAACP Crusade Against Lynching, 1909–1950.* Philadelphia: Temple University Press, 1980.

Index

9 781107 639614